Our Fine Romance

An Autobiography

To MARGART

Enjoy our story!

Maureen & Michael.

June 2023

Maureen and Michael Harbott

Trade Paperback **ISBN 978-0-9880084-0-3**

Canadian Cataloguing in Publication Data
Harbott, Maureen, and Michael - Our Fine Romance
Printed by Printorium Bookworks, Victoria, B.C., Canada

Published by M & M Publications, Delta, B.C., Canada
Cover by Iryna Spica Book Design, Victoria, B.C., Canada.

Visit us at.........www.ourfineromance.com

To our Children ....

Stephen, Nicola, Melanie, Abigail, and their partners

Also, to our Grandchildren ....

Paul, Jennifer, and Michelle Harbott

Jessica, Jeffrey, and Daniel Franklin

Gordon and Sarah Burns

Ryan and Katelyn Watt

To the many people of all races in Southern Africa, who helped us significantly during our time there, expected so little in return, but whose lives deserve so much more.

Enjoy life, because we only have its pleasures for a short time!

Table of Contents

List of Maps
(with permission from Oxford University Press)

- England and Wales
- London and South East England
- Colonial Africa (1914)
- Southern Africa (1964)
- Canada
- South West British Columbia and Vancouver

Photo Credits

- Central Press/ Getty Images

- Union-Castle Shipping Line

- Rhodesia Railways

- British Caledonian Airways

- Canadian Pacific Ships/Railway

- Canadian Pacific Airlines

England & Wales

**London
and South East England**

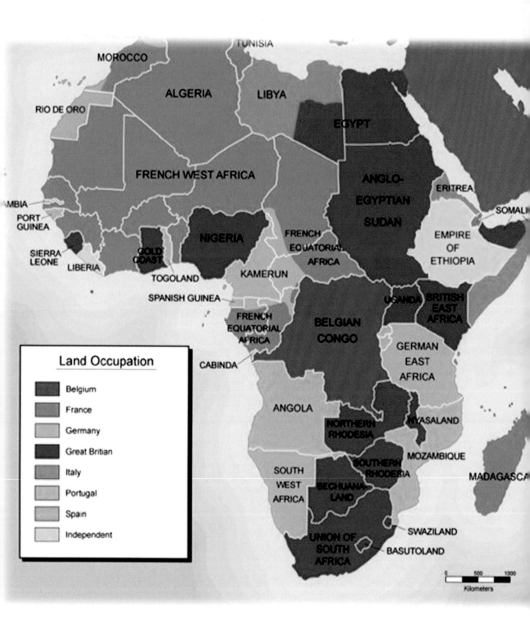

Colonial Africa, Circa 1914

Except for the former German colonies very
few political changes occurred in Southern
Africa until the 1960's

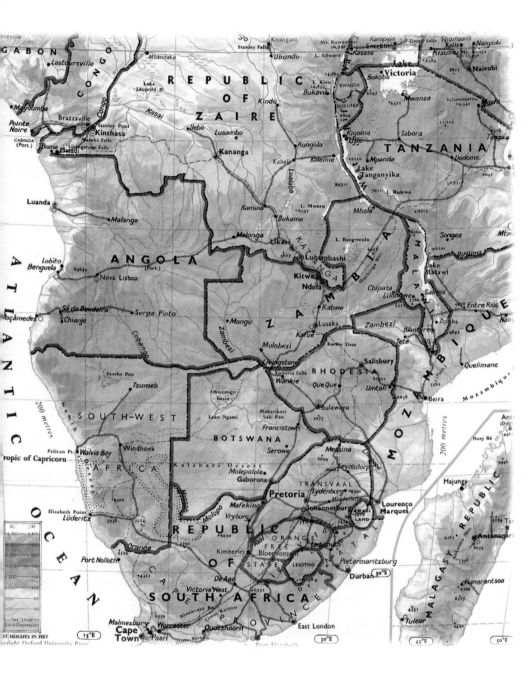

Southern Africa 1964

Rhodesia is now known as Zimbabwe and South-West Africa as Namibia

Canada

**South West British Columbia
and Vancouver**

Foreword

Maureen and I talked about recording our childhood memories and chronicling our life together over more than fifty years, on three continents, long before we first put pen to paper. We wanted to give our children and their children something more than a list of family names. Maureen took the initiative and had several chapters under her belt before I asked, 'What about me, my life, my family?' 'You're responsible for that', she said. And so, we began. Twenty-five years have passed, and as we approach our golden years, we finally have our story on paper. We owe a special thanks to our good friends Nora and Geoff Eldred, who helped us with both the formatting and editing for the first edition. The first chapter is Maureen's story. Then I provide my family background. Subsequent chapters, which document our shared experiences, may switch between our respective *voices*. To assist the reader, a change of *voice* occurring within a chapter is preceded by the symbol.

৪০ ৫৪

English (United Kingdom) language has been used throughout this document.

We hope that you get as much pleasure in reading about our experiences as we enjoyed living them!

Michael Harbott, August 2012

Second Edition Foreword

When we first published our story in 2012, we were surprised and pleased with the warm response it received, not only from our family and friends but from friends of friends in Canada, England and South Africa whose families had had similar experiences either growing up in war-time England or relocating to a new life on another continent. Many felt the story ended rather precipitously, and those closest to us indicated I should add a few comments on our current situation, so a new prologue and revised epilogue has been added to this second edition.

Michael Harbott, October 2020

Prologue

Michael

It was fall in Western Canada, there was a chill in the air, and the leaves were fluttering to the ground as I walked up to the entrance of the Care Home with my usual trepidation.

'Will I always feel this way when I visit Maureen now?' I asked myself.

Earlier I had to make one of the most challenging decisions of my married life twelve months ago when I put my wife into care as I could no longer look after her at home. We had been together for over sixty years; there had been wonderful times and setbacks to be overcome, but we had always gone through everything together, jointly creating our fantastic family.

'Why does it have to end like this?' I asked angrily.

As always I was greeted cheerfully at the reception, I signed in and made my way down the long hallway leading to her new home; it was richly decorated with paintings and artwork that helped to lift my spirits. Keying in the entry code to her unit, I wondered how I would be received. Would Maureen greet me with a smile and a sign of recognition or just a blank stare? Would she be tense and confused, show signs of anger, or just be overwhelmed by tiredness? Entering the communal area, I cast my eyes over the many clients, some of whom were sleeping in wheelchairs, lounge chairs or at tables; a Care-Aide indicated that Maureen was still in her room and led me to her. I was pleased to find that she was sleeping peacefully, pulled up a chair, took her hand, and sat quietly with her, admiring how well she looked. Although she had lost considerable weight, she was still very beautiful, her hair was only slightly grey, and there was hardly a line on her face.

Five years earlier, we began to face the greatest challenge of our married life. Just a few years before that, we had been working together on our joint autobiography, *Our Fine Romance*. We would spend hours together reminiscing about our past in England and Africa, thinking how far we had come and how many changes we had made. Maureen had done the bulk of the writing, and people had remarked how well she expressed herself, how clearly she remembered so many details of her early life.

Now it was all gone, and it seemed it would never come back!

But is it really gone, I wondered, or is it all in some hidden compartment of her brain, like a lost file in a computer, to be magically retrieved later?

After a short time, she stirred, gave me a weak smile, and squeezed my hand. I was relieved and felt there was still some recognition. I asked the usual trivial questions:

'Have you had breakfast?'

'No', she answered, but I could tell by the remains on the plate that she had.

Knowing that our youngest daughter had visited her earlier, I asked, 'Has anyone been to see you?'

'No', she again responded.

Hoping to retrieve some happy memories of the past, I picked up a copy of our book and thumbed through it. I knew that she had lost the recollection of coming to Canada and having a child here. I had tried talking to her about this before, but what about Africa and the adventures we had had there together? What did she remember about the three children conceived and born there? All her responses were negative. I thought of talking about the war years and her evacuation but decided against this as it might bring back some frightening episodes. I was just about to put our book down when I noticed that in the early chapters, she talked a great deal about her father and growing up in England.

'Do you remember your father?' I asked.

'Yes', she replied as a smile appeared on her face.

'What do you remember most about your father?'

'He played the piano, and we sang' she responded.

Trying to retrieve some long-lost memories, in a quiet voice, I started to read our story to her.

1.

The Clouds of War

Maureen

My father, William Starling, was one of nature's gentlemen. He loved his mother and sisters dearly and always treated our mother and his daughters with thoughtful consideration. He was seldom out of temper, and my mother always felt lucky to be married to such a man. He was extremely bright. He was the top boy on his school ladder from about 11 years old. He left school at 12 years old; he had finished all that this school could teach and the school-leaving age then was fourteen, this indicates how bright he was. Born in London, probably Stratford, on 3rd September 1905, he was one of six children. I never knew much about my father's parents. Growing up in the East End of London and with younger children at home, this being somewhat depressing times, it was, of course, necessary that he should find work and earn money. Within a few years, realising that he was interested in engineering, he began to learn a trade, and by the time my father was married, he was called a Jig and Toolmaker. His exceptional skills were in the lathe, turning to very fine tolerances. He was also very musical and learned to play the piano at a very early age. He was self-taught, played by ear, and was much in demand for piano playing at parties, and although a relatively quiet man, he enjoyed the status conferred on him because of being the eldest son, always at the centre of any family gathering.

Ellen, my mother, was born on 17th November 1908, also in the East End of London to Trisscella and Thomas Steeden. She was their first child. When I was a young girl, she would talk about her earliest memories. She reminisced about a time when she lived with her mother and sisters in what she called 'the Buildings' which were tenement type housing developments. My grandfather was in the Army in France during this period (1st World War). While he was away from the family, my grandmother became interested in the Roman Catholic faith, and she was converted. What she was transformed from was a mystery! It was whispered that she might have come from a Jewish background.

There were frequent reports of anti-Semitic activities in the newspapers of the day in Britain, and Jewish people were not generally admired. A young person who had decided to break away from her family might well have decided to keep such a background private. My mother spoke to me about visiting her mother's sister only once, and she hinted that part of the family was connected by marriage to a sizeable soft-drinks business. But we never really knew what kind of a background my grandparents came from. My parents had married in the Church of England. Along with a couple of bridesmaids, her youngest sister June, who was about three years old at the time, was a perfectly sweet little attendant. Mum loved Dad very much but was terrified of having children because Nanny's (Grandmother's) priest was displeased she had married outside 'The Faith' and told her any children she had would be illegitimate and would burn in Hell!

My dear sister Pamela Louise was born on 4th October 1930, a little more than two years after my parents married. My mother once confessed that she was surprised it took so long for her to have their first baby! But she was thrilled to be a mother at last although Dad had reservations because at that time he didn't have full-time work and they didn't have a home of their own. This was during the Great Depression, and many people suffered under-employment. I think at this time he worked for a company called Dexcine in North Woolwich, Essex, which is east of London, on the north bank of the River Thames. He was gainfully employed only three days a week. Grandmother, we called her 'Nanny', was the Assistant Cook in a grand house south of the River Thames, close to London. This was a very respectable life for a girl, so it was quite reasonable for my mother to work in another woman's home, which she did.

On 5th June 1935, I, Maureen Dorothy, arrived on the scene, and my relationship with my sister changed Pam's life. My mother had a complicated delivery with her first baby, so I was born in a hospital that was rather unusual at their economic level. The hospital was in Charing Cross, a neighbourhood in London, which makes me a true *Londoner*. As we grew up, my sister swore this fact set me apart from everyone else in the family who subsequently were all born at home, but I think her feelings were very mixed at finding herself somewhat 'crowded' after being the only child in the nest for five years. However, when she came home from the hospital after the two week's lying-in period, our mother introduced Pam to her dark-haired little sister 'Pam,' she said, 'You are a big sister now, and you can help me look after our baby.' Pam, somewhat mollified by being called *big*, felt quite essential and set to work to be helpful. Being 'Mother's helper' was to become a big part of Pam's identity for the greater part of her life. When I was just two years old, along came brother number one, Brian William, who was born on 23rd October 1937. Of course, I don't remember that. By the time I was four, I remember my parents talking at suppertime about a war that had started in Europe, and there was fear that it might spread to our shores. My Dad told me later that on 3rd September 1939, we listened to the radio as the BBC was going to broadcast a special message from the Prime Minister, Neville Chamberlain. Apparently, we all sat around our small radio set and listened to this message.

'This morning the British Ambassador in Berlin handed the German Government a final note stating that unless we heard from them by 11 o'clock that they were prepared at once to withdraw their troops from Poland, a state of war would exist between us. I have to tell you now that no such undertaking has been received, and that consequently, this country is at war with Germany.'

At four years old, this would not have meant much to me.

Brother number two, Michael Christopher, arrived on 26th September 1939. This was a rather strange occurrence. In those days, children in the family were not prepared for the appearance of a new baby in any way, and my sister and I were packed off to some friends in Cheshire. The reason we were given was that now was a good time for us to be safely out of London as the war had just begun. I know now that was a little *white lie* on our mother's part. Had I been older, I might have wondered why she thought the industrial part of England was safer than where we were, but we were not at that age very worldly-wise. We could not have been there long - this was the period of the *phoney war* - and we were sent home again. I think we travelled alone in the care of the guard on the train. When we arrived back home to our utter amazement, there was another baby! The main reason that I have little memory of Michael as an infant is that the following year around my fifth birthday, the Government was beginning to believe the war was about to come to England's shores. It was decided that school children should be evacuated out of the London area.

Only just five, and about to start school in September, our mother insisted I be included with Pam in the program, and she stipulated we MUST stay together. I remember the vast amount of discussion everyone was having about this, but not the details. It merely sounded to me like it might be another adventure!

My next memory was of saying goodbye to my mother, who was desperately trying not to cry. It must have been midsummer of 1940. Three or four London buses were lined up outside Pam's school, which I have only a dim memory of having attended just a few times. My mother dearly wanted her darling daughters to be safe and was prepared to accept our separation. Pam was put *in charge* of me, and we both were wearing a label with our name and were carrying our gas masks plus a packed lunch, which we had been told we must save for the train journey. I, of course, wanted to climb upstairs so that we could ride on the upper of the bus. Pam permitted this as she liked riding on the top deck too. My memory is of looking down on our mother's upturned face; she was bravely waving and trying to smile and, at the same time, held a handkerchief over her hair as the rain had begun to drizzle a bit and she had just had a new hairdo. I was a plump little thing and wanted a snack, but Pam was adamant. She knew the food was for the journey. My mother could not bear it when I began to cry and called out to find out what was the matter. Of course, I got what I wanted!

I did not understand we would be so far away from home, but because Pam was with me, I felt perfectly safe and comfortable. There was a mob scene at Paddington station, but train stations meant trips to the seaside, and I was undismayed. The train ride seemed to take forever, but eventually, we arrived at Taunton in Somerset. I think our destination had been kept a secret.

The population had to practice keeping secrets quiet because it was wartime. The Boy Scouts were prepared to assist the evacuees with their luggage but Pam, who had been instructed to take care of our suitcase, wouldn't let the tall young boy lay a hand on ours, so he walked beside us and escorted us along a path bordering a field of perhaps wheat or long grass. I remember the warm, grassy, country scent. We came to a church hall where we were served warm tea from large white enamel jugs and little cakes. There was more confusion, but eventually, a group including Pam and me, plus the other girls from her school, were transported to another place, which we learned was the village of Creech St Michael. Here we met the women who were willing to receive us into their homes. It must have been quite an undertaking for these women. They could not have known if the children they were offering to shelter were clean and decent. *Londoners* were all lumped together in country people's minds. Pam, who was about ten years old, and I, just five, stood awfully close together, and I heard it mentioned a couple of times, 'Those two have to stay together.' Some women wanted a girl old enough to help with their housework - they were not all completely altruistic, some would have taken me because I was little more than a baby but perhaps didn't want two children to look after. However, we were lucky. The man in charge of the proceedings was the village school headmaster, Mr Kingdon. When nearly all the available children had been matched up with their billet providers, his wife appeared. Perhaps she had been asked to attend. She agreed they could manage two girls. For us, this was an extremely fortunate circumstance; it turned out that she was childless, and her heart was touched at the sight of us.

The Kingdons had a charming two-level home, which seemed rather luxurious to us. Their house was built of stone and attached to the village school. There was no running water upstairs. The bathroom was across the yard and was attached to the lavatory block that served the school, although there was quite a high sturdy brick wall that divided the house backyard from the schoolyard. The bathroom seemed very spacious, and there was no shortage of hot running water. Their front yard was a very well kept flower garden, and I have the impression that the whole property was elevated as I remember climbing stairs to walk to the side entrance of the house and to get into the schoolyard at the other end of the block. Pam and I shared a bedroom on the upper level and at the foot of the stairs in the right-angle formed by the staircase, stood a huge grandfather clock that chimed the hours. I was a bit nervous about this *personage*. The clock seemed alive to me. They also had a lovely and affectionate golden cocker spaniel, 'Lady'. I fell in love with her - we had never lived in a house with pets before. Pam was not happy about the change in our lives - I guess I was more adaptable and happily basked in the approval of our hosts. Pam missed our mother very much and didn't settle down as quickly as I did.

I remember the whole thing with pleasure. The Kingdons were very kind to us. We went for walks with Mr Kingdon and the dog. He taught me to read, which skill has been an enduring delight to me all of my life. I quickly learned whatever was shown to me, sang, and played and was perfectly happy. Mrs Kingdon did her best for us. She had a 'daily' to help with the household chores, and she cooked and sewed for us and took great pleasure in filling the mother role. I especially remember she made Pam and me matching off-white blazers (which we proudly wore when our mother visited us - Mum was NOT amused). I remember special days when Mr Kingdon made our breakfast, or perhaps it was tea and introduced us to special *hunk* slices of bread thickly spread with butter, jam, and cream. He was clearly the head of the household, said grace before meals, and taught us to stand up when the National Anthem was played no matter what we were doing. Pam had to write a letter to our parents every two weeks to which I had to add my 'M' plus two kisses (xx). Mr Kingdon would also encourage Pam and me to sing together for them. He was altogether a fine upright man with a keen love of home and country. We went for country walks by the canal with the dog and picked blackberries, all new experiences for me. Mr Kingdon would hook down the biggest out-of-reach berries with his walking stick. We did our lessons separately from the village school-children - I think we had separate teachers. We always attended church twice on Sundays. Here, I came to understand the Kingdons had some status in village affairs.

Mr Kingdon always read one of the lessons and sang all the hymns very loudly in a booming deep voice. There were other church events in the Church Hall, and Mrs Kingdon was always a part of the proceedings with her two little girls in tow. I know she loved us dearly because when the time came for us to return to our parents, she and Mr Kingdon had a long interview with our Dad to try to persuade him to let them adopt us. Pam was invited to join the class of girls being prepared for confirmation, but Pam wouldn't do anything that didn't include me. It was thought she was taking mother's instructions very seriously to always take care of me. And this she did, but I also now think that she was lonely for her mother and found a little comfort in being always with me.

There was one near-tragedy when Pam actually saved my life. On one of our joint nature walks with the general school children, we went along by the canal where we had a school picnic. On the way home, we detoured to view the weir (a small dam or waterfall). It was summer again, so we must have been in Somerset for about a year by then. It was cool and pleasant by the water rushing over the weir. I got closer to examine the water and noticed the water was rushing over a flight of steps that looked inviting to me. To get even closer to the water, I stood on the top step and stepped down to the next. Not noticing the green slippery mould on them, I began to lose my footing, and as I began to cry out, Pam was there and held on tightly to my hair. I was very nearly scalped but held safe until people rushed to help her. Pam was the heroine of the day. I should surely have been swept away and drowned had she not been keeping her eye on me. It was a pleasure to see her smiling at all the praise she received. In those days, she was a solemn, skinny little thing.

After about a year of this rather idyllic time, my mother visited us and stayed with someone in the village. I remember her pushing a baby buggy with the two little boys through the village. She was a person of interest in the village, and although Pam and I continued to stay with the Kingdons, we saw her every day. I think I was glad to see her, but she could not help but notice I was less attached to her than Pam. I don't think she stayed long, but the village folk were fairly accepting, and I remember her telling a story of how she was invited to taste just-pressed cider and walked back to her billet 'on-air'. I imagine that when she returned home again, she worried about how her daughters were changing while away from her, and one at least was perhaps in danger of forgetting her. I remember feeling uneasy for part of the time, and Pam was frequently in tears, especially at parting again. Another six months went by, and at Easter, our father arrived to visit us. He brought wonderfully decorated Easter eggs, which were a rare treat. I think he must have come to make a decision about our immediate future.

The Battle of Britain had been fought in the skies above the south of England and 'The Blitz', which was how the following period of intense bombing by German aircraft was described, lessened; perhaps there was a bit of a hiatus in hostilities. I later learned that this was when the question of adoption was again raised. Mum later told me that Mr Kingdon had said to our father, 'Your wife can have other children; my wife can't.' But my mother could never relinquish either of her daughters. She also felt that once that question had been raised, we must be removed as quickly as possible. I'm not sure how soon this was put into effect, but I do remember walking the platform of Creech St. Michael Halt, waiting for the train that would begin our journey back to our home. It was an almost frosty morning; our breath made vapour in the air. Dad walked along with me and showed me how to get the last Nestlé chocolate bars out of the vending machine. He held my hand and said, 'You are still my little Tubby.' This was his pet name for me until I was about sixteen. I loved my Dad and agreed with him. I was very accepting of what the grownups decided. The Kingdons had tried to persuade Pam, and she had been unhappy, but they let us go and even packed the clothes they had bought for us. Clothing was becoming very scarce in London.

So back to the London area we went and to our surprise, to yet another house. Dad later told us he had become worried because our house in Lichfield Road was in almost a direct line from the huge Barking Power Station, which would very obviously be a prime target for German bombers. He must have thought the small gasworks just a couple of miles from this new address was less significant. Number 73 Stanley Avenue, Dagenham, Essex, was to be our family's home for about twenty years. This house was right on the border between Dagenham and Romford, an old market town on the Roman road connecting London and Colchester. So, we were much closer to the open country and a little further away from the industry. It was possible to get to the row of shops (and school) using any one of a number of routes through the estate, but our mother showed us the one route she *always* wanted us to use. This was one of her little rules so that she would know where we were at all times. Halfway along

Whalebone Lane, outside the shops on a wide pavement (sidewalk), large brick air-raid shelters had been built. When the warning sound wailed, these would be unlocked, and people would be crammed in for protection from flying debris. It was quite well known that such protection these buildings afforded would not be effective against a direct hit. We had an Anderson shelter in the backyard, which we used, and my Dad also got a huge table from somewhere, constructed with a heavy solid wooden top on a steel frame, that he installed in our dining room. This was our emergency shelter, and the children were often put to bed under it in the winter when the garden shelter was cold and damp. There were too many stories of ceilings coming down on the upper floors while people were in bed during raids. Parents were vigilant in trying to keep everyone safe.

It was desperate, worrying times. My father was remarkable throughout this whole time. His company converted part of its operation to producing munitions. He never spoke of precisely what he was involved in. The Official Secrets Act was always respected. He went to work in the better weather on his bike, and every day my mother knew he was going to North Woolwich, which is part of the London Docks system, and that area was frequently heavily bombed - it was a prime target. Sometimes he had to find his way around bomb craters, sometimes whole roads had to be closed, but like nearly everyone else, he simply kept going. At home, he was a tower of strength, always finding solutions to problems and making light of difficulties and cheerfully keeping all our spirits up. On rare weekends when he was at home, not working overtime or spending nights on the company roof engaged in fire watching duties (his equipment for this was a tin hat, a bucket of sand and a telephone which frequently went dead!), he would give us a musical selection. At the same time, Mum cooked the Sunday dinner, and we all would have a lively singsong.

He told us amusing stories of events he witnessed, which demonstrated the British *never-say-die* resolve to resist the idea of losing the war no matter how black the future seemed. One of these stories I remember was: when riding his bike to work, which he did to save money, it could get very tricky after an air raid when the road surfaces had become damaged. On this occasion, he was threading his way through piles of rubble and came to an area of small shops. One of these, he passed regularly, and it always had a sign outside reading, 'Open as Usual'. On this occasion, after a particularly wild night, the shop had no glass at all in the large display windows, and the sign was crossed through with paint and another alongside reading 'More Open than Usual'.

Dad invented pet names for the various big anti-aircraft guns that were trundled around the streets in an endeavour to shoot down German bombers and fighter aircraft, which was actually very hard to do. The din during an air-raid could be very frightening. He would say, 'There goes old *Flang-flang* (a gun's nickname), he'll scare them off.' He would laugh heartily at old Mr Nother, a neighbour, capering about outside his shelter, waving both arms in the air and yelling, 'Give 'em hell, boys' into the night sky which was lit up with searchlights and explosions. In his limited spare time, he carved and painted wooden models of British aircraft as Christmas gifts for the boys and came home with specially made metal punches to make confetti for a wedding and designs from which we could make paper chains to decorate our home in the traditional English manner for Christmas. He made me a beautiful brass model weighing scale as I liked to play *Shop*. How I wish I still had that. I expect it was eventually given to a grandchild of my parents.

Strict rationing had been in force from the beginning of the War. Everything was rationed, and sweets and chocolate became almost non-existent. The fruit was scarce unless you lived in the country. Everyone was urged to grow food, and even we had a vegetable garden. Not a successful one really as my mother was very busy trying to feed and care for her family, and my father was seldom at home in daylight, but we did grow potatoes. At Christmas that year, the best my parents could come up with for Christmas dinner was a rabbit! We frequently had *meatless* meals and *eggless* cakes. Eggs disappeared and were replaced by a dried egg powder which we children accepted without fuss. Cheese and canned condensed milk were rationed, and it used to annoy my mother that men who had jobs that required physical effort used to get a higher allocation of these items. Clothing became rationed too, and household linen was quite unobtainable. Everyone became very good at 'make do and mend'. But the strain on everyone, especially the women, was intense. Most people's domestic lives became a constant struggle. Homes began to look threadbare. It was very irritating to the working class of people that wealthy folk could still get a square meal at restaurants in London. But even London was not a happy place with constant air raids, bombs falling, fear, and confusion everywhere.

The laws about blackouts were enforced by vigilant Air Raid Wardens. We dared not show a chink of light anywhere; even people that dared to light a cigarette heard a bellow of 'put that light out'. After a particularly bad and disturbed night, it was very hard to get up and get going with a cheerful heart. As children do, so long as our parents maintained an air of normalcy, we accepted life as it was. It was quite exciting to go and see the big crater where the latest bomb had fallen in our area. Young boys would collect shrapnel (fragments of metal bombs and shells) and ransack homes that had been demolished. Sometimes the whole side of a house would be blown away, and you could see torn wallpaper and wonder if the people had survived. Everyone was interested in 'The News' read by the well-known voices of a few newsreaders on the BBC like Alvar Lidell. Of course, whatever the BBC reported was heard as the absolute gospel truth, and everyone was cheered at the news of enemy losses.

In March 1943, our mother had another baby. Derek, a surprisingly large boy, was born during the night. I think the District Nurse delivered the baby. (In those days, children thought she actually brought the baby with her.) I did wonder why on earth my mother wanted another one, but there was so much going on I never spent very much time thinking about it. The very next morning, we had a real emergency. A low-flying German aircraft came along the backs of our row of houses machine-guns blazing, closely pursued by 'one of ours'. Mum grabbed her new baby and covered him with her own body thinking she would rather die than let the Germans murder her baby, so it would seem her maternal instincts were still in excellent working order.

How Mum planned to clothe and feed this baby, I never enquired, and the ladies of the WVS (Women's Voluntary Services) came to the rescue. Unable to breastfeed this one for long, Mum was introduced to select products developed during this time. There was National Dried Infant Milk in two strengths, half-cream, and full-cream, and exclusive coupons for an extra ration of concentrated orange juice. At the same time all schoolchildren were given one-third of a pint of milk daily, and children from really hard-pressed families, perhaps the sole wage earner was in the Services and, his wife's allowance really didn't cover their needs adequately, could apply for a nourishing container of cod-liver oil mixed with malt to make it palatable. I never sampled this delicacy. I hated the smell of it; thank the Lord, I never needed it. And so, we all struggled on.

Derek's advent gave us all a new interest. He was a beautiful baby and did well on the National Dried food. Knitting yarn always seemed available (in limited colours), and Mum and Pam always had knitting on the go. I was learning, so he had clothing, and whenever possible, Mum would put Derek in his pram and off we would go for a walk - of course, never very far. Pam was still Mum's right-hand helper, but my help was required too, especially during the early 'lying-in' days. This baby had exhausted Mum, and she needed Pam to go with her when she was fit enough to go shopping again. I remember my first efforts at nappy changing and baby rocking, which I rather enjoyed. This early experience of interaction with a baby awakened my maternal instinct.

The raids became less intense, but there were random bombs dropped, and a couple did fall right in our area, one on a nearby school in Chadwell Heath. The resulting crater was horrifying, and once again, our poor mother, whose nerves were in tatters, needed a safer haven for her children. During this time, Mum's family were all doing their bit for the war effort. Nanny and Granddad took in a lodger; there seemed to be a succession of youngish women who generally were employed in a factory in the industrial area of Dagenham. Their youngest daughter June was still at home and would have been about sixteen at this time. June was quite a beautiful, flighty girl. She used to sing with a local dance band, and she especially liked it when her audience included men in uniform - this was her war effort.

I was just getting used to being at school in Dagenham when my friend Patsy reported to me that she overheard two teachers discussing our imminent departure. It must have been an item of gossip in which families were leaving the area, and it may have been a little remarkable that our father could afford to transport his rather large family so far away. One teacher mentioned our plans, and the other reportedly said, 'They are very wise.' If teachers thought it wise, then, of course, it must be the right thing to do. I had begun to admire teachers and wanted to be one when I grew up.

So, off we all went, escorted by our father to a place that became very special to me. Derek was coming up to about a year old, and our mother was not feeling very well. She seemed tired, nervous; everyone was, to a certain extent, after four years of war. The journey to Cornwall was harrowing. It was exciting for us children to look forward to this journey because the train was a special one called 'The Cornish Riviera'; not quite the cache of the Orient Express but still the centrepiece of the Great Western Line and our Dad was impressed. The railway services in Britain were in disarray because of disruptions to the lines, delays due to air raids, and not least, the shortage of able-bodied men to cover all the jobs. We journeyed to Paddington station once again and boarded the train. There was a mob scene there, but we found enough space in a compartment for the family. Mum had packed a modest basket of food as well as our suitcases and a trunk that Dad had acquired from someone at work which contained our bed linen. There was quite a bit of baggage, and because the train was so crowded, some of it went into the guards' van. Our father seemed strong and capable to us and always dealt effectively with this kind of thing.

The train was crowded with servicemen and women, many of whom stood up in the corridors for the whole journey - it was challenging to get to the lavatories, so we weren't allowed to move about very much. This was no hardship for me. I loved the romance of long train journeys and didn't need much amusing. I was fascinated by the passing scene and enjoyed the *diddley-da, diddley-da* sound the wheels made running over the tracks. It was quite a slow journey because of the state of the line, hold-ups outside major cities, etc. Mum passed out the tea while it was still warm and when our supplies were depleted, Dad bought refreshments either on the train, tea and buns were available, or at train stops. Casual men in uniform and some women would speak to us kindly and try to help Mum with her family. Sometimes we were given a sweet or two. People were only mildly interested in each other, except for some twosomes I noticed who had eyes only for each other. Some men slept like logs in the corridors. At one time, I remember travelling through the darkness - we were not allowed to show a light.

Eventually, we arrived at Truro station where my Auntie Louise met us. I think we must have found a taxi to take us out to Callestick, the village where we would be staying. It was about five miles from Truro. The Cornish air is soft and light, and once away from the station, I remembered my time in Somerset. Cornwall is farther west than Somerset, and with Devon in between plus Dorset, these counties make up what is called the West Country. Our initial hostess was called 'Auntie Kate'. I have forgotten her surname. Auntie Louise and cousin, Peter, had been living with her for a year or two, I believe, and she very kindly took us in, too. Her West Country accent was nearly incomprehensible to us at first, but she seemed to like children. Her cottage was quite small, so we all tried to fit in with her ways. Her husband was called Wally - he had been called up into the army - we never met him.

People were very kind, and I was given ancient issues of 'Girls' Crystal', a young girl's magazine. Already an avid reader, I hoarded this treasure and didn't want to share them with anyone. Fortunately, not many were interested! I would carry them into the garden and climb into a tree and lose myself in tales of the exploits of very enterprising, plucky young girls. Pam and I were regularly sent for walks and once picked large bunches of primroses for Louise, who placed them in bowls and vases in every room of the cottage.

We didn't stay long here, but I do remember there was no running water in the cottage. All the water required for the household cooking was carried from the village pump about 50 yards downhill, along the village street. Two galvanized buckets were used for this purpose, and of course, with such a greatly expanded household, there was quite a bit of *to-ing and fro-ing* on this errand. Dad helped for a short time he was with us, but almost immediately, he had to begin making his way back to Dagenham to continue his important work (and earning his wages for us all).

Outside in the garden, there was a huge corrugated iron water butt. This water supply was for use in the garden, for washing ourselves and doing the laundry.

I remember Auntie Kate was amazed when at the end of each day my mother would begin heating water, which was poured into a galvanized bath placed in front of the fireplace. One by one, the boys were washed all over every day. Auntie Louise was amused that before the water was thrown away, I would bring my white ankle socks and wash them with a bit of soap, ready for the next day. We had a washstand in our bedroom, which Pam and I shared. It was an 'up as far as possible and down as far as possible' kind of bath most days. I also remember Kate found jigsaw puzzles for us to pore over, I loved them, but it was hard to see properly; there was no electricity. Almost everyone in the village used old fashioned oil lamps. Soon my mother discovered there was a furnished cottage available lower down in the village for rent, which we soon moved to. Perhaps the owner of this two-level house, facing the stream which ran through the lower village wanted first to see what kind of a family we were before agreeing to let us live there. I am sure we could not have all stayed very long with Auntie Kate.

This house was just fine for us. I remember the staircase, which was installed in a kind of cupboard, was just bare wood and had no floor covering or linoleum. It smelt dusty and made quite a noise when one of us ran up or down, but the house was unattached to any other, so it didn't matter if we made a noise. Also, with no running water nearby, across the stream, fresh potable water poured out of a pipe into the stream. This was the source that served the village pump the upper village used, we learned. Dad later dubbed this feature, 'The Drop'. Pam and I assumed responsibility for keeping the house supplied with fresh water, and we even began to take for granted that the only means of cooking was by lighting a fire, which was also the stove. It was quite a large black monster fitted into the fireplace nook. There were rings in the top cast-iron surface, which could be lifted out when the fire was right for a pot to be placed over the hole for cooking the food. We boiled water and cooked vegetables this way. There were two doors, one above the other on the left-hand side, which gave access to the oven. My mother learned one had to provide whatever was cooking in the oven a half-turn every so often; otherwise, the side nearest the heat source would burn, and the other side would remain uncooked.

Managing the temperature of the heat source was an acquired art. The fire was incidentally, the only source of heat in the house, but resourceful Mum learned and soon began producing Cornish pasties, the local *speciality*.

Our landlord kept the woodpile stocked. This was situated in front of the house right by the stream. To deal with the family's laundry, mother had to light a fire under a sort of black witches' cauldron set up in a small lean-to next to the woodpile and out there she would be every Monday as usual, rain or shine, a fat stick in hand pushing the dirty linen and our clothes about in the black pot. The ironing would be achieved by heating cast irons on the stovetop. Mum definitely did her best to maintain her standards. The village folk admired her industry and probably were surprised how hard she worked. Our landlord was quite impressed, I am sure. He had two daughters who were regarded as *'simple'*. These women were merely slow learners but could perform simple domestic tasks very well. One of the jobs they performed for us was to service our lavatory. With no running water in the house, the lavatory was standing alone outside and to the right of the main entrance door. It was newly painted, clean, and functional. One of these girls would replace the used bucket with a clean one each day before we were up. Our landlord thought mother was too 'ladylike' to do this job! It was Pam's and my responsibility to cut newspaper into squares, which were then pierced with a large nail, then strung on a length of twine and hung inside the outhouse for toilet paper. We learned and survived.

We were better fed in Cornwall. Now and then, a farmer would leave a rabbit on our doorstep. It would have gunshot pellets in it sometimes. A butcher came around in a little van twice a week with fresh meat. Vegetables were available from the Home Farm, where the Squire's wife was managing operations. We also had a village store where Mum used the ration books when she purchased cheese and eggs etc. Two new dishes made their way into our diet: the Cornish pasty and Cornish cream. The cream was produced by scalding the fresh-from-the cow milk and then allowing it to cool. The excellent cream was then skimmed off to be added to our breakfast toast and jam or for topping pies. We had no refrigeration, but we even learned to make a little real butter, which mother craved as we had only had awful margarine, which was also strictly rationed. When summer arrived, we had more fruit than we had ever seen in London. Mum had quickly learned from Kate the skills she needed here!

A twice-daily event for us was watching the cows from the farm across the stream leave for the fields every morning and come back in the evening for milking. They made their way in their own time and always lifted their tails and pooped into the stream. I thought we were lucky our house was just upstream from their usual crossing place but must confess we picked watercress downstream without worrying about it. The stream always looked sparklingly clean to us. And we all were remarkably healthy.

We had a little walled garden just outside the front door of the house, and I have a very clear memory of Derek standing against the wall of the house. Pam and I would move to the garden gate and hold out our arms to encourage Derek to walk. Pam was determined to teach him because he was a plump little boy and was becoming much too heavy for our mother to carry. After a very few sessions, he managed it, and we showed our mother his achievement with great pride. That day she had had a little outing to Truro with her sister mostly for a change of scenery and also for shopping. There was a twice-weekly bus for the convenience of the farmers' wives that made this trip on the appointed mornings and returned home again in the afternoons.

Very soon after our arrival in Cornwall, we were enrolled in the nearest school. The closest school proved to be not very near at all. We had at least a three-mile walk to the village of Perranzabuloe, where there was an old two-room schoolhouse. Our village of Callestick had few children who needed public education. The land-owning families still had their children educated privately. I remember the walk to school very well, Pam and I plus Brian, if it were a fine day, would leave before 8.00 am. The walk was a little too much for six and a half-year-old Brian, so Mum would keep him at home if it was raining hard or cold and windy.

Brian remembers the first time he attended school with us. He told me we had to sit with him all day, probably because he couldn't bear to be left in a strange environment, and when the time came for us to return home, he says he cried all the way. Pam told me to take his hand and drag him along. Eventually, I let go and was prepared to leave him where he sat bawling. Pam lifted him and began to carry him. I think I tried to help - my memory of this incident is not quite the same as Brian's, I have a vague memory of forming a chair with our crossed hands to carry him. We were not successful because Pam and I were not the same height. I loved the walk every morning through the frequently muddy country lanes because I loved school. Along the way, we would pass a farm with a bit of a bog outside the farmhouse. A boy lived here who we sometimes walked with. His name was Dickson, and he would jump onto the bog (when it was somewhat drier than usual) just to show off a little. We were somewhat nervous about Cornish bogs, so he seemed brave. He was a merry soul, and I rather liked him. He was the very first boy I ever thought a little bit interesting.

Pam and I both liked our teacher, Mrs McKinley. Pam felt somewhat affronted that we were now in the same classroom. There were only two classes. The infants, ages five to seven years, were in a separate room, with a motherly soul and a younger helper as teachers, and everyone else was in the primary classroom. But Mrs McKinley was a very competent teacher. She arranged her class by age with the youngest in the first block of desks (on her left), the oldest, those approaching fourteen years of age, which was the general school-leaving age, sitting in the block of desks on her right. All the others fitted into the two centre blocks. Pam, of course, was among the oldest in the class, and Mrs McKinley recognised that this girl was struggling with the changes that trying to absorb an education during wartime brought and the other domestic difficulties Pam faced. It would not have gone unnoticed that Pam was always concerned with the well-being of her younger siblings. Pam later told me she had commented in an essay she hated school and 'if it weren't for Mrs McKinley' she would never go there. Our teacher reacted to this cry for help promptly and called Pam in for a friendly chat to find out what bothered her. The conversation must have soothed Pam's feelings a bit. There were few people in her life that considered Pam's hopes and dreams. But I don't think she was desperately unhappy. There had been just too many changes and responsibilities in her young life for her to imagine a better future.

We regularly had music lessons, and Pam practised the piano a little. This pleased her greatly. The lessons mainly consisted of singing traditional English songs, and I particularly remember 'Cherry Ripe', 'Hark, Hark the Lark', and 'The Sea Songs' etc. We sang rousing marches and hymns. Every day started with Morning Prayers, a hymn, and a short passage from the Bible, which we took turns to read. We said grace before eating our packed lunches - religion was nurtured; it was the help and support of many. We also all shared nature studies, geography, and history. I remember that for geography, we studied South America for some unknown reason, and for history, it must have been about the glory of the British Empire. We were more patriotic then as a people than at any other time. We practised penmanship together. Mrs McKinley would read aloud classic literary works in instalments, which I loved, and each day she would take a particular group for arithmetic. She must have had her hands full because I also remember that she was preparing five 10-year olds for the 11-plus examination. Sometimes we all took part in quizzes created especially for this group. I quite liked these times and, for an almost nine-year-old, did quite well occasionally. I certainly wasn't bored.

During that summer, our mother would sometimes meet us for lunch. By prior arrangement, we would walk part of the way towards the village, and she, having first prepared our lunch and having found a village girl to come in to watch the children at home, would walk to meet us. Sometimes she brought fresh, warm Cornish pasties, I didn't particularly like the meat in them, but I liked the time we had Mum to ourselves. I did like the pastry and the potato and onion and the warm, savoury aroma of the pasties. Other times it was sandwiches. Not so exciting, but Mum, who missed her husband, liked a little time to herself and seeing her girls, was pleased to have a break and share a little relaxation with us.

Almost without our noticing, things changed around us. There seemed to be more trucks rumbling through the village, occasionally a Jeep. Sometimes we would see a man in khaki. We didn't know, but the U.S. Army was arriving. This event changed everything!

Mrs Cattermole came for a short visit with her two children. Perhaps she needed some respite from conditions in the London area where the German bombs were wreaking havoc. At this time, I heard my mother talking with another adult, and little *Miss Big*

Ears heard plenty! It was reported that these 'Yanks' were 'overpaid, oversexed, and over here'. This was a chance remark made by an English general that was frequently repeated. They were indeed, everywhere. What an impact they had! All the women who were living without men were excited. The Americans filled the pubs and made local dances wildly successful. The local inhabitants found their 'jitterbugging' style of dancing rather shocking. It was impossible to be unaware of their presence for very long. Even Mum was visited by a few rather nice types who were satisfied with a cup of tea and a bit of conversation with a woman with a 'lovely family'. Many of these young men were simply homesick.

Pam perked up considerably; she was now approaching fourteen years old and was a well-developed girl. Her figure and her mature air made her seem somewhat older.

My mother was warned gently by her 'visitors' to keep an eye on Pam because not far from our house encamped on high ground a mile or so away were two divisions. One of which was a coloured troop! Mum's visitors were gentlemen of the South, and this was before the Civil Rights Movement. These men were very generous and always handed out gifts. Girls were given perfume and nylon stockings. Mum received gifts of food, sometimes several items. Perhaps they had been instructed to try to make their stay popular with the local residents. They would ask what she would like - apparently, and they could get practically anything. We missed meat and loved the cans of Spam, and what we thought were Vienna sausages. I guess now that they were hotdogs. We were reintroduced to chocolate and other candy, and we quickly learned to say to any man in khaki, 'Got any gum, chum?'

In our experience, the Americans worked hard to make themselves worthy of welcome, but of course, to many Englishmen, their presence was viewed with alarm, and there were many disturbances in the towns. Louise, who by this time had learned to drive and buzzed around the lanes running a mobile library, came to see Mum, and we heard them laughing together about what was happening in the cinemas, much necking, and pubs, much fighting. Dad made one of his rare visits to see us and made friends with some of the guys, mainly when he played the piano in their Mess Hall and got them singing. They would say to him wistfully, 'My mom/sister/brother is a piano player.' Much of what they saw, they related to their own precious home life. Dad thought his family was pretty safe! And so, he went back to his working life.

On the morning of 6th June 1944, we went to school as usual. It was a lovely day, and I had celebrated my ninth birthday on the day before, so I was looking forward to telling my teacher about it. We remarked as we walked along through early summer lanes how unnaturally quiet everything seemed. We assembled in our usual places and stood at the entry of our teacher. It was standard practice in schools in England that students stand at the entrance of a teacher as a mark of respect. She hurried in with an air of suppressed excitement. She said, 'Good morning', as usual, then immediately 'Get out your penmanship exercise books, everyone.' This was unusual, no morning prayers?

She was a little flushed, almost flustered. Her pleated kilt-style skirt flared as she moved. She wrote on the blackboard in a flowing script:

Wednesday, 6th June 1944. Today the Allied forces landed in France. Rejoice, today is the beginning of the end of the War.

Somebody started to cheer, and girls began to clap; male feet were stamped on the wooden floor. We all became excited, and some of the older students wanted to ask questions. Smiling widely, she calmed us and encouraged us to write out the message she had written in chalk and then said when that was done, we could return to the schoolyard for an early *playtime* - our name for recess. Naturally, we were all high spirited when set free, and Mrs McKinley conferred with the infant teachers about this vital news. Of course, many of us didn't understand what this news meant.

As the days passed, we heard of the loss of so many lives that occurred in achieving a foothold in France, but as time went on, it was clear this was the beginning of the Allies' joint offensive to overcome Germany and losses were unavoidable. We became more aware why there had been all those Americans and their equipment in our part of Cornwall and, now that they were all gone, we missed them. But there was one unusual occurrence Pam reported. It happened a week or two later.

When we were playing in the schoolyard after lunch that

day, I was stung on my head by a bee. Such a thing had not happened to me before, and I tore at my hair, dancing in a kind of frenzy. Mrs McKinley came to my aid and realised what had happened, by which time I was sobbing. The sting was removed, and a wet laundry blue bag was fetched and applied (it must have been a country remedy), and I was escorted to the Infants' room to be cosseted, while the rest of the school filed into the classrooms for the afternoon. Pam lagged behind hoping for a word with her special teacher and to her surprise Mrs McKinley was just standing and staring at a figure in naval uniform coming through the gate into the schoolyard carrying a white duffel bag. Mrs McKinley dropped her bundle of papers and ran into this person's arms and was lifted clean off her feet, even though the naval man was not overly tall and swung round. Worldly-wise by now, Pam understood the man to be Mrs McKinley's sailor husband, home at last on leave. She thought this just lovely, so-o romantic.

Pam became quite depressed because she had begun to feel like a young lady from the admiring glances and words that had been directed her way by those American servicemen, which probably illustrates how devastated many a young woman felt. The dances and flirtations and more were at an end. For the first time, we were encouraged to help a local farmer bring in his harvest of potatoes. We worked in his fields and were paid a little money, which we gave to our mother as there was nothing for us to spend it on. Perhaps she bought little treats for all of us. Pam enjoyed this, partly because there was quite a crowd of girls and boys helping the Land Army girls, and a lot of good-natured chaffing went on, which I remember not quite being a part of. And so, the rest of the summer passed. We were now able to go to Perranporth, which is a seaside town and, since it is on the north coast of Cornwall, had been cleared of some of the 'defences' and opened for public use once again. It was felt that as the British and the U.S. navies had won the Battle of the Atlantic, there was no longer any threat from that quarter.

We spent many summertime days here, and I loved it. The sand is a lovely golden shade; there are rocky pools and big rolling waves coming in from the Atlantic. I would turn cartwheels one after the other in a circle, and we all turned golden brown in the sun. It was quite a distance from our temporary home, but we could walk home if we took it slowly. One time a farmer on his way home with two large horses put Pam and me up on one for a ride. The horses' backs were very broad, but I really liked riding a horse!

I remember the country lanes with fruit trees in the gardens. All country children would indulge in a little plum or apple scrumping, but our Cornish idyll was coming to an end. On the last time went to the beach, there was a group of American Servicewomen who gave us a large slab of slightly soft chocolate. These people seemed so glamorous. There was a massive rock like a sentinel on the beach called Chapel Rock. It must have been a Sunday because I remember as the afternoon was drawing to a close, an Inter-denominational Service of Thanksgiving was held, and many of those in uniforms were drawn to it. We couldn't tell American uniforms from British ones. But if we were given gum, they were surely American.

In retrospect, it seemed that our mother did quite well in Cornwall. She certainly had to work hard, but it was peaceful in that part of the country, and our diet had improved. I think she felt quite well again, but she surely missed Dad. I know many letters were exchanged, and Dad did come for brief visits twice while we were there. As the summer came to an end and autumn began, Mum's thoughts turned to home once again, I'm sure, but it wasn't yet safe enough. The Germans had a massive stockpile of weapons and never seriously thought they would eventually use them until the Allies reached French soil. They had to fight for every inch of eastward progress made. I next remember we were involved in rehearsals for a Grand Concert, possibly being prepared for an eventual Victory celebration. Hand-in-hand with a young boy my age, I was going to sing a duet, 'The bells are ringing for me and my gal', a popular song of that time, and I know I was looking forward to taking part in this. It was planned to take place in a church hall. I was provided with a fancy new dress which I had to give back, but as it never happened for me, my memory of the details is sketchy. I was sad at the thought of leaving Cornwall. I loved the English countryside and still do.

By June 1944, we were back in Dagenham, but were now under surprise attacks from a new German secret weapon: the V-1 Flying Bomb (doodlebug or buzz bomb), followed later that year by the larger V-2 missile. Of course, they were aimed at London, and to get there they had to pass over Kent or Essex. Sometimes, these flying bombs would veer off course, or fall short! Launched from the French coast, the V-1 had a characteristic whining hum as they passed over, and then the sound would stop, and we would all hold our breath until the explosion signalled the end of their journey. There was one daylight explosion that happened without any warning. I was emptying the teapot at the time into an outside drain, planning to attempt to make the tea. Simultaneously with the explosion, I was lifted *bodily up* by an unseen force, thrown several feet and deposited firmly up against the coal bunker, which was at the other side of the house. Fortunately, I lifted my arms and was relieved to be able to report to my Mum, 'It's all right Mum, I didn't break the teapot, I didn't break the teapot!' I was terrified of breaking anything as things were hard to replace, and my mother always scolded carelessness. Then I burst into tears as I was really frightened.

There was another quite comical incident. We weren't having many raids but were surprised by a daytime one, and it must have been on a Saturday. Mum wasn't feeling too well, and she was resting in the sitting room, taking a nap with Derek. The warning siren sounded, and right away, we knew we had to take cover. Pam had cooked a quick lunch; I think it was eggs and chips. Mum yelled from the sitting room we should take our plates of food into the hallway and close all the doors. We assembled there in a very orderly fashion, and right away, we heard the sound of a flying bomb passing overhead. We were annoyed that we had been interrupted when about to eat but were safe enough because there were no windows in the hallway where we sat. We were at the end farthest from the street door; the glass there was taped. There was an explosion, Brian and Michael both flinched, and their food slid off the plates onto the floor! Pam and I were quite annoyed because we had to pick it up for them and clean-up, then we all sat down again on the floor in this narrow hallway and with knives and forks, calmly went on with lunch.

I was glad to be going back to school and, to be with my friend Patsy again, although for a time we were a little strange with each other. We had a different teacher now, a Mrs Dubocque. She had a strange habit of speaking out of the left side of her mouth - I realise now she had a neurological problem, but it was weird and, as children do, we used to imitate her and make fun of her. She was assisted by another teacher who was French, with quite an exciting way of speaking with an accent and together they must have been very conscientious because I remember learning lists and lists of spelling words, grammar and sentence construction rules in a very short space of time.

In those days, teachers didn't hesitate to arrange their class by ability. There were tests in reading and arithmetic every Friday, and every Monday, we would be seated in our places according to how we had scored on these tests. A girl called Helen Norman, and I usually took turns at top honours and sat in the first place in the 'top block'. This was very good for me because when I first went back to school, not knowing the system, I was placed in the third block (there were four blocks altogether), and I gradually made my way to this prominent position. I think my competitive spirit had been stimulated in Cornwall.

Once home again, I became much more aware of the progress of the war. Dad always had 'The Daily Mirror' delivered, and each week there would be a special section with a map showing the advance of the various armies towards German soil. Dad would show me this and compare it to the one from the week before. The newsreels in the cinemas showed overjoyed people in French towns being liberated by the British forces. The newsreels were careful not to frighten the population. We seldom saw any of the dead. We also gained the idea Britain was winning the war without much reference to the Commonwealth and American contribution (which was massive). I thought long after the fact that ordinary working-class British people never really recognised the debt owed to the U.S. at that time. Perhaps we do now as the progress of the war has been thoroughly documented in the movies many times. In any event, we all were enormously proud of how well 'our boys' were doing.

Much earlier, when the British Army had driven the Italian and Rommel's German troops out of North Africa, the Allies landed in Sicily to begin the Battle for Italy. Italy was an ally of Germany. Once on the European mainland, the Italians began to welcome the Allied forces, but there were many German units to be defeated. Fighting was fierce and progress slow, but once the Allies entered

Rome, all opposition crumbled very quickly. At the same time, Russia was pushing back German forces, which had overrun vast areas of European Russia. Eventually, the Allies were on German soil, and we knew the war could not last much longer. Unfortunately, the newsreels were full of pictures of refugees and the dispossessed searching for loved ones, homes that didn't exist anymore, and even a completely new life because the old one had been wiped out. While slow progress was made on the ground, the air forces were bombing German targets resulting in even greater devastation than England had suffered.

The family situation during this time was tested. Our mother was very glad to be back in her own home with her husband, but Dad looked very tired and worn. Living in the London area throughout the period of the war was not easy for the working man. He suffered from sleep deprivation due to his fire-watching activities during the bombing and malnutrition because Mum hadn't been there to make meals for him. Our mother became quickly worn out too on returning to London after the Cornish idyll. With four children in school, and one pre-schooler, the house needed quite a lot of work; it looked very dingy and neglected. The bed linen was badly worn, many things needed replacing, and we all needed some new clothes too; there was very little money. But everyone was very hopeful things would improve soon.

And then, suddenly, for us, the **WAR WAS OVER!** VE Day (Victory in Europe) was proclaimed for May 8th, 1945, and everyone went wild with joy. We didn't understand how many long years it would take to recover from that terrible conflict.

Maureen's grandmother, Trisscella at 21 years

Trisscella (left) on her wedding day in 1907, with her husband Thomas Steeden and her sister, Maud

Maureen's parents, Ellen and William Starling on their wedding day August 1928

Maureen (right) with her sister, Pam, about 1942

Michael

My maternal grandmother, Elizabeth Hiscock, was born in Newfoundland, at Scilly Cove (now called Winterton), on 18th September 1874. At this time, Newfoundland was not part of Canada, but a Dominion within the British Empire and most of the families in Scilly Cove made a living from fishing in Trinity Bay and beyond. I remember her telling us stories about the quaint fishing villages with romantic-sounding names like 'Heart's Content' and 'Harbour Grace' but also how hard life was in the winter months. She also spoke about the times if a villager had married into another location, the men would sometimes drag a house across the sea-ice to relocate it for a family in another village. The Hiscock family had been in this area since about 1758, and many of the families here originally came from Ireland, the English West Country, or other parts of Europe.

During her teenage years, my grandmother moved to Halifax, Nova Scotia, and found work in domestic service for a family that had a drapery store. While working in this situation, she was involved in a terrible accident when an oil lamp was overturned and, her dress caught fire. She was left with very severe scarring on her upper body and arms. It was believed in the family that the accident caused deep emotional scars for the rest of her life. She never seemed able to be a happy woman. However, at twenty-nine years of age, she met and married my grandfather Frederick Arliss, in Halifax, in 1903. He was in the British Royal Navy, serving as a medical officer aboard H.M.S. Pallas. She was deeply grateful to Frederick as she had thought for a long time that she was so severely disfigured, no man would want her. She moved to England shortly after the wedding, and they settled in Southsea, a suburb of the naval city of Portsmouth, where my grandfather continued with his career at sea.

My mother, Florence Lalia Arliss, was born on 15th August 1905, quickly followed by a son Reginald and then another daughter, Lilian Grace. A third daughter Hilda was born a few years later to complete the family. Elizabeth made one return trip to Nova Scotia around 1926 aboard the Red Star liner 'Zeeland',

and by all accounts, it seems that she went alone. At about the same time, my grandfather retired from the navy, where he had risen to the rank of Chief Petty Officer, the family moved to Bromley-by-Bow where they bought an Off-License in this dreary suburb in the East End of London, so they were considered reasonably 'comfortably off'.

It was probably around this time that my mother met my father. I have little knowledge of my father's family and must assume he lived all his younger life in the East End of London. My history of him begins in approximately 1925, around the time he had met my mother. He was employed by the London Underground Railway, also known as 'The Tube', and his father was at this time working as a tinsmith. My father spent a short time in the Merchant Navy before this, and my mother remembered later he talked about seeing the Island of Tenerife taking form out of the early morning mist. However, she reported that he never liked life at sea and was discharged after serving for only a short time. These were difficult economic times with general strikes and the beginning of the Great Depression. My mother's parents were forced to sell their business in Bromley and retire with their four children to Manor Park, East London, which is close to the Essex County border at Barking.

After a lengthy courtship, my parents were married on 14th July 1929 at St. Barnabas Church, which was near to her parent's home. She was twenty-three years old, and my father thirty. They began their life together in Byron Avenue just around the corner from my grandparents' house. The next year, my grandfather Frederick Charles Arliss died at the age of fifty-four years from heart failure.

I, Michael John Harbott, was born on 7th October 1935, at Plaistow Hospital in the East End of London, just a few miles from Bow Church, which makes me a true *Cockney*. I often remember my mother saying what a frail and sickly infant I was. Before I was three years old, my tonsils were removed as the doctors felt infected tonsils were the cause of my poor health. I did improve a little but was always a picky eater, and my poor mother, who tried to present a varied diet, still had great difficulty getting any vegetables into me. But I was a wiry youngster and always had lots of energy. My brother Denis, who had been born nearly three years earlier at Stratford, London, was just the opposite – a quiet and seemingly contented child.

My memories of this time are few, but I do remember the horse-drawn milk carts which came by daily and the occasional coal delivery, also horse-drawn, with filthy men heaving huge sacks of coal and dumping them into the bowels of our coal cellar under the house. The dust this exercise stirred up was incredible. Coal fires were our only source of heat in the home, apart from the odd evil-smelling paraffin stove used on extra cold days. My mother had a small garden at the back of the house and liked to gather horse manure, which was used to enrich the poor soil. She would send Denis or me down the street with a particular bucket to collect it after the horses had made a deposit. I also remember the tramcars at East Ham and Stratford and just loved the sight of them lumbering along the tracks and changing lines. There were also still a few London buses with open tops and outside staircases. These were always a thrill to ride on. I seem to have always been interested in transportation as our mother took us out and about a lot, often walking long distances until my little legs ached.

By this time, my father was a conductor on the London Underground trains, and sometimes we would meet him on the train where, much to my delight, he would allow me to push the button to close the train doors. There was much talk about the war at this time. Although I did not understand what was going on, I do remember my parents telling me we listened to the radio on 3rd September 1939. They spoke to my brother and me in serious tones that I hardly comprehended. War against Germany had been declared, and things would get difficult for us. We learned Poland had been overrun, and Holland, Belgium, and France were quickly falling to the advancing Germans.

To save money and to keep my grandmother company, who would otherwise have had to live alone, my parents sold the house they had been buying in Byron Avenue, and we all moved into 187 Browning Road with her. This was a sizeable Victorian-era house with big rooms, high moulded ceilings, and servants' quarters. My parents, Denis, and I occupied a small place next to the kitchen at the back of the house as living space, and my grandmother had a large room at the front and a bedroom upstairs at the back. My mother and father also had a large bedroom upstairs on the front of the house, and Denis and I had to share an upstairs bedroom. In all the main rooms, there was a bell push used to call the maid in earlier days. My grandmother joined us for meals, always cooked by my mother, and it seemed to me she hardly ever said a word except to complain. She seemed to me to be a heartbroken woman. My brother had attended Kensington Primary School just around the corner from where we lived for several years, and I had just started going there. As my father's work was considered an essential service, military service was not in his future, but he did join the local Home Guard. There were rifles for only a fraction of the men, and the rest were armed with shotguns, swords, improvised clubs, and staves. They did serve to give the community a sense of direct involvement in the defense of Britain. From July 1940, the German Air force (Luftwaffe) attempted to gain air supremacy over the Royal Air Force, and the Battle of Britain began over Southern England, lasting over three months. The Luftwaffe ultimate failure was partially instrumental in stopping Germany from invading the island and was a significant turning point in the war. By the summer of 1940, air raid shelters built of massive cement blocks were being constructed in all schoolyards. We were all issued gas masks, which had a distinctive new rubber smell and made a funny noise as you breathed with them on. We had to practice getting to the shelters in an orderly fashion. They were very dark inside, and we would all sit around with our gas masks on looking like a bunch of aliens. It seemed like a game to us.

During the months up until this time, air attacks had been concentrated on air force bases and radar installations in the South-East of England. But on the 24th August, the Luftwaffe was assigned to attack the huge oil storage facilities at Thames Haven just five miles from where we lived. The warning siren sounded during the night, and my mother hustled us downstairs and under the stairs into the coal cellar. I can remember being scared when the tremendous noise from the anti-aircraft guns started. The big guns were mounted on trailers, which were towed around the streets, and it seemed they were right outside our house even though they were likely further away. The trembling ground deceived me in terms of their proximity. Apparently, several bombers had lost their position and visual contact with their leader, and as they were under heavy attack, they unloaded their bombs over London. Two fell in the heart of the city and the rest on London boroughs, killing many people. The British retaliated by bombing Berlin.

The next day my parents cleaned out the area in the coal cellar, as it looked like we might have to spend many nights down there. There was no heat, and we had to use candles for light; also, it was terribly dusty. Our parents told us to dive under the kitchen table if there was no time to go downstairs. My Dad and other neighbours dug a hole in the garden, and an Anderson shelter was installed. The Anderson shelter was constructed from straight and curved sheets of galvanized corrugated iron, which formed the roof and back and sides. This structure was sunk about four feet into the soil, covered with about six inches of earth and closed at the open end by a heavy door. Four bunk beds were fitted to the space so we could all sleep there. However, my father was usually either working or on Home Guard duty.

On the night of 7th September 1940, over 900 German bombers and fighters crossed the Channel, and London was then bombed consecutive nights for almost the next two months, killing over 40,000 people. The raids in our area increased and intensified. Many nights I remember being woken and carried or sometimes walking, down to the shelter. Often the attack had already started, and I wanted to linger and watch as the enemy aircraft were captured in the beams of many searchlights, and the flak could be seen exploding around them. The noise was terrifying. I was hustled to the shelter unafraid of the danger but left wondering why the Germans would want to kill us as we had done nothing wrong. The next morning, I was out in the garden or street scavenging for shrapnel (remnants of bombs and shells). We would also walk over to a small local park where a barrage balloon was based. Sometimes we watched it being inflated into an enormous shape with huge 'ears'. It reminded me of a flying elephant. The balloon was tethered to a truck with a winch and allowed to rise high in the sky when the word of approaching enemy aircraft was received. There were units located around London, and South-East England and the cables were a threat to the planes as they approached their targets. Aircraft did not fly very high in those days. There were many aircraft that crowded the skies, but luckily the particular sound of their engines voiced whether the plane was our enemy or not. One morning in September, just as my brother and I were waking up, a lone enemy fighter plane came low over our house with its guns blazing. We dived under our beds and waited, but it did not return. Another morning we were having breakfast and heard a crash upstairs. Upon investigation, we found a huge piece of ornate ceiling plaster moulding lying on my pillow, about where my head would have been an hour earlier. The constant shaking from the guns firing and bombs falling loosened many parts of these older houses.

By this time, hundreds of children were being evacuated out of London into the countryside, and my parents felt we were in too much danger because the area we lived in was so close to the London Docks which were a prime target. Our next-door neighbours, the Andersons, had left and found accommodation at a small farm in the county of Shropshire, near the Welsh border. My mother had been writing to Violet Anderson, and it was arranged that we could stay on a farm close by them. We were not given many details but were told to get the train to Shrewsbury and then walk to the bus station, from where we could get a bus going to Bishop's Castle. They arranged to meet us at a small hamlet called Plox Green.

Leaving home early one morning with several suitcases, we made our way by Underground to Paddington Station. Paddington was one of the mainline stations, and the sight of all those huge steam locomotives made me feel excited. We left the London area, and I remember looking at all that countryside with farms and animals and bridges over roads, rivers, and other railway lines, all very fascinating for a young boy from the city. My brother was with us, of course, but he seemed to take it all very calmly. We moved very slowly through the city of Banbury, and then the train stopped. The guard (conductor) walked through the train and informed everyone there had been an air raid, and bombs had fallen on Birmingham and beyond. The train could not proceed until the lines had been checked for safety. We were delayed for several hours, and it was late in the afternoon before we finally started on our way again. Then we moved very slowly through the industrial cities of Birmingham and Wolverhampton. After that, we passed a very active Air Force base right next to the railway line. My eyes were popping at the sight of all these fighting aircraft, which I had never seen on the ground before. Arriving very late in Shrewsbury, we were all tired and had what seemed to me like quite a long walk to the bus station where we had to wait for our bus, a single-decker, not the double-decker buses we were used to in London. It was filled with folk returning from a market day in that city. The bus made many stops, dropping people off at farms and small cottages, passing through the small market towns of Pontesbury and Minsterley. It was getting dark when we finally arrived at Plox Green and being very tired. I can't remember who met us or how we got to 'The Farm'.

The next morning a whole new and fascinating world opened to me. The farm 'Capsall' was situated in the Hope Valley; isolated on high ground about a half-mile up a dirt track from the Shrewsbury – Bishop's Castle road. Built of brick and stone, the house seemed huge. One end of the main living and dining area, accessed from the back yard, had a large black stove with an open wood-burning fire, cooking plates and an oven at the side. A big black kettle hung over the open flames. The floors were all stone, and there were few carpets or rugs. On the far side of this room, steps led down into a pantry where large sides of salted beef and pork hung along with plucked chickens and ducks. Strung between them were strips of sticky paper full of caught flies, and there were some live ones buzzing around. There was no electricity or running water in the house. Water was collected as required from a tank located in a stream a short distance from the home, and the light was provided by oil lamps or candles.

We had one large bedroom upstairs with wooden floors, no rugs, and some old heavy furniture. On one piece, a washbasin and a big jug were displayed, and by the bed was a commode for everyone's use, as there were no toilets in the house. For personal bathing, cold water was brought upstairs in the jug, and hot water was added from the kettle to take the chill off. On the oft rare bath nights, a metal bathtub was brought into the kitchen for my brother and me, and warm water was added from the boiler to the right of the kitchen stove. I believe this took place on a Friday or Saturday evening when the menfolk were out at the pub. My mother thought this was all very appalling, and I'm not sure whether she was ever able to take a bath herself. As it was cold at night, my mother would fill a stone hot water bottle, and she, Denis, and I slept in the same large bed. My brother and I soon developed chilblains, an itchy, painful skin disorder, on our feet. With no running water in the house, the toilet facilities were similarly primitive. The only outhouse was situated across a courtyard around the side of the house, built over a stream. It was a wooden structure with a bench seat with openings for two people. There was only torn up newspaper for toilet paper, and the smell and flies were awful in the summertime. My mother was horrified, but as a boy, it did not bother me too much.

The farm family consisted of Mr and Mrs Potter, their son Clifford (about twenty-one years old), and a daughter Olive (about nineteen). Another son George and daughter Doris had married and moved away earlier. Mr Potter was never clean. He wore thick breeches that were caked in cow dung and heavy boots with a cap over his balding head, and he fashioned a heavy moustache. I was afraid of him when he would occasionally take me on his knee. As the whole family had a strong Shropshire accent, I hardly understood a word they said, and according to my mother, I spoke very fast, so I am sure they couldn't make out what I was saying either.

I never saw the heavy front door used, but outside the back door was a stone courtyard leading to the main farmyard, which had cow and pig sheds around all sides, with a gate through to the fields. In the courtyard and adjoining garden, there were two dogs, three or four cats and always kittens, ducks, and a ferret in a cage! I found out later the ferret was used for chasing rabbits out of their burrows so that the farmer or his sons could shoot them. Mrs Potter, a large roundish, cheerful woman, always fed the chickens at certain times, and they would all come running to her when she appeared and called them. We collected the eggs daily with her; it was like a treasure hunt. There was also a big rooster strutting around, and I used to love to tease him. But one day, he got the better of me when he started to chase me, and I ran but tripped and fell in the dirt with the cock pecking away at my legs. Hearing my cries, Olive came to my rescue, and I had much more respect for that rooster after that.

The Potters had a lot of cattle. I do not know how many, but twice every day, they had to be milked by hand. In the morning and late afternoon, they would voluntarily come to the farmyard gate from the fields and wait to be let in. Once inside the yard, they would go straight to their allocated pen in the shed and wait to be milked. Of course, I had to try sitting on the stool with my head tucked into the cows' side, squeezing the swollen teats, but my little hands weren't strong enough to extract any milk. Clifford would always fool around whilst milking and squirt milk directly at us or even at a cat sitting by the shed door with its mouth open. They would milk into a small bucket and transfer it to a large churn by the door. There were cups available, and we would drink the warm frothy milk. Everyone milked except Mrs Potter, who always seemed to be preparing food in the house.

Each morning after milking, the churns were loaded onto a horse-drawn cart and taken the half-mile down to the road where the creamery truck picked up. Once the morning milking was over, the cows were turned loose into the fields, and the cowsheds had to be cleaned out. Layers of straw were laid prior to the cows coming back again in the evening, and the next morning all the wet straw had to be removed with a shovel and wheelbarrow and taken to the middle of the farmyard and piled into a massive heap. This manure was later spread onto the fields. My mother did not like me near this messy mountain of cow poop, but I wanted to help with the cleanup, as did my brother.

The Potters also had pigs, which could wander in the yard, adding to the quagmire, particularly when it rained. A whole bunch of piglets was born in one of the sheds shortly after we arrived, and this was captivating for me to see them all trying to suckle on their mother. Periodically, they would kill a pig for food. I was not allowed to watch but learned that they strung it up by the hind feet with the pig making a tremendous shrieking then cut its throat, allowing all the blood to drain out before butchering it. They would also slaughter cattle, but I believe they would take them away to the abattoir, and everything would come back salted. There was no refrigeration.

Chickens, geese, and turkeys met the executioner's block in the garden. It used to amaze me how they kept running around for a few minutes with no head. Of course, my mother tried to protect us from all this brutality, but I used to sneak out as often as I could. Clifford was always trying pranks on us 'city folk', and I was generally the willing participant. Once, we were in the fields amongst the cows that were all lying down. Clifford said it was all right to sit on one, and I jumped at the chance. He sat on one, and the cow stayed put. As soon as I was comfortably seated, the cow stood up and took off with me holding on to the horns. After a while, I lost my grip and fell to the ground. I was shaken but otherwise uninjured. Clifford laughed his head off but suggested we should not tell my mother. She found out though to my dismay, I believe from my brother who was with us. Clifford also had an old car, and occasionally, when he could get petrol (it was rationed), he would take us for a drive around the fields. I used to love to just sit in this car and play with the controls, including sounding the rubber horn. Once, in a later stay at the farm, Clifford let me steer it while he controlled the pedals.

The Potters also had sheep that were usually kept in a field on a steep slope that ran down to a brook. In this field, there was a long metal trough with sides and a ramp leading up to it. Occasionally we observed this trough filled with yellow liquid and the sheep getting driven up the ramp until they fell into the trough and had to swim through the liquid and clamber out the other end. The Border Collie dogs kept them moving in line while this disinfecting process was carried out. On several occasions, while we were at the farm, the shearer would arrive and shear the sheep with hand clippers. I never knew what happened to the wool, but assume it was sold. And of course, there were beautiful little lambs born in the spring, and I can remember Olive holding some that were frail, by the fire in the farmhouse kitchen, to keep them warm. She would feed them milk by hand using baby bottles. Calves were also born, usually in the cowsheds but sometimes in the fields, and often Mr Potter and his son were up during the night helping a cow in distress. I remember the first time I saw a cow lie down and give birth and then lick the calf clean and clean up most of the afterbirth. It was quite a revelation for a kid whose only experience of animal life up to this time was with the (male) family cat! My brother, Denis, and I were enrolled in a small school in the village of Hope about two and a half miles from the farmhouse, mainly across fields and over fences and stiles. Hope could hardly be called a village as there were only two or three cottages there, and the children came from all the surrounding farms for grades up to about age eleven.

My mother walked with us for the first few days, and then we were on our own, wearing Wellington boots and rainwear for the frequent inclement weather. I did not learn much at this school, and my brother's education certainly suffered, but it was thought that we would not be there for very long.

By June 1941, the air raids on London eased, and the Germans were moving some troops and the Luftwaffe away from Western Europe and tackling the Russians in the east. Many people thought the war would soon be over. We stayed at the farm until later that year when my mother brought us back to London to be with our father. There were still some raids and many false alarms, so we spent many nights in the dampness of the garden shelter, but my brother and I slept well despite the foul location. Our lives returned to almost normal except for the strict food rationing, and there was ongoing talk of the war in Europe, Asia, and the Pacific. I remember my mother mentioning the considerable build-up of American troops in Britain. Their large air force contingent together with the British was bombing Germany and other European targets. There was great excitement in early June 1944 when word spread that there were large troop movements heading south down our High Street, and we all rushed to watch. It was early evening, and I watched in amazement as huge tanks, armoured vehicles, and troop carriers passed in an endless convoy. We waved to the troops, and the people were shouting encouragement to the young men, who perhaps did not know what the next few days would have in store for them. We soon learned from radio and newspaper reports that the D-Day landings had taken place in Normandy, and the Allies had a foothold in France.

Shortly afterwards, we were all saddened to learn that my mother's brother Reginald, was reported missing at sea in the Indian Ocean; his death was later confirmed. His wife Margery and infant daughter Judy were left alone.

We had not had many new toys for the last few years, and my main interest at this time seemed to be kicking a tennis ball around the schoolyard and the occasional game of football (soccer) and cricket at school. Schoolwork I found to be a drag, but we never got homework, much to my relief. One day just when we thought life was getting back to normal, the air-raid siren sounded as we were getting ready for bed, and we rushed to the shelter.

Partway down the garden, we all heard this droning sound above our heads at a low altitude and moderate speed. My father was looking up at this contraption passing overhead, and I remember our next-door neighbour, Mr Anderson, exclaiming, 'What on earth is that!' 'That' we later discovered was a V-1 rocket, which the Germans had been developing for years, and were now launching from France and Holland. Once over the target, the motor would cut out, and the explosive device would plummet to earth, causing considerable damage. We soon learned that if the engine cut out while it was overhead, we were safe as our neighbours a few miles away would get it. These devices were wildly inaccurate, and many zoomed off course, and some were shot down before reaching London. But three months later, the Germans had deployed the V-2 rocket and started sending them over the English Channel onto London. These were more powerful and made a whining noise as they went over and huge explosions when they landed, with significant loss of life.

My parents decided it was again time to get us out of danger, and once again, we boarded the train for the long trip back to the farm in Shropshire. Denis and I were sent back to the same village school, and I began to enjoy life in the country again.

Clifford, the farmer's son, would take me out shooting rabbits, a sport he was particularly good at, and he would also show me how to set a wire trap over a rabbit run to catch them. I saw the caged ferret in action. It would be transferred on a leash to a sack, taken into the fields then sent down a hole to chase out the rabbits. This animal was very ferocious, and I was quite scared of it, but it did its job. I also played with kids on other farms after school and often disappeared with them for hours, having to face my mother's wrath when I finally returned home. I was always out climbing trees after birds' eggs, of which there were great varieties, but the biggest and best were always high up. Once I fell from quite a height and staggered home, never telling my mother what had happened. With other boys, I learned how to make a great catapult. Rubber was challenging to come by, but one of the boys found some good strong square rubber on his farm, and with the shaft made from the fork of a tree, we each made a wonderful catapult and would shoot at just about anything. I remember being upset one day when I was out alone and very casually raised my catapult at quite a large bird flying by. The stone brought it down immediately, and I hurried over to where it had fallen, picked it up and held it in my hand, feeling its little heart pounding away. I could not see any wounds, but a few minutes later, it died, and I was horrified to think I had killed an innocent creature. When I had been collecting birds' eggs, I was always careful not to disturb chicks or birds feeding their young, and this willful act distressed me. I kept my catapult but never again aimed it at a bird or animal.

Back at the village school in Hope, where most of the children were from surrounding farms, we seemed to be learning mainly about nature and would spend a lot of time talking about and painting trees and plants. The 'Three Rs' did not seem high on the priority list. It affected my brother much more than me, as he lost some vital years of education. As in most village schools, we did not have separate classrooms but were divided into age groups, so there were many things going on in the room to distract us.

My mother loved to walk in the country. At weekends we would often go across Mr Potter's and other farmers' fields to get to small villages with quaint names like Snailbeach and Stiperstones. Stiperstones is at the foot of quite a high range of hills, crowned by a massive rock outcrop known as the Devil's Chair, which was often clad in low cloud or mist, making it a very mysterious area. It was a beautiful region to explore as there were several derelict mines with shafts going into the hillside and old locomotives and other equipment just rusting away. A great place for a young boy to get into all sorts of trouble, but I was never allowed to go there alone. Just getting across the fields was quite an adventure as some of the farms had one or two bulls - huge and fearsome beasts, and we had to make sure when opening gates into another field that we knew where the bulls were as they might come after us. They never did hurt us, but I remember once my mother had to run pretty fast when a bull started to look threatening, and there was a reasonable distance to the next gate. We would hike up to the Devil's Chair when it was clear of cloud and pick wild blueberries, and on one occasion, we got somewhat lost and had to come down a ravine just as it was getting dark, ending up wading through a field of stinging nettles to get down. We were all stung severely on our arms, legs, and hands.

Clifford also showed us how to tickle trout in a brook on the farm. He managed to catch fish in this way, but we never did. I loved this stream and together with some other kids, would dam it. There was a deep pool in one place where we could play around. (I could not swim at the time.) There were several girls our age who seemed to be much more mature than we were, so they were always trying to lead us into various embarrassing situations. Apart from the girls, there were other exciting things to be discovered, principally in the stream. I would find fossils of seashells and other creatures in the rocks, indicating that this part of Britain had at one time been under the ocean. My Dad came up from London on several occasions, although he was not comfortable in the country or with country folk. On one visit, we were in a field that sloped steeply down to the stream. As kids, we would run down this incline with no difficulty, and on this occasion, we coaxed him to run with us.

Poor Dad started to run faster and faster until he lost his balance and rolled over and over, eventually coming to a stop. He lay there, motionless with my mother still at the top of the hill, starting to make her way down. Dad was unhurt, no bones were broken, just a little shaken, but he never tried that again. On the same hill during winter, Clifford made a long sledge about two feet wide out of corrugated iron with the front bent up. There was plenty of snow that year, and we built a bank at the bottom of the hill to avoid ending up in the stream. We would all ride together, one behind the other; the only means of braking and steering was Clifford's feet each side at the back of the sledge. One trip, we went right over the bank and almost into the stream.

The war seemed very distant, as the accumulator-powered radio in the farmhouse was only occasionally turned on for the news, and newspapers were rare. We did learn that an aircraft had crashed near the village of Snailbeach, so we were allowed to walk over. It was a Royal Air Force Whitley bomber that had been towing a glider during exercises. The plane went down in a gully on the hillside, burnt, and all five young crew members were killed. We were only allowed to look at the glider that had landed safely in a field nearby. The police had it fenced off, and it did remind us the war was not too far away.

For me, our life on the Potter's farm was an enjoyable experience, but I am not sure that my brother enjoyed it as much, mainly because he was not as adventurous as me. Some other evacuated children had a difficult time. Often, they were sent away to remote places without their parents and were made to work hard to earn their keep. Just before we left, a farmer named Gough on adjacent Bank Farm had been charged for abusing one of two foster children in his care. The elder child Dennis O'Neill died of cruelty and starvation. Both the farmer and his wife were arrested for manslaughter, and the case became an international story when the trial took place at Shrewsbury Assizes in 1945, where the younger brother Terence, who was ten years old at the time, stood up in court and gave evidence against the accused. Terence was in my class at Hope School, and the trial was the talk of the nation, also being instrumental in changing the child labour laws in Britain.

During the spring, the Allied forces were over-running Germany. Eventually, it was reported that Hitler and his mistress, Eva Braun, had committed suicide in Berlin as the Russians entered the outskirts of the city. It looked like the war was coming to an end at last, and my mother decided we should again return to London. On May 7th, 1945, victory was declared in Europe (V.E. Day), and our lives returned to somewhat normal except for the strict food rationing, which remained. However, items that had not been available in England for the duration of the war began to appear again. I remember the first time I was handed a banana and didn't know how to peel it. We would now often visit the local cinema and see horrifying newsreel pictures of the devastation of European cities and the release of prisoners from Auschwitz, Dachau, and other concentration camps. These images made a lasting impression on me.

Michael's mother (centre) with her parents (circa 1912) and his parents on their wedding day in 1929

Michael with elder brother, Denis prior to the war

The Potters (Michael's wartime family in Shropshire)

German Dornier 217 bombers over East London

A barrage balloon in a local park

Michael's family spent many nights in the Anderson Shelter!

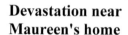

**Devastation near
Maureen's home**

**V1 rockets (Buzz Bombs) and V2 rockets were launched from
France and Holland in June 1944**

2.
Adolescence

Maureen

First, there was great joy. Plans had been made as this wonderful victory day approached, and there were celebrations planned as no one had ever seen before. Street parties were held in almost every street in the country. Parents wanted to celebrate with their children, and our road was marked out for children's races. Prizes were arranged, and everyone made an effort to provide party food. A party wasn't easy as rationing had become very strict – for very many months, we had had no luxuries. We had things like Jello made with a rather sharp-tasting orange juice concentrate and little iced cakes. Fancy ingredients that had been hoarded were gladly donated so that the children could have a merry time. I remember best the evening parties. During the day, a group of six men came and carried our piano between them and placed it on a stage that had been built against our front garden wall. My father pounded those keys until his fingertips were bleeding, and everyone sang their 'party piece' and was cheered. There was dancing in the streets, and there was even a little drinking. Everyone brought out what they had been hoarding. Those women whose husbands were going to be able to come home cried with joy and relief - everyone was quite delirious. Perhaps not quite everyone; so many men had died; many families were mourning painful losses. My father's youngest brother George was lucky. He had been reported missing in action, but he actually had been taken prisoner and eventually returned to his family, very thin and sick but alive.

All the lights had come back on once again all over England. At the end of all hostilities, there was an incredible Victory Parade held through the streets of London, featuring columns of servicemen and women from every service and country involved in the conflict. All the troops marched so smartly with flags and banners flying. I remember the Commonwealth Divisions received a particularly rousing reception. The parade was broadcast by the BBC Live and was also made into a very colourful documentary film which we all saw in the cinemas. Of course, the audiences cheered and cried and cheered some more. I expect the idea was to give the worn-out and exhausted people everywhere a chance to 'let go' emotionally and also an opportunity for everyone to feel proud once again. There had been six long years of war.

In September, after the long summer break from school, our own Becontree Heath Junior School was opened and made available for the first time. We also had a new teacher, Mr Snow. We didn't know teachers could be men too because most of the male teachers had been called up into the Armed Services. He was a calm and wonderful man. By this time, I was beginning to be rather impressed by nice looking men. So, we all set ourselves to do our best for him. It was his job to prepare our class for the 11-plus examination, which would decide what kind of a school we would attend for our Senior-school years. The test would take place in the early spring.

Our family set to work to plan the best Christmas ever. We had beautiful family parties. Mum's relatives came on Christmas Day, and even Dad's parents and family members came on Boxing Day. We had a lovely little tree decorated with lights, and every house had one standing proudly in the window. We really 'went to town' with the home-made Christmas decorations, and we all celebrated the first Christmas of the Peace. This magical season showed us the awfulness was now in the past, and life really would get better. I had a new male 'interest' in my life. His name was Laurence Manley, and he seemed grown up to me because he had left school and worked in a butcher shop. He would walk me home if we met near the shops; such a small thing to arouse my interest.

Pam, now fourteen years old, had left school, and her first job was in the City of London at the Prudential Assurance Company, whose offices were in Holborn. It was quite a journey for her to get to work, but I think she began to enjoy a little freedom and independence. After a few months, when she was adjusted to this change in her life, she took me up to London for an outing. We went on the #25 bus, her usual route to work, and she showed me St. Paul's Cathedral, which was standing alone, surrounded by bomb-damaged sites. The colossal dome surmounted by the gleaming golden cross was an inspiring sight amid the devastation. We walked along the Embankment beside the Thames and saw Cleopatra's Needle and the Houses of Parliament and Big Ben in the distance at Westminster. She shared her love of London with me, and these places are in my memory together with memories of my childhood and family life with her. Of course, I determined I would work in London too when my turn to leave school came.

But in the meantime, I was preparing for the 11-plus examination. The 11-plus exam was quite a big deal, and many pupils became very nervous, just thinking about it. Part of the preparation consisted of working on examination papers from previous years, and it seemed I didn't feel out of my depth very often, so I practised arithmetic and essay writing and hoped it would be enough. The great day dawned in early spring, and the school was prepared with the desks in the examination rooms the required distance apart, and we set to work. The arithmetic paper came first, and I think I answered all the questions, including the problems. Then we had a 20-minute break and returned to the room for the English papers. After a second break, we had the General Knowledge paper, and I felt a bit insecure with one or two of the logic questions but made guesses and then home we went. On the way out of the school, I was accosted by a group of girls from Five Elms Junior School, another Dagenham school, and I was jolly glad to escape from them as they seemed to be rather a rough bunch. I wondered how it would be to attend an utterly unfamiliar school without my friends.

I quickly ran home to my mother, who I knew would be waiting anxiously with tea ready. She later reported to my Dad that when asked how I had done, I had replied, 'I think I passed.' I don't remember being all that confident, but it turned out when the notification came that I, together with four other members of my class of 40 pupils, **had** passed! My parents were enormously pleased and very proud. Even my mother's neighbours congratulated me, so I was convinced this was going to be a good thing and I felt rather important. Pam was a little jealous of me over this, and I remember that she used to play tricks to frighten me when our parents went out. I was terrified of darkness, and being an imaginative child, I was easily made frightened. I used to have bad nightmares for quite a few years after the war ended. Perhaps

Pam was just making sure I remembered she was the 'big sister'. My parents didn't make a fuss about the nightmares; I expect they had plenty of bad dreams too!

I remember another incident at about this time, which illustrates the aftermath of war-time stresses, together with the way family interaction develops. I had always been a nail-biter from about the time we were separated from our mother at the beginning of the war. After I sat for the 11-plus examination, but before hearing the results, I developed an infection at the side of my right thumbnail. This infection sat there for a bit and quite suddenly became a significant infection. My thumb was so painful I could not write and even began to run a mild fever. For treatment, I was sent to a clinic at Five Elms. Since my mother was not feeling well and also because it was hoped I would be going to school the following school year on my own, I was encouraged to take myself to the clinic. There, my sore thumb was examined daily, and a poultice was applied. I was given instructions to take to my mother for further treatment to take place at home each night. In those days, we did not have antibiotics to deal with infections. When the fever mounted, the nightmares intensified, and my bed was moved downstairs partly so that I didn't disturb the whole household, but mostly so that my mother could keep her eye on me during the day without having to keep going up and downstairs. My mother was wonderfully caring when she had a sick child. It was almost worth being ill to enjoy that one-on-one care she lavished at those times, and I think she wanted an opportunity to draw me closer to her, especially as Pam was now moving out into the world and even going out in the evenings with her friends. I enjoyed her attention at this time, but I indeed was very sick and had to sleep sitting up because that thumb throbbed abominably and frequently prevented me from sleeping at all. Eventually, one night the huge swelling on my thumb burst, and I immediately felt such relief that I pushed out of the way the big pillows that I reclined against to sleep sitting up, lay down and slept dreamlessly for the rest of the night. Recovery was quite speedy, but I did lose that thumbnail, and it was many weeks before a dressing was no longer necessary. Such a thing could not happen today. However, it served to improve the love and understanding between my mother and me.

Before the 11-plus exam, we had had many forms to fill up and submit to the Essex Education Committee. One of which was a list of preferences for the schools of our choice. The list of options was quite long, but we had decided on the South-East Essex Technical College as our first choice as they had a very full and varied curriculum. It was very exciting to be purchasing my school uniform. I had never had so many new clothes at one time before, and no one in my family had ever needed a school uniform. It was a good uniform, and I wore it quite proudly for five years. It consisted of three white poplin blouses with long sleeves, a simple sleeveless V-necked pinafore dress (jumper) with a matching belt in royal blue and a lovely school blazer of good quality wool in the same shade of royal blue, piped on the collar and lapels in black. There was a colourful embroidered School Crest badge on the breast pocket. It was to be worn with black lace-up shoes with white ankle socks in summer and lisle stockings in winter. Once at school, there would be added a school tie that included one's 'house' colour plus a school hat or beret, and eventually, there would be PE (physical education) clothes too; a collared golf-style shirt in one's house colour plus pleated shorts in royal blue. Girls were recommended to wear navy blue underwear! The boys' uniform was similar, except they wore grey flannel trousers in place of the jumper.

I think perhaps the attention I enjoyed that summer must have been a little difficult for the rest of my siblings to understand. My brother, Brian, initiated several angry confrontations. He had a real problem with anger management, and I was always ready to stick up for myself. There was one incident that he reminded me of, with a laugh, many years later, where we fought, and he had me pinned down in the back garden. He was about to bring a heavy shovel down on my head when my mother intervened, and Brian was in disgrace once again! Another time when my mother was having a chat to Mrs Wright, her good friend and neighbour who lived across the street, he, together with his friend Johnny Wright, pulled me down on the grass in the front garden, attempted to drag down my navy-blue panties and was about to paddle my bare bottom. Fortunately, Mum heard my yells and once again rescued me. My poor mother was sometimes at her wit's end, trying to outwit Brian's evil designs. I always wondered why she and Dad took me with them when they went out every Monday evening to the movies. Surely, she would have liked to have some peaceful time alone with her husband. As Pam was also out of an evening, she must have been uneasy about what Brian might do to me. But by the end of that summer, I was fit and ready for the next stage of my life.

Around my birthday that year, I had been surprised by receiving special attention from my grandmother. My mother told me she and I would be going to see Nanny for a particular reason. I always liked going to Nanny's home, however. She had a lovely garden, and she kept some chickens. I do remember following her around in her backyard once when I was young, and she showed me off to one of her neighbours quite proudly. I think I could have been rather a precocious little girl with a habit of sometimes saying unnerving things. On this particular occasion, it was to be just Mum and me visiting. It was a bit unusual but had been specially arranged that way. We were all in Nanny's bedroom when she gave me a little gift. The box was tiny, with a name printed on the top. I had never received anything like this before! I was mystified and opened the box to reveal white cotton wool. I picked out the cotton wool and looked up to my mother for reassurance.

'Careful', she said, then 'look'. I looked and saw a very fine silvery chain. Putting the cotton wool back into the little box, I looked more carefully, and there was a very pretty little silver cross on a delicate silver chain. Nanny was smiling in a slightly self-conscious way. This, she told me, was a special gift because she and Granddad were proud that I had passed the 11-plus examination. I was delighted and thanked her properly with a kiss. I wore that special gift on my wedding day and have it still. Perhaps one day, I will give it to one of my granddaughters.

I look back on my school-life with pleasure. At first, there was much to get used to, but I made new friends easily and was interested in all the new subjects in our program. The school was a happy, friendly place, but we were taught to hold our teachers in great respect. The whole class would stand upon the entrance of the teacher, who was to be greeted by name. Should another teacher enter the room during class, we would all stand again, although we would immediately be asked with a warm smile to please be seated. Proper decorum was expected at all times, and we were encouraged to contribute our ideas. We learned the etiquette of debate and how important it was to give everyone a hearing. Any question was always regarded as worthy of consideration, and students were always encouraged to think before speaking but to then stand their ground to defend their views. Our teachers were all university graduates of some standing, and their 'uniform' was the traditional black gown which on Speech Day they wore topped by a hood lined with the shining satin, the colour indicating their alma mater. On this kind of occasion, they were very impressive.

The school was co-educational, and our class was evenly divided. I wasn't too impressed with the boys, but I do remember taking walks occasionally in Barking Park and meeting up with them there. I guess at that age we only spent time eyeing each other. My marks for the first couple of years were unremarkable - I did experience some poor health. It was at this time a growth was discovered under my chin, which necessitated several trips to Great Ormond Street Hospital for Sick Children where an operation was performed, and it was removed. I never knew what precisely the growth was, but I was in the hospital for about ten days and have the scar still; I know my mother was terribly worried. I came home from the hospital with a dressing taped under my chin, which looked as if I was wearing the strings to an invisible bonnet. I was told the surgeon's opinion was that had the growth not been removed, it would have slowly strangled me. I also had my appendix removed at Oldchurch Hospital, Romford, and I remember feeling that I must be like a cat, and there went another of my lives. The convalescent period after these illnesses certainly kept me away from school. Perhaps it was a case of my being 'run-down' after the war. I remember having to frequently catch up on the classwork, and it was somewhat surprising that I remember those school days with pleasure. The Barking Quintet would come to school, and this accomplished Group increased my interest in classical music.

I enthusiastically joined the various clubs and entered the yearend competitions. In this way, I was exposed to public speaking - my talk was about '*Clocks and the History of Time-*

keeping' ((Honourable Mention), and the choir - the Choir Mistress was a Mrs Lee who played the piano beautifully and who encouraged my voice. With others, I helped the gardener take care of the quadrangles when required. Probably my involvement was noticed, and I was very proud to find myself made House Captain in my second year. Our House was Castle (house colour, green); the other houses were Lodge (red), Manor (silver), and Abbey (gold). We could gain points for our House in many ways: getting 'A's for classwork, coming first in the various competitions, and performing services for the school. My friends were all in different houses. In this way, when we had a house meeting, we would have to meet and get to know other students.

Soon after beginning this new life at school, we went to our first Great Assembly. We all assembled in the auditorium in Main School, where we met our Headmaster, Mr J S Arthur, and the Senior Mistress, Miss Williams. Mr Arthur informed us that we were the fortunate elite of the selection process, the 11-plus. 'Our school', he said, 'was the pride of the Essex Education Authority, and we should endeavour to live up to the expectations of the Board of Governors whom we would meet at Speech Day at the end of the year.' If this was a pep talk, it sure worked for me. I was extremely impressed with everything and determined to do my best. As we were at this time, the youngest members, it seemed to me that everyone else was incredibly sophisticated, but I wanted to make a place here for myself very much. He spoke very kindly to us and advised us to begin by learning a new word every day. He would start us off, he said, by giving us the first before dismissing us. As we would be returning to the Annexe, we had brought our school satchels and bags with us to assembly. 'The new word is paraphernalia.' Mr Arthur boomed, then to everyone, 'Pick up your paraphernalia.' We looked around, everyone picked up their books, *etc.*, and we hastened to do the same and then to a jolly tune called 'An English Country Garden' from Mrs Lee on the piano, we all marched out to get the bus back to the Annexe. The habit learned that day of looking up the meaning of a new word in the dictionary as soon as possible is with me still. We only attended the Great Assembly twice each term, but we had our Assembly each day at the Annexe. Much as it had been at Junior School, we had morning prayers, a hymn, and the Senior School Mistress would give out the notices, which usually were reminders about after-school activities, house meetings, etc. I had to wait until the third year to get to know Mr Arthur better.

On the home front, my Dad, with a little more spare time on his hands, became interested in a Concert Party that would meet to practice their musical talents and prepare concerts. I was drawn into this a little and sang on the stage while my father accompanied me. All kinds of people had such a good time at the street parties at the end of the war; they wanted to begin to re-create their social life, which had been sadly neglected during those years. We entered a few talent competitions, and I remember one year my father also entered me with my friend Angela Howe who I did not see very much now as she had gone to a High School in Brentwood. We didn't become famous, but we did have some good times, and Dad's musical talents gained a little recognition, as I did. I used to sing 'Come Back to Sorrento', quite a well-known piece that usually was in the repertoire of operatic tenors. There was always a dance at the end of the season to which we would all go, and I noticed how the older young men and women interacted. Mum, of course, was keeping her eye very firmly on Pam, who loved to dance with any young man that cared to ask her.

Unfortunately, things were not going so well at home. Our mother had become very ill. She had been attending The Middlesex Hospital for an anaemic condition, and she, unfortunately, suffered a miscarriage. She felt this was caused by the medication she had been prescribed, but it may well have been caused by her general poor condition. I had not been paying much attention, involved as I was with my new life by day and homework, which I would do in the evenings in our living room, almost quite oblivious to the family life going on, sometimes noisily, around me. When Mum was admitted to hospital, I certainly took notice then. Pam took time off from her work to take care of the family, and Mum eventually came home, looking quite dreadful but full of admiration for the care she had received.

Our father spoke seriously to us all, and especially to my noisy brothers, as it was felt her poor condition was the result of a combination of malnutrition and nervous worry from the high stress of the recent war and the continuing privations of the aftermath. I later learned that our neighbours had noticed that Mum had deteriorated even further after the war when most people perked up a bit. Some also went so far as to say that they hadn't expected her to come home from that hospital stay at all! I didn't notice any change in my brothers' behaviour, but I do remember that Pam worked very hard, and here and there, I helped her. I learned to cook potatoes and make a custard, and Brian and I would share the dish-washing duties when we would sing together to take our minds off this chore. It must have been a terribly difficult time for my poor mother. Pam was a wonderful daughter; I know she always did the most to help our mother.

The following summer, we actually had a holiday. My Dad arranged for us to have two weeks at Jaywick Sands. This small summer-cottage resort was close to Clacton-on-Sea in Essex on the East Coast. It was thought to be a 'bracing' resort, which indicated the cold east wind blew there frequently. Pam didn't come as she had to go to work, but Mum brought Nanny along, probably to help out a little and for her company, as Dad could only stay for the weekend and one week. I remember Mum made me a swimsuit (I had begun to learn to swim at school) and herself a sundress with a little jacket, so she must have begun to feel better by the time the holiday came along. Even here, Mum didn't relax very much. She would be up early to walk to the shops and bring home fresh rolls for our breakfast. We had the cutest old seaside cottage in Alvis Street. All the streets were named after motor cars. We were to enjoy several more holidays in Jaywick, but I remember the first one the best. It was such a change from our everyday life - we had never had a holiday together before. The cottage had running water and Calor-gas cooking but no bathroom. There was an outhouse, and each evening the 'Lavender' cart would come along accompanied by a fierce aroma. The outhouse bucket would be emptied, which Mum would immediately rinse out with the hose and disinfectant. We went into the sea every day and didn't worry about the absence of a bathroom. My brothers played on the sands for long hours, and I think my mother must have known some peace and relaxation. Her busy hands would always be holding her knitting.

After the holiday we all had to get ready for school once again. I enjoyed these preparations. My uniform was wearing well, and I only needed new blouses, underwear, and socks this time. I believe I later had a school raincoat too. In our second year, we found ourselves at the top of the heap at the Annexe as there was a new intake of juniors again. I began to do somewhat better in class, and now except for those dreadful Physics classes, I felt quite comfortable. It had been noticed, probably by our pretty dancing class teacher, that I had flat feet! My feet were no trouble to me, but we were examined yearly at school and weighed and measured, and I was referred to a therapist for exercises to improve this situation. I liked that my appointments were on Friday afternoons. I presented myself at the clinic for the therapy, which consisted of placing my feet in a bath of water on electrodes, which stimulated the muscles of my feet. I don't think this treatment ever made the slightest difference, but I continued to go because, in this way, I missed many Physics classes. When the course of treatment finished, I still cut Physics class; my homeroom teacher thought I was going to the clinic, and I simply went home. When my mother asked why I came home early so often on a Friday, I told her our class had perfect attendance that week, and this was the reward! I don't think she ever knew I was *playing hooky*; luckily, I was never caught. But I indeed failed Physics.

At the end of the first two years, we were all promoted to the third year. At this level, other students were inserted into the school program as part of a 'late acceptance' scheme. We were all about thirteen years old, and the newer students had passed a further selection process. It was generally recognised by the powers that be in the education field that not all students were adequately prepared to pass the 11-plus examination and this second chance was given to those students who, it was thought, would best benefit by the opportunity to attend a school with somewhat higher goals designed for those with the ability to achieve them. One of these late arrivals was a tiresome short boy who became known as the school 'clown'. He was in the Engineering Department, and we never realised how well he could play the piano. His name was Dudley Moore, and he eventually became a film star.

At the same time, everyone was placed in the program best

suited to their interests and ability. I was placed in the Commerce stream as were most of my friends. My class designation was 3C2; there were three Commerce classes at the same level, still co-ed; one-third of the students were boys, the rest girls. Many of the boys were heading towards Accounting, and one became a Librarian. There were also programs available for those with abilities in the Arts and Trades. In many ways, this was a forward-thinking education system. Still, in hindsight, I realise that all the teachers were of an older generation, so the plan was designed with the recent past in mind.

Up until the Second World War, the United Kingdom had been a real 'player' in world affairs. The traditions of 'The Empire' were still strong, and young people like me were being educated to take our places in the many fields available throughout the Empire and the British Colonies. We lived and worked in an atmosphere that breathed opportunity for us. We did not know that the recent war had brought Great Britain to its knees financially speaking, and we had no doubt that we could fit in. In truth, of course, when the time came for us to leave school, there were still many opportunities, but our world was about to undergo an enormous change. The 'Empire' would collapse, and a Commonwealth of Nations would evolve. This eventually came to mean that emerging nations would enjoy more self-determination and would perhaps not choose quite the same system of government or of acquiring goods, services, and personnel from 'Mother England'. Broadly speaking, I was educated to be a useful and competent member of society, and after earning my living for a few years, I was expected to take my place as a well-enough educated, responsible wife!

So, I was allowed to toss out the dreaded Physics and add Shorthand, Typing, and Bookkeeping to my schedule, along with Domestic Science (learning to sew, cook, and manage a household). I liked sewing so frequently chose that over cooking. Biology class was dropped the following year, and that block was filled with courses in First Aid, Home Nursing, and Child Care. We still had English, German, Maths, Religion, History, Geography, and PE twice a week as usual. My school supported teams and House competitions for various sports, plus a choir, school plays, (I once played a policewoman in a one-act play), and poetry competitions in English and our second language, which in my case was German. I loved the poetry of Goethe, loads of stuff to keep us busy. Once again, my health broke down, and I suffered a bout of scarlet fever, which required a ten-day stay in the London Fever Hospital. I was in the hospital over Christmas that year. When I was well again, I tried out for the hockey team but was more successful in competitions like the poetry festival and the choir. I loved swimming and usually competed in the year-end Sports Day in various events, especially in the first few years I was at this school. But the following year I grew taller very quickly, and this changed my co-ordination somewhat, and I still had those flat feet, so I became a supporter of many activities rather than a participant. But I always enjoyed the P.E. classes and played netball, rounders (a simple form of softball), and a little tennis, all with great enthusiasm. In our final year, we even learned co-ed ballroom dancing!

For my fourteenth birthday, my parents gave me a new bike, which made a huge difference to my sense of freedom. I also had a new friend called Pat Bliss, who lived in Dagenham, somewhat closer to the River Thames. She also had a bike, and we would ride all over Dagenham that summer visiting the many parks in the area and checking out where the boys were. We were really good friends but fairly competitive, too, which was rather good for me. In fact, in our fourth year of high school, I won the prize at the year's end as a top student in Fourth Form 4C2. My parents were enormously proud of me when I received my prize – 'Emma' by Jane Austen - on Speech Day from Mr Arthur in front of the Board of Governors and the whole school, and in the company of all the other prize-winners.

During these three years at Main School, I grew up a lot. In the beginning, I still saw my old friend Patsy each weekend; we attended Sunday School at the Methodist church together and took part in the social activities available there. There were little dances and other social evenings, and there was a Social Committee, of which I was a member, to help plan things. I probably learned to take minutes there. Of course, we were beginning to have an interest in boys now that we were young women, and I was seldom without a partner or someone to escort me home.

On returning to school for my final year, I was delighted and honoured to be assigned as a Prefect. Usually, in the fifth form, each class had two prefects, but in my class, I was the only one, so I felt singled out. Being a Prefect conferred certain privileges and also specific responsibilities. I thought perhaps I had received this privilege as a reward for doing so well the previous year, but we were informed we were chosen because our willingness to perform public service had been noticed too. Now I had new duties; we monitored hallways and staircases during the times the students would be moving about the long airy corridors, we oversaw tardy latecomers and handed out detentions to students who persistently flouted school rules. Failure to observe half-hour detentions resulted in the wrong-doer being reported to the Head Girl or Head Boy, who reported to Mr Arthur or Miss Williams, and it was a rare student who didn't turn up to the appointed room to observe the detention time. Prefects were probably chosen because they were reasonably well-balanced, reasonable individuals who would simply take notice of a minor infraction of the rules but were sparing in actually giving detentions, because that Prefect who gave the detention also had to attend the detention room (or find another Prefect to stand-in for him or her) to ensure the time was served. Detainees were supposed to sit quietly and read or study in detention. Reasonable order was observed at all times, and in such a large school (there were about 1,000 students plus another 500 older students, i.e., over 16 years old), the school buildings were remarkably quiet for much of the time. In turn, Prefects would assist with assemblies, and I was happy to volunteer for reading the lesson from the King James Bible. This kind of exercise was thought to build self-confidence.

Family life was proceeding fairly normally except our mother was frequently highly agitated; it was called, 'having bad nerves'. By this time I was spending between one and two hours each evening on my homework which I still did in the corner of the noisy living room; sometimes I complained about the noise as the radio too was always on. I also used to complain when my towel, soap or toothbrush had been used. I was rather a fastidious creature and tried unsuccessfully to keep my personal things separate.

There were many arguments or 'scenes' which ended in tears; Pam was sometimes out too late, I was not paying enough attention to anyone else's needs, and the three boys were not easy in any way. But taking into consideration that there were seven people living closely together in a tiny house, family life continued more or less the way it should. There was one development that happened during this time that caused my mother a little anxiety and displeasure.

My father was always a man with many interests. During the past few years, after the Concert Party fad passed, Dad looked around for a new interest. He had always been interested in models, and much earlier in his marriage had built a beautiful model of a steam-driven locomotive. Always talented with his clever hands, he used to spend quite a bit of time every Saturday morning repairing our shoes. It seemed there was always one pair that needed his attention, and Pam's high-heeled shoes were regularly handed over every Friday night.

Shoe-repairing was not his favourite work, although it did allow him to escape the turbulent house to his shed at the bottom of the back garden, where he could enjoy a quiet smoke as he worked.

One day he brought home a large, heavy piece of teak timber and showed us a drawing of a model boat and began to mark out this piece with guidelines. This piece was going to be the 'Lady Ellen', the first in a long line of model boats he built. Planning and chiselling this piece created a dreadful mess in our dining room; as it was winter, the shed was too cold to work. Mum was quite flattered this boat was going to be named for her, so she kept her peace. However, it was eventually finished after a couple of years and was much admired by most members of our extended family. Our father built the little two-stroke engine entirely by hand, and everyone was in awe of his talents. Dad joined an enthusiasts' club called the Victoria Park Model Steamboat Club. At first, Mum looked with interest in this activity because they shared the time together, Dad working on his boat and Mum sitting nearby with her knitting, but when summer came, and Dad was deeply involved in model boat 'Regattas' it gradually became less fascinating for her.

Dad's friend in this was a colleague at his place of work, a

Mr Nunn who lived in Leytonstone. They would meet at the Club in Victoria Park, which was quite a journey from our house, and it became a regular Sunday outing in the summer. We would occasionally all join Dad at the park and have a picnic, but after the first season of this, Mum began to think this new passion of Dad's was not much fun for her. However, she made the best of it, she still was able to enjoy their regular Monday nights at the cinema, and occasionally Mr and Mrs Nunn and their son Eddie would be invited to our house for Sunday tea. Eddie took quite a fancy to me, and I remember the first time we met and that intense awareness one experiences when a young man and a girl become particularly aware of each other, and we began to go out together. Eddie was Pam's age, so Mum and Dad thought him a very suitable companion for their younger daughter. Eddie was an apprentice at Standard Telephones & Cables and soon became a fully qualified electrician. By this time I was about fifteen years old and quite keen to embark on this stage in my life, and although I felt only mildly romantic about Eddie, he was a nice young man who took me to nice places and treated me very well; I was quite glad to have a boyfriend.

I had also acquired a Saturday job. The regular school-leaving age was raised to fifteen years old, and those who were still completing their education at that age could legally be employed on a part-time basis. Of course, Mum wanted me to earn my own pocket money, so off I went to Woolworths in Ilford High Street and got a job paying 15 shillings for the day's work. I took home 12 shillings and eightpence (about $2.50 in those days) as I had to pay the National Health Insurance Stamp fee. My old friend Helen Norman also got a job there at the same time, so we used to come home together sometimes. I worked in the kitchen supplies section, and Helen worked within sight in a nearby area. This job was quite a good starter as I was able to work during school holidays too, and in this way, I began to buy all my clothes and to save money for holidays and Christmas, etc. Money was very tight at this time in the family, and I remember my Dad sometimes asking me on Thursday nights if I could lend him 'five bob' (five shillings) because he hadn't enough cash available for lunch the following day which was pay-day. He always paid me back very promptly.

My parents were proud that I was such a good saver, and my Dad and I enjoyed this little interaction: it became a private thing between the two of us. He made me a special wooden box to keep my one-pound notes in, but it didn't have a lid, and I asked him if he could make me a special lid with a ball on the top to hold the paper money flat. He thought this an enormous joke and told everyone I needed a 'crusher' for all my pound notes! The 'crusher' was a lid that would fit just inside the box so that it would hold flat my precious few, saved pound notes. I had, of course, seen such devices in banks. This need of mine greatly amused my Dad, and the story of 'Maureen's crusher' was repeated often and became part of the family lore. So gradually, my world was expanding, but my dreams came to a crashing halt early in the New Year when the subject came up of what I would be doing after high school was finished. At that time, school leavers from my kind of high school would generally sit an examination called the School Certificate, and the results of that would determine if university entrance was possible. I confidently expected to sit this exam and continue my education, but the rules changed. A new examination was introduced called 'O Levels' (Ordinary Levels). The whole system was being changed to better fit the expected more significant numbers of children to be educated for the changing world (the imminent arrival in the schools of a *baby-boom* was beginning to be recognised), and of course, we all had to adjust. I was being prepared for the 'O Levels', but my parents decided it would not be necessary for me to take this examination as I would not be continuing my education. At that time, there was a fee to be paid for each subject examined. It was small, really, but they had decided there was no point in spending this money. I badly wanted to continue at school, complete the 'O Levels' in about six to eight subjects, enter the Sixth form at my present school (this was instead an elite group), and go on to the more advanced 'A Levels' (Advanced) levels for university entrance. I wanted to become a teacher.

I was devastated, numb, and not able to comprehend why my parents didn't want me to continue until we had a quiet conference. My mother quickly dissolved into tears because she didn't like me to be so disappointed, but together they told me that they simply couldn't afford to keep me at school any longer, and I simply had to go out to work for my living. There was no choice because they were sure the courses I had already pursued would equip me to get a job; perhaps one even better than Pam had, and they were sure I would marry, so what was the point! What was the point? I didn't want a job, I wanted a career - I knew for sure I wasn't going to marry Eddie, but there was no choice. I explained the situation to our headteacher Miss Williams, and she had a conference with my mother. She explained they had been looking forward to my being part of the Sixth Form and hinted I could become Head Girl the following year, but my parents were firm; it was to be out to work for me. I would never become a teacher!

Having my hopes dashed, I decided I had better enjoy the last six months of school and didn't try to work very hard at the subjects I liked less such as maths (algebra, etc. had got to be very hard); I hinted in my essay writing my disappointment, and my English teacher Miss Timperley sympathized, but I put it aside and began to enjoy the events planned for the end of the school year. Not having to work for the examinations, I was available for all the social events and spent many happy interludes dancing in the auditorium during lunchtime with various young men who were looking forward to the next stage of their lives, which they regarded as freedom at last. By the time the year-end dance came, we were all pretty good at ballroom dancing. So, my school days were coming to an end.

Two weeks before the end of the term, a group of about eight of us travelled up to London from Barking Station and attended interviews at The Institute of London Underwriters in Lime Street in the City of London (the financial district). We all wore our better clothes with gloves and were invited to join the Institute as soon as we were able. I elected to take a two-week break after school finished - my only small rebellion. Helen, who was part of this group, and several others wanted to start at the soonest possible moment. So, the next part of our future was decided.

The last day of school came, and after our final assembly, I used the centre staircase (a privilege accorded to teachers and Prefects only) for the last time and wept a tear or two. I went to one of the girl's washrooms and waited until everyone had left; I couldn't bear to say 'goodbye' to so many friends with whom I had shared so much, then I walked around the whole school, looked in at the library, the auditorium, the swimming pool and the playing fields I had loved so much. Everyone had gone - I quietly left, walked to the bus stop, and went home from school for the last time.

With little enthusiasm, I prepared for my working life. The school year ends mid-July in Britain; therefore, I had agreed to commence employment at the beginning of August. I used the two weeks I had claimed for a little break from routine, to buy and make a few items of clothing. My wardrobe was sparse as I had always worn my school uniform except at weekends. So, I needed a couple of skirts and blouses plus a jacket to complete my outfit. It was going to be a reasonably complicated commute to work. Lime Street was a short walk from Fenchurch Street station. I was already very familiar with the first part of the journey, which entailed a fifteen-minute walk from my house to the bus stop at 'The Merry Fiddlers' and the twenty-minute bus ride to Barking station. The next part was the half-hour train ride to Fenchurch Street and a five or ten-minute walk from there. So, I had to allow about ten minutes more than an hour to get to work on time. I left the house each day at about 8.15 am. The office began work at 9.30 am.

The office turned out to be a huge one, with about forty typists pounding away. Next door, there was another large office where the information we were entering neatly on forms was converted to key-punched cards and run through machines, which made a terrific clatter, too. It was a very noisy place. However, all the girls were quite friendly, and we were allowed to go out for a coffee break in groups at around 11.00 am, and it was possible to arrange one's coffee break to coincide with friends so that there was a chance to chat then. Conversation during working hours was not encouraged, but the noise made it difficult anyway. Helen, my friend, had started work ahead of me and was in another building, so I sometimes travelled with her but didn't see her at work. She had opted for clerical work. But I was pleased that there was one girl I knew from school in my office.

She was Barbara Osborne, a slender dark-haired, blue-eyed girl with whom I became good friends. Barbara lived in Barking, so we usually went home together after the working day ended at 5.00 pm. For this work, I believe we were paid about £3, 10 shillings per week. The pay wasn't much, and my parents had decided I had to hand over £1, 10 shillings of that for my board and lodging. A 'perk' was that we were also given luncheon vouchers, so each day I did have a good lunch for about five shillings. This was 1951. In the beginning, I had very little money left over as train fares were expensive, and as I was walking quite a bit, I needed shoes from time to time. Shoes at that time cost about three pounds a pair!

So, I gradually got used to my new life. I didn't like the repetitive, tedious work but tried to take an interest. The forms we typed listed first of all the names of the insurers concerned with each consignment, then the vessel, the cargo, the destination, and the classes of risks the insurance covered. Since we were so close to the Port of London (and the Tower), there was a certain romance to exercise the mind, and I felt quite proud to be a part of the commercial world. The Institute of London Underwriters served all the big insurance companies, so I got to know their addresses in the city and absorbed that kind of information because I was very interested in the wider world. After a bit of a slow start, when it was pointed out to the newer girls they simply had to work faster and more accurately, I began to concentrate and took a keen interest in becoming a speedy and accurate typist.

Barbara and I shared our lunch hours, and we explored the interesting little tucked-away streets with jewellers and bookstores in our vicinity. We were both great readers, and we would sometimes take our lunch over to the gardens at the Tower or walk along there by the river and talk about our books and the movies we saw. This part of the City had great possibilities, but we were a little overwhelmed at first and took quite a time to adjust to our first jobs. Shortly it was noticed how friendly we had become, and Barbara was moved to a different section. I made friends with a girl called Evelyn Butler (who was a little older and who had previous office experience), but I still occasionally had lunch and travelled with Barbara.

I was somewhat quieter and inclined to keep myself apart from the family at home, and my mother thought I was still upset because I wasn't continuing with my education, but I didn't think about that too much. I had little energy or interest in our family life and read in my room and thought my own thoughts. I was dismayed how little money I had and wondered how I would ever afford a holiday or new clothes. My mother was slightly concerned and, to my dismay, visited the supervisor of the Personnel Department to discuss this. She, of course, called me in for an interview, and we had a little chat, and she suggested I contact a name she passed on to me with a view to attaching myself to the Girl Guides. My mother had mentioned her concern at the seeming lack of social life I was presently experiencing. I should have told this lady that I didn't feel this particular job was the right one for me. But I didn't know how to handle this situation, being so inexperienced. So always ready to try something new, I did go to a couple of Guide meetings but quickly realised that playing with a group of little girls was not where my interests lay. Little did I know what was in store for me many years later!

When I became quite familiar with the work, I noticed some of the girls assumed a very competitive attitude. They focused on finishing their assigned 'bundle' quickly and accurately. They would then, in a rather lordly way, 'help out' the slower workers so that we could all begin on the next bundles together. Of course, Evelyn and I encouraged each other to compete in a similar way, and our speed improved rapidly. We entered an annual competition to serve notice to the lordly ones; we were serious about this and did quite well. I eventually achieved a speed of around 95 words per minute with less than 0.5 per cent errors, which on a manual typewriter with an extra-long carriage was a pretty good achievement. They were big heavy machines. But this took a couple of years. This experience taught me how to make even dull work a little enjoyable.

At Christmas time that first year, we enjoyed ourselves buying little gifts for all our new friends. Eddie was still my boyfriend at this time. I was getting rather bored with him, but as he was also a family friend, it was hard to change anything. Pam was engaged again for the third time. This engagement was a serious relationship; they had known each other for a long time and were planning their wedding to take place in the spring. Ron Brett was slightly younger than Pam, and of course, my mother had never encouraged him. They had both been members of a cycling club, and I remember joining them in the summertime for a few outings. Ron was always pleasant to me like an older brother might be. He had gone to my school a few years ahead of me, so we understood one another, and I enjoyed his sense of humour. Both Ron and Eddie were doing their National Service, Ron in the army, and Eddie, who had been deferred until the age of twenty-one, when he finished his apprenticeship, in the Air Force. They both became quite good marksmen during their basic training, so they had things in common to talk about. We became quite a friendly foursome, and I remember playing cards frequently on a Sunday evening when both young men were available at the same time. They both had to be back at camp early on Monday mornings, so we never kept late hours, which greatly pleased my mother.

My sister was married to her Ronald Brett at Easter of 1953, and our home seemed to be a battleground over this event. My mother, who didn't really like Pam's choice and positively disliked Ron's family, was making Pam's wedding dress and the bridesmaids' dresses too, so she must have felt a great deal of stress. The reception was to be held at home, and many people were invited. Of course, the wedding 'breakfast' was provided by the bride's parents and was probably cold meats, *etc.* and Mum would have had that to take care of too. My father took care of ordering a very lovely traditional white three-tier, professionally baked wedding cake. It is no wonder there were often 'scenes' and tears over the whole business. I can remember wondering aloud, 'If it would be possible to have a whole evening without mentioning the word wedding.' This ill-considered remark was not well received and resulted in another tearful row erupting. But the wedding day went off very well, and I think Pam and Ron had a happy day.

I had always liked Ron, and he became a wonderful brother, indeed, to me. They had taken rooms in a house nearby, and after their honeymoon in Devon, I knew I would see them often. I think my mother had experienced great difficulty accepting the fact that

Pam wanted an independent life. But she had accepted the inevitable and made those dresses. I was the chief bridesmaid along with Pam's friend Joan Richardson. Ron's Best Man was his brother Bob who I knew from school. He had been just one year ahead of me, and I rather liked and admired him. He was very academic and had always walked away with almost all the form prizes there were for his year, but he never noticed me. It is entirely possible that this marriage was not popular in the senior Brett household, too. At the reception after the wedding, my mother had quite a hard time being civil to Pam's new in-laws, and it seemed very strange in our house afterwards because Mum was very depressed and tired, and everyone seemed very quiet. But now I determined it was time for me to get on with my own life.

Brian, too, was making progress. He left school when he was fifteen and was apprenticed to the electrician's trade. Brian went to work at the same company, Standard Telephones & Cables, where our father was employed. He began to smoke, rolling his cigarettes, just like Dad did. He still had a fearful temper, and I remember he would come home sometimes, having ridden his bike through drizzly weather, in a very black humour and fling the bike inside the house for 'all the world' as if he was the only one who got wet that evening! The skirmishing between us had ceased or at least significantly decreased. I believed he had simply stopped remembering I existed when, to my surprise, he began to ask me to accompany him on outings. Perhaps he was becoming interested in girls and thought he would practice on me.

So, off we would go to the movies. Of course, we used public transportation. Having watched our Dad escorting our mother, I would find myself handed onto the bus and helped to alight. He was most careful to always cross behind me to walk along the roadside of the pavement (sidewalk) when we crossed the road, in the generally approved manner. He was a relatively tall young man now, we probably looked somewhat alike, and this gentlemanly behaviour found great favour and approval. I don't think he went so far as to pay for the cinema ticket because I was probably earning more than he was, but he may well argue with me about that! We would chat in a relaxed, friendly way late at night when I was preparing for bed. Each night I would stand in front of the dying fire, using the mirror above the fireplace to put my hair in about 100 pin curls (according to Brian's memory - exaggerated, of course, he was always a bit dramatic), so that I would look presentable the next day. (He also reminded me when I mentioned I was working on this memoir that I privately gave him a pound note when he passed his first-year Technical College exam, from my little *stash* in that specially sized box that Dad had given me and for which I had requested a *crusher*.) Brian even tried to fix me up with young men he met at work. I remember a rather large Irish man that I was introduced to, who put his arm around me in the cinema. I thought him altogether too familiar and didn't encourage any more similar introductions. I had also purchased a newer, more sporting bike.

The first couple of years at work passed, and Barbara had a holiday with a friend called Josephine Cooper, who had invited her to join a Youth Club that she belonged to, which was associated with the Youth Hostels Association. They went on a hiking holiday in the Lake District, and I helped Barbara shop for young men's Oxford shoes, which were substantial enough for rough walking and available in a size to fit her slender feminine foot. In those days, there was not the outdoor gear available that there is now. The idea of this kind of holiday interested me because I didn't have any plans of my own and it sounded like fun.

Barbara had joined the club, sponsored by the Youth Hostels Association, and after her holiday, she invited me to come along, too. The club met in an old school building in West Ham, which was quite a run-down area, and my mother worried about me riding my new bike through city traffic and rough places. These clubs existed to fill the needs of mostly young people who were interested in getting out into the countryside to enjoy nature. Some of them were indeed very serious about it in the same way that conservationists are serious about preserving the natural world. It was the beginning of that movement.

There were far more young men at this club than there were girls. They came from widely different backgrounds and were a pleasant, lively lot who were interested in cycling through the countryside, having weekends away at Youth Hostels, and organising many other activities every week. The social part of our meetings was sometimes given over to country dancing, which I always enjoyed; we had games' evenings, and it was very nice to meet so many young men. I began to have some fun at last, and it wasn't long before I began to go out on dates, and Eddy was finally dumped!

At weekends, off we would go into the countryside surrounding the London area, two by two in a long stream of cyclists. There would either be a Sunday run or a two-day ride, which included an overnight stay in a hostel. I had ridden a bike since I was about 14 and used to join Pam and Ron occasionally for a ride with the Valence Wheelers. I was quite athletic and never had any trouble keeping up. The YHA group generally went somewhat longer distances than I had been used to, but I soon adjusted, and there was frequently a friendly (male) hand ready to help the girls along on the long ride home. Some of the young men held themselves a little aloof from this activity, and they were usually the *serious* cyclists who also belonged to racing clubs. The weekends away were something new to me because we had a real sense of escaping the constraint exercised by parents when we were at home. We would all arrive at the hostel, claim a bed for the night (at minimum cost), make a light meal with provisions brought with us, then during the evening stroll along to the local pub in a group. Of course, we weren't heavy drinkers, but that half-pint of cider (my choice) was wonderful.

Since we had a curfew at the hostel we would make our way back there through the dark lanes, there would be a few pairings off for a little kissing, etc. and we would all be safe in our segregated beds by 11.00 pm. The next morning it would be up early for breakfast, perform our allocated chores (a required part of the hostel experience), the girls, of course, would do domestic chores; perhaps the guys would get the outside work. Then we would load up the bikes, we each had a large saddlebag, and we were off by about 10.00 am. It was quite delightful on fresh spring and summer mornings. Not so wonderful if we had rainy weather but still better than staying at home.

That summer Barbara and I also began to ride our bikes to work. It was quite a ride to the office, but because the traffic was quite heavy, I could get there at almost the same time one could complete the journey using public transportation. The regular ride of about 12 or 13 miles made me very fit, and I became a well-known sight to other commuters and the local policemen, who would wave me through the traffic. I would arrive at the office a little after 9.00 am wearing a sweater and a pair of short shorts and with a scarf covering my pinned-up hair. A quick wash in the ladies' room where I would meet up with Barbara who arrived from her home in Barking by a different route, a change of clothes for us both and with hair brushed out, and make-up applied, we were ready well before the rest of the office staff arrived for their day's work. Our bikes were stored for us in the basement by the janitor of the building. We managed to save quite a bit of money this way. This mode of transport became a common way for me to save up so that I could afford a holiday in the summertime.

We didn't ride our bikes to work once the weather became too dreary and the days shortened. It was quite treacherous on the slippery streets in bad weather, and I did fall off my bike a couple of times. Never was I seriously hurt, however. But in the autumn, we began to have the dreadful *pea soup fogs*. They indeed were so thick it would be quite impossible to see across the street, hence the name pea soup. No matter what the weather, I was determined to attend our weekly youth club meetings. I had 'gone out with' quite a number of the young men, and there had been many house parties as well as the youth club functions, so this group provided me with a social life that I wouldn't dream of missing. One early November evening, a very heavy fog descended, and my mother thought I was quite mad to go out in it. It was weird, eerie, and I became a bit disoriented a couple of times, and it was only because I knew the road so well that I was able to find the club room.

Once there, I found that not many had come, and we could not have a regular meeting. So, after some random conversations during which we agreed to postpone any youth club discussions until the next meeting, we all decided to return home. I think a couple of the members were a little surprised I had appeared because I had the farthest to come to attend meetings, but we all said 'goodnight', and I began the long ride home. Once on the main road, which was very quiet, I began to be aware someone was following me. I glanced nervously over my right shoulder as the follower got closer, and I discovered it was 'Mick', one of the *serious* cyclists who was a good friend of Barbara's new boyfriend, Harry Pedder. We had occasionally danced together but hadn't exchanged many words because he was a shy young man who became easily embarrassed, so hiding my relief, I just said, 'Oh, hello Mick; I was wondering who was coming up behind me', and we cycled on together for a while. I didn't know where he lived, and I wasn't expecting him to stay with me long, but he asked where I lived and carried on riding beside me. I think we chatted about the horrible weather, always a safe subject, and when we got to Seven Kings where the fog was a little less thick I expected him to turn away to his own home, but he continued with me, and in no time at all, we were riding down Whale Bone Lane to my street. When we arrived at the front gate, he said, 'I'll be off now, but would you like to go with me to *the pictures?*' I replied that I would like that and perhaps we could arrange something at the next club meeting. I had no *special interest* at the time, so I began a relationship which has lasted over 60 years! Boy-girl relationships began slowly in those days. We went to the cinema and agreed to meet at the next club meeting, after which Mick accompanied me home again. We were both about 18-years old and Christmas was approaching, and I remember very well that when we were at a Christmas dance we found we liked to dance together and we were indeed on kissing terms, so we became 'a couple' in the eyes of our friends. Barbara was delighted because as Harry and Mick were friends, we became a foursome, which added much to our enjoyment of the weekend outings. When Christmas came, I was invited to Mick's house. I expect his mother wanted to take a look at this girl he had become interested in, and I learned he was called Michael by his family. I quickly began to call him Michael also, and I liked it better, and I think he did too!

Maureen's first bike and off to College

Maureen (left) with her best friend, Patsy

Maureen's family (about 1962)

Michael

The war in Europe had ended by May 1945, so by early September, we were back in school, and plans were being made for everyone to have street parties. Neighbours got together, and all contributed as much food as they could manage. There seemed to be lots of jelly; they must have been hoarding it for years. The street was closed off, and long tables were spread with food, drinks, and flowers. There was music and dancing, and we all had a good time, as the whole country celebrated. For us, the war was over, and my wonderful childhood experiences in the Shropshire countryside came to an end. My mother, who had developed a very close relationship with George and Gwen Potter of Plox Green, revisited them and the Shropshire countryside, which she loved so much, for very many years after the war had ended.

Then the realisation came of the cost of this war. The newspapers and newsreels in the cinemas were full of the awful conditions discovered in the devastated cities of Europe and particularly the conditions in the concentration and prison camps. Britain was exhausted, and Germany crushed. The bright beam of hope was focused on the United States' generosity and their ability to pour food and supplies into Europe to normalise conditions in the shortest possible time. Unfortunately, Russia had engulfed Berlin before the Allies could arrive and immediately wanted to keep all the territory won. There wasn't much room for negotiation, but an agreement was reached that the city was to be divided into four Occupation Zones – U.S.S.R., the United States, Britain, and France.

The War in the Pacific came to an end on 2nd September 1945, as V-J Day (Victory in Japan) was declared after the United States dropped atomic bombs on Hiroshima and Nagasaki. But sadly, there were to be many other unresolved conflicts to arise in Asia. Here again, the United States spent much time, money, human resources, and effort in trying to get everyday life and trade connections between countries operating again. There was no one else with the energy, monetary funds, and workforce to do this. The *Big Three* powers, the United States, Britain, and the U.S.S.R. discussed how the perpetrators of the conflict in Europe, and the awful War Crimes, were to be punished. The resulting Nuremberg Trials began in November 1945. The newsreels we saw in the cinema and the newspapers were for weeks full of heart-rending evidence presented to the tribunal. The top officials of Hitler's Third Reich were tried, sentenced, and many executed.

As soon as we were settled at home, I was enrolled in the Boy Scouts and became a Wolf Cub. Brother Denis joined a group of Sea Scouts who were located on the banks of the very muddy River Roding in Barking. Although our parents were not very religious, I was sent to the Anglican Church, Saint Barnabas, to study for confirmation. My brother did not go; it must have been felt that I needed religion more than he did.

My mother always liked a walk on Sunday afternoons after lunch and her nap, during which we had to keep absolutely quiet, so we would all walk to Plashet Park or Wanstead Flats and sometimes take the bus to Woolwich car ferry. This trip was exciting where you could watch the ferry's engines as it manoeuvred across the River Thames. I had become interested in machinery. For one Christmas or birthday, my parents bought me a Meccano set! It was only a simple one as that was all they could afford, but it gave me hours of pleasure. The more expensive sets had gears and motors, but I was never to have one of those. As there were not a lot of organised activities for 11-year-olds, a teacher father of a school friend, formed a small boys' club which met at our school one evening each week. I now believe that Mr Tidd must have influenced how my life would unfold. He arranged various games and activities and expected us to be creative. Upon learning that I was interested in trains and travel, he suggested that I could use the school projector to put on a show using slides loaned by the railway companies. With my mother's help, I wrote to the LMS (London Midland and Scottish Railway), and to my surprise, a box of loan slides arrived at my home. I presented these pictures of trains and the beautiful scenery around Britain to the group and, flushed with success, wrote off to the Canadian Pacific Railway, who also responded with slides. These were awesome pictures of trains travelling across Canada and through the Rocky Mountains. I had started collecting stamps a few years earlier, and from this hobby, I learned a great deal about other countries and expanded my knowledge of the outside world. Mr Tidd was also fascinated by Africa and encouraged us to read about David Livingstone, the Scottish explorer, and a missionary, and to see the film about him that had just been released. The group soon disbanded as we moved on to other activities, but I think my desire to travel one day had been ignited. My cousin Pat and I always looked forward to Saturday mornings when we went to the local cinema for *children only* session. The film show started with cartoons and was generally followed by a Western with Roy Rogers and Trigger or Gene Autry, and sometimes, a Lassie movie which I liked. Before the show, they would select several girls or boys who were sitting quietly and give them a tour of the projection room. I was chosen on several occasions. These film shows were exhilarating for children who had been deprived of entertainment for six years.

Even in London, my mother loved to get out of the house at weekends, probably because my grandmother, who lived with us, was so unhappy. We visited all the interesting museums and other attractions in and around the city. My father still worked for the London Underground, and my mother could get cheap fares on the trains. I became very interested in steam locomotives and would visit the large main-line stations, becoming a train-spotter in later years, when I would go with a friend into London on the bus and spend hours collecting train numbers. There were books available with all the names and numbers and technical details of each locomotive. Many adults, as well as young boys, enjoyed this exciting hobby. To me, it was a fascinating pastime, as there were many classes of locomotives, all numbered and some with exotic names like Caernarvon Castle, Mallard and Flying Scotsman, many streamlined and smartly painted. The crews took great pride in maintaining these machines in first-class condition. We took several holidays travelling on these beautiful trains to the West Country. The first one I remember after the war was to Devon, to a small bungalow at Slapton Sands near Dartmouth. Slapton has a beautiful long stretch of golden sand, but this was somewhat spoilt by the miles of barbed wire, which had been laid at the beginning of the war to thwart an enemy invasion. These beaches had also been used as a training ground for the D-Day landings. Other holidays, generally taken during school holidays, were to Herne

Bay in Kent, where we rented a small self-contained cottage. The beach was quite lovely, but often the weather was not, with strong winds blowing across the Thames estuary and we spent many an afternoon playing cards. These holidays are probably where I developed my dislike for card games.

For day trips, we often went to Southend-on-Sea or Chalkwell during the summer months. My mother preferred the later as she felt it had a bit more *class* than all the glitz and excitement of Southend. We always would go down the pier if we visited Southend, which was then the longest one in the world. We would walk to the end and ride on the little train to come back! By the pier entrance, was a motor racing track where I loved to have a ride, but it was only very occasionally that my parents would pay out the money for a 10-minute drive. The noise and smell of the place excited me, but I understood that it was too expensive for many visits.

Looking back to those times, I feel I never really knew my father. My father, Ted, was a gentle and kind man who had worked throughout the war on the London Underground trains, experiencing some ghastly scenes, about which he never spoke. We did not communicate much with each other, and my mother always seemed to be in control of family affairs, including discipline and finances. I certainly cannot remember my father ever laying a hand on me either in affection or anger. I later learned that the war-time stress and rationing, when he was alone for much of the time and didn't eat very well, eventually seriously affected his health, and he suffered 'a nervous breakdown'. After a long period of no work, which occurred during my late teens, he did return to lighter duties at one of the stations, mainly as a ticket collector.

At school, we had to prepare for the 11-plus examination, which determined whether we would go to the Grammar School or Secondary School. I didn't pass, and now I would have to go to Cornwall Secondary School, named after Jack Cornwall, a World War 1, boy naval hero who had stayed at and eventually died at his post, assisting a naval gunnery team. He had also attended this school. It was a very old building in a run-down area. New boys were initiated by being systematically pushed about by the older boys, and there was much bullying and fighting. Some measure of discipline was maintained by caning, usually on the hands, sometimes on the backside. I remember being punished a few times with the cane; once for getting involved in a fight, I did not start. It was carried out in front of the class to set an example. Each day I was glad to escape this hated place and enjoyed the freedom of roller-skating home. The roller skates were not very robust, and my mother was always having to buy new metal ball-bearing wheels to keep me mobile. I had to take the skates (in a bag) into the class, or they would have been stolen, but it was not unusual to do this as several boys skated to school. After less than two years, I was able to sit another exam to enable me to enter a technical college, and this time I passed. As a reward, my parents bought me a new bike for my birthday in October, a Raleigh with Sturmey-Archer three-speed gears.

I seem to remember at this time that I also started to take an interest in girls, a group I had largely ignored in the past, except for my cousin Pat, who I considered as just one of the boys. Having never had a sister, I was somewhat surprised that I now started to pay attention to how pretty they were and that their bodies were developing in an interesting way. My own body seemed to be responding accordingly. My father had tried to have a private talk about this with me, but he ended up just passing me a book with some graphic diagrams, enough to scare a young boy away from sex.

I was about 13 years old when I started at West Ham Technical College, which was quite a distance from our home, but we were issued a bus pass and had to wear a uniform blazer and tie. This school had much higher standards than local Secondary Schools. The teachers all wore caps and gowns, and we were expected to behave and be serious about learning. As many of the subjects were technical, I enjoyed them and also played soccer and cricket for the school. I made friends with one of the boys on the soccer team, Harry Pedder, who was also interested in cycling.

Still going to church at the beginning of this time and studying for confirmation, I was having doubts as to whether I wanted to go on with it. I spoke to my mother about it, and she said I should talk to the rector. He convinced me that it was reasonable to have some doubts about some of the teachings and that it would be best for me to continue anyway. And so, I was confirmed into the Church of England, and I continued to go to Communion for about six months, but, as my negative feelings persisted, I gradually dropped out. I was the only one in my immediate family to attend church.

Before getting my first bike, I used to ride the buses into London, sometimes alone, often with a friend. We would pay a few pennies, the minimum child fare, and take the front seat at the top of the bus, hoping the conductor would not come asking for more money as we generally did not have any. But once I had the bike, I was able to expand my adventures. I had a new friend, Len Nutkins, and at every opportunity, we would go exploring into the Essex countryside and London, often over old cobblestone roads and slick tramlines - very treacherous when wet. Also, at this time, I was given an autograph book and would spend time in the evening waiting outside the stage door of the East Ham Theatre for celebrities to come out. Here I met Vera Lynn, Petula Clark, and many other glamorous entertainers. They would give me their autograph and talk. I could not afford to go to the shows here, but the TV studios and radio stations in London would give out free tickets. I would take myself to shows like 'Take it from Here', 'Itma' and the 'Goon Show', meeting actors Dick Bentley, Joy Nichols, Harry Secombe, Spike Milligan, Peter Sellers and many more. It was exciting talking to these stars and collecting their signatures; my parents did not seem to mind me travelling into the big city alone.

A neighbour helped me get my first job, and it felt wonderful to have some money in my pocket. Mrs Donaldson, who lived next door to us all through the war years, had connections with the Jewish tailors who were located in dingy little shops in the East End of London. My job was to deliver the expensive finished work (generally suits) to the smart Saville Row tailors in the West End of London. It was quite a responsible job as the outfits were custom made and promised for a specific date, so I had to make sure they got there on time. I travelled on the Underground *tube* trains and was always very worried about losing them or having them stolen.

The schooling was going well, particularly in the technical

subjects, and I gained very respectable marks in my final year. My parents had started thinking about what kind of work would be suitable for me. Several years earlier, my brother had started an apprenticeship with Siemens Brothers at Woolwich, and it was felt that I should also go into engineering. As I had an interest in trains, my father took me to the London Underground overhaul shops at Acton and was keen on signing me up for an apprenticeship with them. But I was not very interested in that particular environment and felt that there would be very few job opportunities for this type of work outside London, so it was not pursued.

Early in 1952, I applied for an apprenticeship at The Plessey Company in Ilford, Essex, and was accepted there in a pre-apprenticeship program, which placed me in a drawing office by June of that year. I mainly filed drawings, learned to print them, and made lots of tea for the office staff. My apprenticeship as a Tool and Die Maker started in September, and except for the first few months, which did not go very well, I settled in and started to use machines and make many kinds of machine tools. In one tool repair shop, I met a fellow who knew about and taught me some aspects of watch repairing, and this is when my interest in horology began. Moving from department to department at Plessey, I made quite a few friends and indeed started to take notice of the girls that worked in our offices, meeting them at lunchtime in the cafeteria. I went to dances and the pictures with a few, but the relationships were mainly short-lived due maybe to my lack of cash being just a poor apprentice, and my shyness and insecurity was also a handicap. Once at a Saturday night dance in Barkingside, I thought I'd met the girl of my dreams. She was blonde and slender, and we danced all evening. After taking her home, we arranged to meet at a cinema the following Tuesday, and she seemed enthusiastic. That evening I waited for ages for her, but she failed to show up, and I learned afterwards that she had done this to many boys. I went off girls for a while after this experience. Christmas Eve at Plessey was a wild time as the plant closed at noon, but the partying and drinking started at about 9.00 am. During our training as apprentices, we moved around and made many friends, and of course, they all wanted to give us a drink, resulting in most of us getting quite drunk. Some departments were staffed almost entirely by women, and after a few drinks, their main aim seemed to be to lure as many of the young apprentices as they could into their lairs, causing much embarrassment to their victims. I could move quite fast and was never caught.

My brother Denis was now 21 and having reached the end of his apprenticeship was ready to do his National Service in the British Forces. Denis and I did not seem to have had very much in common as children, and as teenagers, our interests took us in different directions. While I was playing soccer, cricket and cycling, he had stayed on in the Sea Scouts who met in Barking. Denis reached quite a senior position and taught the younger scouts about boats (they had two large whalers), sailing and canoeing. This sport captured his interest, and after meeting a well-known kayak builder, he obtained the plans and built several by himself. This led to many canoeing/camping trips down the various fast flowing English rivers, such as the Avon and the Wye, which involved shooting rapids. He seemed to have little interest in girls but did attend a few dances organised by the scouts and tried his feet at ballroom dancing.

My friend, Len Nutkins, and I were very keen on cycling, and although we had very little money, we tried to improve our bikes and spent most of our spare time touring the southeast English countryside; also, we always followed the fortunes of the Tour de France riders with great interest. The derailleur system of gearing for bikes had just been developed in France, and it was far too expensive for us, but when we joined the West Ham Cycling Club, we met many people who had costly bikes. Len and I went on some long cycling rides, such as to Hastings and back in a day, 120 miles in snowy conditions, and we took a two-week holiday in Devon and Cornwall, staying in Youth Hostels and eating fish and chips every day. Great fun for two young men, but one did get a sore rear end. The hills were very steep in the West Country, and we were able to ride up most of them. Porlock Hill in Somerset defeated us as it had a gradient of 1 in 3½. The cycling club also competed in cycle races, and Len and I started to train and take part in road time-trials and mass start racing, usually run on abandoned airfield perimeter tracks. Some events were just hill-climbing events. All this exercise kept me slim and always hungry and we cycled in any weather throughout the year, using a single fixed gear during the winter. With Harry Pedder, I joined another club associated with The Youth Hostels Association. The club was a mixed club with about thirty per cent girls, and weekend trips to Youth Hostels would be arranged to the surrounding countryside villages, although sometimes we would go camping when all the equipment had to be carried on our bikes. Camping was less restrictive than the hostels. As interested as I was in cycling and racing, I did start to take notice of the girls in the club. Harry liked girls too, and through him, I met a girl called Pat, a tall slim brunette but not much of a cyclist. We became a pair for about six months until, at one of our regular club meetings, a new male member appeared. He was much older and recently *demobbed* from the army, having served in the Korean War. Pat and this newcomer seemed to hit it off right away, and she speedily dumped me and went home with him that night! I was entirely off girls again for a while.

Several months later, I noticed Harry's interest, Barbara, was bringing a friend to the meetings, who seemed to be getting a lot of attention from the other males. She was tall, slim, wore nice clothes, and her dark hair was always shiny and well cared for. By the way she spoke, she seemed to have been to a good school. She generally wore brief white shorts that showed off her long, tanned legs, so it was not easy to overlook her. When autumn came, and London was experiencing extremely foggy conditions that could last for days or even weeks, cycling could sometimes be a rather unpleasant experience. Called smog, this kind of weather was formed by industrial and domestic smoke and usual mist. One very dark and foggy meeting night, visibility was down to a few feet, and one could get very cold, dirty, and lost cycling in it. Most motorized traffic was at a standstill. I had spoken to the newcomer several times, and we had even danced occasionally at our social events. Not many members had braved the poor conditions for that meeting. As we were leaving our meeting place, I noticed the smog was very thick, and Barbara's friend seemed to be about to ride home alone. I followed her for a short while, then moved up and asked if I could escort her home. Her name was Maureen Starling!

Following the war,
Michael became
interested in soccer,
cycling and girls

Michael, on a cycling trip
with his brother,
Denis(left) and friend,
Len Nutkins

Michael (centre back row), as the goalkeeper for the West Ham Technical College soccer team 1951

Michael, competing in a gruelling hilly road race

3.
Our Fine Romance

Maureen

I became a little better pleased with my life, although at first, nothing seemed to have changed. But there were changes. With the departure of Eddie, I began to experiment with high heeled shoes. He was relatively short, so I hadn't felt comfortable about trying heels out. I also joined a social club in the city and played table tennis with a group of young people once a week. The social club was great fun. I met a few more young men and eventually played with one of the better players in the group in a mixed doubles tournament, which was held at Wimbledon. We did quite well together and, to everyone's surprise, won the event and were honoured at the annual party at the end of the season.

Finding the cycling club had provided me with more new friends and activities, so aside from the social element, I also had a new hobby. I loved those busy weekends, and in the space of a few months, after going out with several of those eager young men, I soon had a regular boyfriend. My mother realised that I had a particular interest in one of them. The first time she met some of the crowd was after a short ride into the Essex countryside, a Sunday run on a beautiful winter day, to Abridge in Essex, where the boys got into a soccer game in a rather muddy field. It was a very cold day, and on the way back to West Ham, my home being closer to the open countryside, was the first one we would pass close to, so I suggested that everyone should come to my house where I was sure Mum would, at the very least, provide some hot drinks. My faith in my mother's hospitable nature was not misplaced, as although she was horrified at the state some of the young men were in; they were all made very welcome. The girls were directed to the only bathroom on the upstairs landing. At the same time, the boys were handed soap and towels and invited to make themselves presentable at the kitchen sink for the cakes and tarts she quickly placed on the family dining table. Hot tea and home baking were very welcome, and with great good humour, everyone participated in a merry time. Our family home was quite small; English suburban homes usually are, so an invasion of about a dozen young people was not an event every mother would welcome, and they must have looked like a pretty rough bunch. I think she and my Dad were pleased I had brought my new friends to the house, and perhaps it also helped me find acceptance with the group. They all thanked my parents politely before leaving, and my mother never forgot the occasion.

Up until that time, I had continued to have dates, but once Michael had come to my home, these other young men seemed to accept we were '*a couple*' and the invitations stopped. Realising now that Michael and I were becoming a two-some, my mother issued an invitation for him to come *to tea*. Initially, she seemed to regard the friendship more seriously than I did. When a young man received an invitation to Sunday tea, he recognised this to be an opportunity to be closely scrutinised by the girl's parents. My parents had issued many such requests, and I never realised what an ordeal it might be. The last invitation for my benefit had been extended before Eddie's time; there had been many teatime parties while he was my boyfriend, so I thought nothing of it. The young man that had been invited before Michael's turn was a Welsh boy I met at our Methodist Youth Club. He was studying for his First Officers ticket in the British Merchant Navy. He turned up at the appointed time resplendent in his navy-blue uniform, complete with cap and gold braid. I was quite impressed with the way he looked, and my sister Pam was green with envy, even though she was engaged at the time. That tea went very well as David was quite comfortable socially, and I loved his Welsh accent and easy manners.

Things didn't go so well for Michael. Mine was a rather noisy and opinionated family! Of course, all three of my brothers and Pam were present, and Michael didn't enjoy the scrutiny he was subjected to, and hardly spoke. Because he was quiet, my mother didn't feel comfortable with him and thought him secretive. Since Dad quickly discovered that Michael was involved in a similar line of work to his own, he seemed more ready to accept him, and I never heard a word of criticism from my father either then or later. During one of our many private discussions, my Dad once advised me that one could rely on a man who could earn a living with the skill of his hands; I guess he thought I was following his advice! But at that stage, we really were 'just friends'. I was almost unaware of his discomfort in social situations. If I thought about it at all, I probably imagined he would quickly get over it when he got to know everyone. I never imagined that it would take such a very long time!

So, we continued with our 'cinema' dates and our weekly Youth Club meetings and, when spring came, our weekend Youth Hostel trips. Just before the New Year, my mother had entered my name in a competition open to young women in Dagenham. It was generally called a Beauty Queen competition. They were very popular in the 1950s. Michael was my date on the night of the competition, and surprisingly, I won and found myself being crowned 1954 Press Ball Queen by Jack Warner, who was the famous and popular Number One British film star. It was a very exciting evening, and I had a very pretty white-on-white lacy dress for the occasion. My mother and father took us all to the Poplar Civic Centre Ballroom, where the event was being held. Pam and Ron, who had been married the previous year, came too, and Ron spent quite a lot of money on the *tombola draws* and won a couple of times. This 'gambling' on his part made my mother very nervous. The dance band 'The Billy Tennant Orchestra', which was frequently heard on BBC Radio, was excellent and Michael and I danced together a couple of times, but I don't think he particularly enjoyed the evening. I thought it absolutely fantastic and was glad to represent my hometown, and I didn't have any expectations of this event changing my life.

The most anticipated high point of each year for everyone then was their annual two-week holiday. Remembering Barbara's hiking holiday of the year before, she and I planned a cycling trip through the West Country. This was very exciting. I hadn't had a holiday separately from my family before, so we had to plan carefully and keep our mothers informed about those plans. When July came, off we went, riding our bikes to the mainline station, Waterloo. There we loaded our bikes into the guard's van and settled into a carriage to enjoy the train ride to a lovely old town, Winchester, in Hampshire. Our first night was spent at the Youth

Hostel there, which was an ancient water mill on the river. We thought the sound of rushing water might keep us awake. We were quite excited. Then it was by cycle power and easy stages through Dorset and Somerset to Plymouth in Devon, where my Auntie Louise now lived. She was delighted to see us and cooked lemon sole for supper. We took the opportunity to have a bath - this was not always possible while youth hostelling, so we enjoyed this luxury, rested and freshened up before going on our merry way. Once or twice we got a lift by a friendly lorry driver who would load our bikes onto his lorry and us into the cab. These men simply were glad to have someone to chat to on their long trips. The West Country is quite hilly, and Barbara found this cycling holiday much more strenuous than her walking tour of the previous year, so we were glad of the help.

Each day I mailed my mother a postcard so that she heard from me frequently, and mid-way through the two weeks, I mailed off a parcel containing my laundry and picked up a package of fresh underwear that she sent to me at a pre-arranged Post Office. It was difficult to carry everything one needed for two weeks in one saddlebag even though it was quite large, and I was a fastidious soul. Of course, we met other young people touring, and sometimes we had company for the next leg of our journey. Still, eventually, we arrived home again very fit, bronzed and somewhat thinner but feeling, on my part at least, that we had had a terrific adventure holiday.

For his annual holiday, Michael went with his friend, to a Butlin's Holiday Camp at Clacton-on-Sea. I missed him, and he wrote me a postcard saying that he was having a 'fairly good time, only fairly!' He didn't want me to think he was living it up! The separate holidays had taught us we each did miss the other a little, so we became closer as the summer passed into autumn. Barbara and Harry must have felt the same too. Before long, we noticed that our weekend jaunts were not attended by many of the other cycling club members. We all liked the camaraderie of the rest of the group, but they said we had become so close they didn't want to intrude. Perhaps for all of us, things were changing.

I was promoted at work that fall to a department in the same office where the work was somewhat more complicated, and

Michael's Auntie Hilda came to work in my office. She was in the process of being divorced from her Belgian husband Jean, whom she had met and married towards the end of the war. They had a son Carl, a nice little red-haired boy who at first spoke only French. Hilda and Carl came to live temporarily with Michael's mother, where I met her and encouraged her to apply to the Institute as she was anxious to get into the workforce. She didn't remain at the Institute long but used the time to gain typing speed and the confidence to find a better job. Since she was fluent in French, and as she had used telephone communications during the war, she had excellent marketable skills. We became good friends. I was glad about this because sometime after our holiday, Barbara decided she would prefer to work nearer to her home and went to work at Ford of Dagenham. She didn't tell me, but she and Harry were beginning to think about marriage, and this needed much saving up for.

When Hilda left the Institute and Barbara was no longer there, I began to feel that I needed a change too. When I gave notice, I was offered another position. The head of my department interviewed me together with his secretary (with whom we all thought he was having an extramarital affair), and they told me there were other more exciting positions available, and he would recommend me. I really should have listened as I loved working in the City, but thinking I should be a bit closer to home and maybe save some money too, I declined and took a week off to find another job. I finally found a small company called Engert & Rolfe Ltd., which had a small suite of offices attached to a plant that manufactured and installed bitumen flooring and roofing products.

My mother convinced me that Poplar in the East End was a very colourful place to be, so I settled into this small office where I was the Sales Manager's Assistant. This man, Mr Brown, was amiable and handled estimating duties for the Works Department. I was once again pounding a typewriter and produced very dull and complicated itemised estimates and letters. The girls in this office were quite nice but generally from rougher backgrounds than me, and I didn't make close friends with anyone. This job lasted about two years, and I began to have bad dreams about it after an unfortunate incident that involved a young black man who was taken on and who *set his cap at me*. He was let go, but I didn't like the area even though we were met at the station by the company car and taken care of.

During these two years, Michael and I gradually got to know each other, and we began to want to see each other more often. He was still an apprentice, and his mother probably privately thought I was taking his mind off his studies. The year following my West Country tour with Barbara, Michael and I planned a holiday together. I had got into the habit of visiting Michael's home regularly. We had to arrange our meetings and needed time to communicate. To preserve a girl's good reputation, most vigilant parents set rules for their daughter regarding how frequently they could meet their friends of the opposite sex. It was quieter in his house than mine, and Michael's mother seemed to enjoy my visits. She was a great reader, as I was, so initially, I would visit on a Sunday afternoon, an approved and traditional time for a visit together, and stay for tea. While Michael worked away at his desk on his studies (he also was interested in learning to repair watches), she and I would chat about our books and other feminine topics. Mrs Harbott indicated she was disappointed that she had no daughter, so I felt quite welcome in her home. As time went on, Mrs Harbott confided in me quite a bit. She told me many things about her family and, of course, I was interested in her stories about her sons as small boys and their general family life. Her husband had not been well and was off work for many months with stress-related emotional problems, which resulted in some financial hardship. She had cared for her mother for many years, and when her mother, Mrs Arliss, died, the house had to be sold so that the proceeds could be shared among the siblings. As the house was also the Harbott's home and they wanted to remain there, they purchased it at an agreed price. The struggle to manage this, following what had been a challenging time financially, resulted in her becoming rather worn down and depressed. She was a good and brave woman. It was not at all easy. I was quite flattered to be taken into her confidence. For me, the main event was at the end of the evening after we had listened to the BBC radio 'Grand Hotel' together, a regular programme of light classics by the 'Palm Court Orchestra' which we both enjoyed, Michael would take me home either by bike if the weather was fine, or by bus, if it was not. Then we would have time for private time together. Michael seemed entirely oblivious to his mother's difficulties.

The planning of our holiday together took place at Michael's house. I knew my parents might disapprove of this plan, so we were careful to set up arrangements for us both to spend the nights mostly at Youth Hostels and where there were no hostels on our route at pre-booked bed and breakfast establishments. When the time came for me to let my parents know the details, these were complete and in place. I was not sure how Michael felt about me then, but for my part, I knew we were friends and beyond, so I was able to layout the plans to my mother with confidence. She, of course, was not happy with our arrangement but, realising that I was 20 years old by this time and would be 21 quite soon, at which time I would be legally an adult and able to choose for myself how I arranged my life, my parents didn't attempt to block our plans.

The relationship between my mother and me was a little troubled. When Pam married, my mother did try to transfer her loving attention to me, expecting me to grow closer because she greatly missed Pam. I had always felt somewhat isolated within the family. Pam and Mum had always been such a 'team', and my three noisy, younger brothers were another different group - I had naturally become somewhat independent. My experience of going to a better school than the rest of the family had helped me mature early. So, in the second half of my teenage years when young people are struggling towards independence, it was, perhaps, expecting too much on my poor mother's part to imagine I would assume Pam's dependant role. Initially, in my early teens, I was the only child who had homework assignments every night, which I used to work on in the living room with the radio on and family life going on noisily around me. The living room was the only warm place in the house. When the time came for me to go to work, Pam was looking forward to getting married after being engaged to three different young men. The more significant part of Mum's attention had been nearly fully engaged with these goings-on.

I am not suggesting I was neglected in any way - only that I had become accustomed to working through things by myself. My mother wanted both her daughters to 'marry well'. Many years later, Pam and I discussed this, and we wondered together, where

Mum thought we would meet the kind of men who, in her eyes, would qualify in this respect! When I changed jobs, Mum tried very hard to convince me Poplar in London was an interesting place - she was entirely wrong. So far as I was concerned, I had fallen into the habit of thinking Mum was quite wrong most of the time, so one way and another, Mum and I weren't getting along very well. I never doubted that she loved and was proud of me, but at this stage in my life, I didn't have very much patience with her. I am not proud of the thoughts and feelings I had at that time but understand now that when a daughter is struggling to find her place in the world, many mothers and daughters go through similar experiences and emotions.

So Michael and I set up quite an interesting holiday. We put our bikes on the train; Carlisle in the north of England was our destination, and we began our tour by cycling south to the Lake District. It was another adventure. The Lake District is world-renowned for beautiful scenery, and the hostels were in romantic, quaint sounding places. This part of England is associated with some of the great English poets and is indeed very beautiful. We had quite good weather. We rowed on Lake Windermere and stayed in the little villages. Then it was south to mountainous North Wales, where Michael was quite excited to show me the bridge over the Menai Straits to Anglesey. We saw Mount Snowdon, but the weather was not very fine, which prevented our attempting an ascent, and we cycled on through Betws-y-Coed to Shropshire, where we visited the Potters near Shrewsbury, where Michael had spent much of the war with his mother and brother. This lovely old couple gave us a delicious tea in their remote farmhouse before we spent the night at the hostel in town. Then it was home again the next day by train. We did not seem to find this holiday truly very memorable. In retrospect, this was possibly because, in our separate ways, we felt we were simply marking time, and perhaps we missed the companionship of our friends.

We soon fell back into our usual routines, but in the late autumn, during one of our private moments after a film date, the subject of marriage was mentioned. Michael simply whispered that he thought I was, 'The kind of girl he would like to marry.' This idea was fascinating to me. Perhaps I had been waiting for him to speak. I didn't reject the notion, and I told him, 'That would be very nice' because he hadn't exactly *asked* me. Within a few weeks, we were looking at one another in a different way. Christmas came and went; we now thought we were in love and began looking in jewellers' windows. Being in love, meant to me, that a wedding should be under consideration. My father expected Michael to speak to him about our future together, and I don't know whether this talk happened before or after we became engaged, but it did happen at Easter in 1956. We found my idea of the perfect engagement ring in W Samuels Ltd in East Ham, and right away, I seemed to become the object of some interest to everyone in the family, which was rather nice attention at a time when I felt rather special.

We both realised we needed more money if we ever wanted to put a down payment on a house. Michael's income was increasing annually as he advanced towards the end of his apprenticeship. Shortly after my 21st birthday, in an effort to earn more money myself and when I thought I wanted to be back in '*The City*' which is how the financial and business district of the City of London is described, once again I took a week to find a better paying job. At Engert and Rolfe, I had worked hard, taking on all the typing chores for the whole of the Works Department, including billing. They were sorry to see me go. After the unpleasant incident with the young black man, I had been given my own locked office, but I felt it was time to move on.

After a short search, I became the Second Assistant to the Managing Director of Farrow & Jackson and Purdy Ltd. This company was a neat little company involved in the manufacture of bottling, corking, and labelling equipment for the wine and beer trade. I shared an office outside the Chief Executive's office, and I assisted his personal secretary and also acted as secretary to the Sales Manager. My superiors used dictating machines, and I quickly learned to combine them with my fast typing skills. This little company was situated quite close to the Tower of London, and I made friends with the company Chief Accountant's secretary Joyce Robinson, who is my friend still.

I probably liked this job best of all those that I had. I enjoyed the location and the people I worked alongside. I also knew I was planning to be married, which was something that I realised I had long hoped for. At this time, London was being rebuilt at last, as the recovery from the years of austerity following the end of the war, was coming to an end and I seemed to walk on air in the sunshine of that summer; I was very happy, and around London, young women were constantly serenaded by the young bronzed and muscular men engaged on the building sites, who would utter *wolf whistles* and *cat-calls* at every likely female. It was great fun and not regarded in any way as sexual harassment in those days. We felt instead complimented and desirable.

It was soon time to plan another holiday and this time we chose the West Country. Perhaps this time a holiday together was not such a good idea. Once again, we took a train part of the way and began cycling around Devon. By the time we got to Barnstaple, we could hardly keep our hands off each other. We had booked a week at Ilfracombe, planning to have short trips to the lovely places nearby. Unfortunately, we both arrived in Ilfracombe with food poisoning. We had to visit the hospital as we were both so sick, but with the resilience of youth, we were soon better, and being young and in love, our kisses and physical explorations of each other were getting very passionate. We did have separate rooms. Landladies expected guests to behave circumspectly! And we tried to comply. After a particularly passionate encounter, on our ride the next day, I was so bemused when cycling along a path at the side of a river that I nearly fell in, so I implored Michael to please let us wait until we were married. Somehow we managed and eventually arrived home with such a glow that everyone must have known how much in love we were. This waiting time was quite stressful. I shall never know how Michael felt about it because he was never one to communicate feelings.

Home again and back to the usual routine, we ran into Harry Pedder one day. We hadn't seen either him or Barbara for many months. He was driving a little car and told us without getting out of it that he and Barbara were about to be married and said with great pride, 'And we have collected our entire home together.' It seems they had saved hard and were to be married in the New Year, and we were invited to the wedding. I felt quite envious that they were ready ahead of us but soothed my feelings by beginning to buy linen and blankets for our own eventual home. When I told Michael's mother, about this, she wondered why I was buying these things 'so soon'. I replied that we would need them, but although she had said she and Mr Harbott were pleased about our engagement, I got a very strong feeling that she thought Michael too young to be married yet. So, I thought I had better be discreet about the progress of our preparations and stay home a little more.

The following spring, we attended our friend's wedding, and it was a charming small affair. The reception was held at Barbara's home. I was greatly amused after the reception when the bride and groom in their *going away* outfits said goodbye to all of us and then walked down the road to the station together; Harry was carrying the suitcase, to begin their honeymoon! That wedding seemed to be a signal, for we attended many weddings for friends during the next couple of years.

Michael had a new friend, Vic Monteith. He persuaded Michael that we should all have a cycling holiday together the following year touring Scotland. I was always willing to see new sights, and we would be a foursome with Vic's girlfriend, a quiet little person making the fourth. After Christmas, we began to make all the plans together. They suggested we stay at B&Bs, and as there would be two girls and two guys, we booked two double rooms at each overnight stop. Michael and I were looking forward to the trip and the chance to be together for two weeks. We took an overnight train to Edinburgh and set off in pouring rain. At our first stop, after greeting our hosts and getting settled, when bedtime came, Vic and Christine said 'goodnight' and to my great surprise disappeared together upstairs. We looked at each other - what could we do? We waited a bit wondering if they would reappear, and when they didn't, up we went to the other room. The sleeping arrangements had never been discussed - I was amazed that quiet, mousy little Chris was so liberated. She looked as if butter wouldn't melt in her mouth! After our trip up and the wet ride, we were cold and tired, so snuggling up together in bed was a great way to get warm. It was the same story all the way to Inverness by way of Pitlochry, where we saw a fish ladder, the first I had ever seen. It never stopped raining, and those two grabbed the best room every night!

By this time, I was quite fed up. Every stitch of clothing I had was wet, but I was determined to seem to be a 'good sport' about it. At Inverness, we were treated to a bagpipes concert in a dreary, grey park - it was still raining mistily. From there, we had to set out on a chilly, blustery, long ride across Scotland towards the Isle of Skye - this was a tough holiday; I remember struggling with this ride, which was about 60 miles. Eventually, we came to Kyle of Lochalsh and the ferry to Broadford on the Island. We planned to stay there for the weekend. Big mistake - everywhere seemed to be closed up and we had very little food, but the sun had decided to come out. It was a very memorable weekend nevertheless because, with nothing else to do, we had incredible nights. I devoutly hoped Michael knew how to take care of 'things'.

The next day (Monday) we were to take the ferry to Mallaig and then by the 'Road to the Isles' to Fort William. Another long ride on an exposed road, but there was almost no other traffic, and the day was beautiful. I was a bit bemused by the events of the night before, and we were coming up to the monument for the 'Bonnie Prince Charlie's Rebellion' when I saw a mountain up ahead. 'Is that Ben Nevis?' I asked. Michael took out his map, let go of his handlebars, and sat straight up, still peddling, as I had often seen him do, to examine his map. 'Yes,' he said, 'it is' and right away, I saw him turning a somersault flying high through the air, his bike, likewise airborne, upside down. Everything inevitably hit the ground. He had neglected to notice that the road we were travelling on had minimal shoulder, and every so often, there would be an unguarded culvert where a little mountain stream passed under the roadway. He had run off the paving just where there was no road at all. We slammed on our brakes and ran back to examine the damage. Michael was wet, having landed in the stream, had a very badly bruised thigh, and scraped shin but no broken bones. The bike was practically in two pieces. The crossbar was broken close to the handlebars. His precious lightweight bike was no longer rideable. But he could have killed himself, so, though a calamity, the situation was not completely hopeless.

Michael arranged at a small nearby train station to have his bike sent to our next destination in Fort William, and while we road on, he hitchhiked there. The next day he had some temporary repairs performed on his bike at a blacksmith's shop in a small village, and although the bike looked very shaky and creaked ominously when Michael began to ride it, we were able to continue on our journey.

So, we set off once again, along the edge of Loch Lomond to Stirling, which was our destination that day. We saw the castle which was the home of Mary Queen of Scots - I think it was there that her Court Musician, David Rizzio, was murdered before her eyes. Since the bike was holding up, we went to Edinburgh for the train journey back to London. Once in London, we had the ride to Michael's home at Manor Park. A good part of the road east out of London was laid with cobblestones, and Michael's creaking bike held together just long enough. We really had a tale to tell about this holiday, but of course, until now, we never did tell 'everything'.

Once home again, it was time to seriously begin planning our wedding. As always, this initiated much discussion in both families. As a working-class family of relatively modest means, a wedding was quite a big deal, and the success of the event relied on some co-operation between the two families concerned. Michael's mother didn't like my mother very much, and she disapproved of Michael getting married 'so soon'. However, realising we were quite serious about this and possibly guessing how far our relationship had evolved, I assumed she had decided the matter was somewhat out of her hands. My father asserted he wanted to do things 'right' and provide a decent reception, etc. My mother loved weddings and probably thought her best attitude was one of warm encouragement. She was not in the best of health at this time. At 50 years of age, she must have been going through menopause. She also was suffering from shingles and seemed fairly content to leave most of the decision-making to me.

We set the date, 29th March 1958. March was a popular time for marriages to take place because it was at the end of the tax year, and a married couple could then get a refund on a portion of the income tax paid for that whole tax year. This year it was also the weekend before Easter. We had to book the church quite early, so these arrangements were made immediately following our

Scottish holiday. I purchased a roll of 10 yards of heavy ivory satin for my dress from a speciality fabric store in Petticoat Lane, where I was a fairly regular customer. The fabric turned out to be a heavy and unwieldy thing to carry home, and I remember I met my friend John Gillings, with whom I sometimes travelled home on my usual train, and he carried it right to my door for me. His face gave no sign of what he thought when I told him it was for my wedding gown, but I never saw him again.

I decided we would have only two attendants, my sister Pam who, since she was already a mother, would be my Matron of Honour and Michael's cousin Pat, who agreed to be a bridesmaid. Both young women would wear lilac dresses, which I planned to make myself. At our economic level, the typical wedding style people like us adopted was that the bride would wear the best white dress her father could afford, but it would usually not have a train. However, my dress would look quite formal with long sleeves and shoulders covered, and there would be a modest train. The climate didn't allow for low-cut dresses. Short veils were usually worn, but faces were not covered. Because I was tall, I elected to have a long wedding veil, which was my *'something borrowed'* and the dress would have a half-train. My sister lent me the wedding veil she had worn to her wedding five years earlier. Our menfolk wore dark suits from the best tailor they could afford, although fathers often bought *off-the-peg*. The fashion for renting wedding attire was not unknown but was infrequently adopted. We were proud to wear our own clothes, and if we saw a very formally dressed wedding in our neighbourhood, we all regarded it as people trying to look 'better' than they were – showing off, in other words.

Pat and I shopped for headpieces for the attendants in Ilford. This was not difficult as every head decoration I picked up looked pretty good on her. We were quite good friends, and she knew an excellent dressmaker who would make a beautiful wedding gown to my specifications. But the dresses were not to be started until after Christmas. With my attendants, we decided the flowers I would carry should be white roses. White and mauve lilac for my attendants would be a little unusual but pretty. The flowers were intended as a little compliment to my mother. She was very fond of the lilac that grew in our back garden, and her favourite flower was the white rose. I purchased a set of 'Prestige' saucepans and other useful household items and basked in the warm interest of all my female relatives. Invitations were examined and a style chosen. I enjoyed making these decisions and arrangements, but I was beginning to get a little nervous as I remembered the period before Pam married as one of constant tension. I knew the road ahead simply could not be completely smooth.

I followed what had become my habit when Christmas came. I had Christmas dinner with my family and then went by taxi to Michael's house for the evening. They liked to see me; I think Michael's mother felt it made their day a little special, and I felt complimented by her attitude. However, this year I began to hear some grumbles because Mrs Harbott felt perhaps a little 'left out' of the arrangements. When we were relaxing after teatime in the sitting room, she mentioned that she thought they should be more involved in the planning of this event. So I explained how far the arrangements had come and asked what she would like to do, knowing full well that as Mr Harbott had been on reduced wages because of ill health, there was probably not very much they could do. I knew that even buying new clothes presented quite a problem for them. Michael didn't seem to take much part in this. I believed he very much wanted the wedding to happen and was quite prepared to let the women decide everything. I never heard him express any contrary opinion, so I assumed he felt everything was going along just fine. I knew he planned to buy an especially nice dark suit from the best East Ham tailor. I helped him choose the fabric and accessories. We also went out together to choose my wedding ring. We purchased a special gift for each other, too. I bought a Roamer watch for him (which was stolen some years later), and he bought a lovely gold bangle bracelet for me. I treasure it still.

Michael's part in all this was to buy the ring, pay for his own expenses, the cost of the actual wedding ceremony, and arrange and pay for our honeymoon, which we were really looking forward to as we planned to spend the first night in a hotel in London and then travel to Alassio on the Italian Riviera for two weeks. I don't remember whose idea the Italian honeymoon was, but I know it sounded rather novel and exciting to me, and I think we decided together about where to stay for our first night and how we would get there.

I was a little uncomfortable feeling the approval regarding our forthcoming marriage had lost some lustre and tried to put it out of my mind. Still, the following week Michael's mother had a little more ammunition. She announced that her friend Mrs Wells, who I had met a few times, had decided she would make our wedding cake as a gift. I was assured Mrs Wells was experienced with wedding cakes and would only use the very best ingredients and finish the cake with the best royal icing. She would begin preparations in January to give the cake (which in England was traditionally a rich fruit cake) the time to ripen. I thought Mrs Wells meant well, and perhaps this would help Michael's mother feel part of the event, so I told my parents of this development when I returned home. We had not yet discussed the wedding cake or the arrangements for the reception, so this development precipitated the kind of period of lengthy 'discussion', I remembered from Pam's wedding preparations.

My Dad didn't want anyone else's 'interference'. He was determined I should have a 'proper' professional and beautiful store-bought confection. I eventually suggested we go together to buy a unique ornament to decorate the top of the cake and the pillars etc. that a three-tiered cake would require and reminded him we would need a hall with a kitchen for the reception. At this, my mother realised that with the number of invitations we planned to send, caterers would have to be engaged, the 'bar' would have to be stocked and music provided for the dinner-dance planned for the evening. Therefore, they had to consider their expenses, and perhaps someone else taking care of the cake was not a bad thing. It had been quite an extended period of discussion, but eventually, I was able to see Michael's mother and be suitably grateful for Mrs Wells' kind offer.

I began work on the bridesmaids' dresses, and even though my attendants were quite buxom young women, I was quite pleased with the way the dresses started to look. It was quite a challenge, and I spent many weekends through the winter with the dining room table covered in a sheet while I worked on the many yards of fabric the two dresses required. I used a little electric sewing machine, my Mum and I had purchased together. Food was not allowed in that room while I was working, so everything had to be cleared away in time for the family's evening meal and out came everything once again when the meal was finished if I wanted to continue sewing in the evenings. Thank goodness my parents had the television in the 'front' room now, and I could sometimes have the dining room to myself while I worked. My sister Pam seemed unusually quiet throughout this period. I wondered afterwards if it was because she was so involved with her own home and family affairs – she had been married over four years by this time and had one child, Geoffrey - but I later understood my wedding was shaping up to be a bit fancier than her own. Pam was my dear sister, but I had to admit she never had much sense of style and had been prepared to let our mother make all the decisions and arrangements for her. I loved her for the way she simply fitted in with my plans and was never openly critical.

In late January, Michael and I had to attend Preparation Classes with our Vicar Mr Tom Pownall at his home office, which adjoined the Parish Church of St Mary's, Becontree. There were several young couples in the group, and the purpose was to introduce us to the ritual of *Solemnise of a Marriage* according to the rites of the Church of England, where we could later hear our *Banns* being called on three consecutive Sundays during regular services before we could be married. I was happy to know the Book of Common Prayer in use followed the King James Bible style language. Some congregations were moving to the New Version, but I was quite a traditionalist and liked the beautiful old language. Since we could hear well the shouts of several small children from his home next door, we all laughed when he got to the part in the service of the reasons for Christian marriage, the bit about the procreation of children. Our vicar had clearly honoured that part of the contract. Each couple had a short private interview with Mr Pownall to make sure he had the right spelling of our names etc. and he politely enquired how our arrangements were going, reminded us we must not be late as there were many weddings to fit in on 29th of March and finally, he wished us well.

About this time, Michael and I had a quiet talk together about birth control and decided together that he would be responsible for it at first. I promised to visit the Birth Control Clinic at Five Elms, which was in Dagenham near where my parents lived, after a month or so. I was a little shy about going there before we were married. Since the end of the war, when all the young men had returned to their homes, there had been a tremendous surge in the number of babies born everywhere. This was the 1950s 'Baby Boom'. During our courtship, articles appeared in papers and magazines about sex and the need for birth control. Government departments and services were overwhelmed in the post-war period because there were limited funds available for housing and the health services required for the booming population. Up until this time, this subject had been kept rather 'under wraps'. Suddenly, sex education and birth control clinics were everywhere. It became all the rage! Respectable 'nice' girls were not, up until this time, supposed to know much about it. 'Unmarried mothers' were always talked about in hushed whispers, if at all, when I was growing up, and my mother indeed never mentioned the subject. So, having engaged a photographer, wedding cars, our suitable attire, and the caterers for the reception, we thought we were just about ready.

Our long-awaited Wedding Day finally approached. The last couple of weeks were taken up with making lists of those guests who had accepted our invitation, lists of wedding gifts received, and lists of what we thought we needed to take on our honeymoon. In England at that time, wedding showers were unknown, so family members would usually deliver their gift, or have it sent by mail, and others would bring a gift on the wedding day. Together with my mother, we had discussed the menu for the wedding breakfast, and my father planned to visit the hall we had rented and decorate it appropriately early on 'The Day'. We had found quite nice rented furnished accommodation, after quite a lot of looking, in a quiet street off Little Ilford Lane, which joined Barking to Ilford. It was at number 26 Laxford Lane and was the second level of a well-kept two-story house that belonged to a middle-aged couple who had never had children. The owners of the house were Mr and Mrs Arundel. Mr Arundel worked at night; he was a fireman. Mrs Arundel worked part-time at a Bendix Laundromat. They didn't want us to begin paying rent until we moved in; they seemed really, very nice. I thought everything was as ready as it could be when the great day dawned.

My poor mother was quite unwell with the pain from shingles, but she had a lovely new royal blue dress which she was going to wear with her fur coat, and did her best to put her poor health out of mind. She cleared the big front bedroom to become the dressing room for me and my attendants, and I remember Auntie Olive coming up to see us while I was still in my slip and trying on my headgear, which was a simple circlet which I'd had made, composed of leaf shapes covered in the satin of my dress. I had decorated this with hand-sewn pearl beads to make it look a bit fancier. It looked quite nice with Pam's veil attached, and I could see how it would look on me. My dress was still hidden under wraps. I didn't want anyone at all to see it until I had it on. I had a pair of white low-heeled pumps, which were not new, as my 'something old'. They were very comfortable. I knew the dress was very close-fitting – in fact, I could hardly bend my arms with it on; I knew to manage the full, bell-shaped skirt of this dress was going to be a challenge. The flowers had been delivered early in the day and were placed in the bath, which was a cool place – they were exactly what I had ordered.

Everything went very well. Everyone left ahead of us, and my father helped me into the car for the ride to the Church. With the 'good luck' cries from the neighbours ringing in my ears, we proceeded at a somewhat stately pace to St Mary's church. Approaching the church, my Dad was looking a bit grim, then catching my eye, he suddenly said, 'You can still change your mind if you want to, you know!' I was feeling excited and nervous, so I simply shook my head and didn't respond, and then we were pulling up to the church. The chauffeur opened the door on my father's side first, so I suggested he get out and come round to help me. It was hard to move with those tight sleeves and all that skirt, so Dad came round and took my flowers and helped me out. He tried to help with the dress, about which he had heard so much, but Pam was there ready to help. I took his arm in the doorway of the church and gave it a little squeeze and smiled at him. At the head of the aisle, I could see Michael standing beside his brother. The church seemed very full. The organist struck up 'Here Comes the

Bride', everyone stood as was customary, and in slow-march time, with Pam and Pat following, we proceeded up the aisle. I felt very beautiful and very proud, like a Queen-for-a-Day; it was a beautiful moment, and I was beside Michael in no time. Michael was tense and nervous but seemed somewhat pleased to see me. He handed over his gloves to his Best Man, and I handed Pam my flowers, and so we were married. Everything was very near perfect and absolutely wonderful.

I listened very carefully to the lovely ceremony being read, and we made the required responses as clearly as we could. I remember feeling breathless, but I managed to remember to lift my gown slightly before we knelt for the Blessing so that air made the dress billow very nicely around me. In a very short space of time, with the kiss, it was over, and we retired to the Vestry to sign the register and receive the warm congratulations of our immediate family. My Dad looked a bit better by this time and was able to smile again. I never realised at the time how emotional he was about the business of 'giving away' his youngest daughter. I had thought he would be quite glad to have all the *to-do*, which had been going on for several months, over at last. As we exited the church, the next wedding was entering behind us as we paused to have some pictures taken by the photographer. We received the good-luck tokens that accompany English weddings, silver horseshoes, small posies, and, from Mrs Arundel, a prettily dressed, small bride doll, while the rest of the wedding guests looked on, calling their good wishes. Then it was into our beautiful wedding cars, decorated with white ribbons and a few private moments, and we both breathed a huge sigh of relief.

When we arrived at the reception hall (the Boy Scouts Hall), I had a sinking-feeling kind of moment. The caterers were there, but the room which my father had worked so hard to clean and decorate was not in very good condition. However, I decided I would simply ignore the shabbiness, and everyone must have resolved to do the same; Dad's white and silver wedding decorations disguising the rafters were much admired. It was a lovely reception. Everyone seemed very happy, the food was quickly served and eaten, the speeches were short and lovingly delivered, and everyone drank our health. There was just one near-catastrophe. Before we got to the cutting of the cake, a sharp-eyed person on the catering team noticed the famous Mrs Wells' wedding cake was developing a bit of a list. It seemed the 'very best royal icing' was not quite firm enough to support the two top tiers, so we had to quickly move to the cutting ceremony, and the cake was whisked away to be cut up for the guests. But I had never really liked rich fruitcake myself, and it had looked very nice when we all first sat down at the beginning of the reception when the pictures were taken, so that little *hiccup* was hardly noticed.

After the meal, the tables were cleared away, my mother's brother manned the bar, and we all enjoyed a party, but the time soon came for me to change. Pam and I returned to the house for this, and my new blue dress and jacket outfit was laid out and ready, so it didn't take long. Michael was quite anxious for us to be off and quickly had our suitcases into the car, but before we left the party, I gave my white rose bouquet to my grandmother and kissed her. I don't think I ever was her favourite granddaughter, but I hoped my dear Mum would appreciate the little gesture. The gentleman who used to drive me to Michael's house at Christmas time, Mr Fine, was our chauffeur for the evening. He drove us to The Ladbroke Hotel in Oxford Street, London, and still wearing some of the confetti from the happy 'send-off', we checked in for the first time as Mr and Mrs Michael Harbott, a married couple.

Michael

Maureen and I did not see each other until the following week when we met again at the Wednesday evening cycling club meeting. Once again, it was a miserable damp, foggy evening, and after the meeting, we went to a local milk bar/cafe (we called it *The Caff*), where we could enjoy coffee, a milkshake or an ice cream bar. I again escorted her home and, having discovered she loved going to the cinema, suggested we should see one the following Saturday evening. We arranged to meet at the Odeon in Whalebone Lane, which was fairly close to her home.

Arriving at the agreed time, I became somewhat anxious because she was not in sight and I thought she might have changed her mind, but she soon came along looking very attractive. This was the first time I had seen her wearing anything other than cycling clothes - she gave me a wonderful smile, and we held hands in the 'one and nines'. One shilling and ninepence was the cost of the second-best cinema seats. This was the first of many such enjoyable outings. Later, she was often late for our dates, and I soon came to understand that she always wanted to look her best when leaving her home and this was probably difficult in her house where there was only one bathroom. Maureen loved romantic or musical films, so the choice was generally hers.

I had not had much exposure to music, as my mother seemed to feel that the popular music of the day, which she called *'that boogie-woogie'*, was sinful and corrupting. The music she permitted was rather dreary, light classical stuff. I enjoyed the current 'pop' music that I heard at local dances but never at home. However, I soon discovered that if I stayed up late after my parents had gone to bed, I could tune in to Radio Luxembourg, broadcasting from Europe, on our rather old radio, and listen to all the latest recordings. It was refreshing to go to the cinema with Maureen and to be exposed to some of the great music that she loved. We saw many good musicals together: 'Oklahoma', the Doris Day romantic films, and 'Annie Get Your Gun'. I remember that we once waited patiently in a long line-up outside the cinema, and then stood at the back of the auditorium for the whole performance of 'The Glenn Miller Story' with James Stewart and June Allyson.

We were now into the winter of 1953, and things began to go much better at work when I was transferred from the main Plessey plant at Ilford to a smaller department a few miles away at Seven Kings, which specialised in the manufacture of gauges and other measuring equipment. I liked the people I worked with, many of the machine operators were women, and I felt I was learning a lot and also making a contribution to the operation of the department.

That year had been a good one for the British. Mount Everest had been climbed for the first time by Edmund Hillary and Sherpa Tenzing, and the coronation of Queen Elizabeth II had taken place in the summer. The previous year Britain had developed the first commercial jetliner, the 'Comet', and it was now in regular service. The countries within the British Commonwealth were becoming more industrialised and were advertising for skilled people. Many responded and left for Canada, Australia, New Zealand, and Africa. Although I still had years of apprenticeship ahead of me, I began to feel that one day I would like to do the same. I was also doing well in my engineering studies. I was working towards the Ordinary National Certificate in Mechanical Engineering, for which the Company allowed me one day each week to attend South East Essex County Technical College, which happened to be the same school Maureen had attended.

My first meeting with Maureen's family occurred one cold, wet Sunday, early in December. Our cycling group had been out for a short ride into the Essex countryside, where we had played soccer in a muddy field. The girls sat on a five-barred gate and watched this activity. As it was a damp and cheerless day, we all became rather cold and tired. Passing close to Maureen's house on the way home, she invited us there. Perhaps she hadn't noticed how muddy all the young men were, but her mother was amazing. The whole bedraggled group was invited in, and she quickly arranged for us all to get cleaned up, warmed up, and fed!

Maureen and I seemed to be *going steady*, and I was invited to her house one Sunday afternoon for tea. Coming from a small, quiet family and being rather shy, I quickly found this family to be loud and opinionated. Her mother seemed suspicious of me as I did not talk much about myself or my own family. I did have a talk with her father when the others left the room. He seemed to warm to me when he learned that I was serving an apprenticeship in a similar trade to his own. Their house seemed small for their family of two daughters and three sons, although Maureen's older sister had recently been married. I think their father had learned to light up his cigarette and simply tune out the commotion going on around him. Over the Christmas holidays, we went out together to several dances, and Maureen was invited to my house for our traditional Boxing Day family party. It was an opportunity for her to meet my parents.

Maureen's mother, who was always very proud of her bright, nice-looking younger daughter, had submitted her picture to the local newspaper, the 'Dagenham Post' for the Press Ball beauty pageant. This annual event was organised by all the local papers published on the east side of London. From the photo and an interview, she was selected to represent Dagenham. The ball was held at the Poplar Civic Theatre Ballroom early in the New Year, and I had very mixed feelings about this event, even though I was invited to be her escort. Her father, mother, and sister Pam with husband Ron, Maureen, and I arrived in a chauffeur-driven hired car, which was quite an event in itself. The occasion was much bigger than I had anticipated. There seemed to be thousands present, and there was a sizeable popular dance band. I felt very insecure seeing my girlfriend interviewed on stage, and her name then announced as the winner! 'Perhaps she would lose interest in me now', I thought. Of course, her family was delighted and watched with pride when she was photographed, crowned, and kissed by Jack Warner, who was at that time a much-admired British film star. She had a short dance with Jack Warner and a few other people, then it was my turn at last, and I did try to share her excitement and pleasure. Of course, I was pleased for her, but I was really concerned this might change things between us. I need not have worried. On our theatre date the following week, her manner was as natural as usual. Clearly, for her, nothing had changed.

Late in that winter, my grandmother, with whom we were living, became very ill and rarely left her bedroom at the back of the house. Her condition deteriorated steadily, and we expected her to be admitted into the hospital, as my mother was becoming exhausted caring for her, which she had done for many years. Mother was eventually told she was dying, and grandmother would remain at home. A few weeks later, following a day and night of disturbingly loud rasping sounds, she was silent one morning, and my mother calmly informed my brother and I that she had died. We went off to work as usual, and she said she would telephone the doctor from a nearby call box. By the time we returned from work that day, the body had been removed, the evening meal was ready as usual, and my mother seemed relieved. Within a few days, all my grandmother's possessions had also disappeared from the house; my mother had called in a scrap dealer. Two antique clocks that I had had my eye on were gone! The funeral followed shortly after. I didn't understand until many years later, what a hard, early life my grandmother had experienced.

'Courtship' necessarily became a rather long-drawn-out affair when we were young. Although we were together frequently, we were seldom alone. Neither of our homes had a telephone, and phone calls at work were frowned upon. After a date or a weekend trip, we would spend a short time in Maureen's parents' house, standing in the hallway by the front entrance door, 'saying goodnight'. This was the only opportunity to be really close and share a few passionate moments.

As well as the theatre dates, our outings, when we had reasonably good weather, would frequently involve a cycle ride at the weekend, with the other members of the club. Generally, we would go 30 to 40 miles into the countryside surrounding London and sometimes would include an overnight stay at a Youth Hostel in Essex or Kent. Often the hostels were old manor houses, large farmhouses or rectories, frequently of historical value, situated close to small villages in the country. The dormitory-style accommodation was usually spartan, to say the least, but adequate, and everyone had to help with the various chores. The sleeping arrangements were segregated of course, but we would usually go to the village pub and have a cider or two (even though some of us were technically underage for drinking), and the walks back to the hostel resulted in a few couples loitering behind in the usual way of young people. The Youth Hostel Association had strict curfew rules, so time was limited. It was all fairly innocent but exciting, just the same.

Maureen's parents' home had the first television that I ever saw in a home. They were very proud of this purchase - the screen was about 12 or 13 inches across, and one of the first programmes I saw was a variety show introducing a new type of music with a thumping and energetic beat. Pam and Ron were also there, and Ron said he thought this new music would become very popular. I disagreed and said, I thought it would be just a passing fad. The band was Bill Haley & His Comets, and the music was called 'Rock and Roll'. This new television interfered with our developing romance. When there was a fire in the sitting room in the front of the house, usually at the weekends, we had got into the habit of taking over the best place when everyone went to bed to say our 'goodnights' privately. It was more comfortable than standing in the front hallway. With the advent of the new television, no-one wanted to go to bed, so we were once again forced into the cold hallway where it was too cold to linger very long.

But we were enjoying this time, and spring was approaching, which signalled to most people that it was time to think about a summer holiday. I heard quite a lot from Maureen of her plans for a two-week cycling trip with her girlfriend, Barbara. They were quite ambitious and planned a cycling trip through Somerset and Devon in the West Country, which left me at a bit of a loose end. So we went our separate ways; I, choosing to try a newish idea and go for one week to a Butlin's Holiday Camp, situated not far away on the east coast of Essex at Clacton. I didn't particularly enjoy my first and only experience at a holiday camp, as I really missed my girl. So, subsequently, I spent quite a bit of my time alone watching the band during the evenings, and I did not seem to connect with any other people there. Maureen came home with all kinds of stories about their adventures and the other young people they had met, so we were soon all back together again, and we resumed our usual activities. At Plessey, I was moved back to the main plant at Ilford and spent the next year receiving training in the various sections of the machine shop, and once again, I wasn't pleased with the work. Many of the journeymen I was assigned to were not very good instructors and didn't seem to be very happy in their work, having been in the same trade for many years. They seemed to me to lead very narrowly, unfulfilled lives. I began to wonder if I had taken up the right profession.

At this time, National Service in one of the armed forces was still mandatory for all healthy young men in Britain, and due to my apprenticeship I, and others in a like situation, were allowed a deferment until age 21. I was beginning to feel that from a working point of view, there had to be more to life than what the future held for me. My studies at the Technical College had gone well, and I had obtained my Ordinary National Certificate in Mechanical Engineering. I decided at this time to continue studying toward the more advanced Higher National Certificate rather than the City and

Guilds Examinations which most apprentices were taking, as I felt this qualification might help me eventually gain a better career, maybe tool design or drafting. It also meant further deferment from National Service.

Maureen and I continued to see each other regularly. She was much admired, and there was one fellow at the cycling club who had taken a fancy to her. He was a little older, had completed his National Service, and had seen a little more of the world than many. But she didn't seem to pay him very much attention, and to my relief, he left the country and went to Australia. I still cycled a lot and was still involved in racing, competing in time trials, mass start races, and hill climbs. It was a challenging sport and kept me lean and hungry. Most of the races started early on a Sunday morning, and Maureen would sometimes be at the finish to welcome me in. Often we would cycle through the lovely English countryside and, when we needed a rest, we would hop over the gate of some farmer's field, unroll our waterproof cycling capes so that we could sit on the grass and after eating a packed lunch, enjoy a little passionate time together. It was a wonderful time to be young.

My brother Denis had now finished his apprenticeship and was due to do his National Service. He had much enjoyed his experience with the Sea Scouts, eventually moving into a position of leadership; also, he was quite anxious to join the Royal Navy. Our mother's father and brother had been men of the sea. After having his medical examination, he was extremely disappointed to learn that he had been rejected from any of the forces due to having varicose veins in his legs. Arrangements were made for him to have the necessary operation (cut and tied off), and within a few months, he reapplied to the Royal Navy but was again rejected.

Denis did not take rejection well, and he was depressed for quite a while, but then he decided to apply and was accepted for immigration to Canada. We had some distant relations on my mother's side in the eastern part of the country, with whom he visited before finding work as a toolmaker in Montreal for the winter. The following spring, he left Montreal and accepted work much more to his liking, at a resort in the Laurentian Mountains where he was responsible for the boating programme. He taught the guests how to sail and canoe.

Back home, Maureen and I started planning a cycling holiday together even though our parents were not at all keen on the idea. Our plan was to go by train to Carlisle in northern England and cycle south through the Lake District, then see a bit of North Wales and Shropshire, where I had been during the war. We would then get the train home from Shrewsbury. We intended to stay at Youth Hostels and where one was not available at a couple of *bed and breakfast* establishments. That spring, Maureen began writing letters to book our accommodations, and by July, I had serviced our bikes, and we were ready to go on our first big adventure together. Somehow, my memories of this holiday are rather vague. Maybe our relationship was not going well at that time, or perhaps I was feeling weighed down by my lacklustre working life and the responsibility the trip entailed. However, we completed the trip as planned, but I did wonder if we would remain friends.

But we did! We settled back into our regular life and saw each other two or three times a week. My work was now centred around the main tool room at The Plessey Company, and I continued to study some evenings and repair a few watches and clocks in my spare time. Generally, on Saturday evenings we would have a 'date' and go to the cinema. Our primary means of getting about, apart from our bikes, was the London Transportation bus system, which was extensive, quite reliable, and cheap. As we lived about eight miles apart, I would generally meet her about halfway at a cinema. She was sometimes a little late, but always arrived immaculately groomed and pleased to see me, so the wait was worth it. At the weekends our 'goodnights' began to take much longer - the relationship deepened. My mother became concerned, thinking I was much too young for such a serious relationship, telling me it could interfere with my studies and affect my future.

I began to hope my future would include Maureen, so I raised the subject with her in a rather vague way. On Saturday, after one of our nice outings, when we had got to the 'goodnight' stage, I said I loved her, and we talked of marriage. I believe her response was, 'That would be nice.'

It was still traditional then for a young man to ask

permission of a girl's father when they wanted to marry, so when a suitable opportunity came along, and I was momentarily alone with her Dad, I asked him how he felt about my marrying his daughter. To my surprise, he didn't ask me any questions at all, and he just said he was delighted and had been expecting it. Maureen and her mother reappeared, and her mother was equally pleased, even shedding a tear. I told my parents later in the week that we were going to be engaged. My mother did not seem happy, still believing I was too young to tie myself down. My father, on the other hand, was delighted; he had always liked Maureen. We began looking for an engagement ring together and found one we both liked in H Samuels in East Ham High Street. It cost £25, which seemed like quite a lot of money. We became engaged at Easter in 1956 and planned to marry when my studies were finished.

Meanwhile, my brother had left Canada and gone to work in the United States at Niagara Falls in New York State. Denis had only been there a few months when he was drafted into the United States Navy and was sent to the huge naval base at San Diego in California, for basic training. At last, for him, a dream came true; he became a sailor.

Maureen celebrated her 21st birthday on 5th June 1956, and her parents invited my family to a tea party. Everyone seemed to enjoy the occasion. Her father took some snapshots with a Brownie Box Camera.

In the spring, we had started talking about our annual two-week holiday when we were both at my house. Since we never wanted separate holidays again, we decided we should try another cycling trip together; this time to Dorset, Somerset, and Devon, with the first and last parts covered by train travel from London. Maureen began the process of arranging by mail, the overnight accommodation needed for our trip using mainly Youth Hostels where they were available, and a few bed and breakfast addresses. Our holiday began with the train ride to Dorchester, where we unloaded our bicycles and started cycling. Only a few days into the trip, I nearly lost Maureen for good. We cycled along a narrow path beside the River Exe on the way to Exeter, the county town of Devon. We found a comfortable spot to eat lunch and enjoyed a few passionate moments. Afterwards, continuing along the path, Maureen's front wheel skidded on a wet patch, and she very nearly overbalanced and could have fallen into the fast-flowing river. With my lack of life-saving skills, I am sure I could not have saved her, and explaining to her parents what had happened would have been difficult.

Continuing to Plymouth, where we visited Maureen's Aunt Louise, her mother's sister, we stayed for one night then headed north across Exmoor to Ilfracombe on the North Devon coast where we planned to stay for several days. Shortly after we arrived at the B&B that we had booked, we both became violently ill with food poisoning. We even took ourselves to the local hospital as we felt so sick. We had eaten a rich roast pork lunch at mid-day in Barnstaple. But in a couple of days, we were recovered well enough to take a steamer trip to the remote island of Lundy, which is situated in the Bristol Channel. After toiling up quite a steep hill from the dock to the village pub, we then drank the cold and delicious local cider. It was a hot sunny day, and there was very little to eat. So, we hopped over a gate and fell fast asleep in a cornfield. Still feeling relatively weak from the food poisoning, we just wanted to lie down in the sunshine until it was time for the steamer to leave. Awakened by the sound of the ship's horn, we had to run headlong downhill and just managed to get to the gangway in time. Our accommodation in Ilfracombe was in a narrow older house, two rooms of course, on separate floors. The landlady was a bit of a dragon, but that didn't stop us from getting together in Maureen's room a couple of times. Following our few rest days, during which we explored this pretty town, we negotiated the steep hills of North Devon to Taunton in Somerset, where we loaded our cycles once again into the guard's van at the rear of the train and enjoyed the final train ride of our holiday back to London.

Maureen and I were now definitely a couple and generally saw each other twice during the week and, also, at weekends although communicating with each other was difficult with no phones available in either of our homes. We talked about getting married in the spring of 1958, which appalled my mother, who thought we were much too young still, and we should see more of the world before settling into the responsibilities of married life.

She didn't know about the ideas I had for our future!

I was nearing my 21st birthday, and my apprenticeship was coming to an end. I was transferred to the main tool room at Plessey and assigned to work with a good journeyman toolmaker, Vic Monteith. His son Victor also worked there too, and I learned he also was a keen cyclist. We became friends, and the following year he suggested a cycling holiday with his girlfriend, Chris. We would be a foursome and together decided on a tour of Scotland for the next summer. Once again, Maureen, who liked this idea, began the process of making the arrangements for our accommodation. This time since it was two girls and two guys, we would go the B&B route.

At home, things had not been going too well. My father had not been well for some time and was now off work, having had a nervous breakdown. To supplement the family income, my mother had been working at her sister Grace's shop in Ilford. She travelled to her work daily by bicycle. Denis was still away in the U.S. Navy.

In October 1956, I was 21, had finished my apprenticeship, and was presented with my journeyman papers. I was asked by the company if I wanted to remain in the Tool Room as a Journeyman Toolmaker, or as I was studying for my Higher National Certificate in Mechanical Engineering, I could transfer into an aircraft Tool Design Office as a Junior Tool and Die Designer. I chose the latter, even though the pay was less. The Department dealt with tooling for the manufacturing of aircraft components, and I felt this would be more interesting and might lead to other opportunities. I had only had limited drafting experience at Technical College, and being the junior person in the office and from the 'Tool Room' did not get much help from the others who had always worked in an office and felt they were a little superior. I did make friends with one of the drawing checkers, and he certainly helped change the course of my life. Frank was a friendly New Zealander who was very homesick for his native land. He had come to England 10 years earlier as a young man and married an English girl, who promised him she would go back to his homeland with him, but after having a child decided she did not want to leave her mother. Frank always talked about New Zealand and felt there were ample opportunities for young people, particularly those with a trade. He showed me pictures of his house and family, and I became interested. But I realised that at this time, with wedding plans well underway and my studies to complete, I would have to put any ideas about leaving on hold.

Our cycling vacation to Scotland in July, with friends Vic Monteath and Chris started with an overnight train trip from London to Edinburgh, which seemed a long way away, and so was quite exciting. We did a little sightseeing in grey and drizzling weather and found our lodging for our overnight stay. The next day in the pouring rain, we crossed the Firth of Forth by ferry and headed north. It never stopped raining to Inverness, which took several days. We battled wind and rain across the mountainous highlands to the Isle of Skye, where for the first time, the sun came out. We stayed for two nights in a little village called Broadford. Our last night here in the Scottish Highlands was indeed one to remember. All the shops stayed closed on Sunday, so we had no food all day, and we all went to bed quite hungry. But it turned into a memorable night, nevertheless.

The next morning, rather wearily, we left the island, and after crossing to the mainland by ferry, we proceeded along the infamous but beautiful 'Road to the Isles'. It was a good but chilly day, and about 15 miles along this rather exposed road a moment's inattention on my part changed the course of our holiday rather abruptly. Maureen noticed a mountain up ahead - we were travelling south. She asked if it could be Ben Nevis, which is the highest mountain in the British Isles. Studying a map whilst riding along was not an unusual endeavour on my part, and this I proceeded to do. Unfortunately for me, the gravel edge of the narrow road suddenly dropped away; there was a small culvert carrying a sparkling little stream under the road surface. Into this space, my front wheel fell, catapulting me about 10 feet into the air, and I landed off the road in the stream with the bike.

Maureen and the others quickly halted and turned around to find me wet and bruised, with a small scrape on my shin but otherwise uninjured. But my bike! It was in very poor shape. The thin-walled alloy frame was severely cracked, and as I retrieved it from the stream, it broke into two pieces. We now were in quite a predicament as we were in a somewhat isolated area and about 15 miles from our night's lodging in the town of Fort William. By chance, we also happened to be close to a rail line, and there was a tiny train station called Glenfinnan. Time was moving along, and it was now about 4.00 pm. We were informed by a solitary man at the station that the next train would be on the following day, but we could leave the bike with him, and he would have it shipped to Fort William. Since there was no other option, this we did, and I advised the others to ride on, and I would meet them at the appointed B&B. I planned to hitchhike utilising the first available vehicle. I felt quite shaken up, and my left leg was very painful, but as they rode away, I began walking along that 'Road to the Isles', famous in legend and song, expecting a vehicle to come along at any time. I walked (or slightly limped) through spectacular scenery, past the memorial to Bonnie Prince Charlie at the end of Loch Shiel and walked on and on, but no vehicles passed me in either direction. Finally, after what seemed like an eternity, a small van came along, and the driver picked me up and gave me a ride to Fort William. After hearing my story, he took me right to our lodging, where Maureen was getting very anxious about my whereabouts.

The next day we had to reassess our situation. After retrieving my bicycle, which had already arrived at the station, we went to a local bicycle shop and discovered they could not help with any replacement parts. The store owner suggested that a blacksmith in a small village on the train route to our next destination might be able to help, as he had welding equipment. So, altogether, we took the train to Arrochar and located the blacksmith shop. He set one of his apprentices on the job to weld the frame back together, and I watched in despair as the flame welder ate through the light-alloy tubing. But after about an hour, he had the bike back together with two plates surrounded by perforations forming the join. He charged little for this service, and understandably could not guarantee the work. We mounted our bikes and moved off. The bike creaked, the front and back wheels were out of alignment and I had severe doubts whether it would hold together, even to our next destination. We were headed for the city of Stirling, where we had planned a two-night stay, which gave me time for my aching thigh muscles to recover a little. By some miracle, that bike did hold together, and we made it right back to Edinburgh. With relief, we loaded everything onto the train to London, and I rode it home over the cobblestones of East London. Once home, the bike sadly had to be scrapped.

Back at work, I needed to pay attention to my engineering studies because if I was to become a Tool Design Engineer, I would need the Higher National Certificate. Without that, I would just remain a draftsman, a job I intensely disliked. Another consideration was that by October 1958, when I had my next birthday, I would be unable to defer my entry into the British Armed Forces any longer. Some of the people I worked with had finished their two years in the Forces and returned to civilian life dissatisfied, feeling it had been a complete waste of time. As this compulsory conscription was shortly coming to an end, I was reluctant to do the same.

Maureen generally came over to my house on Sunday, afternoons by bus and would sit and talk to my mother after tea whilst I worked on my engineering studies. I think she liked the peace and quiet of my place after her own chaotic one. About 9.00 pm, we would take the bus to her house and after spending a little time with her family, would wait until they all went to bed, when we could have some private time to ourselves on the front room couch. By this time, our relationship had developed into quite a passionate affair. I would often stay late, sometimes missing the last regular scheduled bus at around midnight. Maureen lived in a small terraced house with her three younger brothers, her older sister having recently married and moved away. The rooms were small; Maureen's bedroom being slightly less than six feet square! There was one bathroom for six people. Maureen was very particular about her appearance, so this led to some conflict with family members, and she looked forward to the time when she could leave the family home. As we moved from autumn into winter, Maureen and her mother were very involved with plans for the wedding.

I was to look after the honeymoon arrangements. Maureen had mentioned that a friend at work had been to the Italian Riviera and I liked the idea of a trip outside Britain for the first time. As most of our contemporaries were going to local English seaside resorts for their vacations, this seemed rather exotic. So off I went to Thomas Cook, the well-known travel agent, in East Ham High Street and came away with brochures and prices of holidays in Italy. Maureen and I browsed through all the information and decided on an all-in package to Alassio. It seemed quite expensive, but we thought we could manage it. By Christmas, the church, reception, and honeymoon were booked.

During the dreary winter months, I was still no happier in my job, and I had to take my studies seriously if I was to stand any chance of passing the examination in March. My desire to make a life in another country was still strong, and together with Maureen, we visited both New Zealand and Australia House in London. New Zealand told us that due to severe housing shortages, they would only accept unmarried people, and we could go and marry there later. This, of course, was not acceptable to Maureen. Australia was taking immigrants but warned that there too, the housing shortage was acute, and many were living in barrack-like complexes. We heard about some *would-be* immigrants who returned to the U.K. at their own expense, and their low opinions of Australian living conditions were reported in the London newspapers and, also in Australia. So, with the wedding and honeymoon arrangements to be made, and the attention that had to be paid to my studies, any thoughts of emigrating were put aside at this time.

Christmas came and went with the usual parties and celebrations with our respective families and work colleagues. In February of the New Year, we arranged to rent a furnished upper storey of a terraced house in Ilford, which was approximately mid-way between our two families' homes. We would be moving in on our return from our Italian honeymoon in April. I prepared for my examinations for the Higher National Certificate in Mechanical Engineering. With so much on my mind and the late nights I was keeping, I felt under some pressure and wondered if I would indeed pass. After taking the examinations, I worried I had not done well, and when the results were published, this proved to be the case. I had passed in all subjects except Applied Mathematics. So, this was a big disappointment, and I did not know how this would affect my career plans. I could, of course, repeat but, at this time, did not have any enthusiasm for another year studying.

We were to be married at the end of March, and Maureen suggested that I should look into birth control devices, which somewhat surprised me, as she did not seem to have worried about it up until now. I was concerned about her getting pregnant and agreed to look into it, as I knew that a baby would sabotage my ideas for emigrating. She said that she would look into some female diaphragm devices later, but in the meantime, I should get some contraceptives. So, one Saturday morning off, I went to the chemist in Ilford High Street to look into birth control supplies, not knowing what to expect. 'What should I ask for?' They were called by so many names, Durex, condom, contraceptive, sheath, rubbers, or *French letter*! You couldn't simply pick them up off the shelf then but had to ask the assistant for help in selecting the right kind as they were all under the counter. 'Would they ask about size, large, small, or somewhere in between?' I guessed I was the latter. 'And what about options like lubrication and other features to enhance the female sexual experience?' 'Did I need these?' And what if it was a girl behind the counter; my face would be so red it would light up the whole store. Fortunately, it was a man waiting to serve me. He brought out the various kinds of items available and explained to me in great detail the benefits of each different type. I bought what he suggested, but I just wanted to get out of there as quickly as possible.

I also needed to open a bank account, which at that time required a member of that bank to sponsor you. My cousin Pat's father, who had a business, offered to do this for me at Barclays Bank. Maureen had been very busy since Christmas, sewing the bridesmaids' dresses. The bridesmaids were to be her sister Pam, and my cousin Pat. Maureen came with me, and from a well-respected tailor in East Ham High Street, we ordered my suit to be made. We also went one Saturday morning to buy the wedding ring, a plain band of 22-carat gold.

My Best Man was to be my brother Denis, who was somewhere in the Mediterranean with the U.S. Navy Sixth Fleet, but he had assured me he could make it home for the wedding. As the big day approached, I was somewhat apprehensive; I did not like to be the centre of attention and still easily felt embarrassed. To add to the tension, we had not heard from my brother, and on Friday evening before the big day, he had still not arrived by the time we went to bed, and my mother was practically having hysterics. But to our relief at around 2.00 am, there was a loud knocking on the front door, and there was Denis, all smiles with my mother scolding him for creating a disturbance and cutting it so fine. He had apparently used U.S. military aircraft and had experienced many delays travelling from Marseilles, France, where his ship had docked.

The wedding was to be held at St Mary's Church at Becontree Heath, and my parents, Denis, and I had a taxi there in time for the noon service. Standing at the altar steps with my brother, I did not look round until Maureen appeared at my side, giving me a lovely smile. In her ivory satin gown, she looked absolutely stunning. The young Minister conducted the Church of England service, and we made our vows then signed the register. Maureen received her Marriage Certificate and her brand-new passport in her new name, and we were husband and wife. Photos were taken outside the church, and we were showered with confetti. I was somewhat tense having all those pictures taken and was very glad when we left for the reception in our decorated wedding car for the short drive to a small hall a few miles away on Whalebone Lane. Maureen and her mother had done a fantastic job of organising the reception, and the room was beautifully decorated. More pictures and some home movies were taken on the grounds of the hall, and after the chicken dinner, the toasts, the speeches, and some dancing we went to Maureen's old home, which was close by, to change for going away. After another short time at the reception saying our 'goodbyes', a taxi arrived to take us to London for our first night together as a married couple. On the ride into the city of London, I realised just how exhausted Maureen was after all the work arranging the wedding and then the excitement of the day. Arriving at the Ladbroke Hotel, it was obvious to the staff that we were newlyweds as we were shedding confetti in the lobby, but they gave us a friendly greeting and showed us to a nice, quiet room. This night was to be our first time ever staying at a hotel. We adjourned to bed right away.

Maureen and Michael's first pictures together, 1953

This photo was submitted by Maureen's mother, from which she was selected as 'Miss Dagenham'

A kiss from film star Jack Warner for 18-year-old Maureen Sterling of 73 Stanley Avenue, Inverham, after being chosen as East London Press Ball Queen in February.

Maureen is crowned as East London Press Ball Queen by movie star, Jack 'Dixon of Dock Green' Warner, February 1954

Good times Youth Hostelling in the English countryside.

**Michael and Maureen's
Wedding Day
29th March 1958**

4.
Married Life

Maureen

As most newly married young people do, we felt rather silly checking into our hotel. Coloured confetti, which our guests had showered on us as we departed, still clung to our clothes and hair, but the hotel staff just smiled – they had seen this before. It was about 10.30 pm by the time we arrived at the Ladbroke, so we were soon shown to our room and lost no time in getting our 'going away' clothes off and falling into each other's arms in bed. I think Michael had high hopes about the romance of this night, but I don't think it was precisely memorable. I was so tired and fell asleep in an instant and slept as if I had been drugged. We were awakened by the maid bringing in early-morning tea. We had to get going very early for we were travelling to the Italian Riviera. This was to be quite an exercise, and I was feeling rather strange and unreal as I watched Michael take charge. After a light breakfast and checking out, a taxi appeared to take us to Victoria station, where we boarded the Boat Train to Paris. It had seemed so glamorous when we were making plans, but we quickly discovered that foreign travel could be quite disturbing. Our final destination was Nice, France, so we had to make sure we got into the right train carriage. We had to share a compartment in a Wagon Lit carriage, and two or three similar carriages were shunted onto the ferry at Dover for the English Channel crossing to Calais. Here our carriage was attached to a French train to take us on to Paris, the Gare du Nord.

In Paris, we had a two-hour wait. Our carriage was to be shunted around Paris to the Gare de Lyon for the overnight journey to Nice. Michael wanted to stretch his legs and suggested we leave the compartment and take a look around. I was feeling tired and anxious and didn't want to leave the safety of the compartment or our luggage unattended, and I also worried the train might start to move without warning. Nevertheless, off, Michael went to take a look around. I was very relieved when he reappeared after about half an hour, and after being shunted around Paris, we were joined by two other couples for the overnight journey to Nice, a young couple and an older experienced looking pair. It is the nature of English people to avoid striking up conversations with strangers on trains, so just smiles were exchanged. This seemed like a very unreal situation to me. When we got underway, a porter came into the compartment and unlocked and let down the six bunks. I regarded this as a signal to prepare for the night and went along to the cramped toilet compartment to remove my make-up, brush my hair, and change out of my travelling clothes. I put on a short but respectable *nightie* and a dress-length cotton cover-up. When I returned, the other couples had been chatting a bit, and the older lady said to me she had never travelled in France before with two honeymoon couples. We laughed a little together, and I climbed up into my bunk, and eventually, everyone else in the compartment followed suit. I was so tired; I wanted desperately to be alone in my own little bed in Stanley Avenue. I had no idea how Michael was feeling; there had been no opportunity for private conversation for hours. To me, this whole journey had the strangest feeling. I felt as if I was behind thick glass, not quite able to be involved in the scene I was witnessing.

The morning came after a restless night; the sound of the train on the tracks prevented genuinely restful sleep. I was unaccustomed to not sleeping well and felt very little better in the morning. However, of course, we tried to behave normally. We noticed right away the air was warmer, the sun was coming up, and the countryside looked fresh. I longed for some privacy, but a murmured greeting was all we could exchange as we made ourselves ready for the day as quickly and with as little fuss as we could manage. Leaving the station at Nice, still wearing the 'going away' outfit, which was beginning to look a little creased, and my new high-heeled shoes, we made our way to the bus station. The next part of the journey would be by road along the magical world-famous Grande Corniche, passing through Ventimiglia and San Remo to Alassio. We had some time to kill, however, and Michael, always ready to expend some energy, suggested we walk to the Promenade des Anglais which ran along the seashore beside the Mediterranean and was not far away, where we could probably have some lunch. I thought lunch would be an excellent idea, and perhaps the sea breeze might help to revive me. So, stowing our suitcases in a locker, we set off. It turned out to be about a mile or so, but even though I was wearing high heels, it was certainly worth it because I have always loved a glimpse of the sea, and as expected, the 'Promenade' was spectacular. Lined up along the seaside were benches with porticos providing shade. Seated facing the water were many elderly looking matrons, no doubt from the apartments on the opposite side of the road. They all seemed to be wearing black dresses, and their hands, which rested on their plump stomachs, glittered with the (to me) most fantastic display of their diamond rings! I had never seen anything like this in quiet, respectable, English south coast resorts! As we walked along hand-in-hand, I felt we re-connected with each other; we experienced that ease between us that somehow had got lost on the train, so we were in accord when Michael suggested we examine the menu-boards of the restaurants across the street. We enjoyed our first French meal. I think it was a small steak with salad. It was entirely novel to us, having hot and cold food on the same plate. The blond, excitable (in a so-French way) waitress called me 'Mademoiselle' and then quickly corrected herself. I rather liked being addressed as 'Madame'.

We might also have had a glass of wine because when we got on the bus for the next leg of our journey, I had a hard time staying awake, and I remember Michael saying to me, 'You could try to take an interest, Maureen.' He was getting a little impatient with this 'new wife' creature he had married. But I was exhausted by this time; my feet were killing me, and I could hardly keep my eyes open to take in that marvellous scenery. Except for the way the driver swung around the hairpin bends, I don't think I even remember that part of the journey. Arriving at our seafront hotel eventually, we found it everything we hoped for. We had a room on the third floor (called a 'piano' in the creaky, slow elevator), and we could see the sea from our balconied window on the east side. 'Le Beau Sejour' was everything we thought a honeymoon hotel should be. We had a wonderful large room with a beautifully comfortable double bed. The bathroom was just a little way down the hall, and this was not a problem because the hotel was not full, and we were not at that point used to en-suite accommodation anyway. We had a nice table in the dining room where we ate every meal – this was a full-board hotel, and there was a delightful Maitre d' hotel to take care of us. So, after a couple of days, we began to take notice of our surroundings. The weather was hazy and sunny but only mildly warm. We explored the seaside village, always coming back for lunch when we would be greeted by the Maitre d' hotel and served by one of his waiters. Maitre introduced us to Orvieto wine, so after a glass or two of that, we needed a nap or some afternoon delight in our quiet room. Around 4.00 pm, we surfaced and took another walk. We sometimes explored Main Street. We bought some Italian sandals and a rather elegant basket holdall with a leather lid, and Michael gave me a present of a beautiful umbrella which caught my eye. It was pale pink with small fuchsia pink flowers over the whole – it had a curved Malacca handle. I had that precious umbrella for about ten years. Italian goods seemed very interesting and rather exotic to my English eyes, being used to plainer styles.

I came down with a feverish cold and stayed in bed for a day but was soon feeling better, and we met some other couples who were guests there. One pair was 'just-married' like us. The husband confessed his wife was nervous about '*keeping house*' and especially the cooking. I was quite impressed with this pair because the young woman showed me a picture of her wedding gown, which had come from The House of Worth. It must have been quite a 'Society' wedding! The other couple was from Belgium, and the English wife was happy to have friendly people to speak English with. Our second week went better. We were quickly getting accustomed to the married state and so became a little more adventurous with our explorations. The weather was getting warmer, and we could sit at the water's edge on the sand. One day we took a picnic and hiked up into the villages above Alassio. I look back on that time with fond pleasure. But our two weeks soon came to an end, and I remember nothing of the return journey, so it must have been merely uneventful.

I do remember feeling quite proud to be a married woman, and I think we both were delighted with our fabulous honeymoon and the married state. I honestly thought we were ready to deal with the next phase of our lives. We returned directly to our new home on the upper floor in the Arundel's house in Ilford. We were on our own now! We both went back to our jobs; me to Farrow & Jackson in Aldgate near Tower Bridge and Michael to Plessey in Ilford. During that first week home, we visited our families so that they would know all was well. Neither Michael's parents nor mine had a home telephone at this time, so making arrangements about when we should visit was not easy. I knew we wanted to keep in touch with both sets of parents and go about the countryside of East Anglia during our first shared summer, so when Michael surprised me by suddenly arriving home on a Lambretta scooter, I recognised the advantages of this mode of transport immediately. When we were single, we had always travelled between our two homes in the summertime on our bikes. Still, since we now had more domestic duties, or at least I had (I found that cooking the evening meal after coming home from work time-consuming, especially as I didn't have a great deal of cooking experience), Michael must have decided a quicker, less physically demanding means of transportation was indicated.

So, we made our first major purchase together. While I had been deeply involved in wedding arrangements, his mind had dwelt on another matter which I knew about, but which had seemed rather like a flight of fancy to me. Michael was quite a restless young man. His boundless energy caused his mother to label him a 'heedless youth'. I had always found his youthful energy and enthusiasm for 'doing things' attractive. After all, not everyone had cycled all over Scotland, England, and Wales; I liked our adventures. He made life much more interesting. During our courtship, I had learned that Michael's grandfather had been a sailor. He met and married his wife in Halifax, Nova Scotia. Their son also became a sailor. Michael's uncle lost his life during World War II, and brother Denis had managed to become a sailor in the U.S. Navy! Michael's mother was of a somewhat restless disposition. She yearned to be able to travel abroad but had always lacked the opportunity, which partly accounted for her sometimes, depressed spirits. In our conversations together before I married, she had often spoken of her desire that her sons should travel to 'broaden their minds'. So, I accepted that for this family, a restless eagerness for travel was in their blood. My mother, on the other hand, found the idea of foreign travel a dangerous one. She thought Michael's mother's thoughts about this a device to brainwash her offspring so that they would quickly be out of the house and off her hands!

Soon after our return from Italy, Michael's mother very kindly invited us both, together with my parents, to a 'Sunday Tea'. His Mum and Dad thought it a good opportunity to be together and to hear all about our honeymoon trip. The evenings were now lighter, so off we went to Browning Road on the scooter. Hilda, Michael's aunt, who had bought a house just around the corner in Byron Avenue, was also present. In a lull in the conversation, Hilda's voice was clearly heard to say to Michael, 'Did you ever do anything about that sailing we enquired about?' Our 'secret' was out. My mother's head jerked up, her face registering concerned puzzlement even though Michael responded quickly enough with a shake of his head, saying, 'No, our plans aren't really at that stage yet; we didn't follow up'. Although normal conversation resumed, I realised I had to make my parents aware of the kind of things we had been considering for the future. As we were parting at the end of the evening, my mother asked about Hilda's remark. I simply said we had things to talk about with them and would like to come home to see them the following weekend.

In our noisy, lively home, there was always so much going on I had frequently 'kept my own counsel', having early developed a greater need for privacy than Pam had ever required. To the end of her life, our mother was Pam's closest confidante. My mother yearned for the same close relationship with me, but poor Mum had to be satisfied with my response. When we made our visit during the following weekend together, we explained what sort of plans we had been thinking about. Since he had been 18 years old, Michael had been deferred from the National Service programme which was mandatory for all healthy young men in Britain at that time. It was planned that this conscription programme, which had been in place since the end of World War II, would, at some point, be discontinued. After working so hard on his Higher National Certificate for Mechanical Engineering, Michael regarded a possible two-year stint in one of the Armed Forces as a useless interruption to his career and a complete waste of time. For myself,

I certainly didn't like to think we could be living apart so soon after our marriage. Since his family regarded travel as important, and we both enjoyed a little adventure, it wasn't such a big step to begin considering emigrating to one of the British Commonwealth countries which desperately needed young people with specific skills. We had visited New Zealand House and made enquiries. Our enquiries had come to nothing because we were advised that New Zealand, experiencing severe housing shortages, could not accept married couples. Michael also told me at some point that at Australia House, the verdict was that we could apply and, assuming we were accepted, we could be housed in barracks for an unspecified period upon arrival due to that country's housing shortage. Communal living was certainly never part of my plans, so, being busy with wedding preparations, I had simply put the whole idea into the back of my mind. In my euphoric state following our wedding, I had not thought about Michael's adventurous idea at all for some weeks. Hilda's remark reminded me about Michaels plans to depart England before he got too much older.

A couple of times during the previous year before our wedding day, we had met a young woman from South Africa at Hilda's house. Margie, Hilda's lodger, was married to an Englishman whom we never met because he was working in the north. She had a small child, and together, Michael and I had a couple of conversations with her. Margie was trying to be cheerful in spite of our rather dull English weather. She told us about the wonderfully sunny climate South Africa enjoyed. Opportunities existed in her country for skilled people, and household help was readily available too. Our interest was aroused, but we had done nothing more before we married, and since my mother, who had been suffering from a painful attack of shingles, had expressed rather negative opinions about foreign travel for young people. I hadn't thought it appropriate to talk about our dreamy ideas and perhaps upset her unnecessarily. But now we had to talk about our plans because Michael was becoming pretty serious about seeking a new opportunity away from England. Back at work, I had met a new employee. Christine was from Port Elizabeth in South Africa, and we had a few useful conversations together. She told me stories about the beautiful climate, the beach parties, and how easy relations were with the black community; how cheerful and friendly they were and how her family had a couple of trusted employees who had been with them for many years. Our plans hadn't got very far, but Michael was extremely keen on the idea, so we related all this to my parents so that they knew what was in our minds. But we now had this lovely scooter and the first summer of our married life to enjoy, so Michael's plans still didn't weigh very heavily on my mind. I decided I would listen and go along with his ideas as a good wife should, waiting to see what happened next while concentrating on learning to become a happy wife and homemaker.

It turned out to be a wonderful summer. We were very happy together – I loved being out of the crowded, noisy family home, always having to explain my plans to my mother. I did miss the service she had provided and to which I had become quite accustomed. My mother had always been ready to be helpful; the early morning tea was always there, as was the hot meal in the evening, she even took pleasure in taking care of my laundry for me. She always said she wasn't so keen on looking after men's and boys' things. Perhaps I had not properly appreciated her attention in the past, but now it was all up to me to do these things for the two of us, as Michael had been similarly 'looked after' by his mother. I loved coming home from work, knowing we would be together all the time and I think Michael enjoyed our early months together as much as I did. I appreciated using the household things I had purchased: the kitchen equipment and household linen. Ours was a furnished apartment, so the furniture and appliances didn't belong to us, but I took special pleasure in those things we could call our own.

We did not have laundry facilities. At that time, it was 1958, the first launderettes were appearing in every High Street in Britain, so it was an easy matter to take a load or two to 'the Bendix' (the brand name of the machines used), and wash out my 'smalls' at home, allowing them to dry overnight on a folding frame 'dryer' placed in our living/dining room near the fireplace. Michael now went to work on the scooter, and as the early summer evenings grew longer, we could have a little run out whenever we felt like it. At the weekends, we had long day runs to enjoy the

English countryside or to the coast, and when my mother took her annual holiday with my dad at a holiday camp on the south coast, we went down to see them for a weekend and had a lovely romantic time. But we were both happy to be on our way again, just the two of us; we never found the crowded holiday camp scene very appealing. When Mum and Dad came back to Stanley Avenue at the end of their holiday, we had to tell them we had been accepted for immigration and planned to go to Africa.

ഇ ഈ

Soon the honeymoon was over, and we were making our way back to England, a quiet, uneventful journey, to be greeted by the usual dreary Essex weather. We had so much enjoyed the warmer weather and lovely blue skies of the Italian Coast and longed to have more of it. Upon our return to our newly rented upstairs apartment in a home in Ilford, which was quite close to where I worked and an easy bus and train ride into the City of London business district for Maureen, we needed a better means of getting around together. A car was financially out of the question, so I decided to buy a Lambretta scooter. I had noticed how popular and useful they could be while we were in Italy. Having not ridden one before, I had to quickly learn to drive it and obtain a Learner's License, which did not allow one to carry another person, but I did anyway.

Back in my drafting job, my thoughts turned again to emigration. Australia and New Zealand were out as far as we were concerned. Canada and the United States, we did not consider, so I started to have some interest in South Africa and Rhodesia. My Aunt Hilda had introduced us to a girl from South Africa, and we got some ideas from her about that country. We had very little money, and as we would have to pay for our passage to where we might decide to go, we had to carefully consider any offers.

Upon visiting both Rhodesia House and South Africa House, which were side by side in Trafalgar Square in London, we were advised we were suitable candidates for immigration and were provided with the appropriate application forms. Another staff member told us about an organisation called the 'The 1820 Settlers

Association'. If you were accepted for immigration, this group, which had been created by some of the first English-speaking immigrants, was available to help with all arrangements regarding accommodation upon arrival in South Africa, job interviews, etc., although there would be no financial help. Because of the large auto industry in Port Elizabeth, I was advised that there would undoubtedly be work for me there. The Apartheid policy was briefly mentioned, and as it was obvious that we were white-skinned, we were informed it would not be a concern for us.

After some discussion, we decided we would apply for immigration to South Africa. I had kept my parents informed of our ideas for leaving England, but Maureen, busy with wedding plans, had not mentioned anything about this idea to her family for many months. It is possible that she thought such a grand adventure might never happen. Within quite a small number of weeks, we had several interviews at South Africa House, medical examinations, and we were advised that our application had been approved and our entry visa would be valid for six months. At this point, Maureen realised her parents should be made aware of the possibility we might leave the country, as she now understood that it might indeed happen.

We had both used our summer holiday time for our two-week honeymoon, so we just took a few days in July to enjoy a little tour on our Lambretta scooter. We visited Maureen's parents, who were on holiday near Eastbourne, where we briefly mentioned our plans over a shared dinner. As the summer continued, we decided we would leave after my birthday in early October for South Africa. Having received our entry papers, I again visited Thomas Cook and booked the voyage from Southampton on the Union-Castle Steamship Lines vessel 'Pretoria Castle' for 29th October 1958. The South African authorities had advised us that Port Elizabeth was the best city to go to, as there were many engineering plants there, and the '1820 Settlers' would set up interviews for me in this city. The ship, a regular weekly mail, and passenger service was to call at the Canary Islands and then would come the long cruise south to Cape Town where we would spend eight hours. Leaving there, we would round the Cape of Good Hope to disembark at Port Elizabeth in the Eastern Cape.

We were planning a wonderful adventure, and it did not appear to bother us that after paying our fares for the train and ship, we would have very little money, probably just a few hundred pounds left. By the end of the summer, our plans were entirely in place, and we had to update our parents. My parents had been kept informed and had encouraged us as we went along, but Maureen's parents, probably thinking that my plans would not come to anything, were shocked and upset.

They had good reason to be unhappy. Over the past few years since the end of the war, there had been much turmoil and bloodshed in some former British colonies. In Africa, the prominent trouble spot had been Kenya with the Mau-Mau atrocities. Many of our friends and other family members thought it very unwise to go to Africa, but we knew that at that time, South Africa was a peaceful, stable, very law-abiding country. Apartheid (literally meaning 'separate development') was legally the rule of the South African government, and everything seemed to be very well controlled by their police and military forces.

We now had to make plans for shipping our few possessions. It was mostly wedding presents, household linen, etc. that Maureen had collected. We also had to give two weeks' notice at our places of work, make arrangements to settle the Income Tax Collector, and sell our precious Lambretta scooter. The steamship company sent a truck to pick up our effects, which they carefully packed into a wooden crate measuring about four cubic feet.

We moved in with my parents for a few weeks before our sailing date. My mother thought we could save some rent money that way. I managed to sell the scooter to a colleague at work. Most of my friends were not at all surprised that we were leaving because I had been talking about it for some time. We went to see Maureen's family at the weekend before the Friday departure to say our goodbyes, not knowing when we would see them again. Here we discovered that no one was coming to see us off on our grand adventure.

Michael and Maureen's honeymoon in Alassio, Italy

Our new mode of transportation prior to leaving England for South Africa in 1958

5.
Off to Africa

Michael

We sailed on Thursday, 29th October 1958, a damp, dreary day. My father accompanied us as far as Waterloo station, where we caught the boat train to Southampton, having bid a sad farewell to my mother at her house in Browning Road, where we had been staying for a few weeks. I believe she would have come to the ship but probably could not face the emotion of the slow departure. At precisely 4.00 pm, our ship, the 28,700-ton RMS Pretoria Castle, started to pull away from the pier. For us, it was all exhilarating. I don't think we had given a great deal of thought as to how our parents felt about us leaving. Earlier, we had been shown to our cabin, after checking in our previously shipped personal effects which had been professionally packed in a large crate. The cabin was small, with two fixed bunks one above the other, a washbasin with mirror above, and no porthole. It was an inside cabin, located low down in the centre of the ship. The toilet and bathing facilities were along the corridor; not quite what a newly married couple would prefer! The ship carried 540 Tourist passengers like us and about 214 in First Class. We watched the ship move slowly away from the jetty, but it was now getting dark, and the wind was cold, so after following the usual lifeboat drill, we went below to the dining room for our first meal at sea. We were assigned to a table with four other people, two returning South African residents and a Scottish couple, planning to visit family in the Cape. The meal was quite good, and as we were exhausted, we retired to our cabin early.

When we awoke the next morning, we learnt that we had left the English Channel and were soon to enter the Bay of Biscay, notorious for its stormy weather. Fortunately for us the weather, although cloudy, was quite good for this time of the year, the ship was only rolling slightly, but enough to make me realise that I was not exactly a good sailor and might quickly become seasick. It didn't seem to bother Maureen at all; she looked forward to every meal, whereas I was careful what I ate, and did not have much appetite. For our first day at sea, we simply explored the ship. We spent some time on deck, but the wind was too cold to stay long outside. We enjoyed the social aspect of the three daily meals served by our steward. After another good night's sleep, we both felt fine, and the ship was steaming along at 22 knots, well off the coast of Spain. During the day, we played a few deck games. It was starting to get warmer now, and the clouds had gone, although the wind was still chilly. After dinner, the crew put on a show. They enjoyed dressing up in drag and seemed to me to be a very effeminate bunch, but it was quite good fun. We would have a drink or two but did not stay up late. We were much more interested in retiring to our private cabin. Steaming through another night, we woke up early to watch the ship approach the volcanic Canary Islands and enter the port of Las Palmas on the island of Gran Canaria, having travelled 1,548 nautical miles from Southampton.

A few passengers disembarked here, but the main reason for calling at this port was for cheap bunkering (taking on fuel) as these are Spanish islands, close to the rich oil fields of North Africa. We were advised we had six hours here and went ashore, where we joined a small group for a bus tour around the town of Las Palmas. We visited the house that Christopher Columbus lived in before sailing to the New World in 1492, had a drink in a bar, and then were driven up to the rim of a volcano, which was shrouded in mist. On the way out of town, we were shocked to see people living in caves on the side of a hill. We had not realised that this type of primitive existence still prevailed among the poor in some parts of the world. The islands have a mild dry climate, and we were quite comfortable in summer clothes, a wonderful feeling after the gloomy weather we had left back home. Maureen, who always started to get anxious as any departure time approached, made sure we were back on the ship in plenty of time for the 5.00 pm sailing. Once more at sea, our course was set south for the tropics and a ten-day trip ahead, with no land in sight until we reached Cape Town. For the next few days, we relaxed into the leisurely pace aboard the ship. We met many interesting people. There were lively groups of young South Africans and Rhodesians, returning home after adventures in Britain and Europe, business people on contract to various companies, a few immigrants like ourselves, and some tourists. They all seemed a friendly, happy bunch and certainly kept the parties going at night, long after we had gone to bed. As we were now in the tropics, the sea was getting calmer, but with overcast skies and the odd rain squall, it made it very humid. With the sea temperature about the same as that of the air, the ship became very hot below decks, and the air conditioning did not seem very effective. We spent our days lounging on the deck or around the rather small pool. During the morning, the deck steward would offer beef tea, the traditional brew which was thought to help settle a queasy stomach, and of course, afternoon tea was at 4.00 pm. The bar was open most of the time, but we were not accustomed to much alcohol, and we also had to watch our expenses, having no home, no job, and limited funds.

It is an old navy tradition that anyone crossing the Equator for the first time is duly acknowledged, so at about 10.30 am one morning, we assembled on deck. Captain Fisher gave a short speech telling us that we were now at 0 degrees of latitude and crossing the line. A crew member dressed as King Neptune then took us through the ritual of 'The Ancient Order of the Deep'; we received a certificate that proclaimed, should we fall overboard, that all sharks, dolphins, whales, mermaids and other denizens of the deep were to treat us with due respect. It was a lot of fun and helped to pass the time. We were now in an area of very calm seas known as the 'doldrums'. Early sailors so named it as in the old days of sailing ships were often becalmed for weeks, the men becoming depressed when the sails would not fill. The Captain would order the ratings into the boats to tow the ship and 'find the wind'. It was grinding hard work. About this time, we also had a costume party night. Maureen selected some suitable items from the ship's shop (very limited offerings) and worked a whole day on her outfit. We went to dinner, I dressed as a pirate, barefoot in a bandana with my long pants rolled up a little and Maureen, in a green crepe-paper 'grass' skirt, and a flower lei was a barefoot hula dancer. It was fun seeing all the dreamed-up costumes, and we could see that the seasoned travellers had brought their outfits with them. After dinner, drinks, and dancing, the costumes were judged, and prizes awarded. For the next six or so days, we seemed to just get into a lazy schedule of lying around and taking part in the ship's organised activities. It was sweltering during the day and only a little cooler when the sun went down. As we travelled further south, out of the tropics, the skies were much clearer, and at night, we would look at the stars, noting they were in a different orientation to the northern hemisphere, and the Southern Cross was clearly visible. It was very romantic strolling hand-in-hand to the stern, watching the moon on the water and the phosphorescence glowing in the wake of the ship, then retiring to our cabin in a very relaxed and happy frame of mind. We had one more evening show put on by the crew members, and then preparations were being made for our arrival in Cape Town. Our arrival time was to be 7.00 am, but seasoned travellers told us that it was a beautiful sight entering Table Bay, and we should be on deck about 5.30 am, so we went to our cabin early. Up at dawn the next morning, dressed in warmer clothes, we went up to the promenade deck. The sun was just rising, and we were in Table Bay, with Cape Town ahead and Table Mountain looming above the city. Clinging to each other, against the brisk cold wind, we were both excited at our first sight of Africa and somewhat apprehensive as to what the future held for two 23-year-olds on this vast alien continent.

The Pretoria Castle docked at Cape Town precisely on time on 13th November 1958, late spring in the Southern hemisphere. Standing on the promenade deck, we were fascinated by the immediate hive of activity on the dock below us. The cranes soon started to unload huge packing cases onto the dolly carts, and the many Africans below started to move them. We noticed the crane drivers were all white. It was quite a calm, warm day, and after a while, we were bothered by a rather pungent smell drifting up from below. Noting our concern, a South African close by said, 'That's the scent of Africa; the blacks seldom wash. You'll get used to it.' The previous night we had been assigned a time to meet in the lounge with the Immigration authorities, so we proceeded to go below. Our meeting with the officials, who were mainly Afrikaners, was relatively brief and official but friendly enough. After stamping our passports, we were free to go ashore for the day. The ship was due to sail for Port Elizabeth at 9.00 am on the next day. Before leaving England, we had been to our local branch of

Barclays Bank to buy travellers' checks. On the ship, we could use English or South African pounds, but now we needed to find a bank and acquire more South African currency. Leaving the ship, we walked the short distance across a newly reclaimed area of land called the Foreshore and soon reached the city, where we found a bank open. Although the notes and coins looked strangely different to us, the currency was still in denominations of pounds, shillings, and pence. Also, there was a silver three-penny piece called a *tickey*. The city impressed us with its beauty, sunshine, moderately tall buildings, and the friendliness of the people we spoke to.

I noticed the young women on the street seemed very attractive, tanned, and healthy-looking. There were many people of various races bustling around, but they appeared polite and cheerful. We noticed there were separate service counters in many places for white and non-white patrons, and the toilets and sections on the buses were also segregated. Strolling along the main street to the city centre, taking in all the new sights, sounds, and smells, we went into a large department store called Stuttafords. We saw strawberries and cream were on the menu in the elegant restaurant. Strawberries in November were a novelty to us, and we enjoyed them, seated on a terrace that was open to the blue sky. They were by far the best we had ever tasted and were served to us by a neatly uniformed, smiling young woman who we would have described as '*half-caste*'; we later learned to call these people 'coloured'.

Afterwards, continuing in the warm sunshine to the top end of Adderley Street toward Table Mountain, we came to many government buildings on the edge of a beautiful semi-tropical garden area. The 'Company's Garden' is a well-known landmark and public space. We sat for a while and studied a map of the city and surrounding areas, to decide what we should do next. We noted there were some beaches to the southwest of the city around a rocky headland called Signal Hill, and as the buses left from close by, we decided to catch one to a place called Sea Point. Having bought the return ticket from a kiosk, it was easy to board the next bus, and we made sure we were in the right area for whites, always near the front. It turned out to be a very scenic ride, and after arriving at Sea Point, we walked along an esplanade by the Atlantic, which was lined with beautiful homes and modern apartment buildings. Noting the many *coloured* nannies with little white children and nursemaids for the elderly, we thought we must be in quite an affluent area. There was a large, modern oceanfront swimming pool where we had lunch in the well-appointed restaurant and enjoyed our surroundings for the afternoon. Returning to the city, we walked back to the ship and were in time for the evening meal.

The next morning the ship prepared to sail and at 9.00 am left the dock in Cape Town and headed south, passing Robben Island. We passed Sea Point, the resort suburb we had liked so much, and continued south by other beautiful suburbs guarded by the western flanks of Table Mountain. Many passengers had disembarked in Cape Town, so Maureen decided to do some washing in the ship's laundry, to get our clothing in clean and fresh order ready for our arrival at our Port Elizabeth destination. As we approached the Cape of Good Hope, the ship started to pitch and roll heavily, and I did not feel too well, so I retired to the cabin. Lying down did not help very much. The Cape is notorious for heavy seas as this is where the cold waters of the Atlantic meet the warmer Indian Ocean. We went on deck as we rounded the 'Fairest Cape', but the wind was very strong and cool, so we found a sheltered spot. Our journey to Port Elizabeth took two days, and we enjoyed the luxury of a less crowded ship. We passed the southernmost point of Africa at Cape Agulhas, steaming eastwards along the beautiful coast of the southern Cape Province. On Sunday morning, our ship moored at the dock in Port Elizabeth, having travelled 6,430 nautical miles from England, and our long journey was over.

We claimed our cabin baggage and made arrangements for our packing case to be held at the docks until we had a permanent address. We were happy to be met by a young English couple, Dave and Margaret, who were representatives of the 1820 Settlers Association. A few days' accommodations had been booked for us at a local guest house by them, and we were driven by car up a rather steep street away from the dock area and dropped off. This friendly couple arranged to pick us up again later for a tour of the town and surrounding areas. They seemed anxious to be helpful. During the afternoon, they took us all over the small city of Port

Elizabeth, including the industrial areas and the beaches. I was also informed that two job interviews had been arranged by the *1820 Settlers*: the first to be with The Ford Motor Company on Monday morning. When we retired to bed that night, I had somewhat mixed feelings. The guest house, although clean, did not seem to have a very friendly atmosphere. The clientele were mainly older Afrikaners, who seemed reluctant to talk to us, but gave me the feeling they were talking about us. The city had undoubtedly not impressed us very much, and the beaches seemed bleak and windswept with few of the usual services and amenities we expected and had observed in Cape Town. But at the appropriate time on Monday morning, Dave appeared at our lodgings to take me to Fords for the interview. The factory was quite large and assembled various types of cars, trucks, and tractors for the southern African markets, with many of the components manufactured there. They had an urgent need for skilled toolmakers, and after a good interview, I was offered a job; the pay rate proposed to be slightly more than I was making in England. However, having come from an industrialised area, close to the enormous main Ford factory in England, I was not exactly keen to enter this kind of work environment again and told the man who interviewed me I had other interviews lined up, so I would let him know.

The next day, after breakfast, following a somewhat restless night, Maureen and I walked down into the centre of town in warm sunshine and discussed what we should do. We both agreed we did not like Port Elizabeth very much. After travelling all those miles, I was very reluctant to go into a work situation similar to the one I had detested back home in England. There seemed to be a much higher percentage of Afrikaans-speaking people than we had expected, and this seemed to create a barrier between the two language groups, and we didn't feel very comfortable. After another restless night, we decided that rather than try to make a go of it here, we would return to Cape Town, even though we realised that the cost of returning would deplete our meagre resources. Another job interview had been arranged for Wednesday, so instead of attending that interview, I phoned to cancel it, and we walked down into the city again and made an inquiry about transportation back.

We discovered that the cost of rail fares and ship passage were about the same, but we had that packing case at the docks to move also. The ticket agent at Union-Castle Shipping Line offices advised that our crate would go as personal effects at no extra charge, and we realised that the ship would therefore be the most cost-effective way for us to go. The next available ship to Cape Town was the same Pretoria Castle returning from Durban and would arrive in six days. We pondered our predicament for a while at a snack bar, but without any further hesitation, we went back and paid the fares for the ship. Now the small amount of our available funds was a concern. The following day we met again with Dave and Margaret to let them know we would not be staying in their city. They were quite shocked and disappointed that we had decided to leave, and I felt we had let them down, but they wished us well, and we never saw them again. It seemed best to stay on at the same guest house for the remaining time because it was reasonably cheap lodging. Now we had to pass the time for almost a week, spending very little money. The guest house did provide breakfast and an evening meal, so we just made do with a light snack during the day. We walked around the city a bit, enjoying the warm, sunny climate, visited a snake park close by, but got quite bored waiting. Finally, on the scheduled day, the ship arrived in port, and we made our way to the docks to board as soon as we could. By late afternoon we were again back at sea heading toward Cape Town. The journey must have been quite uneventful as we both have little recollection of it.

ꕥ

My thoughts during the whole exciting emigration period were decidedly mixed. I certainly didn't like saying ‘goodbye’ to so many people. It seemed in those moments to be so dreadfully final. I was quite attached to my extended family, and dearly loved my parents and my sister Pam. But the idea of a two-week cruise after the sweet summer months of our marriage, which we had enjoyed so much, beckoned me. I had only read about such events and was happy to look forward to what could turn out to be a rather captivating experience. Our time together so far had been fantastic. We'd also said 'goodbye' to our friends at work. We sold our nifty scooter and our touring bicycles and sundry gear; we were pretty sure we were not going to need them again. I thought Michael was the sort of young man who would be thinking about eventually owning a car! I set myself to enjoy the passage to South Africa as an extension of our honeymoon. Along the way, through my reading habit, while I was growing up, I had gained a little insight into how one behaved in these circumstances, and I knew I had enough of the 'right' kind of clothes. I had been steadily working towards the goal of getting set up to begin our married life during the whole period of our engagement. My husband seemed unsure about dealing with waiters and cabin stewards and other strangers, but we managed to fit in well enough by working together.

Michael has detailed how much we were impressed with Cape Town. When we arrived in Port Elizabeth, it soon began to dawn on me that everything here was very different; something changed in our thinking. Perhaps our previous life close to the amenities of London had been no preparation for small-town life. The two distinct *white* language groups seemed to generate an uneasy feeling. We didn't discuss our feelings about this very much. Michael was never verbally very communicative; he became quiet and introspective. Since he naturally would be the one who would earn the more significant portion of our income, I waited for him to indicate he was satisfied with this choice and was so relieved when he confessed that he wasn't very impressed with this town and didn't much look forward to the working environment here either. I acquiesced immediately when he suggested we go back to Cape Town, little realising how much it would deplete our funds. But once the decision was made, I never doubted that somehow all would be well.

℧ ℭ

After docking once again in the harbour in Cape Town and making arrangements for our packing case containing our household effects to be stored, we made our way, suitcases in hand, to the Visitors' Bureau and were given the addresses and telephone numbers of a few guest houses in the city area. After choosing one located in the higher end of the city in the shadow of Table Mountain, I phoned and was told they had a room available for us, so we made our way to Leeuwen Street, which was close to the *Company's Garden* we had previously visited. The guest house seemed bright and clean, and the landlord was friendly, so we took the room for a few days. Now we had to get our bearings and seriously look for work and more permanent accommodation before our funds completely ran out.

On Friday, the weekend edition of the Cape Argus newspaper, with the *Classifieds*, appeared on the streets. We scanned it for jobs and rental accommodation. There was a brief advertisement in the Employment section reading 'Toolmakers Urgently Required', giving a phone number. Calling right away, I was relieved to hear an English-speaking voice on the line, informing me that the business was called 'The Metal Box Company' and that I could come for an interview on Monday. Explaining that I had just arrived in the country and was without a car, the voice suggested that I make my way from the mainline railway station in the city to Mutual station for 9.00 am. At this time, there would be someone to take me to the plant, which was located out on the Cape Flats, the flat, dry, sandy area northeast of the city.

We also found in the newspaper several 'places to rent' in Sea Point, the area we had liked so much on our previous visit, even some in other resort-type regions to the southwest of the city on the Atlantic side. We made a phone enquiry about accommodation and decided to visit a few on Saturday. One in particular at Camps Bay sounded very interesting. It was now approaching the end of the month, and it seemed that rented places customarily were 'to let' on a month to month basis. The buses left from nearby, at the top of Long Street, so the next morning we caught the double-decker bus for Sea Point, noticing we had a white driver and conductor; *Coloured* passengers seemed to choose to sit on the upper deck. After looking at a couple of apartments there, the ones we could afford seemed a bit dingy, so we continued on the same bus route to Camps Bay. This part of the ride was very scenic, with the road skirting around small coves, past some lovely sheltered beaches with the rocky cliffs towering above us on the left. There were modern apartment blocks and beautiful homes clinging to the mountainside above and below the winding road. It reminded us a little of the French Riviera. Our first view of Camps Bay from the bus was awe-inspiring; it was so beautiful. Before us was a wide golden sandy beach edged by a palm-fringed promenade, and the steep, mountainous western flanks of Table Mountain dominated the scene. We noticed the sea looked very choppy at the far end of the bay and realised when we alighted from the bus why this was. The Cape can be a very windy place. Twenty-five miles to the south, at the Cape of Good Hope, the cold water of the Atlantic meets the warmer waters of the Indian Ocean, and the currents and opposing air systems generate extremely strong winds. The mornings are generally calm, but during the afternoons, the south-easterly wind increases, often to gale force, creating an unusual effect on Table Mountain, which overlooks the city and suburbs. As the cold air picks up moisture from the back of the mountain, it creates a blanket of cloud that continuously pours over the top of Table Mountain like a waterfall but soon evaporates and disappears. It is known locally as the *Tablecloth*, and the cloud will change colour showing gold, saffron, and pink bands in the setting sun. The wind, considered to be a healthy feature of city life, is known as the Cape Doctor and germs are routinely blown away into the Atlantic. Although the Sea Point area is protected from this wind by the mountain, we soon realised that parts of Camps Bay were not. We alighted from the bus by a small parade of shops across from the wide, sandy beach, where we asked directions. It was only a short walk uphill to 88 Camps Bay Drive, a small neat looking bungalow, where we introduced ourselves to Mr and Mrs Spearman. We thought Alex and Marta Spearman to be a slightly unusual couple. He was a relatively small Englishman about 40 years old who had spent a number of years in India in the Colonial Service and was Sir Alexander Spearman, the son of a baronet. Marta, of Afrikaner descent, was somewhat younger than her husband. She spoke quite good English. They seemed friendly and showed us their home, which was all on one level, but since the terrain sloped down towards the ocean, the rooms along the back of the house had wonderful ocean views over the roofs of the homes below. The north wing, which accommodated the bedrooms, had been divided by a two-sided built-in cupboard, which created a completely separate apartment. This wing, extending towards the ocean, comprised a living/dining room, a tiny kitchen and bathroom, and a small bedroom that accommodated a double bed. Entry to this portion was gained by walking down a path at the side of the house into the back garden and up a staircase to the door of the completely separate flatlet. It was sparsely furnished throughout with rather old but serviceable pieces. They were still in the process of making the place habitable, and it would soon be available to rent. The monthly rent would be £22 per month, payable in advance.

We liked this area, the ocean, the beach, and the beautiful location of the house attracted us very much. On the other hand, we knew there were cheaper places to rent in the somewhat mixed southern suburbs of Cape Town, and our available funds were a real concern. At this point, I still did not have a job. We sat down and had a chat with Alex and Marta. They seemed to like us, and we agreed to rent the flatlet, also because we had no other plans, we offered to come out the next day, Sunday and help them finish cleaning up. We explained we could not move in until Tuesday, 2nd December as I had a job interview on Monday, but this would give us time to recover the crate from the docks, which held our bed linen and blankets, among other things. On Sunday, we again took the bus to Camps Bay, paid our rent for the first month, and spent a few hours helping clean up the flat. In the late afternoon, the Spearman's kindly invited us to stay for dinner. It was a simple meal, and we appreciated their hospitality.

My job interview on Monday went well. The person that I had spoken to had advised me to catch the 8.30 am train from Cape Town to Mutual station, about 15 miles out on the *Cape Flats*, where I would be met. The trains were segregated, and each carriage was clearly marked *Blankes* (meaning White) or *Nie-Blankes* (non-Whites). The journey took about 30 minutes, with many stops. Quite a number of people alighted at Mutual station, and there were some cars and vans waiting for passengers, including a large, flashy American Chevrolet with a chauffeur,

137

probably waiting for someone important. American cars were somewhat rare in South Africa. After a few minutes, when all the other passengers had left, and I was still awaiting my ride, the coloured uniformed driver of the big car approached and said to me, 'Mr Harbott, for Metal Box?' Hiding my surprise, I said, 'Yes' and he led the way to the Chevrolet and opened the back door, I got into the vehicle, and off we went. Located in an Industrial Park called Epping, a few miles from Mutual station, The Metal Box Company was the South African branch of an English company that produced machinery and tooling for the canning industry. Much of the African labour for the many factories and businesses here lived in the Locations (native African neighbourhoods), which were sub-divided into nearby townships called *Langa* and *Nyanga*. My interview was to be with the plant manager Ken Overton, another Englishman. He reviewed my training and experience, gave me a tour of the plant, told me what the salary would be, and then offered me the job. As I needed to start work as soon as possible, and the pay was more than I had been getting in England, I accepted the position right away, although I had no idea how I would get to work from Camps Bay. Explaining that we were moving into new accommodation the next day and that I had to retrieve our personal effects from the docks, as my toolbox was in the packing case there, we agreed that I could start work in two days. With a handshake, we said goodbye. I was driven back to the station in the same style, and took the train to Cape Town, then walked to Leeuwen Street, where Maureen was anxiously waiting to hear my fantastic news. We were both delighted and relieved. In a very short space of time, we now had not only somewhere to live that we liked, but also a good job lined up. I lost no time in arranging for our crate to be sent out to Camps Bay the following day, and we prepared for what we hoped would be our last move for a while.

On the next morning, we paid our bill at the guest house and once again carried those suitcases containing our clothing and a few belongings and got the bus to Camps Bay. After letting Marta Spearman know we had arrived and picking up our keys, we let ourselves into our new home. In the afternoon, we were very relieved to see our packing case arrive. While we waited for it, we talked about how we were going to manage financially until the end of the month when I would be paid. We had to spend what little remained of our cash very carefully. But we were not dismayed. We had found a place to live in, and the weather and our surroundings were beautiful. We needed to conserve our money for fares to work and for food. Maureen was anxious to begin looking for work as soon as possible and would be taking the bus to work in Cape Town.

We had discovered that bananas were very cheap, and fresh milk, which we didn't have to pay for until the end of the month, could be delivered daily right to our door. We would buy a few essential foods and could have a cooked meal at a little café by the beach two or three times a week; also, we would consume a lot of bananas and milk. We were sure we would be fine, and our available funds would cover our needs well enough. We had to open and unpack the crate in the back garden because it was too big to go up the narrow stairs and through the entrance door to our apartment. Everything was in perfect order, and it was reassuring to see our belongings once again. Since leaving England in October, we had not been able to communicate very much with our families. We had sent a few postcards and letters from various places, but as we had no fixed address up until this time, they could not write to us. No one in either of our families had a home telephone. Our living room in Camps Bay had a small dining table by the window. We sat there where we wrote to our parents, telling them of all that had happened and providing them with our new address. It would always be two or three weeks before we had a reply. Settling into bed early that first night, it was wonderful to relax with our own linen and pillows after all the travel and anxiety. The next day was to be my first day at work in a new country, in a trade I had not practised for two years, and I had no idea how I would get there with my heavy toolbox.

We were up early Wednesday morning, had a quick breakfast, and I walked down the hill, toolbox in hand, to catch the bus at 6.00 am into Cape Town. It was almost midsummer, and the sun would soon be up over the mountain as the bus made its way along the beautiful coastal road into the city. I again took the train out to Mutual station, and from there I hitched a couple of rides to get to the factory. The morning went quite nicely with routine paperwork for employment, a brief medical check-up, and introductions to my fellow workers. There were a large group of semi-skilled white workers operating various machines for the manufacture of parts for production machines, and a group of about six toolmakers who manufactured tooling for the canning industry. A few coloureds and Africans worked throughout the plant as storekeepers and labourers. The toolmakers, considered the elite group, comprised several South African, a Dutchman, a German, a Russian, and Peter Howison, another Englishman with whom I made friends. I asked the foreman, who also was English if he knew of anyone who lived near Camps Bay, who might be willing to give me a ride to work. He suggested I talk to the big Russian, Harry, but warned me he could be a troublesome fellow. It turned out Harry lived in a rented apartment in the small seaside resort of Clifton, perched on the cliffs just a few miles from Camps Bay. He agreed to give me a ride to Clifton after work and indicated that if I wanted a ride the next morning, to be at the same place at 7.15 am. This arrangement worked well for me as Clifton was only a very short bus ride from our home. Harry Raak was both different and difficult. He was a big man, about 16-stone (220 lbs). He had poor English and a very volatile temper. I learned later he was from Estonia, and when the Russians took over his country during the Second World War, many of his countrymen were killed. Harry, a youth at the time, was sent to a forced labour camp. The dreadful conditions and what happened to him there had affected his mind. We did not say much at first on our journeys to and from work, but by the end of the week he seemed to have warmed a little toward me, and I asked him if I could travel with him until I had a car and that I would share with him the cost of the petrol. 'Ja, okay', he said, and we shook hands.

At last, the pieces were starting to fall into place. We spent the weekend in Camps Bay, enjoying the beautiful scenery and the beach, but found the sea was much too cold and rough to swim in on this coast. In order to save money, light meals were the order of the day, as payday was still two weeks away. By mid-December we were both established in good jobs, my company had a Christmas party, but not having yet made many friends we spent Christmas alone. I received my first paycheque just before the holiday, and we were able to buy some badly needed food, which included ham in an odd-shaped can. Opening this on Christmas morning with a knife (we didn't have a can-opener), it slipped and cut deeply into my hand. It was apparent by all the blood that stitches were required. Fortunately for us, we had noticed a Jewish doctor's office in a house just down the road from us. We went there with the hand crudely bandaged. He kindly stitched me up while listening to our story and would not accept any payment.

As the New Year approached, we reflected on the great adventure that had changed our lives and looked forward to our financial situation improving rapidly, as we began making our way, creating our life together in this new country. We hoped things would work out satisfactorily as it was a long way home and, even had we wanted to; we did not have the means to return to England.

Our first view of Africa was from the 'RMS Pretoria Castle' arriving in Table Bay, 13th November 1958

Union-Castle Line mailship leaving Cape Town

During our long wait in Port Elizabeth

Beautiful Camps Bay

6.
The Fairest Cape

Michael

One weekend, after visiting *Cape Town Castle*, we learned that this region had a fascinating and colourful past. The first Europeans to visit Table Bay were led by the Portuguese explorer Bartholomew Diaz in 1488. On his round-the-world voyage in 1580 the Englishman, Sir Francis Drake, sailed around the Cape of Good Hope in the *Golden Hind* and the ruggedness and breathtaking beauty of the peninsular caused him to write, 'This cape is a most stately thing, and the fairest cape we saw in the whole circumference of the earth.' It was many years later in 1652 before the Dutch, under Jan Van Riebeeck, established a permanent settlement in Table Bay. The purpose was to supply their fleet of ships en route to the Spice Islands (Dutch East Indies), now Indonesia. At the time of his landing, the indigenous population consisted of a few Bushmen and Hottentots in the southern and central areas of the Cape and the Bantu (the Xhosa tribe) in the northeast. Over time, the Dutch East India Company established a supply station and brought many Dutch settlers to Cape Town; they were to become known as *Boers* (farmers). Their objective was to develop gardens to grow vegetables and barter for livestock with the Hottentot tribes. They also built a hospital and a safe harbour for the repair of the company ships. By 1689 French Protestants called *Huguenots*, fleeing religious persecution at home, arrived, intermarried with the Dutch, and helped develop the wine industry in the region. Except for a time during the French Revolution and Napoleonic wars, 1795 to 1803, when the British took control, it remained in the hands of the Dutch until ceded to Great Britain in 1806. The British named the territory the 'Cape of Good Hope Colony' and encouraged emigration from England. The new British settlers soon came into conflict with the *Boers* (the Dutch-speaking people, later called *Afrikaners)* over the anglicising of the Courts of Law, the control of farm and pastureland, and slaveholding. Slavery was abolished by 1833 in the British Empire.

Beginning in 1835, many Boers left the Cape Colony and started on the *Great Trek*, taking their slaves north with them, to seek more land and escape British rule. They eventually founded the Republics of the Transvaal and Orange Free State. By 1867 diamonds had been discovered at Kimberley, and this region was annexed by the Cape in 1880. Six years later, gold was found in the Transvaal. When Cecil Rhodes became Prime Minister of the Cape Colony, he sought to unite the Transvaal, Orange Free State and Natal with the Cape. The Boers strongly resisted this development, and the conflict became the Boer War, which ended in their defeat in 1902. In 1910 the Cape Colony became one of the founding members of the Union of South Africa.

In 1948 the Nationalist Party, under the direction of DF Malan, won their first general election, which marked the beginning of the *Apartheid* era. For the first time, Afrikaners were in control, and legal segregation on racial lines became the main policy initiative. By the time we arrived in South Africa, apartheid was firmly established by the Nationalist Government. We always understood the British influence could not be held responsible for this.

᠒ ᠌

I had set out on this journey with my new husband dazzled by the romance and excitement of our first long sea voyage together. Now we had to come down to earth. We had become somewhat uneasy during the time spent in Port Elizabeth, and I was glad we didn't remain there. I didn't know what we were going to do next, but as the 'living in South Africa' idea had been initiated by Michael, I thought my best plan was to follow his lead and support his opinion in our discussion about what we should do next. Returning to Cape Town had seemed the only possible option; we had been so favourably impressed on our first visit. I had also noticed then, without thinking a great deal about it, that there seemed to be more tall people in Cape Town, especially among the younger men and women. I was rather tall for an Englishwoman; I was pleased to note that my stature was unremarkable there.

When we docked once more at the foot of Table Mountain, gathered our belongings, and went ashore, I recognised it was now time to deal with real life. Always keen to make a good impression, I dressed with care, wearing a hat, gloves, and high-heeled shoes, carrying a couple of soft bags, and with Michael having our suitcases, we walked across the foreshore/harbour area and into the downtown part of the city.

It was quite a long walk in the hot sun. I should have realised that, although he didn't say much about it to me, Michael was deeply concerned about our low funds; he must have decided taxis were out of the question. When we were settled in the guest house in the Gardens area, I changed into more comfortable clothes and sandals. In a remarkably short space of time, after staying just two nights in a bed and breakfast home in the Gardens area, together, we found a lovely place to live, and Michael had secured a job. So early in December, after seeing Michael off to work on his first day at The Metal Box Company, I set to work in our little apartment in Camps Bay to put our personal belongings in order and investigate the kitchen equipment. We had a small fridge for our milk supply, which worked well, but the electric stove was not very serviceable. There were two solid hot plates for cooking with a rather dirty and inefficient little oven below. I thought we would manage with the hotplates well enough. I spent the first day in our new small home, getting our clothing in order and finding places to store our belongings. I needed to press my good clothes to enable me to be suitably dressed for the job of finding work. It was so easy to become distracted from my domestic chores and waste a little time whenever a ship left Cape Town. I could look out over the roofs of the houses below us and watch the passing sea traffic sail past our window on that incredible shining blue ocean and dream a little.

I did not know it then, but Michael had never had to attend work-related interviews before coming to South Africa. He had been recommended to The Plessey Company in England by the principal at the technical college he attended. I, on the other hand, had some experience of going for interviews and decided that it would be best to go to an employment agency because I knew successful, well-established businesses preferred to use them rather than putting an open advertisement in the newspaper. So, with a few 'butterflies' inside, this was a strange country, and I didn't yet know how they managed their affairs, I boarded the bus and went to make enquiries in an agency I had noticed at the upper end of Adderley Street, thinking I would simply register with them. That very day, without my having to do any kind of a test, I was advised Syfrets Trust, a prestigious financial entity, had an opening suitable for my abilities, which I had briefly detailed on the registration card. Since Syfrets Trust was just a few steps away, around the corner on Wale Street, I went there immediately. These offices had an imposing entrance and looked somewhat similar to the office environment I was used to. I had a short interview with Mr Stanley, the department head, and was engaged to begin work the following Monday. Syfrets, along with other banking and trust-type financial dealings, was heavily involved in facilitating the buying and selling of stocks and shares for their many wealthy clients. South Africa was, and is still, world-famous for its valuable natural resources, the gold and diamond mines. The inevitable paperwork involved in the legal transfer of these commodities formed the more significant part of the department's work. My responsibility would be to operate a special kind of typewriter and produce the official 'notes', which detailed all buying and selling transactions of these stocks, shares, and bonds. Extreme accuracy was required, and each working day's transactions were to be completed, and the 'notes' in the mail by 6.00 pm at the end of the business day. This was a legal requirement. At the beginning of each day, before business became brisk, I was to report to a Director's office and assist his two secretaries if they needed my help and in turn, one of them would help me at the end of the day when the pace of business increased, to make sure all those vital 'notes' were dealt with in a timely manner. These two girls were Diana Van Reenan and Cynthia Dean, two nice young women who seldom needed my help, explained to me what they did, and became my friends. The working hours were from 9.30 am to 5.30 pm. Sometimes, on extra 'high volume' days, two of us would have to remain until 6.00 pm to ensure all the notes were completed. Both Michael and I had secured employment very quickly, and the people we had met so far had been helpful and very nice. I thought we had been very fortunate.

I spent a few days before starting work, getting acquainted with my new surroundings in Camps Bay. I visited the few local shops and the library while enjoying the sunshine and novelty of at last being able to live so near the ocean. I felt lonely while Michael was working and looked forward to his return each night when we would have a light meal or a couple of bananas with milk. I saw Marta Spearman, our landlady, one afternoon and told her I was going to work at Syfrets. She invited me in for tea, and we got to know each other a little. She was quite impressed I had got a job so quickly in such a prestigious, well-known financial institution. As I left, she mentioned her neighbour's cat had produced kittens. I liked cats but had never been able to own one, and before I knew it, I was offering to take a kitten off her neighbour's hands when they were old enough. I was soon able to pick one out. He was just an ordinary little grey tabby but became the source of much pleasure to us both. He was the first of many feline friends I was able to own and love. I named him Ruffy because he was a feisty little puss with sharp claws and teeth. Ruffy's advent made us aware of one of the problems of living in South Africa. We had been told there were many snakes residing on and around Table Mountain, but we seldom saw any. What we were not prepared for were the significant number of fleas. Everyone had to deal with them. Poor little Ruffy easily picked them up, and they were plainly visible on the light grey fur of his tummy. When we realised what was happening, we would pick them off with tweezers each evening until he got bigger and could take care of them himself. Marta, who grew up on a farm, was very *matter-of-fact* about pests and advised me to sprinkle flea powder around the perimeter of each room to keep them away. The flea powder would also deter the ants, which would march long distances in black columns more than an inch wide in their search for food. The Spearman's had a dog, Lady, a beautiful young German Shepherd just growing out of puppyhood, that needed obedience training; they had a cat, too. Marta was well used to dealing with household pests!

After a leisurely weekend spent at the beach and writing letters to our family in the early evenings after we'd had enough sun, we both prepared for work on Monday. Michael had to leave quite early each weekday morning, which left the tiny bathroom free for my turn. I was a little nervous but tried to enjoy the ride into Cape Town, which took about half an hour. I was shown where I was to sit and introduced to my neighbours, and I prepared to set to work. Just in front of me and to the left, outside Mr Stanley's office door, sat his second-in-command, Mr St John (pronounced 'Sin-jon'). He had a refined English 'public school' (i.e., private school!) accent but was a very cheerful, friendly man, willing to help me if I had trouble deciphering hand-written information. He kept an eye on me, but after a couple of practices, I was soon turning out the 'notes' in good order. Accuracy with no alterations was required. He would check them, and occasionally I had to retype one. The official number of the spoiled ones had to be noted in a little black book before they were destroyed. It was interesting to me how very closely each step of the process of stocks and shares changing hands was monitored, to satisfy legal requirements. Towards the end of the day, a director, Diana and Cynthia's boss came by and spoke to Mr St John. I heard another upper-class English accent. Cape Town clearly had quite a large British contingent. Their conversation ended by this gentleman saying, 'So don't forget, St John, Friday about seven – it's black-tie of course!' as they parted. I was to learn that Cape Town society was very active for six months of the year when Parliament sat in the offices adjacent to the Company's Garden. During this time, there were many formal dinner parties and receptions. The rest of the year, South Africa was administered from Pretoria in the Transvaal. But the white community remained rather formal in their manners and style. Manners and habits learned in colonial days endured!

We were amused to notice everyone got quite 'dressed up' simply to go to the cinema (it was called 'The Bioscope') and ladies going into town for an afternoon shopping trip always wore hats and gloves. A shady hat was a good idea in view of the hot sun beating down for many months of the year. I didn't wear a hat to work because working women usually didn't, and we weren't exposed to the sunshine in the hottest part of the day. I had always had a good supply of white gloves. The first couple of weeks passed, and Michael and I received our salaries. We decided we would open a joint account at the main branch of Barclays Bank

DCO (the initials standing for Dominion, Colonial, and Overseas) on Adderley Street, which would make it very easy to pay our bills. I quickly learned there was little interaction between the different sections of the community. Apartheid which is an Afrikaans word meaning 'separateness' (the official English translation was 'separate development') was an official policy of the government which was dominated by the Nationalist (Afrikaner) majority, although in the Cape Province alone the English speaking United party held a majority and their influence was growing in Natal on the east coast of South Africa. Therefore, the different colour groups did not live together, work together, or play together. Officially the groups were designated 'White', 'Black' or 'Coloured'. The 'coloured' group was made up of persons of mixed blood and those whose heritage included Asian influences. Some of this group were also called Malays and lived in a separate quarter on the east side of the city. The earliest immigrants of this community had been brought to South Africa by the Dutch East India Company to cultivate the gardens they required to re-supply their ships. Their descendants were generally Muslim, very hard-working, and quietly maintained their own traditions and culture. They were active in small business and maintained a relatively low profile – they kept to themselves but were definitely non-European.

In conversation, the people we met spoke of those belonging to the Black and Coloured communities as 'non-European'. This seemed to them to be a somewhat kinder way of describing them than labelling them by their skin colour. We noticed signs everywhere, which said 'Europeans Only' on restaurants, bars, and public toilets. We were amused – we thought we certainly qualified and, therefore, confidently used these facilities. The majority of the other white folk had probably never been anywhere near Europe! From time to time, we read in the newspaper of legal wrangles regarding Classification. It was interesting to discover Japanese were classified as White, but Chinese Coloured! A special court was convened to decide if a person classified either Black or Coloured' could possibly be wrongly classified. There were a lot of people who fell between the cracks, and these cases were always reported in the newspapers. At Syfrets, there was a pretty young light-skinned married woman who had a thick Afrikaans accent and clearly was of mixed parentage. She seemed to be cautiously accepted by the White community; her husband was white. There was always gossip about her because her brother, who would occasionally meet her at the end of the day, was definitely coloured. I also heard on the local radio about a much-discussed play currently attracting attention in Johannesburg called 'Try for White', which was about a similar situation. This was discussed at coffee time in low voices. It was a really hot topic. Many people did not completely agree with *apartheid* but went along with the official law because it made cheap labour and domestic help very accessible.

A short time before we arrived in the country, the Immorality Act had also been passed into law. This law made sexual contact between the races illegal. A conviction would result in a prison sentence. But there had been very many such instances in the past and the young white people we got to know used to laugh about it, because it was frequently the Dominie, the minister in a rural Dutch Reformed Church, (therefore part of the Afrikaans-speaking community and almost certainly a Nationalist) who was 'caught' and made the news. When we had been in the country a little longer, and I had made friends with some of my co-workers, we were able to carefully ask more about these questions. It was important that we understood. Many people would employ a black or coloured girl as a domestic worker in their home. Some might employ a young black male gardener. All these people had to be out of the White areas by sundown. Certain jobs were reserved for Whites only. Offices employed young black males to act as messengers, storekeepers, doormen, caretakers, and janitors. They, too, had to leave the white areas by nightfall. Unemployment among the black community was high. Teenage boys on the Grand Parade (the central public square), which was used as a car park and where a Farmers' Market took place at the weekends, offered to 'take care' of your car while you shopped. This meant, if you were willing to reward them, your car would not be broken into or otherwise interfered with. Respectable looking English-speaking young black men were employed at 'OK Bazaars', a budget department store and supermarket, packing the purchased items into bags. They would carry them to your car for a small tip. The cashiers at the till were always white. There was much to learn and adjust to here.

The Pass Laws also came into force at about the same time the Immorality Act was passed. This required all black persons to carry their pass with them at all times; the Africans called it their *situpa*. The Pass was a document of identity that detailed place of birth and current address etc. and was similar to a passport. Having this Pass made it possible for wealthy people to have live-in servants, and for farmers to have Bantu (indigenous native people) permanently settled to work on their land. A black person found without a Pass was punished. White people used to carrying their identification, driving license, or passport, wondered why the native people hated the Pass Laws. But it meant they weren't able to move about freely in their own land, so they found the law repressive. It was clearly a means of controlling the black population.

We celebrated a quiet Christmas together and moved into the New Year. Our life settled into one of routine. We desperately needed a car, so we were carefully saving our money. January became very hot. It was difficult to sleep at night. Air conditioning was practically unknown in Cape Town. We welcomed the 'South-Easter' when it blew; that wind at least moved the warm air about. It was not possible to cool off in the ocean, although we both enjoyed the beach when it was not too windy. The sea was rather rough and extremely cold. There was a strong current brushing up the Cape peninsular, the Benguela Current, which originated in the Antarctic. My friends at work talked about the comfortable, warmer waters off the beaches along the eastern side at Muizenberg and Fish Hoek on False Bay. This was a popular resort area where one could enjoy the warmer waters of the Agulhas Current from the Indian Ocean. But until we had our own wheels, we weren't able to travel that far. While at work, at least my south-facing office was not in direct sun, but by the end of the day, it was sweltering on the streets, and the bus ride home was steamy with so many bodies crowded together. But the days passed quickly enough because I was keen to take charge of my new responsibilities. In less busy moments, I helped out other colleagues by typing covering letters to accompany new share certificates purchased by clients. They were mostly form letters, but I was interested in learning all I could. I made a good friend at the office, Pam Nichols. She and her sister Jean both worked for Syfrets. She would happily tell me about the new house she and her husband had recently bought in Meadowridge, a new 'Garden City' development near Wynberg on the eastern side of the mountain. They had two little girls and not a great deal of money because Pam's husband George had served in the South African Army during the War and this had prevented him from remaining in college to improve his career prospects. Pam kept a '*girl*' who acted as a nanny/housekeeper. Pam's sister Jean lived with them to help with expenses. Michael and I were invited to their home one weekend for afternoon tea. It was a nice, modern one-level home with a garden, which was George's pride and joy. I thought everyone was very kind, and I was anxious to learn how people arranged their lives and what was important to them so that we could fit in. Michael was making friends too. We had met a nice-looking couple, Jo and Denis Goodwin. Denis had met Jo when he stayed for six months in London. Many young English-speaking South Africans travelled overseas to visit England. Such a trip was regarded as a 'coming of age' rite of passage. They enjoyed being away from parental supervision and felt that they became worldlier by the experience, as they undoubtedly did! Denis, since he had an understanding of English ways, was able to explain many things to us about life in his homeland, and Jo, as a relatively newly married Englishwoman, seemed friendly and happy to have some English friends. This couple was highly social; they appeared rather sophisticated to us because drinking was always part of any occasion. They had other young friends; some were married, some not. Every weekend there would be a party somewhere, all their friends lived in apartments on the mountain slopes above the city, and they invited us to join them a few times. I was introduced to South African brandy, very good mixed with ginger ale! Our life was pretty normal for a young newly married couple, but the continued hot weather was beginning to wear me down. I was unusually tired at the end of the hot days in February; I had never been bothered by the heat in England – I loved sunny days. I felt headachy and a little nauseous at the thought of cooking dinner each evening. In fact, I would struggle through getting the food on the table and then not eat anything except perhaps our old standby, a banana with a glass of milk. Michael was also working hard, getting used to his new work and daily routine. He hadn't worked at the tool-making trade for two years, and he had to deal with an oven-like workshop too, although he did have a labourer to help with lifting, etc. He didn't seem to want to notice my lethargy. I thought perhaps my malaise was due to a reaction to the excitement and stress of the past few months. Then another thought struck me, and I really did feel sick; perhaps I was pregnant!

Our life together so far had been most exciting, with some anxious times, too; we hadn't thought much about this possibility. I had kept my appointment at the Family Planning Clinic after we had been married for a few weeks and had been fitted with a device called a 'Dutch Cap' to be used with a special cream. Birth control had been around for many years, but no method was fool proof. That wretched Dutch Cap could easily become dislodged, with some hilarious consequences. I mentioned my worry to Michael, and he was equally dismayed. He quickly asked me if I could be sure. Of course, I was not convinced. One missed period given the circumstances of the changes that had happened in our life was perhaps not remarkable, so we walked about in the sunshine in a bit of a daze for a whole weekend and then decided to put the idea aside while we waited a few more weeks. Early in March, I was no longer in any doubt. My nauseous feelings at the end of the day had reached a point where I couldn't abide touching meat or fish and had to go and lie down for a while when I arrived home each evening until my body temperature cooled. We had got into the habit of eating fish regularly, as it was a good quality cheap meal. 'Stockfish' was less than a shilling (about 25¢) a pound – I had been introduced to this healthy bargain by my friend Pam.

ଚଠ ଔଷ

By March of 1959, four months after our arrival, I was starting to feel that things were beginning to work out for us in this new country. We both had secured relatively well-paying jobs and were living in a beautiful location overlooking the South Atlantic

Ocean. The climate was ideal, and we spent our weekends enjoying the local beaches and travelling by public transport to local attractions in and around Cape Town. Maureen seemed very happy, enjoyed her work, with only a few moments of homesickness from time to time. She was very tanned and looked radiant. We were very much in love and lots of opportunities for passionate moments. But there did seem to be a little glitch developing in our idyllic life; it appeared that Maureen was pregnant. The news should not have surprised me, as we had been rather casual in our birth control methods, but I did start to worry again about how this would change our plans for saving any money. As the days passed and we moved into the winter months, we both relaxed about it, and I began to realise that Maureen actually enjoyed being pregnant and was looking forward to the birth of our child. But I knew I had to think about how we were to manage an increasing family size.

ༀ ༚

One day when my new friend Pam and I both happened to be in the 'Ladies' room together, and no one else was in any of the stalls, I confided my concern to her. She and George belonged to the Roman Catholic Church. She certainly understood birth control could be a problem, but she smiled and embraced me and advised me to see a doctor to make sure. All would be well, she said. I told her I had seen a doctor's office with Dr Humphrey King's name on it, and she said she knew him and his partner Dr Henry Silberbauer, and she said, 'Go ahead, see one of them. You'll like them, and they will take good care of you. Tell them what you suspect. It is generally polite to leave it to the doctor to make the diagnosis.' Pam made me feel somewhat encouraged. I made the appointment for a Saturday morning and off I went. Dr King turned out to be a sizeable genial sort of man with whom I was immediately comfortable. He confirmed the diagnosis and gave me some informative leaflets reminding me I should see him or his partner every month for the next little while. And then I was on my own to deal with this. Michael never said much about this situation. Later he confided he was genuinely concerned about financial considerations and worried about what we would do when the baby came, and I couldn't work. I thought that wasn't going to happen for over half a year – it seemed like ages to me, and before very long, I began to like the idea I was an expectant mother; I had always loved babies.

So, fascinated about the whole process, I bought a very good 'Before the Baby - and After' book. Having no family to talk to, I found everything I needed to know in my book, which I studied quite devotedly, and Michael ignored completely. I wondered if he was trying to convince himself this wasn't going to happen. As time went along, my body didn't seem to change much. Dr King said at another appointment that it was because I was tall, but nausea would sometimes overwhelm me in waves, especially towards the end of the day when I was a little tired, and I wasn't exactly eating very much. I was beginning to struggle with my workload. For various reasons, I was delayed until 6.00 pm quite often now. The Stock Exchange was experiencing a boom. Cynthia or Diana were quite willing to stay behind if I asked them to, but sometimes when things were quiet at around 5.00 pm, and I told them I could manage alone, there would be a last-minute rush, and I didn't like to go back on my word just before they were due to leave the office. They were young single girls looking forward to evening activities. I, on the other hand, had quite a long wait at the bus stop after frantically typing the notes. Then I would stand in line for the later bus, the bumpy bus ride around the mountain, and a long walk up Camps Bay Drive, sometimes in a 40 mile an hour gale with my feet hurting. My journey home did not seem so pleasant now.

Early in April, a new girl had appeared in my office. She was engaged for a brief time as a temporary relief typist to fill in for another girl who was on holiday. She seemed a confident, well-educated girl who told me she simply didn't like full-time work; she preferred to work in different places for short periods and not be stuck in one job with the same bunch of people, always doing repetitive work. So, I decided that perhaps being a 'Temp' typist would give me more flexibility in view of my condition, which I hadn't revealed to my employers or anyone other than Pam. So, I requested an interview with Mr Stanley. I hadn't had any conversation with him since the first interview. When he indicated he could see me now, Mr St John said, to everyone's amusement, 'You know, Mrs Harbott, you have to have at least £10,000 to invest to talk to Mr Stanley.' This statement caused everyone to laugh. I simply smiled and entered the office. Mr Stanley greeted me kindly and said they were pleased with my work, and I thanked him but told him a new consideration had entered my life. I told him I was pregnant, and it wasn't yet public knowledge. I had requested to speak to him because I wanted to give notice. The long working day was proving a little too much for me. He asked if I could continue until the end of the month, and I agreed that I thought I could, and we shook hands. He wished me well, and I left his office, went back to my desk, and got on with my work.

Of course, I soon had to share my secret. Cynthia and Diana showed great interest and concern and made sure I was never left alone to finish the notes the remainder of the time I was employed there. I learned these nice girls were so interested because they had never been given any information about sex education, and they perceived in me a source for all the information they wanted and needed. Both had gone to private schools; Cynthia was 18 years old, and Diana, the daughter of a wealthy farmer who grew winemaking grapes on the family estate at Constantia, was 20. She was planning to go to England the following year to work and 'see the world' a bit, as so many young South Africans did. Her plans were already known at a higher level, which is probably why Mr Stanley had attached me to them. I very matter-of-factly gave them what basic informative leaflets I had and showed them my baby book. I couldn't believe young women were still so 'sheltered', although I remembered my mother had once told me she went into marriage and having children knowing absolutely nothing. So, I continued working through the month, planning to have some time to myself at the end of it and then to look into getting temporary work.

Cynthia, who lived the other side (the protected from the wind side) of Camps Bay, and whose father was a banker, invited Michael and me to a *Braai-Vleis*, the Afrikaans word for barbecue, at her home to meet some young friends of her family and her parents. We had shared a meal in the homes of some of our young friends, but this was the first time we had received an invitation to a well-established older couple's home. I knew it would be a lovely home. We took our usual care with our appearance and made our way to the given address. It was a beautiful home, but the party was outside on the patio, and the other guests, another young married couple, were already assembled. They were casually dressed. We didn't know a *Braai* meant casual wear. Anyway, it was a pleasant group, and we had a nice evening. When the meat was ready, Cynthia went around doling out half-yards of toilet paper – she apologised for the absence of paper napkins. We didn't care; this was our first experience of outdoor dining. We'd never known anything like it in suburban London! Michael told me, as we were walking home in the still, velvet night, the young man who was also at the party had chatted with him about cars. The idea of getting one was still Michael's main ambition. This young man kindly advised him that he should look at Jaguar cars, because 'they are built so well, you know, and have such good resale value.' Apparently, he had a Jaguar, and his young wife had a Mercedes, a wedding gift from her father! We laughed. What did *they* know about being a new immigrant, especially a *hard-up* one! Michael was thinking about a second-hand older Hillman Minx. Towards the end of May, we bought that car! We were so excited. The only problem was that Michael had no experience of driving cars. And, he didn't have a driving license.

ಬ ಚ

Now it had been confirmed that Maureen was indeed pregnant, it became immediately clear to me that we *had* to have independent transportation. My weekday ride with big Harry was causing a little anxiety as he was a strange person with a very uncertain temper. I never had any driving lessons or even a driving test in England, only ever a learner's licence for the scooter. I had obtained a learner's licence here, but it required a qualified driver to be with me. Fortunately for me in South Africa, as in most British possessions abroad, they drove on the left, thus reducing some of the anxiety. We had seen an older model (1952) Hillman Minx, on a car lot on the outskirts of the city. I remembered in

England they were regarded as reliable family-type cars. The salesman was offering an extended payment plan. This meant, with a small down payment, we could pay it off in one year. I believe the total price of the car was around £200. As I could not afford to have driving lessons, we decided to buy the car anyway, and I would teach myself to drive, totally illegal, of course. We paid a deposit and arranged to pick the car up at the showroom at about 6.30 pm on a Friday evening when we had both finished working. After signing the papers, I asked the salesman if he would drive us to the edge of town, saying I was not used to much traffic. I didn't mention that I only had a learner's licence and had never driven a car in my life. After explaining the controls, he left us on a slight incline. Following a few stalls and a jerky start with the manual gearshift, we were on our way to Sea Point and home. But fate was against us as the sky darkened in the form of a very heavy thunderstorm. After a while, we could barely see where we were going in the heavy rain and lightning flashes, so decided it would be safer to pull over until the storm passed. As we were on a busy road, I decided to turn into a side road, which went down a steep hill and ended in a 'no exit'. My attempt to make a turn resulted in the car stalling. We sat for a while until the rain began to ease up. Now the car would not start. I had very little knowledge of car engines, and the night had become very dark, so I decided we had to abandon the car, find the main road somewhere below us and catch a bus home.

We both felt very disappointed, and I hoped the car was not a lemon. The next morning the sun was shining, and I told Maureen to stay put, and somehow, I would get that car home. She was very anxious about the whole thing. Taking the bus back to Sea Point, even though I was not at all sure where I had left it, I located the car surprisingly easily, and to my relief, the engine started at the first attempt. I now had to turn around on a steep hill, a task I cautiously managed and drove very carefully back to Camps Bay, feeling rather pleased with myself. Maureen had been watching the road and waiting anxiously for me and came running out to greet me with a big hug. On the following Monday, I made an appointment for a driving test to take place in two weeks, so I had very little time to brush up on my driving skills.

My work was going well, and I found it interesting and not overly challenging. Harry was becoming more difficult. He had agreed to give another fellow who was having car troubles a ride. This guy had a habit of whistling as we drove. Harry became annoyed with the whistling, so he abruptly stopped the car and told him to get out and walk the rest of the way to the factory. No one argued with Harry! Our route to work took us through the downtown part of the city; I did not feel confident about city driving yet, but I felt the urgent need to become legal. So each evening for the next two weeks, after a quick supper, Maureen and I jumped in the car and headed south where there was very little traffic, and I taught myself how to drive. If we were short of time on weekdays, we took a route down the winding coast road, across a pass behind Table Mountain, through the vineyards at Constantia to the higher southern suburbs of Cape Town and back into Camps Bay over another mountain pass called Kloof Nek. When we became braver, we went further south towards the Cape of Good Hope - a much longer drive. This required travelling on a very beautiful road that had been carved out of the mountainside at about 500 feet above sea-level, with a sheer drop into the ocean below. This road, Chapman's Peak Drive, descended quite steeply, twisting and turning with few safety barriers. There were car wrecks visible in the surf below. At night, when going around the curves, the beams from the headlights would shine off into black space. On 28th April 1959, I went into Cape Town and successfully passed the test. Were we relieved!

Since arriving in South Africa, we had been able to enjoy the sun, and the beaches and Maureen looked very beautiful with a nice tan and very trim figure. Now that she was pregnant, she seemed to have an extra glow about her, and I knew she was looking forward to being a mother. I, on the other hand, had lost weight. Being so far away from our family and expecting a child, we felt we should create a record of our activities here. Since our marriage, we had hardly taken any pictures and had little record of our voyage to Africa or our early days in the Cape. We had taken a few shots with a very cheap box camera, and I had borrowed a cine-camera for a short time from a friend, but we decided we would now buy our own. As money was scarce, we bought a cheap

Kodak Brownie cine-camera and started to take a few moving pictures.

ॐ ☙

Buying the car brought greater freedom and interest to our lives. I seemed able to put nausea and tiredness aside and was always ready to accompany Michael on those wild rides around the mountain every evening. Before I left Syfrets, Pam had advised that we ought to look for a cheaper flat. So, we looked into accommodation in the Southern Suburbs and thus began another chaotic period. Michael was never one with much patience for 'shopping', whether it was for regular purchases in stores or searching for a more suitable place to bring a baby home to. The next few months were not as happy as those first few months had been. If I had been able to look around on my own, perhaps the search would have been more productive, but since Michael, now a completely legal driver, had to take me to look at places, we made the mistake of deciding too quickly on the first one in Rosebank, which was close to a better suburb called Rondebosch which I really would have preferred. This apartment, which we viewed when the current tenants were present, was quite well furnished, had a good bedroom and a large bathroom, but hadn't been very well looked after. It was a bit bleak-looking and was right next to the railway tracks.

We moved in at the beginning of June. There weren't many trains, but the early morning one would pass with a piercing whistle, which concerned me a bit. The drying yard for the laundry was dank and smelled of dogs; I refused to use it. I hung my laundry on the *stoep* (front porch), and the next day Michael came home from work quite annoyed with me because someone in the block had complained to the landlord, who had called him at work to tell him all of Rosebank was in an uproar. I realised I could never be happy there, especially as a closer inspection had allowed me to see that the kitchen floor in this place was coated with a considerable layer of dirt, which I knew I could never shift. It was not at all suitable for a child. Feeling very 'down' and depressed, I suggested to Michael he should tell the landlord we would be moving out at the end of the month. Then another place for us had to be found. Off he went to look at a place in Oranjezicht, which was an area close to Leeuwen Street, where we had stayed in a guest house when we arrived in Cape Town. He came back from his foray and said he had just the place. It was the second floor of an old but well-kept house where the landlord, who was in a wheelchair, and his housekeeper lived on the ground floor. It was a pleasant location, very clean and well furnished, close to town and the 'Company's Garden' so we thought it might be very nice and we agreed to move in at the beginning of July.

My mother sent me a little money to help me buy a second-hand sewing machine that I had seen. I had made a few clothes for myself ever since I was about 13 and knew if I continued to do that, it would help our financial situation a little. When I was no longer working, I would have plenty of time available for what was, to me, a useful and pleasant pastime. Realising that I probably needed a little help, she also sent me two summer dresses she had quickly made from one of my old patterns, to wear after the baby came. I thought that a very loving and thoughtful thing for her to do. We bought the sewing machine, and I made a dress for my friend Diana's 21st party, which would camouflage my slightly expanded waistline. I didn't look very pregnant until I got to the eighth month, but I knew my shape was definitely changing.

At the party, we met Diana's twin sister Maria and their family. It was a wonderful experience driving to that lovely estate in the Constantia valley, where the family had been growing wine grapes for many generations. It was a glimpse of the gracious life that had been lived in the beautiful old Cape Dutch style farmhouse for a few hundred years, and I was delighted to get out of that apartment for a few hours. No longer working, I enquired at the Employment Bureau about temporary work. Immediately I was offered six weeks with an insurance company called Legal & General. I knew this name – Legal & General was a well-known, old established English company. I hadn't known that, like the big banks, they had branches throughout the British Commonwealth too. I was to act as the Branch Manager's secretary, seated right outside his door in a general office while his regular secretary, a very nice woman who showed me the work, had an overseas vacation with her husband. I began with this company mid-way through June, and the position would last until the end of July when, according to Dr King's calculations, there would be about six more weeks of my pregnancy. I began the happy task of collecting a few of the items I would need for our infant, using my trusty baby book's recommendations and looking forward to being in brighter, happier accommodation.

On 1st of July, we moved yet again to Oranjezicht. This quickly turned into a disaster. When Michael returned from his first visit there, he told me he had been invited into their living room in a pleasant way, where Mr Van der Merwe and his housekeeper were having a drink together. He was offered a glass of brandy because they said they were celebrating the gentleman's birthday. Michael chatted a little and was shown the accommodation and thought it superior to any that we had yet had. A few days later, we had gone together to see the property. On this occasion, they were enjoying a drink with their current tenant, a young woman who worked for the government who would be leaving at the weekend because government employees would be departing Cape Town for their regular six-month session in Pretoria. Once again, a glass of brandy was offered, which I declined, indicating my condition. We asked if having a baby and our little cat in the house was acceptable to them. It was a very spacious house with a sundeck on the upper level – they thought having a new baby in the house would be very nice and there was a big garden for the cat. I was shown up the wide staircase, which made three turns to reach the top, by the younger woman who spoke careful English, but she told me she was bilingual; Afrikaans was her native tongue. The upper-level apartment was indeed bright, spacious, and very clean. I liked what I saw. So, Michael wrote a cheque for the first month's rent, and we returned to Rosebank rather pleased with our 'find'.

All went well on moving-in day. We only had personal belongings to move, including bed linen, clothing, pots and pans, and an ironing board. Our car held everything. Oranjezicht was a lovely area of Cape Town just above the Company's Garden. I would be able to walk down a couple of old-established tree-lined streets and through the gardens to my office on Adderley Street in about 20 minutes. Walking home would take a little longer because it was all uphill. I realised the very first day that although walking was a good exercise at the end of a day's work, it was also tiring. When I reached the house, the main idea on my mind was getting off my feet and relaxing on the bed with a cup of tea. Mamie, the housekeeper, always seemed to be hanging around the entrance when I arrived home and I would exchange a word or two with her, and quickly head for the stairs. We became aware that Mr Van der Merwe and his housekeeper would drink together every evening – sometimes they were a little noisy. On a day in the second week of our tenancy, I hardly paused but smiled and greeted Mamie on my way to the staircase. She began muttering to herself, but I went on up and closed the kitchen door and put my kettle on. When Michael came in, she met him with a tirade against me. She had taken a dislike to me because I wouldn't 'be sociable' with them; they must have begun drinking earlier that day. She followed Michael up the stairs, becoming more abusive. He had never had to deal with a situation like this. He almost pushed the old girl down the stairs. Poor Mr Van der Merwe in his wheelchair was yelling up the stairs for Mamie to leave us alone and come down. It was a terrible scene, and I was quite frightened and now in tears. Now, what could we do? When things quietened down, Michael went down to Mr Van der Merwe and told him regretfully we really couldn't remain there and would leave at the end of the month, and he didn't want any repeat performance from Mamie. Once again, we had to begin house-hunting, and we had learned we should avoid a live-in landlord.

Preferring the proximity of the city, we now researched Vredehoek, which was quite close to Oranjezicht, but towards Devil's Peak, which adjoins the eastern part of Table Mountain. This was a well built-up area of a few nice older homes and many apartment blocks, mostly owned or managed by the same company. Once again, we found a partly furnished one-bedroom ground floor flat on a quiet road, with a wonderful view of the mountain behind us. This block with eight apartments was called Herzlia Court. Our living room looked out onto the entrance pathway, bordered by a narrow garden. It was furnished very simply with a dining table and four chairs and two armchairs flanking a small coffee table. There were no carpets or rugs and only skimpy curtains. The bedroom had a not very comfortable double bed and a chest of drawers. The kitchen had a small table and two stools, a clean electric stove and a small fridge. The wash lines were out the back in a nice grassy area, and from here, we could observe the back of the apartment block next to us, and most neighbours we noticed employed a 'coloured girl' as a housemaid to help take care of them.

My temporary job had been completed, and I signed up for childbirth and relaxation classes with a well-known teacher, Lore Sternweiler, and went to study with her twice weekly. Natural childbirth was thought to be the best and most appropriate method of delivering a healthy baby for a healthy mother. In the United States, many women preferred to have a painless birth, with whatever help modern medicine could provide. The U.S. seemed to have some influence on South African life. There were many American women's magazines available, and I had already seen that having an 'American kitchen' was an important feature of new homes being built. But St Joseph's Hospital, where we had registered for the delivery of our baby, staffed mainly by an order of German nuns as well as many forward-thinking doctors in South Africa, believed 'natural' childbirth was the only way to go. I joined in with a class of six other women all in the third trimester of pregnancy. They were quite surprised that I was now in my eighth month, and there were some breathing exercises I could do better than they could, because of the way I was carrying this baby. It was a bit expensive to have these classes, but I thought that in the absence of having my mother or sister to talk to, this was probably the best course. I hoped Dr Sternweiler's advice would help me feel confident about the birth. So now began the time to get ready! We bought a second-hand baby crib that Michael carefully painted and a new mattress. I had purchased crib sheets and a blanket, waterproof pants, and English-style nappies (diapers), undershirts, and back-fastening nighties. These were quite expensive, but I knew they would stand up well to washing. I discovered that South African girls tended to buy cheap flannelette squares and fold them into 'kite' style for nappies. In the absence of a washing machine, or a girl to do the laundry, I knew I would have to launder everything by hand in the bathtub on a rippled washboard. But I had always enjoyed taking good care of the fabric, so it didn't matter. A local drug store provided me with a baby scale, which I could borrow for a few months. In return, they, of course, wanted me to buy everything I needed from their store. Since they offered free delivery of anything I needed, of course, I agreed.

I made friends with an English girl, Pam, who lived above us with her husband, Brian. They came from the Lake District. She was a tiny, pretty little thing who had been a ballet dancer. They had a son a few months old, Andrew. I met her when she came down with her *nappies* to peg them out on the wash line. They were a quiet, private couple, but I thought when our baby arrived, we probably would be able to enjoy a chat over a cup of tea occasionally.

My due date approached, and I was getting nervous. Michael had been working hard and not saying much about the approaching event. He had taken me to meet a new friend of his, Alan Penfold and his wife, Joan. They lived in Mowbray in a tiny little cottage and had a baby girl, Lynette. Joan was a sweet girl, an excellent housekeeper and cook. She seemed very friendly and interested in seeing us after our baby was born, but shortly after this, they moved away to live in Northern Rhodesia. I have to confess I was getting thoroughly fed up with wearing those same old clothes and being pregnant and became depressed when the due date came - and went.

My doctor had been pleased with my progress and asked me to telephone him as soon as I knew I was in labour. I saw him weekly now. He was not concerned about my being overdue and planned to deliver the baby when the time came. After waiting two whole weeks, one night after falling asleep, I woke at about 2.00 am, and I felt something might be happening. I woke Michael, and together we walked down the road in the bright moonlight to the public telephone box. We had never had a telephone because our parents in England didn't yet have phones, so we had no one to call. The call box was circular, and Michael pulled the door open, but I couldn't lift my foot high enough to step inside, there seemed to be a dark mass in the way. I softly said to Michael, 'I can't get in.' He pushed the dark mass with his foot, and a young black man lifted his woolly head and scrambled out. He should not have been in that 'white' area so late at night, but we felt a little sorry for him having nowhere else to sleep. I stepped in and made the call. Dr

King suggested we go home and, if my slight cramping continued until morning, we should go to St Joseph's Hospital. The staff there would call him and let him know what was happening. We allowed the young black man to re-enter the call box, and Michael put his arm around me, and we walked together back to our home. I knew these moments together were precious; we soon would have another life to care about.

At home, I ran a warm bath, checked over the contents of my suitcase, and crawled back into bed for a few hours. Michael usually was a good sleeper, so he quickly went back to sleep, but I dozed a little here and there; I was quite sure this was not a false alarm. At 6.30 am, I woke Michael and asked him to make some tea. He had a little breakfast, and by 7.00 am, we were on our way to St Joseph's at Pinelands. The admittance formalities were soon over, and I was shown to a private labour/delivery room. Michael stayed a little while but decided he should go to work and call in again around lunchtime. We had no idea how long this was going to take, and the staff needed to 'prep' me and observe how far apart and how strong the contractions were. I was encouraged to walk around. It became a very long day. Dr King looked in and told me things were going rather slowly, but the nuns would keep him informed, so off he went again. Michael came in a bit sheepishly at lunchtime. I wasn't very hungry; in fact, I felt a little sick, so he ate my lunch, then decided he would go back to work, leaving me to struggle on, but he spent the evening with me. I was still walking around managing to remember my breathing exercises and pausing when there was a contraction – I was getting exhausted. It was a horrible night. Michael left for a few hours of sleep, promising to come back early the next morning. By then, I was really in trouble – I didn't think I could go on anymore. Dr King came in and had a conference with the supervisor nun, who was my midwife. They were monitoring me carefully and decided that if we didn't get to the pushing stage soon, the Operating Room would be the place for me. I was moaning and gasping when Michael arrived. Not a pretty sight. This 'natural childbirth' was tough. Michael tried to keep me company that morning, but I hardly cared. I began to hear sounds overhead with things being dragged around. Michael was banished. They were making the Operating Room ready, and suddenly I was in the transition stage, and it was time to push. I was so-o-o tired. I didn't think I could, but with the encouragement of the patient nun and Dr King, I began to gather my strength together. When I put my mind to it, I pushed so hard they had to slow me down. So, I did the work, and Stephen slid into the world at 12.30 pm on 30th September 1959, weighing 7 lbs 7 oz. Poor baby, he must have been shell-shocked, too.

The nuns wrapped up the baby and put him in my arms. I was overjoyed but felt incredibly weak – my arms could barely hold on to him. He was taken off to the nursery. Michael appeared, and I told him we had a son, and then I seemed to drift away and didn't know what was going on for the next little while. Our parents in England had become very anxious as the baby was overdue, and they had had no news from us. Michael's first thought when he left me was to go straight to the main Post Office to send telegrams to both sets of parents. I became aware of my surroundings several hours later in another room, I was sore all over, but fresh and clean, wearing one of my own nighties and feeling very drowsy. In those days, a new mother had an opportunity to get a good rest after having a baby. Because I had such a hard time, I needed more bed rest for a few days. The staff was terrific. I had a perky, young, but very experienced nurse, not a nun, to care for me. But at feeding time, it was always one of the gentle Sisters that brought Stephen to me. The first time he was brought to me, I recognised him but checked his hospital bracelet just to be sure! Breastfeeding didn't go very well, but we all tried very hard. On day five, I was allowed to join Dr Sternweiler's class for gentle exercises to help my body begin to recover its normal form. She came twice a week to help 'her' mothers in recovery. Since I had a private room, it was very nice to see other new mothers in the class and swap our various stories. Mr Bob Hinings, one of my colleagues from Legal & General, surprised me with a visit and brought flowers. I felt a little shaky about going home. After about nine days, Dr King, on one of his regular visits, asked me if I would prefer to bottle feed my infant. He thought since the supply was so limited and because I had no one to help me at home, having the total care of my baby and my home responsibilities would likely make breastfeeding too difficult. I had sweated through those feeding sessions, but I was sure my strong boy would prefer a better supply than I seemed able to provide, so I accepted the formula that was offered, and on the 11th day after delivery, Michael brought us home. It was a beautiful sunny day, my dear cat, Ruffy came to greet me; I felt well and ready to assume the role of Stephen's mother fully.

Our rented house in Camps Bay

Pleased with our first car and being pregnant!

Chapman's Peak is not an easy place to learn to drive!

7.
Motherhood

Maureen

Michael took our picture on the beautiful sunny day we took our first child home. We were so proud and happy, and I felt just wonderful. Since Stephen was to be bottle-fed, I had to get set up, and off Michael immediately went to our chemist to buy the supplies we needed. The formula I had been given required regular cow's milk, which had been brought to the boil, modified with boiled water plus sugar. Fortunately, we had a refrigerator in this apartment, so I could make up a batch and store it safely. Every ten days, I had to adjust the amount of water added to one pint of milk, until at the age of three months or so he would be drinking straight whole cow's milk. The formula seemed to suit Stephen very well. It was necessary to observe a high standard of hygiene and sterilise everything. In a hot climate in Africa, many babies are lost through various intestinal infections. I was quite determined to be extra vigilant. My trusty book gave me all the information I needed.

The first few days at home with a new baby are always chaotic. Michael had to go off to work, leaving me all alone with Stephen. My doctor had arranged an appointment for the postpartum check-up in November and told me to give his office a call if I became worried about anything. So, until then, I was on my own. Stephen was a fairly good baby, but I was amazed at how much laundry he made and how much time I spent feeding, changing, sterilising the equipment (in my new pressure cooker), and doing the laundry, as well as making meals and keeping the flat tidy. There seemed to be very little time for simply rocking my baby. Within quite a short space of time, I was more tired than I had ever been, and Michael must have felt neglected. It was quite hard to greet him each evening with a smile!

As do most new-borns, Stephen needed feeding every three to four hours around the clock at first. He only drank about two and a half ounces each time. My book advised not to take a new baby out for four to six weeks. It was thought wise to protect them

168

from other people's germs. The sunshine was very bright; I knew his eyes needed protection from it. But when a few weeks had passed; we could have a little trip out in the car at the weekend.

I was anxious to get a baby carriage, and foolishly, I wanted an English-style pram. We bought a second-hand one, a Silver Cross – it was beautiful, a wonderfully smooth wheeling, quite impressive carriage, but much too large. We lived on a hill, and on my first visit to the well-baby clinic, I realised right away that I had made a mistake because coming home uphill was a challenge. I continued to go to the clinic, although I knew my baby was gaining weight and progressing quite well. Here Stephen was able to participate in the free infant immunisation programme, and because I felt so isolated and lonely, I wanted to begin to make some new friends. I saw my neighbour from upstairs, Pam, but she was always with her other friend whose baby was the same age as hers, so getting to know her was a slow process. At home alone, I could quickly become depressed, but I was busy all the time. My back was very sore still; it had become painful towards the end of the pregnancy, and leaning over the bathtub to scrub the laundry was not my favourite thing. The worst item was Michael's workshop coat, which I washed about every two weeks. That took some scrubbing. I wished I could be relieved of that job. A few days before I was to keep my six-week appointment with Dr King at his downtown office, I was sitting one afternoon as usual peacefully feeding the baby with the sunshine slanting into our living room. He had been focussing his eyes on my face for a while. It was a very intent look, and I almost thought he was wondering who I was. Suddenly his mouth relaxed, and the nipple popped out of his mouth. His eyes met mine, and he smiled at me. What an amazing moment. I fell in love with my son right then – that moment of a connection made such a difference. I understood the love between us could flow both ways.

I forgot my fatigue and other difficulties – motherhood was wonderful. Stephen loved his feedings, and I began to know when he had taken almost enough milk because the smiles would begin. I survived to the six-week mark and went down, quite triumphantly, on the bus to keep my appointment with Dr King at his downtown office. My infant was admired, and I was welcomed and congratulated and pronounced fit. Carrying him in my arms, wrapped in a hand-knitted shawl my sister Pam had made for him, I walked along Adderley Street, where a street photographer snapped our picture. I was on my way to Stuttafords. I needed at least a window-shopping fix.

Stephen was beginning to sleep longer at night and was soon sleeping right through from about 11.00 pm until Michael got up for work at 6.30 am. He gradually assumed a very happy, outgoing personality and charmed everyone who saw him. It took his Daddy a while to get used to the ways a baby behaves. Michael never had contact with any baby before becoming a father. Very occasionally, he would help feed Stephen, and he tried to join in our playtime when it was bath time. Michael was very good about agreeing with my suggestions with regard to Stephen – he didn't have enough experience to offer any other ideas of his own. He took pictures of Stephen and me and seemed proud of us both, and I knew he loved us. But I think the responsibility of having a wife and child weighed heavily on him.

When Stephen was a little older, I gave up on that big baby carriage and sold it, and we bought a stroller. Occasionally we would go out for an early dinner to a nearby restaurant at the top of the Company's Garden. I would feed Stephen before we went, and he would sit in the stroller, smiling at everyone. I would keep him busy by passing him pieces of bread – he loved food from the beginning. The staff would be so complimentary about how well he behaved; then, it was quite evident his Daddy was proud of him. Another outing we could enjoy now Stephen was a little older was going to see a film at a Drive-in Cinema. We didn't go very often, but we still loved a good movie. We would cheerfully drive over 20 miles to spend a couple of hours with the speaker, transmitting the soundtrack of the film, hooked onto the slightly lowered car window. Stephen would be fast asleep on the back seat.

We lived at Herzlia Court for just over a year. We had been on short trips and appreciated the magnificent beauty of the Cape Peninsular. Stephen was a joy. Such a happy, friendly boy who was growing fast; a good traveller, he seldom cried. He was a big chubby fellow. Of course, I thought him the most beautiful baby ever. I began to want us to buy some furnishings of our own. My back was still bothering me – we badly needed a better bed, our own bed! We had acquired more stuff for Stephen, who slept in our bedroom. We took a daily newspaper, so I soon discovered from the Cape Argus how much things cost and where the best prices were. Our apartment was very sparsely furnished. There was an oiled parquet floor in the living room, but no carpet. I thought that as my energetic baby began to move around, he would get too dirty. He didn't seem too ambitious in that area. He seemed very happy sitting outside the kitchen door in his highchair, waving his arms and kicking his legs to the delight of the people (and their maid) that lived opposite.

I still craved for Camps Bay. Perhaps Michael wanted to please me – life was not that easy in Vredehoek, there were no shops or parks nearby. So once again, we began looking at apartments - unfurnished ones this time. I had learned that some stores allowed qualified customers to pay over three months, with no finance charges, on certain items. I had been very frugal, and we had spent almost no money on clothes, entertainment, or recreation. We found we could just about afford a very nice two-bedroom unfurnished flat in a newish, attractive, modern block of 15 apartments on three levels right at the top of Camps Bay Drive. There were no buildings at all at a higher level than this one. The view behind was of the upward sloping bush where flowering proteas and other indigenous plants grew up to the base of the Twelve Apostles, the western flank of Table Mountain. At this new location, the living/dining room and main bedroom faced the spectacular view of the ocean, and I knew I could easily make some curtains for those beautiful picture windows. The smaller bedroom, kitchen, and bathroom were on the back. This apartment was ideal because it meant the baby's room would not get too much sun in the late afternoon. Throughout the apartment, except for the kitchen and bathroom, which were tiled, the floors were dark red Rhodesian teak, polished to a gleaming shine. The flats were approached up a flight of stone steps; also, it could be very windy. At the street level, there was a garage for each apartment, and lawns and gardens surrounded the block. A coloured general handyman attended each day. Johannes was a little slow, but kept the grass cut and collected up the garbage daily. He was generally available to help the residents if heavy lifting was required. In Vredehoek on Mondays, I'd had to start my laundry at 6.00 am and get it on the wash lines before 8.00 am. Because of the bright sun or brisk wind, it never took very long to dry the laundry in Cape Town. If I delayed getting my Monday wash out there, the maids from the other apartments would use up all the space and 'forget' to take in their clothes when they dried. In Camps Bay, there was a big paved area with wash lines that were never full. These things were rather important to me. I always wanted to get the chores done quickly and efficiently and early!

We moved back to Camps Bay on 1st September 1960. I had met a very friendly salesman at a store, and we bought a good double bed and a small dining set veneered in Sapele mahogany. He arranged for the 'no finance charges' when we made a down-payment. Like everyone else, this man was very impressed with our lively, friendly boy just 11 months old and seemed to want to help us. I never realised that a happy, beautiful child could be such a useful accessory. Michael, who liked to listen to the radio, bought a good one made by Pye. It was in an attractive wooden case and could receive short-wave signals. He wanted to listen to the Overseas Services of the BBC (British Broadcasting Corporation) and Voice of America. A talented coloured carpenter at his work made him a beautiful cabinet to hold the radio and our record player. We started collecting a few LPs; Ella Fitzgerald, Johnny Mathis, Doris Day and Frank Sinatra were our favourites and very popular with the general public. The galley kitchen at the apartment included a good electric stove; we bought a small used fridge from friends who were leaving Cape Town. My precious set of stainless steel, copper-bottomed cooking pots were proudly hung on the kitchen wall, and I set up my sterilising 'station'. Although the early introduction of 'mixed feeding' was widespread in the 50s, Stephen still liked his bed-time bottle. I was determined to make this place our home. I was delighted to be back in Camps Bay and didn't mind at all that those Rhodesian teak floors needed hand polishing.

I renewed my acquaintance with Marta Spearman. It was nice to have someone who almost qualified as an old friend. Marta was going to have a baby. Due to childhood illnesses, she had only one lung. Having a child was a hazardous business for her. I guessed her husband needed a son to inherit the title. She presented him eventually with a daughter, Wendy. Ruffy, our cat, came with us to Camps Bay; he'd been very happy in Vredehoek. Across Ludlow Road, opposite Herzlia Court, there was a large park-like private piece of land with big trees. He used to roam and hunt there. One day Michael found him just outside the apartment block. He thought poor Ruffy had been hit by a car. We were dreadfully upset to see our pet in such a condition. We put him in a box and hurried off to the SPCA unit. The vet soothed us when he said they could help him. He came back to us a few days later with his tummy sewn up; he'd had surgery for internal repairs. I wouldn't let him out until his stitches were removed, but in no time at all, he was back to his old wandering ways even though he had been neutered as a kitten. He would sit on the brick half-wall of our *stoep* and leap high into the air to try to catch the birds that nested in the trees in the lovely garden of the house opposite our apartment. It was a wonder he didn't break his legs when he came down onto the pathway. I thought he would be safer in our new home because there weren't many cars on Camps Bay Drive, and there was plenty of natural bush for him to explore.

We celebrated Stephen's first birthday quietly in our new home. Our parents and my sister sent cards and gifts. Michael's mother sent a beautiful two-piece scarlet suit. I thought it would fit when the cooler weather came. He was a large, very healthy child weighing over 30 lbs at 12 months. He would sit very happily in one place with his toys strewn around, watching me go about my work. Of course, I was his slave and would put in his hand whatever he wanted. I didn't encourage him too much to try out his legs because he was so heavy – I worried about the possibility of them not growing straight. He eventually devised his own method of moving about. Sitting straight up, he would shuffle along on his bottom by pushing both heels together, first to the left side, and then to the right. He would do a few extra paddles to one side to steer himself around a corner. In this way, he made his legs strong, and when he did walk at just over 17 months, within a couple of weeks, he was walking and running as well as any other boy of his age. I had left him to work out the problem of learning to walk on the advice of my doctor.

I was seeing Dr King again. There must have been something special in the air of Camps Bay; I was pregnant again. At my request, Dr King had fitted me with a diaphragm after having Stephen. It was bigger than the Dutch Cap and similarly ineffective. Further proof, we were not very good at birth control. Once again, I had the bouts of nausea and tiredness. Of course, I now had a lively toddler to keep up with, but I loved our home in Camps Bay, I knew all about what having a baby entailed now and was sure we could manage another child. Michael wasn't so sure!

To help out financially, when Legal & General called me to fill in for another six-week stint, I thought it might help fill the waiting time and augment our income if I accepted the temporary job. My neighbours, Paula and Jack Kilgour, who had a little boy called Murray, sometimes used a day-care in Bantry Bay, which was next to Sea Point. I thought since Stephen was such a placid and happy, friendly boy, he would probably be happy enough there and get used to the idea that there were other small people in the world at the same time. I accepted the job. I could drop Stephen off with his supplies in the morning, catch the next bus and arrive in the city in good time to do a day's work. I knew the job very well, and I was glad to see the friends I had made at the office again.

That little interlude went quite well, although I didn't mention to Michael that I thought the day-care person did not allow as much exercise as I felt her charges should have, and she was not as careful about diaper hygiene either. But Stephen came to no harm. When Christmas came, I was invited to attend the Christmas party with the other Legal & General employees. I quickly made myself a white dress, which set off my tan, and we all went out to dinner and had a social time in the restaurant lounge afterwards. Bob Hinings and another young man I worked closely with, Keith Shaw, were extremely attentive, too attentive to my way of thinking. I guess I had forgotten how the men in offices behaved over the Christmas period, passing out drinks, flirting, and expecting kisses. I didn't care for too much of that. Bob Hinings, who was a widower, had visited me at home and once very kindly took Stephen and me for an afternoon drive to show me a pretty spot in Kirstenbosch Public Gardens. The next time he asked if he could call, after that party, I told him I was too busy now. He was not seen again. Perhaps I was still a little naïve – I thought him too old for that kind of thing! And Keith Shaw was just a young man trying his luck! It was hard to miss the fact that young South Africans had a very healthy, athletic look; generally tall and handsome men, they were not used to having their attentions rebuffed.

I settled into my second pregnancy as best I could. The nausea that could strike at any time caused me to eat very little, so I tended to lose weight to start with. By the seventh month, I had gained it back and put on a little more but was never more than 12 or 13 lbs above my normal weight. The best part of this was that I didn't need very many maternity clothes. I made a couple of over-blouses and bought a skirt one size larger than usual and made a couple of simple fairly straight dresses with no waist seam, for the last few months. My dear little cat had another accident. It was a car again. It happened on a Sunday, and Michael was home. Ruffy was rushed to the animal clinic again, but alas, when I called the following morning, I was given the sad news that he hadn't survived. Poor Ruffy. I had loved him dearly and was quite grieved. He had been my companion and had always enjoyed the outdoors so much. With another baby on the way, we thought it best to wait a while before having another pet, as Stephen was getting so active; I needed to keep both eyes on him all the time. We enjoyed the lawns at the back of the apartments, and there were opportunities to chat occasionally with the other young mothers. There were several young married couples with little children. The children seemed to prefer to play independently but watched each other. I got books from the library about early childhood education. I wanted to give my children a head start, and have them grow up properly informed and able to fit in. Having such good neighbours meant that occasionally we could babysit for each other and in this way Michael and I were able to enjoy an outing to the cinema.

After Christmas, we visited our friendly furniture salesman again, and using the money I had earned plus a little more 'no interest' credit, we bought a grey carpet for the living room, a small sideboard to match our dining set and two comfortable chairs in the modern style. We had kept in touch with Pam and George Nichols, and now we had a respectable home we invited them over to Camps Bay and served a cold meal, which Pam advised me was the easiest to manage. I was happy to be able to begin to reciprocate the kindness that friends had shown us. We continued to see Jo and Denis. They were still involved with their sophisticated weekend parties and didn't seem too interested in having a family yet, but they were planning to move into their newly built house in Meadowridge. I dreamed perhaps one day we might be able to afford to do the same. Michael had made a few new friends, too. We went to see Barry and Margaret Van Niekerk, who had a cottage at Fish Hoek. Margaret was a trained nurse before her marriage and the birth of their son. She very kindly volunteered to take care of Stephen when the time came for me to have our next baby, due in July. While we were thanking them for this great kindness Stephen, sitting quietly on the floor just in front of me, leaned forward and tried to take a bite out of the edge of their new coffee table. His four front teeth left a perfect imprint. We were mortified, but the invitation wasn't promptly taken back as I thought it might be. What wonderful friends we had!

Our baby was due about 21st July and once again, the big day came – and went. I wasn't surprised. Except for some tiredness, I always felt slightly better towards the end of pregnancy and soldiered on for another two weeks. Then I thought I'd had enough but felt nothing happening until early one morning on the 11th of August. Because our friends lived in quite the opposite direction to St Joseph's Hospital, where I would once again be delivered, we left Stephen with our neighbour Paula and Michael took me to the hospital in Pinelands. I didn't like being separated from Stephen and took his picture with me to display in my room. With the previous experience in our minds of the long labour, Michael kissed me goodbye and left me in the capable hands of the caring nuns once again, drove back to Camps Bay, picked up Stephen and his packed suitcase of clothes and supplies, and took him to Fish Hoek. He was almost 22 months old. Our kind friends Barry and Margaret had a boy of the same age, so she was a brave, kind woman to take charge of our son too.

Meanwhile, I was once again shown to a private delivery/ labour room, going through the now-familiar 'prepping' routine. The midwife nun, who was attending me, examined me and shepherded me through the various procedures. I was feeling well, and I felt that everything was under control – I was ready for this as the contractions were regular, but not uncomfortable – yet! Before she left me, she passed me a call-button and said, 'I'll return when you call. You're going to be out of here before lunchtime.' I responded, 'Thank you, Sister, but I've been here before, you know. I know how long it takes.'

She left with a smile, but she was absolutely right. Our daughter, Nicola Louise, emerged just after Dr King entered my room at about 11.00 am on 11th August 1961. She weighed a little less than 8 lbs and, to me, was very beautiful. A daughter! How wonderful! Michael was amazed when he returned, and the baby was already born. He went along to the nursery and came back quite red in the face. He was so excited. Later he said that he had been concerned because her nose was pushed a little to one side, and she had a pressure haemorrhage in her eye on that side. She had lain in one position for three weeks extra time. I never saw any irregularity with her nose, and Dr King told me the pressure haemorrhage would soon disappear. I just thought I was the luckiest woman in the world, 'Two beautiful children now, how lovely.'

We had some lively discussion over choosing her name. I had chosen Stephen's name (Stephen Michael) before he was even thought of. My childhood friend Patsy and I had made a pact before we left England, that when we had children and if we each had a boy, his name would be Stephen. I had been considering Melanie, but Michael thought Melanie was a made-up name; he had never looked through a 'Name Your Baby' book! I thought Nicola a very pretty name and knew right away it would be perfect for our child if we had a daughter, so Nicola Louise it became. My mother's sister, my favourite aunt, was Louise. I liked using family names too. After staying with me for a while, Michael needed lunch and rushed off to spread the good news, which once again included sending telegrams to our parents, and he was hungry. He came back with a beautiful pink blanket from the Baby Department at Stuttafords. I was so pleased he had thought of it and purchased it himself. He certainly was thrilled with his daughter.

Once again, the milk supply was inadequate. Before we left St Josephs, I was introduced to a new baby food from the United States called SMA, which Nicola tolerated very well. Like her brother, she was a very contented baby. She began trying to smile at me before she was four weeks old and quickly became as pretty a baby as we ever saw. It was my great delight to keep her fresh and clean, well-fed, and happy; her contentedness was my reward. Of course, our son required a great deal of attention too – he was growing taller and weighed about 35lbs at two years old. One month after his second birthday, our efforts at potty training finally took hold, which made my laundry work lighter. Disposable diapers were appearing on the market, but initially, they weren't very kind to a baby's skin, and we couldn't afford them anyway.

About this time, Stephen had a little accident. One weekend I was busy with Nicola in the bathroom, where the baby-changing station (a board set over the bathtub) was; Michael was with Stephen on our little balcony, which was accessed from the living room. We were on the ground floor, but as the ground sloped downhill on the front side of our building, the railing of the balcony was about eight feet from the ground, which here was formed into a cement trough designed to drain rainwater away from the foundation. I heard a yell from Michael, and he rushed past to the flats entrance door calling, 'He's fallen over the balcony!' I dumped Nicola in the middle of our bed, ran into the living room, and before Michael appeared around the side of the building, I somehow flew over that railing onto the ground, and there was Stephen staggering towards me, crying loudly and holding his head. He had a large bump rapidly swelling on his forehead. I gathered him up into my arms and thrust him at Michael and ran back the way he had come, into the flat because Nicola was now unattended on the bed. I was very upset with Michael for not realising how closely you had to watch Stephen. On the balcony, climbing was absolutely not allowed! But Stephen had come to no lasting harm, so peace was soon restored. Not being used to small children, Michael was unfamiliar with the need to set limits. He simply remarked that he was glad we didn't live on the second or third floor!

Various friends dropped in to see us. Joan and Alan Penfold came to see us too. They were having a holiday in the Cape visiting from Kitwe, Northern Rhodesia. They brought Lynette with them, only two and a half years old. They seemed happy with their life there, and while Alan and Michael talked, Joan told me about her home, which was a nice one-level, three-bedroom brick-built house on a large corner lot. Gardening was one of her hobbies, and they had African servants, a houseboy, and a gardener to do the heavy work. She told me many women also employed a live-in nanny for their children. It was a surprisingly comfortable way of life. Kitwe was a pleasant little town where everything for a normal life was readily available. There was even a cinema and a television station, although Alan had not yet bought a TV set. South Africa had no plans to allow television because, as a bilingual society, the Nationalist Government elected to wait until there were enough people trained to produce programmes in both official languages.

Before very long, Michael was talking about 'opportunities' on the Copperbelt in Northern Rhodesia. Totally involved with caring for the children and my home, I didn't at first pay much attention. I had engaged a woman of colour, a motherly soul who worked for another resident in the apartment block, soon after I brought my new daughter home. Her name was Dora, and she came one day each week to help me. Her duties were to take our wet laundry out to the wash lines (I was very particular about clean laundry and would never turn the actual washing chore over to another), general cleaning chores, and especially to polish the floors as needed. On Dora's day, when Nicola was sleeping, I could also take a little walk just with Stephen. He was getting to be a mischievous handful, and I still wanted him to have an afternoon nap, so the walk had to be before lunch. Dora's work was completed by about 4.00 pm – she ironed the bed linen and Michael's shirts for me in the afternoons. I was happily satisfied and very engaged in my life at that point.

In late October, Michael told me that when Alan had visited, they had talked about the possibility that he, also, could find work on the Copperbelt. Alan had very kindly offered help by saying we could stay with them for a short time while he found a job. Michael, realising that we didn't have a good enough income to allow us to visit England to let our parents see their grandchildren, buy our own house or to even have any kind of a holiday, was seriously considering this idea. He had been working at Metal Box Company for three years and didn't think there was any possibility of advancement or of increasing his income there. I wasn't exactly enthusiastic about this idea – Michael trusted Alan's opinion of job prospects in Northern Rhodesia completely, and his offer of hospitality was very kind. But leaving South Africa to go to the Federation of Rhodesia and Nyasaland was another emigration. I wasn't sure I could cope with taking such small children north almost to the border with the Congo, which I thought of as Central (darkest) Africa and possibly not a very healthy place for them. I was so happy living in Camps Bay and had thought we would remain there for many years. However, never one to pour 'cold water' on Michael's schemes, I also thought about Joan's pleasure in her environment and that maybe it could be another adventure – we would have an opportunity to experience what I thought of as the 'real' Africa. Life in urban Cape Town was so influenced by the English style – I knew the real Africa was out there somewhere. I was also very aware that in Northern Rhodesia, we would be about 2,000 miles geographically closer to England, and air travel was beginning to be more available and affordable.

I had got into the habit of watching the lavender hulls of the Union-Castle steamships leaving Cape Town as they turned north for England, on Friday afternoons. My mother had always read a British weekly magazine called 'Woman's Weekly' and sent her copies to me every two weeks. There was always a hand-written note tucked inside the pages. Our regular correspondence and those magazines had helped me form a warmer connection with my mother, and although I can't really say I suffered great homesickness, perhaps because I wanted to share my children with her, I wanted to see my mother.

Early in November, our minds were made up. I had mentioned our plans to my doctor. Dr King brushed aside my concern about my children's health. He simply said, 'If it is a promotion of your husband's career, of course, you must go. Many young couples are raising children there.' Michael made all the arrangements; we had medical examinations in Cape Town and a regular dental check-up and received our papers for entry into Northern Rhodesia with very little fuss. Among many other things, I had to devise a strategy for maintaining the safe handling of Nicola's bottle-feeding equipment without access to sterilisation. The journey by train to Kitwe would take four days. I decided to invest in a set of brand-new bottles for the journey. Each day I planned to use a fresh new bottle and nipple. At the end of each feeding, I would carefully wash out the used bottle and put it aside in the 'used bottle' designated bag at the end of the day. The SMA powder very easily combined with previously boiled water that had cooled. And this was indeed the time to try out disposable diapers.

On this migration, we planned to take our furniture, and an appointment was made for Stuttafords Removals to pick up our precious household effects early on the morning of our departure. Nicola had a new two-in-one baby carriage. The 'body' of the carriage and the chassis could be separated. She had been sleeping in her carriage and could continue to do so for a couple more months in Kitwe. Stephen was almost old enough for a single bed, which would make his crib available for her later when we were settled. The plans were falling into place. I made myself a two-piece dress as a sort of going-away outfit and began to say a rather tearful 'goodbye' to my friends.

Our departure date was to be in mid-January – our rent was paid to the end of the month. On our final weekend, Michael wanted to have a party for his Metal Box friends and their wives. It was quite a lively affair, and we all promised to keep in touch. Michael sold our faithful Hillman car, and so the day of our own 'Great Trek' dawned. The large removal ((moving) van arrived, and loading began. I dressed the children and myself. Everything was ready. The train to Ndola, Northern Rhodesia, ran twice weekly, and my friend Cynthia very kindly drove us all down to Cape Town train station. It was hard to say 'goodbye' to her, but we were soon installed in our four-berth compartment. Nicola's baby-carriage was stored in the guards' van along with some of our luggage. Pam Nichols, in the sixth month of pregnancy, appeared –

she wanted to make sure there was a friendly face to wave us off. We both had tears in our eyes. Those last few minutes were agonising, but right on time, the train slowly pulled out of the station, and we saw Table Mountain receding into the distance against a beautiful blue sky. I wondered what might be ahead - what would become of us now?

Stephen with Maureen on Adderley Street, Cape Town and with his proud father

Michael's brother Denis visited Cape Town

A newly arrived Nicola

8.
The Wind of Change

Michael

Now that Maureen was expecting our second child, I must admit that I was again concerned about how I was going to support my growing family on my income alone. My wages were quite good, but there was no opportunity to earn any extra money with overtime, and we needed furniture. Our car was not exactly completely reliable; I was always working on it at weekends to keep it on the road. I still had an interest in watch repairing, so set up a small area where I could work at home. There was a parts supplier in Cape Town, and the hobby brought in a little money. We had now been away from our families for nearly two years, and we both felt a desire to see them and show off our beautiful offspring. Still, I realised that in our present financial situation, it would be impossible for Maureen and me and two children to make a trip back to England in the foreseeable future.

However, things were starting to change in Africa in the early 1960s. Following a tour of Commonwealth countries in Africa in February 1960, the then British Prime Minister, Harold Macmillan made a speech to the South African Parliament in Cape Town and stated that 'A Wind of Change was blowing throughout the African continent.' He acknowledged that black people in Africa were, quite rightly, claiming the right to rule themselves. He suggested that it was the responsibility of the British government to promote the creation of societies in which the rights of all individuals were upheld. This speech, of course, did not go down too well with the Nationalist government of South Africa. The next month, at Sharpeville in the Transvaal, 69 Africans were killed and over 200 injured when the police opened fire on a crowd of black people who were protesting the Pass Laws. This event signalled the start of armed resistance in South Africa and prompted worldwide condemnation of their apartheid policy, including an arms embargo. In February 1961, a new currency, the South African Rand, was introduced replacing the South African Pound, and later that year, South Africa declared itself a Republic and withdrew from the British Commonwealth. Active also at this time were two relatively unknown African lawyers, named Oliver Tambo and Nelson Mandela, who were later charged with treason. They were sentenced to life imprisonment on Robben Island in Table Bay. The ANC (African Nation Congress) party was also banned. Life was getting seriously interesting. One day at work, shortly after an African had been shot at Langa Township, which was the next-door community to where I worked, all of the African workers decided to leave their jobs and march into the city as a protest. Word soon spread, and thousands marched peacefully, over the Cape Flats, and onto DeWaal Drive into the city's Grand Parade, passing very close to where we were living at Vredehoek. I was very concerned about Maureen's safety and hurried home as soon as I could, only to find she had not had the radio on and knew nothing of the protest. That time, fortunately, the event was peaceful, and after some speeches, the mob dispersed without incident.

Another different but interesting event occurred in 1961. On the island of Tristan da Cunha, administered by Britain, situated about 1,500 miles away in the South Atlantic, a volcano erupted, forcing the entire population of about 300 to evacuate. We saw them when they arrived by ship in Cape Town. Wearing clothes that looked as if they had come from the 18th century, they spoke a form of old English with a West Country sounding accent. With only seven family names among the whole group, most of them were descendants of shipwrecked seaman. They were taken to England, but we later learned that after a few years, they nearly all returned to Tristan, even the young people. They simply couldn't happily settle into the modern world.

I had made several friends at work, and one, Alan Penfold, was to have a significant influence on our future lives. Alan was a qualified Toolmaker and worked on a very accurate machine called a Jig Borer, which was housed in an air-conditioned room. After I had been working there for about a year, Alan confided in me that he was leaving the company and joining his brother in Northern Rhodesia. There were large copper mines in a region close to the Belgian Congo. The mines offered excellent wages for white employees in technical trades. Alan had some experience in heavy maintenance, and his brother, who was an engineer, said he could get him a job. So, Alan left us. I also made friends with several other South Africans, and we occasionally socialised, always having a good time at the Metal Box Company Christmas party.

Once we had the car, we were able to travel to various places around the Cape Peninsular and over the Cape Flats, to the mountain ranges where, among the beautiful scenery, were many vineyards. We enjoyed our first vehicle but soon discovered the Hillman was prone to overheating during the hot summer days. Once, climbing a mountain pass near Ceres, the engine simply cut out from the heat. We sat in anxious silence for a while, but then I managed to turn the car around, and we cruised down with no engine running while it cooled, then we drove home without further incident. We made several trips down to Cape Point and the naval base at Simonstown, also to the beaches at Muizenburg, but it was nearly always very windy there. The southern part of the peninsular beyond Simonstown was a nature reserve, where troops of very aggressive baboons roamed. They seemed to be afraid of nothing and would steal anything. It was unwise to get out of the car when they were nearby. There were very few other wild animals roaming free in the Southern Cape Province, just penguins, baboons, and a few snakes.

Shortly after buying the car, we discovered the best place to buy fruit and vegetables was at a market held Fridays and Saturdays on the Grand Parade in Cape Town. The vendors were mainly Cape Malays and were the most helpful people, so we chose one and always went back to the same stall. They were extremely polite and cheerful, and some of the women very beautiful, although white men were not allowed to fraternise with them, of course. They were classified as 'coloureds' and lived in an area just to the east of the city on the slopes of the mountain, an area called District Six. When we went to the market with Stephen, which was generally on a Friday evening, they always made a big fuss of him, and he responded by being very friendly. You could drive right up to the stall. We would leave Stephen in the car while we chose a selection of fruit and vegetables. He would call out to them '*Narna, narna,*' and in no time, he had several bananas in his hands. They were very excited when we showed up with our beautiful new baby daughter Nicola and crowded around to admire her. We went home with plenty of free fruit that night.

Meanwhile, back in England, my brother Denis had returned and was once again living with my mother in Browning Road. After three years in the U.S. Navy, he had been given the option of leaving or signing on for 20 years. He chose the former and left the U.S., but after only a few months at home, he joined the British Merchant Navy and on one of his first trips to Australia onboard the P&O Shipping Line vessel 'Orion' he spent a day with us in Cape Town, just a few weeks before Nicola was born.

Nicola was born in August, mid-winter, which can often be quite cool and wet. As at Stephen's, I was not present at the actual time of her birth as I had taken Stephen to stay with friends. I expected there to be another long labour, but when I arrived back at Pinelands, I was immediately taken to the nursery and shown my new daughter. I was concerned as she had one very bloodshot eye and her nose seemed to be pushed over to one side. Maureen seemed fine, not too tired, and thought her baby was utterly beautiful. She was delighted to have a daughter. We discussed names. After Nicola was born, we seemed to settle into a contented routine, with Maureen being very attentive to the children's needs while I was given some additional challenges at work. We had now settled in a nicer apartment and been able to furnish it quite well, but although I had three weeks' holiday each year, we had not been able to go away anywhere. This problem did not seem to matter too much as we were living in a wonderful place and, during the summer, were able to enjoy the beach and the ocean. Everyone felt very safe and could move around freely, knowing the South African army and the local police force were alert, and any disturbances would be very quickly dealt with. I always had the feeling that it would be difficult for us to save enough money for a trip home to England, and just thinking about buying our own home was completely out of the question.

Around October 1961, another turn of events set me thinking. My friend Alan Penfold, whom I had met at Metal Box, had driven nearly 2,000 miles south to Cape Town for a vacation. He and his wife, Joan, came to visit. Alan told me about how well they were doing in Northern Rhodesia. He explained that he worked for a large mining company owned by the Anglo-American Corporation, in an area known as the Copperbelt, adjacent to the former Belgian Congo. The modern town of Kitwe had developed around the mine, and all European (white) employees were provided with a house and basic furniture at a very nominal rent. They even had television service, which was still not yet available in South Africa. All the mining and support staff received an excellent base pay rate and were paid an annual bonus based on production and the current market price of copper. At the time of Alan's visit, the bonus amounted to about 80 per cent of their annual salary; it had reached over 100 per cent a couple of years before. This seemed almost too good to be true. He did mention there was some concern about a problem that was developing in a neighbouring territory.

Kitwe was only about 25 miles from the border with Katanga Province in the Congo, which had become independent from Belgium in 1960. At this time, a bloody civil war had erupted over the possible secession of Katanga from the rest of the country. This province, led by self-proclaimed President Moïse Tshombe, was the wealthiest province, with vast reserves of copper and diamonds, and the unrest was widespread. To restore order, United Nations troops were sent into the Congo. On 17th September 1961, while on his way to meet President Tshombe to secure a ceasefire, Dag Hammarskjöld, the Secretary-General of the United Nations, was killed in a plane crash just outside Ndola, Northern Rhodesia. The crash was only about 30 miles from where Alan was living, and it was rumoured that Katangese rebels had shot the plane down. Alan assured me that the trouble was contained over the border. If it were to spread south, it was believed the South African or Southern Rhodesian military would send in troops to protect the residents and the precious mining interests.

During the next few weeks, after Alan's departure, I considered the pros and cons of making yet another move, which also meant immigration to enter the Federation of Rhodesia and Nyasaland as permanent residents. The political situation did not seem to be changing much in the Congo. Earlier, some white missionaries had been murdered by rebel forces at Stanleyville and other centres, creating an exodus of Belgian civilians south into Rhodesia and South Africa. After some consideration and as there had been no other unpleasant incidents, I decided we would look into going. I applied to the Federation offices in Cape Town for the necessary entry papers and, after a brief medical, we were approved and had six months in which to enter Northern Rhodesia. We decided we should wait until January to give Maureen and Nicola a little more time to get ready for the four-day train journey. It would be hard leaving the beautiful climate and scenery of the Cape, but I felt another move was necessary if I was to provide a better future for my lovely wife and expanding family. Many of our South African friends thought we were crazy to make this move, as in their opinion, South Africa under apartheid was going to be the only 'safe haven' for white people in the future, but I had my doubts about this. Most had never been to Northern or Southern Rhodesia and had no idea of the development and way of life there. We needed to have smallpox and yellow fever vaccinations. The area we were going to was malaria-free, but as we were passing through tropical regions, we were advised to take anti-malaria tablets with us for use on the journey. And so, by Christmas, I had booked the train, which ran three times a week through to Northern Rhodesia. A notice had to be given at work, where they probably thought I was not of sound mind, and we had to give notice on our apartment. We spent Christmas quietly preparing for the trip, except for my company party, where we seemed to have a good time with the many friends we had met. The weekend before our departure, we had a 'farewell' party at our apartment, with several of our friends, and made it a night to remember.

On the morning of our departure, 16th of January 1962, a large moving van from Stuttafords arrived to take all our possessions, and later Maureen's friend Cynthia MacKenzie drove us to the station. At precisely 3.00 pm, the train pulled out of Cape Town. We both felt sad as the life we had created together was left behind, and I wondered yet again, 'Are we doing the right thing?'

We had a nice but small four-berth compartment to ourselves on the train, with fold-up beds and a hand basin in front of the window. Toilet facilities were situated at each end of the carriage, and there was a full-service dining car. The South African

Railways line was electrified and took us over the Cape Flats and through the vineyards and Hottentot Holland Mountains into the Great Karroo desert. It was well into the night when we arrived at De Aar, where our carriage and others were transferred to a steam locomotive, and we branched north toward the Northern Cape. From here, the train was on a single track, and by the next morning, we stopped at the town of Kimberley, famous for the discovery of diamonds in 1887. Stephen had a good night's sleep and was very active. Being a very lively and friendly little boy, almost two and a half years old and well able to talk, he would often disappear into other people's compartments, and I would have to locate him by going along calling his name, until we heard him reply 'Pardon, Daddy.' He was usually sitting talking to other passengers, who seemed fascinated by him. At Kimberley, we could get off to allow him to run about and let off steam, but Maureen was always anxious when the train was due to leave, fearing that Stephen may be left behind or lost. It now began to get very hot on board; there was no air conditioning. We would try opening the window, but then the soot from the steam locomotive came in all over Nicola, who didn't seem to mind, but Maureen worried endlessly and tried to keep her infant comfortable and pristine; she somehow managed to keep her clean and well-fed under challenging conditions and Nicola never cried. The train steamed on through another night, and early the next morning, we arrived at Mafeking in the Northern Cape, close to the Bechuanaland border. This town was famous for having been under siege for many months during the Boer War. After another brief stop, we headed north across the edge of the Kalahari Desert. We made stops at some small settlements, and at each, a crowd of Africans would be waiting to sell food and their other wares. The poverty was more intense than anything we had ever seen before. Many of the people had lost limbs and were begging. Others looked as if they had leprosy or some other terrible disease, and mothers had very undernourished babies on their backs. It was painful to observe. As the train left, they ran beside it, crying out with outstretched hands. For the rest of that day and through that night, we made our way north, crossing the Tropic of Capricorn into the tropics. The next morning it was much greener as we were leaving the desert, and the temperature was more comfortable. After a stop at Plumtree, where we went through Rhodesian immigration on the train, we proceeded to Bulawayo, the second-largest city in Southern Rhodesia and the ancient gathering place of the Matabele nation, where we had a four-hour wait. Bulawayo was the end of the line for South African Railways. Here we had to unload our baggage and move to the waiting rooms until the departure time of the Rhodesia Railways train to Ndola. It was a well-organised waiting area, which included a restaurant and full bathroom facilities. We each had a fabulous bath, there was plenty of hot water, and black attendants handed out fresh towels. Stephen and I shared one bathroom while Maureen and Nicola used another. Everyone felt much refreshed with a complete change of clothes. After leaving a small tip for the attendants, we again boarded our train. We had remembered to take our anti-malaria tablets several days earlier, needed for the next part of the journey because we would soon be entering infected areas.

It was a beautiful warm sunny afternoon as the train pulled out of Bulawayo and once again headed north on a single track, for the final stage of our journey. For the first 20 miles or so, the scenery was green rolling hills with rocky outcrops, but then it gradually changed into a flat country with tall, thick bush on either side that obscured any view. We seemed to be travelling through a tunnel of low trees; this continued until nightfall, which comes quickly in the tropics as there is virtually no twilight. The train trundled along at about 40 mph all night, stopping only for coal and water, as there were no towns on this stretch of track for about 200 miles until Wankie, a coal mining area, by which time it was just starting to get light. The vegetation was now becoming more tropical and jungle-like, very hot and humid, as we slowly descended into the Zambezi river escarpment. We were approaching the famous Victoria Falls, and the train went very slowly over a high bridge very close to the falls. The morning mist had not yet cleared and combined with the spray from the falls; our view was somewhat disappointing. The river was the border between Northern and Southern Rhodesia, and we shortly pulled into the small town of Livingstone, where our papers were once again checked. We were able to get off and stretch our legs and allow Stephen to run about to relieve his pent-up energy.

David Livingstone, the Scottish missionary, was the first European in 1855 to see the waterfalls, called '*Mosi-oa-Tunya*' ('The Smoke that Thunders') by the local natives. It is one of the world's most spectacular waterfalls, with the river over a mile wide at this point. After a brief stop at Livingstone, we again got underway, climbing out of the Zambezi River escarpment, passing through many small villages, where sometimes the train would stop, and we could buy fruit from smiling local Africans. They seemed well-fed and happy with their life. The vegetation here was very lush, and we could see that various crops were being grown and water was plentiful. Crossing over the Kafue River, we had our only glimpse of wildlife on this whole journey when we saw several hippos wallowing in a large pool. Generally, the noise of the train frightened any game away. Stops were made at Lusaka and Broken Hill, and with one more exhausting night spent sweating on the swaying train, we eventually steamed into the town of Ndola, where we were so relieved to see our friends. Maureen had spent some time before arrival, making sure she and the children were looking tidy. Alan and Joan gave us a very warm welcome.

The long train journey north from Cape Town, past the Victoria Falls to Kitwe, Northern Rhodesia

9.
Our First Real Home

Maureen

After four days on a moving train, the solid ground felt unfamiliar as we alighted from the train to be warmly welcomed by our smiling friends, Alan and Joan Penfold. The men shook hands, and they both gave me a kiss and spoke kindly to the children. I had dressed myself and the children carefully, being anxious to make a good impression. I didn't know this couple well, having met only two or three times in Cape Town. We thought it an extremely charitable act for them to offer accommodation to us on such short acquaintance while Michael found work. Perhaps Alan had seen something he liked in Michael when they worked together for more than a year at Metal Box Company. They led us to their car, which fortunately was quite big, and our luggage was stowed in the trunk. Nicola's baby carriage had to be tied down on the roof rack, and in no time at all, we were travelling, too fast I thought, although there seemed to be little other traffic, down a long straight road to their home in Kitwe. As we arrived, we noticed that where they lived at Nkana, a suburb of Kitwe, the houses built to accommodate the Rhokana Mine employees all seemed identical. Rather square, with a corrugated iron roof, the Penfold's home sat diagonally on a nice corner lot surrounded by a neat hedge of hibiscus which enclosed lawns, trees, and shrubs. The houses were well spread out, the lots being about one-third of an acre. Joan and Alan employed a houseboy James, immaculate in a fresh white uniform and a gardener who I didn't see very much of. Each house had a long driveway ending in a brick-built garage in the backyard, which had a servant's room attached. The servant's room was called '*the Kia*', the Bemba word for 'house'.

They had prepared bedrooms for us and, for the duration of our stay, their little girl Lynette, who was a few months older than Stephen, slept in their bedroom. Everything seemed very different here. I noticed right away that Joan was expecting another baby; we hadn't known about this, but she assured me she was in absolutely wonderful health. And she did look well – she was a pretty young woman, always nicely turned out; she paid attention to her clothes and hair. Her baby was due in about four months. We soon discovered that Joan was also an excellent cook. We had learned in Cape Town that South Africans were extremely welcoming and hospitable. Still, even many years later, when we thought about the kindness of Alan and Joan, we marvelled at the generous hospitality they offered us.

For registered servants of mine employees, The Rhokana Corporation would make accommodation available in the African Township. Most people preferred this option for married servants. If servants lived on the property, in no time at all, their relatives would come to visit, and then there would be no peace with all the little children running about. Having adult servants accommodated in the township would give them access to health care for themselves and their own family too. Gardeners, usually younger, more transient males, sometimes occupied the *Kia*, which was a bare room with a cement floor and a flush toilet. Everything seemed very orderly and civilised. Ample filtered fresh, drinkable water from the nearby Kafue River was readily available, and every home was connected to water-borne sewage. We were assured that there was no malaria in Kitwe – the boundaries of the town were regularly sprayed with DDT.

Except for the difference in the temperature and humidity, life seemed perfectly normal to me. It was pretty warm; there was no air conditioning. We were warned there would be fierce tropical thunderstorms for the next couple of months. We had arrived at the weekend, and it took us a couple of days to get ourselves organised and rested after that long train trip. Nicola had been an excellent traveller – she had hardly ever cried. By maintaining her usual schedule, she had responded very well. She smiled at everyone and, best of all, had come to no harm. Now there were so many new experiences ahead for all of us. But first, we had to recover and learn how Joan ran her home so that we could fit in. Michael, of course, planned to look for a job immediately. Over our first meal together, Alan very kindly suggested he could borrow their car when Joan didn't need it, to begin the search. I don't remember there being any difficulties during the time we spent as guests.

I greatly admired Joan's careful housekeeping and the friendly but firm way she ordered her servants. She managed her kitchen and cooked delicious meals for us. Generally, the houseboy did the clean-up after meals, but when he wasn't there, I helped with the dishes. I had my usual chores to perform, taking care of the children's needs. I again established my routine of sterilising Nicola's feeding bottles, sanitising her diapers, and laundering all our clothes. I didn't want our presence to increase the workload more than necessary. Alan worked exceptionally long hours, so Joan and I were together with our children all day. We spent some happy hours in the afternoons when the housework was done, and the children were having their naps. Accompanied sometimes by the sound of heavy rain falling outside, we knitted baby jackets and got to know each other really well. At this time, I learned a great deal from her. I paid attention to how she managed her servants. She was an excellent homemaker and was very focused on going about her domestic duties in an orderly, economical fashion with a quick, light step. Her home and garden were well kept in every area. She showed me around the town and introduced me to her friends. I was deeply grateful to her; she truly helped us make a reasonably smooth transition into a new life in a strange environment.

Joan and Alan had a well-bred young female Boxer dog. Tammy came into season while we were there, and Alan would wash her down at an outdoor faucet, which flowed into a ground-level concrete sink, to keep her clean and fresh. Lining the driveway to the garage were tall avocado trees. The fruits from these trees were the biggest avocados we had ever seen, and we quickly developed a real enthusiasm for them, although we had never eaten avocados before. The ripe ones would fall from the branches with a rustling sound and hit the ground where they burst. Tammy would bound forward and devour the fruit with a slurping sound. She loved avocados too. There were several guava trees in Joan's garden and some lemons and papayas. They grew easily and bore fruit very quickly. The local name for papaya was 'paw-paw'. The fruit salad was a frequent favourite for dessert.

Michael began his job search. It soon became apparent that this would not be the easy task that he had anticipated. During the first week, he visited the mines that were closest to Kitwe. The Nkana mine was his preferred choice, but there were no openings there, so he left an application form and began to look further afield. Since the other mines were all about 40 or 50 miles away, he realised he couldn't continue using the Penfold's vehicle, so each morning he would leave, sometimes with Alan, and beginning in the centre of town he would start walking in the direction he wanted to go and thumb a ride. He always got a lift quite quickly, but it was a soul-destroying, time-consuming business, and naturally, he had to hitch another ride to return to Kitwe. We had no income and not very much money in hand. Michael never complained and always seemed upbeat and optimistic. After a couple of weeks, I began to feel a little depressed about the situation – I knew we didn't have enough money to return to Cape Town, so I wondered what we were going to do. I felt a little bit at a loss, not being in charge of my household, but continued to concentrate my attention on the care of the children and their routine. I cheered up a bit when our furniture arrived from Cape Town – all in perfect order. Of course, we had nowhere to store it, so we simply piled it into the garage and covered it up, hoping that it wouldn't be stolen. Although this was generally a peaceful enough community, because the local natives had so very little, everyone had a story about break-ins and petty thieving. Many people had a dog, usually because a barking dog would at least raise the alarm if there were intruders about.

At last, after nearly a month, when Michael had been away all day - I think it was a Wednesday - he arrived back at the house in Geddes Street around supper time driving a green and white Vauxhall Victor motor car. We all ran outside, amazed, and asked whose vehicle it was. 'Mine', he said, 'I've bought it, and I've got a job.' I think this was the best possible news for us all. He came inside, and we began supper while he told us about his search. He had heard of an engineering company in Ndola called Raine Engineering and had gone there to make enquiries. He was immediately given an interview and offered work in a trade he was familiar with: Engineering Maintenance. Needing work so badly, he accepted the offer immediately; it seemed to be a reasonably good wage. When he signed on, he was advised to contact the

Ndola City Council offices where he could find rental accommodation to house his family. It was all very exciting. Michael still planned to try to get employment on one of the copper mines later, but he had to begin earning money immediately.

Early the next day, soon after breakfast, we dressed the children and off we went in our 'new' car to Ndola to begin the house search. At the City Council offices, we met with the Housing Supervisor, a bald Englishman, and after a short interview was directed to an address in an area called Kansenji. This community was recently developed with red dirt roads, but there was a small row of new stores nearby for food and necessities. The house, 24 Sussex Gardens, was a freshly painted one-level three-bedroom bungalow, with an affordable monthly rent. When we looked it over, I could see there were no fences or hedges between any of the houses, and although the house was on quite a large lot, aside from a banana grove and rough grass, there were no shrubs or trees. But I did notice there were other white families with little children in the nearby houses. Our house had all the usual facilities, and everything looked spotless, so we decided to take it. Back at the Council office, we paid our rent to the end of the month, signed for the keys, and let them know we would probably move in at the weekend. Michael was to start work on Monday.

We were quite excited to report our good fortune to Alan and Joan. Once again, Alan was accommodating – his brother had a truck he could borrow to help us move on Sunday. It wasn't going to take very long to pack our clothing etc. so Michael and I went into Kitwe together to buy a 'thank-you' gift for our hosts. We chose a decorative copper fire screen. Joan had a collection of small copper items, created by local artisans, on the fireplace, which was hardly ever used, and I remembered she had admired the fire screens when we had been shopping in the town. Because of all they had done for us, it was a small gesture, but we were very grateful.

The truck was packed on Saturday evening, ready for departure early the next day, so after breakfast, when the children were prepared, we were off. Before we left, Joan invited us back the following weekend for lunch so that we could let her know all was well. Once again, we were on the move to yet another address.

Our moving day went smoothly. The new house had a small cooking stove, and I was happy we had included our small refrigerator in the possessions we had sent to Kitwe. Beside the back door was a little pantry, more than adequate for storing canned goods, dry goods, and other kitchen equipment. I had learned long ago that when undertaking a move to a new address, the first thing one should always do was make up the beds. Stephen's crib was placed in the smaller front bedroom, our bed in the larger bedroom, and in the third little bedroom, we put everything else we couldn't immediately find a home for. We didn't own night tables, so Michael placed a closed packing case at his side of our bed to accommodate the alarm clock, etc. We had curtains packed away, but I needed help to hang them. The windows were bare, but as we weren't really overlooked, it didn't seem to matter very much. Nicola used her carriage a lot; now, six months old, she really needed a full-size crib, but Stephen was still using the one we had, and the first week in our new home quickly passed. There were no fences or gates on the property, and I spent quite a lot of time looking for Stephen. He would get out of the house somehow and go in search of other children to play with. He had found having a playmate his size, while we were with Joan, very agreeable, and he was a friendly little boy. Somehow whenever I was busy caring for Nicola, he would disappear, and I would get quite anxious when I couldn't find him. But a good thing about this problem was that I soon got to meet the neighbours.

At the end of the week, we returned to Kitwe and picked up from Joan and Alan the few things we had left there and had a meal with them. We drove back to our new home after the sun had set; it was a wonderfully clear night, and the moon seemed huge, and we were not prepared for the frightening experience that this night would bring us. Stephen went to his crib without any trouble, and I fed Nicola and pushed her in her carriage just inside the door to the 'spare' little back room. She had been sleeping peacefully through the night since we got on that train to come to Kitwe. Michael always left for work relatively early, so we soon went to bed too.

Sometime in the night, I have no idea of the time, I awoke. I felt a hand stroking my thigh. I slept on Michael's left. I always turned to my right to face him. The hand was approaching me from

MY LEFT. I turned my head and saw a shape at the side of the bed and heard an intake of breath – Michael was still sleeping soundly to my right. In the same instant, I realised I could smell sweat, and there was an intruder, and involuntarily I screamed. Immediately I saw the shape rear back as Michael, silhouetted against the uncurtained window, seemed to come up out of our bed in one huge leap to land on the floor at the end of the bed. I heard the intruder run down the hallway towards the kitchen, with Michael in pursuit. I was shocked beyond belief but didn't want Michael pursuing the intruder into the darkness outside. At the back of our lot, there was a dense stand of banana trees – anyone could be lurking in there. I screamed at Michael, 'Come back, come back!'

When we switched on the lights, at the end of the hallway, there were two large dirty, black handprints at about shoulder level, where the person had thrust out his hands so that he could quickly change direction and leave by the back door to his left, which was still open; what a horrible experience! But I was not hurt and didn't want to upset Stephen, who was saying, 'What's wrong, Mummy?' in his little childish voice. I gathered him up and soothed him, which helped me to calm myself. It was about 3.00 am. We locked up once again and looked around to see if anything was missing. It was a bit hard to tell since I hadn't yet found places for all our belongings. I noticed right away that the intruder had lined a few things up by the back door; one of them was my woven blue sewing supplies box. He obviously meant to take things with him when he departed. He also had been into every room. Even my precious little girl's carriage had been pushed much further into the small room. And Michael's Roamer wristwatch, which had been my wedding gift to him and his wallet which had been on the makeshift packing case/night table, was gone! The wallet included some identification, but not very much money. We called the police. Within 15 or 20 minutes, two white BSAP (British South Africa Police) with a couple of African policemen arrived in a Jeep. But there was nothing they could do. They spoke gently and asked us for statements. They left, assuring us they would find the culprits and be nearby on alert for the rest of the night so that we did not need to worry. They also told us they would return in the morning with a female police officer to take a full statement from me. We tried to relax and sleep but were much too upset.

The next morning, Michael telephoned his workplace and explained the situation and stayed at home with me. When the police officers returned, they took fingerprints and determined the intruder had gained entry through the small pantry window, which did not quite close securely. The female police officer took my full statement. She was determined to make much of the fact that his hand was moving under our bedclothes on my bare upper thigh – but we soon learned that similar incidents were not exactly uncommon. We heard of people waking in the morning to find everything has gone, even the blankets from their beds. This was becoming a scary country.

A couple of days later, when Michael had returned to work, the two BSAP policemen returned with an unkempt, ragged black man. They asked me if I could identify him. I had got such a fleeting impression of his back and head, as the intruder left our bedroom, that it was quite impossible for me to say this was the man. But the policemen were sure this was the one. They probably had a network of paid informers in the black townships. They told me he had just been released from prison! I told them his head and his stature looked about right, but I really couldn't give a positive identification because it had been so dark. But would they please get him away from me just the same. Then I went inside the house, bolted all the doors, and waited for Michael to come home. It was all a very frightening experience. We informed the Housing Officer of the incident, and he sent someone over to make the pantry window secure, and that was the end of it.

A week or so later, some gardeners arrived, and they planted hedging on both sides of the house to mark the extent of the lot. I knew those frail little hibiscus cuttings needed attention. I was asked to water them. Those violent tropical storms had decreased, and the dry season was beginning. Still, I wasn't yet very interested in gardening, we hadn't yet purchased a hose, and therefore I had to carry water back and forth in a bucket. I didn't have very much time or energy for that. Michael came home with a little gun; it was a starter's pistol. A young man he'd met at work told him the Africans wouldn't bother you if it became known you had a gun. Michael felt a little more secure, but it didn't help me too much. However, I began to make friends. I met a woman whose husband was a sergeant in the army. She also had a couple of children. They came from the Midlands in England. I thought this pair a little rough, but she was someone to share a nice cup of tea with occasionally.

Then I met another quieter, nicer woman whose name was also Maureen. She had a boy a little older than Stephen. I was pleased to find other children for Stephen to play with in the afternoons – I had to keep him locked inside the house all morning while I did the daily chores. I was rather taken aback to discover Stephen had become a little light-fingered. Before leaving anyone's home, I had to frisk him. He loved motor cars so much; he developed a bad habit of picking up other boys' Dinky cars and pocketing them, hoping to add them to his collection. He soon learned that it was absolutely not allowed.

When I got brave enough to penetrate the grove of banana trees at the bottom end of our garden, a week or two later, I found another friend. Gail was a quiet slip of a girl who had a little boy called David. I met her because I heard of a motherly lady, who had created a small business by running a playgroup for pre-school age children, in the next street where Gail lived. The playgroup was a Godsend. She had a fenced play yard, had a regular schedule of games and activities, and would give the children a little lunch. Some of her 'students', children of working mothers, were there for the whole day. I enrolled Stephen for two half-days a week. In this way, I could get on with my laundry or other cleaning chores, on those two mornings, without worrying all the time where Stephen was. The first time I spoke to Gail, it was to ask her if she would mind if I took a short-cut through her garden to take Stephen to the group, and again after lunch when I would return to fetch him. Of course, when leaving the house, I had to carry Nicola with me. Gail was quite lonely and was happy to agree. Her son went to the group too. Gail, being very shy, didn't easily meet people, so we became friends.

I tried to have help in the house. Michael engaged a young boy, and on the first morning, I set him to polishing the smooth red cement floors. The polishing was a miserable job. The red polish had to be spread on the swept floor and polished with two brushes. The African servants used to put the brushes on their bare feet and dance. They got quite warm in the process, and I couldn't stand the smell. When Michael came home from work, I said, 'You have to dismiss him – I can't stand the way he smells.' Michael thought, giving him some soap to wash at the garden tap would do the trick, but the poor boy didn't know what to do with soap and didn't 'catch on'. After quite a comical demonstration from Michael, there was no difference in the aroma. So, he had to go! I wasn't very comfortable with an African in the house anyway and soldiered on.

Michael was working hard Monday to Friday with a half-day on Saturday. He had soon confessed that he wasn't very happy with this job. Raine Engineering was such a dirty, evil-looking place with old, inefficient machinery; he felt it wasn't even a safe environment to work in. Since he still intended to get a job on one of the mines, he decided that each month he would take a day off – I don't know how he squared this with his employer. On the day off, we would get up and dress the children and, after breakfast, take the car and visit one of the towns which adjoined another of the mining towns on the Copperbelt. Since I found it quite challenging to be living in that house on a dirt road, I enjoyed a day out. So off we went with him. In this way, we visited the towns of Luanshya, Mufulira, and Chingola; he wasn't going to give up.

I went through a period of not feeling so well. I developed severe ear infections, and it was hard to sleep with the pain. Perhaps I wasn't accustomed to the climate and was also reacting to the stress we both were experiencing. It was not the most relaxing time of our lives. I went to see a doctor in Ndola who prescribed some medication and advised me to rest more. Of course, when the ear infections cleared up, I soon felt more like myself again. I usually was very healthy. I was happy that I had got to know a general doctor. Now an experienced mother, I hadn't worried that Nicola had not had the regular 'well-baby' clinic check-ups that Stephen had. She was growing well, had never been sick, and was beginning to get mobile. One day, when I was preparing our evening meal, and Michael was telling me about his working day, she managed to get her feet under her body when she was in her high-chair, and before we knew what was happening, she toppled out. The fine, fair hair on the top of her head was covered in the red polish from the stone floor when we picked her up screaming. What a terrible accident! We soothed her, and she quietened, but soon began to look drowsy. This didn't seem quite right to me, so we all piled into the car to revisit my doctor. He diagnosed a mild concussion and advised us to keep her awake. He wanted to admit her to the hospital, but I said I would stay by her side all night if necessary. We would take turns waking her at intervals. We brought her crib into our room, and I sat up with her. Before long, after we each had taken a few turns at rousing her, inevitably, we both fell asleep. We awoke as usual with the dawn, and when we looked, there was Nicola standing up in her crib right next to our bed, smiling happily at us. She was absolutely fine. Highchairs didn't have safety straps in them in those days. Neither did we have safe car seats. It's amazing how we did without them. But from then on, I did tie Nicola into her highchair.

At last, soon after this episode, when we didn't go with Michael on one of his job-hunting trips, he called in at the Nkana mine in Kitwe to remind them he still wanted a job with them and heard there was a vacancy - a man had unexpectedly died in the tool room. Michael came home quite excited. The interview would be within a week, and he became the successful applicant. It had taken six long months, but what rejoicing! This job sounded much more promising. After six months of struggling, I could give up on that bare little house in Kansenji, where I had tried to create a home. We would be moving yet again! When we gave notice to the Council, the Housing Officer came to see me. He wanted us to know there were other nicer houses available if we were not happy with the house. I realised he had wanted to do his best for us. I thanked him and told him we were leaving the area for Kitwe, where housing was provided.

ဆဝ ငၺ

Maureen was very courageous after our robbery and attempted assault. Of course, we were both very frightened at the time, not knowing whether there were more intruders in the house or if they might come back. I considered us to be fortunate that there had been only one who became scared when Maureen screamed, but there could have been others who may have been armed. The next morning, as I had not gone to work, I walked over to our neighbour, who I had not yet met, to tell them of the incident. A white Rhodesian came to the door and invited me in when I explained who I was. It surprised me somewhat when he introduced me to his pretty coloured wife and children, a relationship that was forbidden in South Africa. He was not at all bothered that we had been robbed and implied that it happened all the time, advising me that I should arm myself. 'The Africans will stay away,' he said, 'if they know you have a gun'. I had absolutely no experience with firearms. The next night we made ourselves very secure, and the night passed without incident. Back at work in the morning, I told a few fellow workers what had happened, and one advised me to 'buy a gun, and if you shoot anyone, make sure they are on your property, if not drag them there'. Another had a more civilised idea. He said to purchase a small starting pistol that looked like a real gun, made a loud noise when fired, but could not harm anyone. Another colleague said he had one for sale, and we made a deal. The next day I took it home and immediately felt more secure. This device suited me fine as I was not yet ready to go around shooting Africans. Maureen remained very calm through this difficult time, and never once mentioned that we should pack up and leave. I think she realised that this was not an option anyway, as we did not have enough money to return to South Africa - let alone England.

My job at Raine Engineering was very hard. The company did contract work for most of the mines on the Copperbelt and had one of the few foundries in the area. The work is hot, dirty, and smelly where molten metal, usually cast iron, is poured from a large furnace into sand moulds. Now was late summer and toward the end of the rainy season, so everywhere was very humid, particularly in the late afternoon. The casting was done by bare-footed Africans, who would use a ladle to tap molten metal from the furnace and pour it into a row of prepared moulds; dancing around as the hot sparks landed on their legs and feet. The maintenance of all the equipment and preparation of the moulds was done mostly by skilled white employees. One of my first assignments was to maintain a huge mechanised conveyer belt that was set below a furnace and used to cast four-inch iron balls used in the ore crushing process on the mines. It would often stop during the casting process, and I, together with an African helper who spoke no English, had to free the jammed doors and get it moving again. It was sweltering, hard work. Most of the Europeans who had been working here for some time could communicate with the Africans using a dialect developed in the South African gold mines called '*chikabemba*'. The dialect was a mixture of English, Afrikaans, and Bemba. It was very simple and easy to learn, but I never did manage to speak it. My first experience with a large African snake occurred at work one day. The Africans, who were very frightened of snakes, had cornered a large poisonous Black mamba (I believe) and were trying to kill it with sticks before it bit anyone. Eventually, it did die, and they paraded around, dancing and singing, with it held high above their heads. It probably became a tasty meal that night.

The tense political situation in the Congo had eased somewhat, when the Province of Katanga, which adjoined Northern Rhodesia, agreed to end their secession, although United Nations' troops were to remain there in a peace-keeping capacity. An aircraft carrying the United Nations' Secretary-General, Dag Hammarskjöld, had crashed into a hill near Ndola some months earlier. The damaged aircraft had been stored at the airport for six months, and now the pieces were being brought to Raine Engineering, for melting down prior to being shipped to the USA. United Nations' security personnel were present; it was part of a secret investigation as it had been reported the plane had been shot down by Katangese forces. I believe nothing was ever proven. Many of the men at Raine Engineering had been trying for years to get a job on one of the mines because, with a low rental house provided and all the other benefits, it was considered a plum job in the area. Even this did not discourage me, and I regularly visited the mine personnel offices, letting them know I was still available. After about six months, my persistence paid off, and I was offered a job in the tool room at Rhokana mine in Kitwe, the town where Alan and Joan lived and the one we liked the best. Within a few weeks, we had left Ndola to move into the mine temporary quarters in Kitwe.

ဆ ೦ಶ

During the six months, we had been in Kansenji; my children had been my special pride and joy, worth any amount of effort to keep them happy and comfortable. They were beautiful children. Now nearly three years old, Stephen was quite a challenge, but it was because he was so lively and interested in everything and everybody. He never noticed that the girl across the street was the child of a black house servant, who was from The Congo and spoke French as well as her native language. He would sit with her on a low wall outside the gate to 'her' house, and together they would sway back and forth sideways and sing Bemba songs, which is what I assumed the language was. They couldn't communicate with each other but seemed happy in each other's company just the same. Because the street was not paved and the weather was now very dry, at the end of the day, they would both be closer to the same colour, a dusty brownish grey. The family in that house had a friendly German Shepherd dog that also was very willing to play with Stephen. We have a movie fragment of them playing together. Nicola was a special delight. She had always been such a smiley, happy baby and was now about to reach her first birthday. But once again, I had to prepare for moving and was delighted that we were moving to Kitwe. During the time we had been in Ndola, Joan had given birth to another baby girl, Janine, a sister for Lynette. I was looking forward to spending time with our special friends.

The first step was to visit the housing manager at the mine offices. The Rhokana Mine at Nkana was a division of The Anglo American Corporation, which had developed every facility for the mine employees, including a hospital. Aside from the housing and recreational facilities, across from the Mine Club, which quickly filled up with thirsty men at the end of their working day, there also was a large dining room/restaurant. The Mine Club was supported routinely by the many single male employees but was available to every white employee, so I did not necessarily have to cook a meal every day. The Africans, in the South African way, had a service window on one side of the building and would be served their kind of food there. There was no apartheid here, but all the facilities were naturally racially segregated. We learned from the housing people that we would be given access to temporary accommodation right outside the mine gates for a month. At the end of this time, we would be allocated a regular mine house similar to the kind that the Penfolds had. The temporary accommodation was a grungy one-level fully furnished half-duplex, quite close to the single men's quarters and the Mine Club. The whole area, including the interior of the house, was, as most mining operations are, thick with black dust. But it was only going to be for a short time, so I thought we could tolerate it. When our furniture was delivered from Ndola, we had to find room and stacked it in one of the bedrooms. One of the black delivery crew thought it extremely amusing. He said, 'Madam, everyone must walk on top of all this furniture now!' I just had to laugh with him; there was certainly no room for a pathway on the floor between the furniture. Fortunately, the Mine Club recreational property included a beautiful first-class, large swimming pool almost opposite where we were living, and we could go there every day. Stephen could play safely in the children's pool. This house was so dirty I had nowhere to put Nicola down except on our bed. Now a year old, she was beginning to test her mobility, but I certainly wasn't about to allow her to crawl about on those filthy floors, even though I did my best to deal with the dirt.

There was a good-sized, clean bathroom and plenty of hot water, and we all had a bath every night. One night, Michael and I were in the bathroom together. I was standing in the tub drying my back using the usual 'towel shimmy' method, while we talked about the day when a movement at the dirty little window high up to my right caught my eye. There was the face of a young white man watching me! Another fright - and I let out a surprised shriek! Michael rushed outside making quite a noise, but the figure had vanished. He quickly returned and put his arms around me; he really didn't like me having these horrible experiences. Of course, he reported the incident at the housing office, and they promised to let us know as soon as they could when there was a house available for us. I desperately needed a decent, safe place of our own. So, we struggled on. When Michael began working at Nkana Mine, he seemed to be happier, both with the challenge of the work and with the people he worked with, and at last, we were advised a house, 101 Geddes Street, was available for us. Alan and Joan's house was just a few blocks further down the same street! Yet another moving day was not going to dismay me. At first sight, our new home didn't exactly look inviting. It was clear the previous tenant had not taken much care of the place and hadn't been any kind of a gardener. But it was exactly the same as Joan and Alan's home except it sat four-square on the lot. I was pleased it was a little closer to Kitwe Centre for the shopping; it was just within walking distance. The house had been carefully swept, and the walls and ceilings were freshly painted, so I was pretty sure we could soon improve the look of its interior. For a very nominal rent, each mine house included what was called 'basic furniture'. The furniture consisted of a sturdy, family-sized wooden table and four chairs plus a painted cabinet in the kitchen for china and cutlery. Two heavy-duty wooden armchairs in the simple 'Mission' style with loose, square, seat, and back cushions were in the large living room and twin beds with ugly mattresses in the main bedroom. There were two three-drawer chests; one with a mirror. All the furniture was stained the same dark walnut colour. There were no curtains, no kitchen appliances. So, we had to take stock of what we needed immediately. The first thing was a kitchen stove to cook on. The necessary electrical outlet had been recently installed; we could see where there had been a wood-fired stove that a native cook had used in the past. We sure didn't plan to hire a cook, so we purchased an electric stove on Hire Purchase (payment plan). It was no problem for the mine employees to get credit. Our small refrigerator from Camps Bay would serve until we could afford a larger one. On an interior wall, the kitchen had a second rather narrow door, which revealed a deep narrow pantry with lots of shelf space, which stayed cool if we kept the door closed. The pantry was a valuable feature with storage space for dry goods, canned food, and small kitchen appliances. Outside the high pantry window, I was pleased to see a wonderful lemon tree full of fruit. The tree was planted fairly close to the house. The tree's prickly branches reached up to the small window. No intruder would try to get in that window! Our double bed fitted easily into the back bedroom with the three-drawer mirrored chest. There was a built-in closet in each of two of the bedrooms that were lined up on the south-east side of the house. The bathroom was between our bedroom and the one the children would sleep in. Opposite the bathroom was a huge two-door built-in cupboard for household linen etc. The living room and adjoining kitchen looked out onto the driveway, which was planted with an avenue of mango trees. Half-way along the driveway was a small patio that was shaded by well grown, tall pink and purple bougainvillaea. The door here gave entrance to the kitchen. We decided to dump the mattresses from the twin beds and bought Stephen a new mattress. He was a big boy now – it was time for a regular bed. He shared his room with his sister. Nicola was able to enjoy the safety of the crib. The second twin bed we placed in the spare room which opened onto the adjoining 'breeze' room. These two rooms formed the front of the house. Rather like a 'summer' room in that, it simply had fine wire mesh in the place of glass windows right across the width of the room, and the 'breeze' room was a nice place to sit at the end of the day as the sun was setting. It was going to be wonderful to have so much space. The kitchen, like the 'breeze' room, also had sheets of wire mesh instead of glass at the windows. In every case, for those rooms that had the wire mesh windows and which connected to the interior of the house, locks, and bolts on the living room side of the doors had been installed for added security. Later we were able to buy second-hand wonderfully strong, louvred glass windows for both the breeze room and the kitchen. The windows made the whole house much more secure and, when opened, would permit airflow right through the house even when it was sweltering outside. Michael cheerfully went off to work. His hours were 7.00 am to 3.30 pm with a half-hour allowed for lunch. He took a packed lunch, which I made up for him each morning. We would get up at 6.15 am each working day and have time for a quiet chat together over breakfast before the children were up. On Saturdays, he would work until noon. Later on, should overtime work be required during the week, he would come home at about 5.00 pm for the supper hour and then go back to work until about 10.00 pm.

ഇ ൦ൠ

Rhokana mine was massive, producing large amounts of pure copper and smaller amounts of other minerals. There were four shafts that went a vertical distance of 4,000 feet into the ground and then a labyrinth of tunnels, connected by trains. The ore was blasted in the tunnels and brought to the surface, where it was then crushed and concentrated using tremendous amounts of water, which came from the Kafue River that ran very nearby. After further processing, the ore was smelted and refined. Further ore was collected from an open pit mine, where large machines excavate just below the earth's surface. All this activity required a significant amount of heavy equipment, and the large machine shop was there to support and maintain it all.

I was assigned to a small, well-equipped tool room, and we were responsible for repairing and making new parts for the smaller machinery and equipment on the mine. There were three other men working in this area, the charge hands, Harold Wenman and Brian Lowe; these two were South Africans and Jim Green from Southern Rhodesia; all these men were a few years older than me. From my very first day there, they made me most welcome and were prepared to help me in any way they could. Now 26 years old, I was told I was replacing a man in his early forties who had died suddenly of a heart attack. The work proved to be very interesting and also a challenge as we had to make many parts that were not readily available. Being so far from the spare parts' suppliers in South Africa, the UK, or Europe, it was necessary to provide well-equipped repair facilities and competent tradesmen, as the mine never shut down – it was a 24-hour operation, year-round.

Northern Rhodesia has a tropical climate, modified slightly on the Copperbelt by an altitude of 4,000 feet, with a rainy season from October to April. During the winter months, the skies were cloudless, and it cooled comfortably at night. The mine buildings had corrugated iron roofs, and from mid-September, the clouds would start to form in the late afternoon, with an increase in humidity. With no air conditioning, the temperature in our workshop would soar to over 100° F, and then the rains would come about 4.00 pm, and you could always smell their impending arrival. With the heavy rain, there would be severe thunder and lightning, which often continued well into the night. A problem at the mine was the very obnoxious fumes from the mine smelter, which drifted over our workshop and into the open windows. Sometimes the visibility was barely 100 feet, but the town and European housing were built to avoid the prevailing winds, the African Townships not being so fortunate.

I had only been working at Rhokana for a few months when Jim, in my department, also had a heart attack during the night and died. The mine officials were worried that these fatalities were caused by work-related stress, but it was more likely due to the excessive drinking and smoking lifestyle that many adopted there. The mine club bars were always full when each shift ended, and the main bar could seat about 100 men. Jim was replaced by Vincent Esposito; an Italian married to an Irish nurse who later became our good friends. At lunch and coffee breaks, we would sit around in the shop and talk, and another quiet fellow Peter would occasionally join us. Harold and Peter had lived on the Copperbelt for a long time, and they used to reminisce about their early days there. I asked them if there were any wild animals in the area then and they said there were. I asked Peter if he ever went hunting. He said he did and then somewhat reluctantly told us of a terrible experience he had. He and a friend had located a big cat (I believe he told us, leopard), which they thought was behind a large anthill. Anthills here can be the size of trees. He went one way around it and the friend the other. Suddenly he heard a terrible noise and rushing forward, found his friend being mauled by the animal. He shot and wounded the big cat, which then ran off. But his friend died from his injures later and Peter said he never hunted again.

At last, we were beginning to feel settled, and both enjoyed the social life with some new friends we had made. I also was able to relax a little because I thought we were doing much better financially. Around Christmas 1962, we heard of charter trips being arranged for travel to England and, at last, began to think we soon might be able to make a visit to England and see our families again.

ℬ ℭ

Just after we moved into the Geddes Street house, Stephen and Nicola began to run fevers. Before we had left the temporary accommodation, we had gone back to Kansenji for a children's party we had been invited to, and in return, we invited the people we had met there to come and see us in our new home. I remembered that two of the children there, their parents being a couple that we did not know, were flushed and fractious. I guessed we had picked up something then. Michael called in at the hospital to explain the situation, and a doctor came to see us and diagnosed measles. I was very thankful we could get such prompt attention. Because Nicola was so young, a nurse came to the house a couple of times to check temperatures, etc. She explained they were vigilant because Nicola was only just a year old, and in this climate, a very high fever could be dangerous for so young a child. When she was satisfied, I was competent to take proper care of them, she left a thermometer and medicine and advised I should call the clinic if I became worried. Stephen recovered, and soon, all was well with Nicola too, but we were a little concerned for the first few days. Briefly, there were a few episodes of 'night terrors' experienced by Stephen. I learned from my Dr Spock handbook this was not unusual in children under four or five years old. This was the age at which the imagination was developing. Stephen had indeed experienced considerable change in his young life – perhaps the violent nightmares were the result. While awake, he seemed completely happy, well adjusted, and healthy.

Because we felt we could properly settle down here and to give Stephen a new interest, we decided to buy a dog for him. We chose a sweet black cocker spaniel pup and took him home. I'd never had a dog, but I fondly remembered the spaniel in the home in Somerset that my sister and I went to as evacuees so long ago. I thought Jasper was a good name for him. We kept his bed in the kitchen at night and hoped he might add to our sense of security. He was a nice little pup, but he began to get a little snappy at about three months old. I was a bit uncomfortable about this because of our children, so we took Jasper back to the pet store to ask for advice. Michael held him in his arms while we spoke to the store owner – there was quite a lot of yapping going on. Jasper sat there looking about him with great interest and was so good while the pet store owner talked to us. He thought Jasper was simply teething, and all would probably be well quite soon, so we simply took him home again, and I made sure we treated him carefully for a while. The store owner was proved to be entirely right. Stephen liked animals and loved to help his Dad bathe Jasper at the outside sink. They would take turns after the bathing exercise running around the house with Jasper on the leash to prevent him from immediately rolling in the dust and getting his shiny black, slightly curly coat dirty as soon as he was clean. Jasper thought he was my dog because he always sat underneath my chair when I was in the garden and would follow at my heel wherever I went. He was very good with the children. We also acquired two cats: Dixie, a tabby female, and Captain, a black long-hair male with a white 'bib'. Dixie, of course, soon had a litter of kittens, which we found homes for, but both animals were swiftly spayed and neutered.

I was so happy when I was able to completely unpack ALL our belongings at last. We had full-length curtains for the living room, which I had made in Camps Bay for the apartment. There were three casement windows in this room. All windows were guarded by plain burglar bars on the outside. I decided we could have new curtains for our bedroom. The ones I had made for the apartment, which were rather boldly striped, would look good in the breeze room. And I was sure I could get some playful fabric for the children's room. The stone floors in this house needed a few applications of the red polish to restore the shine, but we had a dark grey carpet for the living room, so we didn't have to polish the whole floor. We had moved in on 1st September, and although there weren't any party guests, at the end of the month, the two children were well enough to enjoy Stephen's third birthday. Gifts arrived from England, special Dinky models of fire trucks, and 'work' related vehicles, which pleased him. We bought him a pedal car that looked like a little Jeep. He was so fascinated by cars; we couldn't have chosen a better gift. He was thrilled speechless. Alan and Joan dropped by for tea, without their children because of the recent measles and wanted to see how we were getting along. Alan remarked how nice our furniture looked in this house. I felt quite complimented.

It was a pleasure setting up this home, and I wanted to make the stark bare rooms seem comfortable. To us, it seemed quite a big house, so there was much to do. September was a hot, dry month; the tropical rainy season would begin in early October. We decided to try again to find help in the house. Word was soon passed around that we were not yet set up with servants, and often early in the morning, there would be several hopeful black youths waiting at the kitchen door. After a few false starts, we found a pleasant, clean-looking young man named Peter. He had some experience and understood English quite well. He was ready to do whatever I asked of him and had some training at a mission near his village. I never employed a cook or a nanny, as some women did. Many women lived a very idle life, allowing their servants to do everything. Peter's duties were to clean the floors and the bathroom, dust as required, and hang the laundry on the line.; I liked to make our beds and take care of our clothes, so I still did the laundry myself. He ironed in the afternoons under my watchful eye and did a lovely job with my husband's shirts. He also scrubbed at the outside sink Michael's 'shop' coats. I never again had to toil over them. It was necessary to iron everything that would be dried outside, even the nappies. There was a flying insect called a Putzi fly, which would lay eggs on the drying laundry. If the eggs hatched out, babies and adults could get a nasty boil from the burrowing, almost invisible worms. Ironing would render the clothes safer. He also always cleaned up in the kitchen after our meals, which I cooked, and he did a thorough job of it.

After the first month with Peter, when we thought he would suit us, we bought him two white uniforms to work in and showed him how to take care of them. We also arranged accommodation for him in the African township and purchased a second-hand bicycle so that he didn't have to walk the three miles to our house. His working day started at 8.00 am, he had a free hour in the middle of the day, and he was free to go home after our evening meal, around 6.30 pm. We deducted a minimal amount from his modest wage and let him know that if he stayed with us, after a reasonable time, say six months, the bicycle would be his. We also engaged a young gardener. Alfred didn't understand English at all, but once shown what to do would work willingly enough but rather slowly. The 'boys' seemed to love cutting grass. They would provide themselves with a home-made tool, which was a length of steel with a curved, sharpened end. The other end would be wrapped with dirty fabric to prevent blisters on their hands, and they would swing this tool backwards and forwards like a metronome. We called the boy and the tool together a Rhodesian lawnmower – we saw them everywhere. Alfred's particular skill lay in digging. We engaged him at the end of the dry season when there were so many leaves lying around. Michael set him to dig a hole to compost the garden debris and then forgot about him. When he called for Alfred to wash the car, he went looking for him. His hole had almost swallowed him and, Alfred was quite out of sight. He must have been working on that hole for several days. Michael also decided to try his hand at growing a few vegetables, with Alfred's help. They were both proud of the beans they harvested.

Within just a few months, the children were well and thriving, and we had things running along smoothly. We began to talk about the possibility of having a holiday in England. Michael would probably get six weeks' holiday the following year. Regular charter flights from the Rhodesias to London were becoming popular. Quite frequently, these flights for mine employees were organised by the Mine Club. This was a very exciting idea; we had never thought of travelling by air before. When the copper bonus was declared towards the end of the year, we were delighted to find Michael's bonus would cover the cost of one return fare to London, so we set ourselves to save up for a trip and wrote to our parents to tell them what we were planning. Naturally, they were delighted to hear the news, and they became excited, too.

While we waited, I learned about the Rhodesian way of life. Most of the women there had the use of a car. The day always began early, with the men going off to work. It was also wise to get any chores also done before it got too hot. Then it was perhaps time for a coffee party with a few friends. If that was not on the programme, the women would go off to town to have their hair done or to shop. Many women's husbands were actually miners.

They went underground and supervised a team of black workers who did the hard work, setting the fuses and clearing the rock. These men were regarded by the rest of us as an elite group; they earned a higher income, their work could be dangerous, and their wives usually had a generous dress allowance, which enabled them to buy very nice clothes frequently. There were several high-quality dress shops in town, and any number of hairdressers and the Elizabeth Arden Salon was a busy place too.

I wasn't yet able to join in all this kind of activity as we were saving up for our holiday, but I certainly looked forward to learning to drive and being a part of everything soon. In the meantime, I would walk into town once a week, usually on a Tuesday, for the pleasure of buying what we needed and for the change of scene. Michael and I would, like most of our contemporaries, do the family shopping together at the weekend when the car was available. On our Tuesday walks, Stephen would ride his little bike, and I pushed Nicola in the sun-shaded carriage. Stephen was still a little boy, and it was quite a long way. It became a habit to buy a package of Smarties in Kitwe. On the return journey, in the approaching mid-day heat, Stephen's little legs would get tired. I would encourage him to keep going by giving him two Smarties every time we reached the end of a block, and we had to cross a road. He was very tired by the time we reached our house and would begin to fall asleep over his lunch. We all had a rest and a nap in the early afternoon on those days. I found some beautiful Sanderson floral printed curtain fabric, for our bedroom windows, in the department store in town, and kept busy with my sewing machine. I began to make clothes for the children: pyjamas and comfortable little shirts for Stephen and pretty dresses for Nicola. These fabrics came from a small store owned by a family from India. I was always served by the husband, and his lovely wife, dressed in a traditional sari, would smile and admire the children. My children's clothes were a pleasure to work on as they were quick and easy to make. I made a few things for myself too but kept my eye on a very nice dress shop and made up my mind that I would get a couple of fashionable outfits for our trip to London. It had been ages since I was able to spend a little money on myself. We were planning to be in England in late summer so, thinking the children might feel a little cold there, I knitted them matching blue sweaters with fair-isle yokes.

I was rather dismayed when, just a few months after we arrived in Kitwe, Joan and Alan announced they were returning to Cape Town. Alan was then working with a Work/Study group at the mine, which examined time and motion in the workplace. He didn't particularly enjoy this work, perhaps because those employees who were studied didn't appreciate being watched all the time by someone holding a stopwatch. This kind of research was frequently in the news. The industry was beginning to recognise the need for greater efficiency. Even kitchen design was coming under scrutiny; I read about how to have a 'step-saver' kitchen in magazines. We didn't realise it, but the computer age was just over the horizon. I was disappointed my friend would be leaving; I had been looking forward to being part of their circle of friends and knew I would miss them, but the time continued to pass quickly, I was busy, and soon we would be preparing for our first trip home.

Before they left, Joan and Alan had shown us a local recreational spot called Cheesemans Farm. It had initially been a small farm operation out along the Ndola Road, and the owner had dammed up a small tributary of the Kafue River to make sure there would always be enough water for his crops in the dry season. But he had discovered he could also make money by inviting the white folk to use his property at the weekends for picnicking and swimming – there was a small entrance fee. To make the water safe, he had imported some special snails to control the insects that spread *bilharzia*, which was a tropical water-borne disease, and he tested the water frequently. It was regarded as a safe place. We had a wonderful day there together with the Penfolds. It was my first experience of a relaxed picnic in Africa, and I needed Joan's advice on what I should bring. A picnic in England meant sandwiches and lemonade – since there were facilities to light fires at Cheesemans, I didn't think the English picnic fare would quite fit in.

I was anxious to get my driver's licence. Michael had taught me a little about driving a car in Ndola. Now we were more settled, and he would take me to a quieter part of our community where there was less traffic, and, with the children sitting quietly in the back, he would allow me to practise. Since we didn't have seat belts or children's safety car seats in those days, it became second nature to drive smoothly and carefully. After a short time in Kitwe, I felt competent to go for the test but didn't pass the first time because, feeling a little nervous, I couldn't reverse the car between the large cones representing a parking spot without the car touching them. But two weeks later I was less nervous, all went well, and I passed. And gradually, we began to develop a social life. Our friends usually were young marrieds, like ourselves, maybe with a couple of children. A garden barbecue was the preferred way of casual entertaining. In Southern Africa, a barbecue is called a *braai-vleis* (pronounced bry-flace). This is an Afrikaner phrase, which literally means burnt meat/flesh. Usually, children were welcome at a 'braai'. They would play together as the sun went down while the adults enjoyed their 'sundowners'. On special occasions, there might be an adults-only party; should it happen during the rainy season, we would remain inside the house.

Of course, when the children were not included, it was necessary to find a baby-sitter. Most teenage girls would do a little babysitting to earn pocket-money when they were available. However, generally, they needed to leave the Copperbelt for secondary and higher education. As that standard of education wasn't available locally, the times they were available to babysit were infrequent. Occasionally there were also dances at the Mine Club; I especially enjoyed the Christmas dance – a big affair for which we dressed up. We still enjoyed seeing a movie now and again. We had two movie theatres in Kitwe, the Rhokana Cinema near the Mine Club and the Astro Cinema in the centre of town. We couldn't leave the children at night very often, so we didn't see very many movies.

The Copperbelt had a television station based in Kitwe. We didn't have a TV set but decided that when we returned from our holiday in England, we would probably be ready to consider buying one. Nicola celebrated her first birthday in Geddes Street and learned to walk when she was approaching 14 months old. Kitwe used to have a Town Fair early in the dry season, and I entered my lovely little girl in the Baby Show. These affairs were popular in the post-War period. I had made her some cute simple dresses which set off her light tan and took pleasure in dressing her light blond hair. She was looking at her best when the day of the show came. It was an important social event, and of course, all the mothers there thought their child was the most beautiful baby. After an interview with two nurses from the hospital, who were the judges who counted teeth and examined limbs for straightness, Nicola made it to the last six, then there was a pause to enable the mothers to enjoy a cup of tea together and a chat in the shade of the beautiful trees at the show grounds. Then all finalists were summoned for the final judging. A fine boy about nine months old was declared the winner, and Nicola, who proudly demonstrated her walking prowess, was the winner in the 'Toddler' class. Her prize was a certificate entitling her to a half-hour sitting with Andrew Hayward, the best portrait photographer in town. She was a little shy in front of his camera when we had the sitting, but we got some very nice framed pictures.

Our life assumed a regular pattern, and the time quickly passed. Our plans for our long-awaited holiday were all in place, and the great day of our departure approached. We had devised a plan to make the house secure and decided to leave our car in the garage, which wasn't equipped with doors, so Michael purchased lumber to board up the opening when we left the house. Arrangements were made for Jasper to go to a kennel, and my next-door neighbour, Ingrid Fanner, promised to feed the cats. They could sleep in the room attached to the garage. Fortunately, the neighbours in the house on the other side, at 103 Geddes Street, had a dog who would alert them if intruders were about at night. The Africans didn't have a curfew as they had in Cape Town, but generally, we never saw many in our residential area after dark. If the patrolling police found loiterers, they would see to it that they returned to their township. Nearly all dogs belonging to white people were very suspicious of unfamiliar black people and would set up a racket when strangers wandered past the house in the daytime. They usually accepted familiar house servants, so we were reasonably sure the neighbourhood dogs would sound an alarm if strangers were abroad at night. So, having made the best arrangements we could, with some anxious feelings, we packed for our long-awaited holiday in England.

৪০ ০৪

As soon as I settled into my job at the mine in August 1962, we began to think that we would quickly be able to return to England for a holiday visit with our family and show off our two beautiful children. At Christmas, when the copper bonus was announced, we knew it would be possible. This bonus for all employees, including Africans, was reported just before the holiday season and was a percentage of one's annual salary, based on the current world price for copper and the mine's output for the year. This year it was to be 49 per cent, far below the record 105 per cent of a few years earlier, but still in our minds very encouraging. The money could be taken at Christmas or saved and used at the time of the employees' next annual vacation. We choose the latter, and, as charter flights to England were being advertised at the Mine Club, we made a booking for August, by which time I would have been working for the company for one year and thus entitled to six weeks' paid holiday. While I concentrated on my working life and Maureen busied herself with creating our home and caring for the children, the time for our trip home finally arrived. The flight had been booked with Dan-Air Services from Ndola and was to be on a DC-6 aircraft. Refuelling stops were to be made at Entebbe, Wadi Haifa and an overnight stop in Malta, before proceeding to London (Gatwick).

Our new friends, Jill and Otto Bousema, drove us to Ndola airport in the early afternoon for a 4.00 pm departure. On arrival there, we were advised the flight was delayed in Salisbury and would arrive in about two hours. Later we were informed there would be a further delay, and by 8.00 pm it seemed they had no idea when the plane would arrive, so we were taken to a reasonably old Colonial type hotel in Ndola and instructed to be ready for a 6.00 am pickup for the airport. By now, of course, we were all very tired and, after settling the children down, tried to sleep. At 4.00 am, there was a knock on the door, and we were told the plane would be arriving soon, and we had to get ready for a ride back to the airport. When we got there, the aircraft had indeed arrived, and we boarded and took off just as the sun was rising. At last, about

14 hours behind schedule, we experienced our first plane ride and were on our way home to the 'Old Country'. We had no way of letting our family in London know about the delay.

After an interesting stop in Entebbe, Uganda, where we had a light meal and bought some souvenirs, we again headed north, over the thick jungle at first, which gradually changed into more sparse vegetation and then became desert. The sun was now setting, and it was quickly dark, as, in the tropics, there is very little twilight. After just a few hours of sleep, the plane landed at a small airstrip in the desert, beside the Nile, for yet another refuelling stop. This was Wadi Haifa in the Sudan, very close to the Egyptian border. A few years later, this whole region was under the waters of Lake Nasser when the Aswan High Dam was completed. At this stop, we were escorted across the tarmac, lit by a single lamp, to a small white hut and given something to drink. After about an hour's wait, we again boarded and took off over the Nile, which we could see clearly illuminated in the moonlight. Stephen and Nicola had been very good on the flight so far and were soon asleep again. During the daylight hours, they had kept themselves amused with the many small games and books Maureen had assembled prior to our departure. By early morning we were still over the Sahara, approaching the Mediterranean coast. The crew pointed out remnants of the World War II desert war, tanks and wrecked buildings, still visible in the area. It was a thrill to see the coast of Africa receding beneath the aircraft. Soon we landed on the island of Malta. We were scheduled to have a night's sleep here in a hotel, but due to our leaving Ndola so late, this was cancelled. Instead, we were bussed to a hotel in Valetta where we were served a meal. But after two nights with very little sleep, we were all starting to feel pretty exhausted, so our meal did not seem too appetising. After about an hour and a half, we were back on the plane and taking off on the last leg to London. Maureen and I started to get quite excited at the prospect of seeing our family again after all those years.

But our good feelings were short-lived. After flying over the Mediterranean and crossing the coast of France, the air started to become turbulent, and we could see substantial dark clouds ahead with spectacular flashes of lightning. The captain advised that there was a severe storm ahead, and he could not climb above it as the plane was not pressurized for a higher altitude. He would try to steer around it. It seemed he was not very successful because shortly, the plane began to be tossed around violently and, at times, plunged frighteningly, losing what seemed like many feet in altitude. Fortunately, Stephen and Nicola were fast asleep in their seats, and soon Maureen, who appeared to be okay, was given several babies to hold by a stewardess, as their mothers were all being sick. I started to feel very unwell, too and tried to make my way to the bathroom, passing two stewardesses who were giving passengers and another younger stewardess, oxygen. The bathroom was busy, and it did not appear that it would be vacated any time soon, so I returned to my seat.

Maureen, who was still balancing three strange infants on her lap, who were all crying lustily, looked across at me, asking if I was okay. The green colour of my face told her I definitely was not, and she wouldn't look at me again. After a while, the turbulence started to subside, and I began to feel a little better. I managed to hold on to my food, although many didn't. In the late afternoon, we landed at London's Gatwick airport, about 10 hours late. So ended our eventful first flight to our homeland – what a 'memorable' experience!

At our temporary home in Kansenji, Ndola

Our first real home at 101 Geddes Street, Nkana, Kitwe

10.
A Homeland Holiday

Maureen

After the terrifying last leg of our long journey home, my eyes misted up when I saw the patchwork green fields and little country lanes of pretty England below us as we lost height on our way into Gatwick Airport. The children roused, and we began to gather our belongings together in preparation for landing. Stephen and Nicola had been so good during the long flight, even when I was trying to hold three not-my-own screaming babies on my lap; they had simply slept through the drama of that dreadful storm. It was August, and I was wearing a light pants suit, and the children, too, were still wearing the clothes they had boarded the plane in. But we didn't look too travel-stained as we trudged through what seemed like endless elevated corridors to get to the Customs and Immigration Hall. I wondered if there would be anyone left to meet us as we were so late arriving, but as soon as we reclaimed our suitcases and passed through the final doorway, there they were, and I was in my mother's familiar arms. What a wonderful welcome! They had been anxiously awaiting our arrival all day and hadn't been aware that charter flights were often unreliable timekeepers. Michael's mother was there too, with Denis, his brother. My mother had come with Ron, my brother-in-law. My sister had been with them for much of the day, but as she had her third child, nine-month-old Amanda, with her, as the waiting time lengthened, she needed to go back to my parent's home to wait.

We hugged and kissed and cried a little; we were all so relieved to once again be together on English soil; absolutely nothing else mattered. We collected ourselves and had a cup of tea and decided how we would arrange ourselves for the two-hour journey across London. Both Denis and Ron had brought their relatively small cars. Michael's mother had offered us accommodation at her house in Manor Park, so Michael and Stephen went with Denis and, his mother and, Nicola and I joined Ron and Mum. We put the children to bed at Michael's mother's house, and they obligingly fell asleep quickly. Even though it was quite late in the day and we were both tired, I couldn't wait to see Pam, so Michael and I joined Ron, and we took a quick trip to Stanley Avenue so that I could see my dear sister right away. We could just spend a half-hour together. She was already preparing for bedtime, and we were beginning to realise we were tired beyond belief. So, after hugging each other, Pam and I made arrangements to be in Dagenham in a day or two, and Ron drove us back to Browning Road, and we could fall into bed at last.

It was very kind of Michael's mother to allow us to make our temporary home with her because her husband was not well. She gave us her big front bedroom, which could also accommodate the children. She and Dad had moved into their back bedroom, which had twin beds. She needed her own space to be able to sleep well to look after him. Mum told us he was to be admitted to the hospital for tests. Poor Mum, since the deprivations of the war, she had spent many anxious months nursing her husband through emotional and physical trauma. But Mum was thrilled to see her grandchildren and have them near her. The very first morning, when they awoke, she appeared and invited Stephen to come downstairs and have breakfast. Nicola awoke too and was happy to join him. Michael and I drifted off to sleep again, and when we finally surfaced a little while later, they were having a lovely time getting acquainted over breakfast. Michael's mother had always wanted a daughter, so she was happy to pay special attention to Nicola, who was still in diapers at night. She was going to be two years old in a day or two and was learning to talk. Stephen, of course, was already quite a conversationalist. Naturally, Michael's mum understood we wanted to spend time with my parents and family too, but as their house in Dagenham was somewhat smaller, she invited us to use her home as much as we could. Michael also thought we could perhaps have a little private time together without the children since we had babysitters available. So, we began to plan how we were going to spend our six weeks holiday.

ℬ ℭ

It was wonderful to see our family again. My mother was looking quite well, but my father was not feeling very good and could not make it to the airport to meet us. He had been on sick leave from work for some time. The doctor diagnosed stomach ulcers, and he was waiting to attend the hospital for tests. My brother Denis had recently left the British Merchant Navy. He was once again living with my mother in Browning Road, working as a toolmaker at the very same place, The Plessey Company, where I had served my apprenticeship.

Maureen and I were quite keen to have a little time away together, and as my brother very kindly offered his car to us, we planned to have about eight or ten days in Europe. The holiday would be the first time we had been apart from the children since they were born. They were to be left in Maureen's mother's care. Several days before we were due to leave, my father was admitted to the London Hospital at Whitechapel in the East End of the city. We visited him there, but he was not doing well, and we were concerned, although the hospital said he would probably be released in a few days. As my mother still did not have a home telephone, I made arrangements for while we were away, to call my brother at a predetermined time and date on the next-door neighbour's telephone. My brother kindly lent us his Volkswagen Beatle, and after dropping Stephen and Nicola off with Maureen's mother, we crossed the River Thames and drove through the County of Kent to a small airport at Lympne. This airport had a small fleet of cargo aircraft that specialised in transporting cars and passengers over the English Channel to various French towns. We were quite excited. Although we had been to Italy for our honeymoon, this was our first experience of travel in Europe entirely on our own. Everything was a new experience. We spent several days driving at a leisurely pace across France, had a brief detour into Germany, and then to Zurich in Switzerland. Here we located a nice 'pension' above a pub in the old part of the city. That evening, I had arranged to make the call to my brother back in England. We were directed to an International Telephone Office and were amazed at the operator's ability to speak a multitude of languages. After a short time, they connected me to the number I requested, and my brother Denis came on the line. Maureen picked up the extra earpiece provided, and he quietly informed me that my father had not left the hospital and had died the day after we left, on 28th August 1963. Of course, we were both very shocked by this news, and I just said to Denis that we would come home immediately. The next few days were a blur. We proceeded west across Switzerland, barely able to take in the beautiful scenery we were passing through, stopping briefly at Interlaken and staying the night at Neuchâtel in the French-speaking sector. Up early the next morning, we drove right across France to Calais and took the ferry across the English Channel. The British customs at Dover did not seem to quite believe my story and were suspicious when I said we had been to Switzerland and had only been away five days. They searched our car very thoroughly! Maureen quietly explained what had happened, and the Customs' official sarcastically responded, 'You're breaking my heart', and walked away. That night we were back home with my mother and brother.

It was a sad homecoming, but my mother seemed busy with the funeral arrangements and allowed herself little time to grieve in public. In just over a week, the funeral took place at the City of London Cemetery at Wanstead, where my father was cremated. Maureen stayed at home with the children and helped some neighbours prepare the food for a small reception in the front room of my parent's house. There were not a significant number of people at the service. My father was 64 years old when he died, and I was sad that I had not been there at the end of his life and also that we had never really got to know and understand each other as adults. He loved our children but was only able to spend a short time with them. We now only had a short time left until our return to Northern Rhodesia, the place we now called home. I went one afternoon to The Plessey Company, where I had spent seven years in the drawing office and toolroom and where my brother was now employed. Meeting a few of the people I had worked with was quite interesting, but it reinforced my feelings that I did not want to live there. The truth was I was now very keen to get back to Africa.

The day soon arrived for our return flight, and we were somewhat apprehensive because of our bad experience on the way over. My brother took us to Gatwick Airport, where we said a hasty goodbye. This time the flight left on time, and soon we were soaring up over the southern England countryside and turning due south over the Channel. After a smooth flight, we landed at Malta and spent the night in a Valletta hotel. After an early breakfast, we were soon in the air again, crossing the Mediterranean, then the Sahara Desert, landing in Khartoum, the Sudanese capital. Here, in the terminal restaurant, we were served a nice meal, attended by impressively tall Arab men in white robes, each wearing a red fez on his head. We were soon on our way again on the final leg to Ndola, where we landed on time, and our friends Jill and Otto were there to meet us. I was relieved and delighted to be home again in Africa.

⁎ ↰ ↱

On the Sunday following our arrival in England, we all had lunch together at my parent's home, and my mother, who always preferred little girls, got to know Nicola a little; she wasn't too sure about Stephen, however. Stephen, coming up to four years old, was such an articulate talker, she found him a bit unnerving. I guess she still retained memories of the trials she endured with her own three boys when they were small. But she and Dad did agree to have our children for a few days if we should be able to get a little time away together. Of course, we spent quite a bit of time with Michael's mother. She was simply ready and willing to love her grandchildren and thought they were practically perfect. Michael took pictures (as he always did), and we are lucky to have some photos of the children with his Dad, who was about to go into hospital 'for tests'. It was so good of Denis to lend his Volkswagen to us. It made it possible for us to move about quickly. It was summertime, and Denis liked to ride his bike to work. We needed to take the children out quite a bit – my parents-in-law's home wasn't accustomed to the constant activity surrounding caring for two lively little ones. One outing was to Brighton on the south coast, which was a place I had always enjoyed.

The beach was rough and stony, and the chosen day was cool and breezy, but the children, wearing those sweaters I had knitted, enjoyed a trip to the English seaside. In Kitwe, we were three or four days' drive from the beach!

We naturally visited Pam and Ron several times. Auntie Pam especially loved boys, so for her, Stephen was 'the one'. Uncle Ron, who had three brothers, was enchanted by little girls. When we had our little trip to France and Switzerland together, we left the children with my mother. When we returned, we quickly discovered that she had kept Nicola and handed Stephen over to Pam, who cheerfully assumed responsibility. She and Stephen were destined to develop a loving connection, and although they didn't meet often, they would always be good friends. These South African children were an object of great interest to my sister's neighbours. One asked her why Stephen wasn't black since he came from South Africa! Another was quite horrified because he would run about without anything on his feet. In our own faraway home, the children always kicked off their shoes and socks at home because it made them feel cooler, and I had been advised their little feet would become stronger if they were allowed to run barefoot wherever it was safe to do so. I didn't exactly approve of Stephen running across the street in Basildon, doubting those streets to be 'safe', but he came to no harm.

Michael has written about his father's sudden death; this was very sad. Just before we left on our trip, I spent an afternoon with his mother. It had been determined that her husband had cancer, and she thought he would be coming home to die. She visited him tirelessly but encouraged us to take the time for a little break together. This time with their other grandparents was indeed appropriate. Michael's family agreed that our planned short trip should go ahead, and when his father was released from the hospital, we would decide upon our return whether we should continue staying with his mother and father. Of course, everything changed when we spoke to Denis from Zurich. We both have little memory of our journey back to England; we functioned normally but felt frozen. When we arrived, Michael's mother was resting on the couch in the living room. She was so pleased we had returned quickly and was very glad we were back. She was calm and in control of the funeral arrangements and other legal and financial details. She told me of her trips to various offices to deal with certificates and pensions etc. and managed to smile – the kind representative from her husband's place of work who helped her was unusually attentive. She thought having the children back would be a good idea. Of course, I was anxious to have the children in my arms again, so we gathered them up from my parent's home, where we told them of Mr Harbott's recent death.

My mother immediately volunteered to continue to look after the children, but we explained Michael's mum had asked for them to return. She then asked if she could perhaps be of help on the day of the funeral. I appreciated her kindness because I had no experience of what happens when there is a death in the family. I didn't know anything about how these things were arranged and would have been pleased to have her sympathetic presence, but my concern was focussed on Michael and his mother and what they wanted. We took the children home, and Michael's mother was so pleased to have them around, especially Nicola. She told me their presence was a great help to her – their daily life just had to proceed as if everything was normal, and the routine helped her. I greatly admired her calm steadfastness; I never saw her weeping. I knew my own mother, a much more emotional woman, would have behaved differently. On the day of the funeral, I had my instructions. I was to take the children out for a walk before the cars came for the mourners. Then when we returned, I was to promptly open the drapes at all the windows in the front of the house. At that time, when there was a death in a family, it was customary for all the window curtains to be closed to indicate a house of mourning. It was regarded as a sign of respect. But Michael's mother hated this convention and any action she called 'making a parade of death' and wanted life to return to normal - or what approximated normal - as quickly as possible. Two of her nearby neighbours who she knew well were to be let in; they would prepare tea and be ready to serve the light refreshments already prepared. I simply thought it best to do just as she directed. Out we went and, when we returned, I realised I didn't have a house-key to open the front door. I had to knock at a neighbour's house and jump over the fence in my 'good' clothes and high heeled shoes into the back yard, and fortunately, the back door was not locked. I was able to accomplish my appointed task, whisked back all the curtains, and was ready with a clean and tidy Stephen when everyone returned. Nicola was having her afternoon nap.

So that sad, long day passed. Michael's aunts, his mother's sisters Grace and Hilda, had gone to the funeral and came back to the house afterwards. I was delighted to see them. I knew Michael's mother depended on her sisters for so much. She was such a disciplined, reserved woman who had for many years looked after their elderly mother; she didn't have many close friends. She thought, as the eldest sister, she should be the leader of the three, but in fact, she loved and depended on them in place of having 'best friends'. On a day towards the end of our holiday, we took her with us and visited the London Zoo. This day was pleasant and warm, and the children were happy and had a very good time. It gave Michael's mother some lovely memories to reflect on, and we told her that when she felt the time was right perhaps, she would feel strong enough for the long journey to come and stay with us in Kitwe. Michael and I realised this tragedy would define our first homeland holiday, and we both began to look forward eagerly to returning to our African 'home'.

Stephen and Nicola meet Michael's father in England, for the first and last time.

Maureen's childhood home (photo taken during a later visit)

11.
Home Sweet Home

Maureen

The journey back to our African home was routine – there were no delays, and our friend Otto Bousema was waiting at the airport to meet us. Despite the various difficulties we had encountered, especially the sudden death of his father, Michael and I thought the trip had been well worthwhile. We had allowed our parents and other connections to see that after five years of marriage, we were happy together; we were content with the way our shared life was unfolding and that we thought we had made a good choice in going to Africa. We were thrilled to be 'at home' again. We planned for the next few years to continue building our savings and to think about spending fairly modest holidays exploring and learning about the many fascinating and beautiful parts of Southern Africa in the future. In a private corner of my mind, I still nurtured the hope that when we had saved enough money, we would return to England, buy a house in a decent neighbourhood and resume our life there; I definitely wanted our children to have the benefit of an English education. But in the meantime, I was happy to settle back into my comfortable life in the sunshine.

&0 C8

I, like Maureen, was happy to be back in our home in Africa. Although we had enjoyed the holiday, the unexpected death of my father had undoubtedly made it a very sad trip. I was glad he was able to see his only grandchildren, even though their time together was brief. Because he had always been a cheerful, friendly man, I was sure that if he had got to know them, he would have loved them very much. Being in England had reminded me again of the many reasons I had wanted to leave five years earlier. In Africa, I think we had started to appreciate the vast open spaces and the sense of greater freedom that this gave us. After a brief visit to my old company Plessey again, I believed that my work situation was much better now. I enjoyed the challenges that the work for the mining company presented and the camaraderie of the men that I worked alongside. I also felt we had many good years ahead of us in Northern Rhodesia, and a very good opportunity to save money for a house of our own, perhaps in England or possibly South Africa.

But as Mr Harold Macmillan had predicted in 1960, there were specific political changes beginning to occur in Southern Africa. The governments of France, Belgium and Portugal had started to leave their African possessions, often with disastrous results. Britain, too, was making a start on the negotiating process towards independence for Northern Rhodesia and Nyasaland. These two colonies, together with Southern Rhodesia, had together formed 'The Federation of Rhodesia and Nyasaland'. We felt the change if it ever happened, was many years away; we quickly settled back into our comfortable way of life on the Copperbelt.

The type of work on the mine gave me many opportunities to learn new skills and procedures, but I still felt I needed to improve my technical education further. So, I signed up for a correspondence course to study for membership in the Institute of Mechanical Engineers, a professional organisation. This higher education, I believed, would help me to get a much better job at a later date. It meant studying most evenings after work, and I somehow also managed to fit in a little watch repairing. We frequently worked late at the mine. Occasionally, when there was a real panic situation, we would continue working through the night, to be relieved by another person at 7.00 am. We were paid double-time for that working period and given the next day off to recover.

On 22nd November 1963, I had worked late until 7.00 pm. It was a stormy night, and I listened to Radio Rhodesia as I drove home. The programme was interrupted, and it was announced that John F Kennedy had been shot in Dallas, Texas. At home, I had a short-wave radio and tuned to 'The Voice of America'. We sat and listened to the events unfolding and learned that night, the President of the United States had died of his wounds. It made us both feel very shocked. I wondered what was going wrong in America. There had been much racial unrest in the south since the 1950s, and now they were also involved in a very bloody war in Vietnam. We thought we were safer in central Africa. But by the end of the year, we started to feel the 'Wind of Change' that Harold Macmillan had spoken about was beginning to blow our way; the political situation had noticeably started to change. On 31st December 1963, the Federation of Rhodesia and Nyasaland was dissolved, and Northern Rhodesia became a separate political entity, with talks in progress toward achieving independence.

ဆ ඥ

We came back to our Geddes Street home just before Stephen's fourth birthday. Hence, my first project, after checking that all was well with our house, was to plan and arrange a birthday party for him, which became an excellent opportunity to gather together our new friends and their children and resume the social part of our life. We had continued to pay our houseboy Peter reduced wages while we were away. We had asked him to check the house once every week or two and to report it if the outside had been compromised in any way. He turned up with Alfred, the garden boy, in tow a couple of days after we arrived home. They were happy to see us back and wanted to resume their duties. All was well. He took over the housework, and I was free to begin baking and planning Stephen's birthday celebration. Stephen's party was the first I had ever attempted. We were lucky that his birthday was at the end of September. The weather was warm and a little humid at that time of the year because it was just before the rainy season, which usually began around early October. We were pretty sure we would not have to deal with rain, and the children's table could be set outside in the shade, where the adult guests could sit comfortably in the shadow of the trees. It was quite a nice party. But I soon learned that such social events owed their success to early preparation and paying attention to the details and because I was not yet a very confident hostess or cook, the effort made me quite tired.

A week later, after the party, we celebrated Michael's 28th birthday on 7th October, by which time the rainy season had begun. The mornings could be beautifully clear, sunny, and fresh after the overnight rain, which always started in the late afternoon and, as the season progressed, heavy thunderstorms would continue very noisily, often right through the night.

During one violent dinner-time storm, the lightning seemed to flash right in the kitchen at the electric stove. My neighbour declared it was a 'thunderbolt', and a giant tree next door came down and damaged the roof over their kitchen area. Now we truly appreciated the ugly corrugated iron roofs on these houses and why they had such a wide overhang protecting the walls, which were surrounded at the base by a broad, shallow cement trough on the ground. It was all designed to make sure the rainwater was quickly guided away to the ditches, which eventually connected to the Kafue River. So much moisture in the atmosphere made the air too humid – I would sometimes get a sick headache and need to lie down and had little interest in food at dinner time. I realised that I had been feeling tired and lacking in energy since our return from England. The thought occurred to me that I might be pregnant again, and as soon as THAT thought came to mind, I began to feel nauseous. Surely not! A few more weeks confirmed my suspicion and off I went to the hospital clinic to have the diagnosis confirmed and to be registered in the prenatal programme, by which time I was becoming quite pleased with the idea we might add another baby to our family.

The nausea was a nuisance, but with two lively children to look after, I was really busy, and time never hung heavily on my hands. The lemon tree outside the pantry window seemed to bear fruit for many months of the year, and it became my helper. I lived with a glass of cold, home-made sweetened lemon juice always at hand, which I sipped frequently. It helped to hold down the early pregnancy nausea. As usual, I lost weight for the first few months – regular food didn't seem attractive, and the birth date seemed far distant. I realised I felt a little depressed.

The children, Stephen, mostly, were a handful, but I took great pleasure in looking after them. Stephen always preferred to play outside with a couple of boys who lived almost next door and in the dry season, they all played together, either in our garden or theirs. By lunchtime, he would be covered in reddish dirt. They liked to create miniature roads in the sandy soil and run their Dinky cars and trucks about imaginary errands, accompanied by '*vroom, vroom*' noises. When lunchtime came, and the boys returned to their own home, Stephen had to be picked up outside the kitchen door and deposited in the bathtub, where I would strip him and bathe him, so he began lunch cleaned up. We all had a rest in the afternoon. Nicola, however, in my mind, was a practically perfect little girl. She liked to play very close by wherever I was. I never lost her in a store; she was always within arms' reach. At the time, I didn't think this remarkable and, remembering the many times I had gone looking for Stephen when he was around three years old, I was grateful. If Stephen was available, they would often play quite happily together. To help the time pass more quickly, towards the end of the third month, still looking slender, I answered an advertisement for temporary work, mornings only. I became the temporary personal secretary to the Senior Partner in a law office, Mr Longman of Longman & Co., in Kitwe and was engaged in taking care of his personal correspondence for a period of three months. When not busy, I was to offer assistance to the five other women in the office, four of whom were secretaries to other lawyers in the group. My work, in this instance, would be mostly typing Wills.

I had discovered a very lovely Early Childhood Playschool group run by two women in Kitwe, who would take care of Stephen and Nicola during my hours at work. The mornings-only job made it a simple matter for me to take them to and pick them up from the playgroup now that I could legally drive. Stephen could enjoy supervised play with boys his age, perhaps good preparation for school days. He was quite ready for this and Nicola was such a charmer, I knew the two 'teachers' who had the help of two coloured nannies would respond to her sunny nature, and she would see and interact with other little girls. I didn't immediately confess my condition to Mr Longman – it was a temporary position for a specific period after all. Mr Longman, a member of the Rotary Club, was planning an important overseas trip to New York and Chicago, where the head office of Rotary International was, as the Southern Africa delegate to the Annual Conference. He was excited at the prospect of this trip and the opportunity it presented to meet lawyers in America. The planning of his itinerary and travel arrangements created a lot of mail correspondence daily, aside from his legal work. His Legal Assistant, Vicki Smits, was too busy to take care of this easy stuff. I was happy to have the opportunity to brush up on my fast typing skills. Mr Longman used a dictating machine at home at night for the work I did. I had used a foot-operated dictating machine in London so that, too, presented no problem.

This little job gave me a new interest as I met new people. I was invited to a wedding shower for a pretty young girl in the office; Wilhelmina was getting married, and Vicki, who had five children, became my friend. This was my first experience of a North American-type shower party. The important part for me now was that I would earn a little money and enjoy, for a short time, a small sense of independence. I had plans for that cash and eventually bought a beautiful top-of-the-line *NECCHI* sewing machine for myself and a fair-sized refrigerator for our kitchen. The little one we had brought from Cape Town wasn't adequate for our growing family or the climate in Kitwe. For that space of time, it was a perfect little job. It took my mind off my condition, over-riding that slightly sick feeling I always had, I made a new friend and the children had an exciting time, which was also a valuable learning experience. I would collect them and arrive home at about 1.00 pm, and we would eat a light lunch and then all have a rest for an hour or so and be refreshed when Michael came home from work. When he arrived home, we would have a cup of tea together, and then I would begin preparing our evening meal. By this time, the children would have got rather dirty again, so when Michael was in the bath, we used to put the two of them in by his feet, and Michael would wash them down. They would play a little together, and he would then call me to take the children, dry them, and put their pyjamas on. It was an easy way for Michael to enjoy a little playtime with his children.

During this time, we naturally had been in touch by mail, as always, with Michael's mother. She was calm and, although sad and lonely, was not overwhelmed by becoming a widow. She had always longed for the opportunity to experience foreign travel, and we encouraged her to consider flying out to spend a little time with us. I thought she might like to come and stay for however long she wanted. She could get to know her little grandchildren and experience a way of life that was quite different from that she had always known. She had always been the 'head' of their family. Michael's dad had been a dear, loving man but not very ambitious either in his working life or socially. We were both excited when she said she was coming and we purchased a single bed and other furnishings, which included an armchair and a picture depicting an English scene, for what would be 'her' room.

There was an alcove in our bedroom, which would accommodate a crib for the new baby. Nicola, nearly three by this time, was sharing Stephen's room, but we liked to have a new infant in our room at night for the first few months. I was completing the final weeks of my temporary job and was now in the seventh month of pregnancy. Again because of my tall stature, I didn't look as pregnant as many women did that far along, so my colleagues at work had only recently become aware of our 'expectations', which of course didn't matter at all because I now had less than two weeks still to work. At the weekend off, we all went to Ndola Airport when the happily anticipated day of mother's arrival came. She was flying on a BOAC (British Overseas Airways Corporation) VC-10 aircraft. These new aircraft had recently come into service, and many fresh young 'contract' mine employees were arriving weekly from England. We called these newcomers 'VC-10ers'. In previous years most new employees for the mines had come, as we had, via South Africa and Southern Rhodesia. It was a truly happy occasion to greet Mum and take her to our home. Of course, she was somewhat disoriented by her long, unfamiliar flight, but arrived in pretty good order and had decided she loved flying. She knew she would need a little time to get adjusted to the change. Since I was still at work on weekday mornings and I wanted the children to carry on at the playschool (I didn't think it appropriate to ask her to supervise the children as soon as she arrived), I asked her if she would like to prepare lunch for us. I thought she might enjoy a bit of peaceful relaxation initially, early in the day while she got used to this new environment, and perhaps a little light food preparation, which she had always seemed to enjoy at home, would give her a small project to work on. I only had one more week to work, so when

Monday came, off we went as usual. Things went quite well that first week, but she expressed some diffidence about having the houseboy in the vicinity while she was in the kitchen. This was all part of the different way of life here. We generally prepared dinner together, and it was strange to her that we didn't have to do the washing up! But the following week, I was at home and able to take her about a bit in the town while the children continued to go to playschool in the mornings for another month. On our shopping expeditions, we purchased baby clothes and knitting yarn, and in the afternoons after a bit of a rest, we would sit knitting companionably together. I remember discussing names with her. Once again, I thought Melanie would be a nice name for a girl and, should the baby be a boy, David was a strong traditional sort of name. Michael still did not think Melanie at all suitable. One evening, when Mum was finishing her white knitted baby jacket, she looked up and said, 'I think this one looks like Melanie's jacket'. Michael realised the matter was out of his hands. He had established a desk in the *breeze* room, where once again, he would quietly work away on his studying or repairing watches.

As I reached the weeks towards the end of pregnancy, I naturally became a little weary. Michael bought a second-hand bicycle for Mum's use (she had always ridden a bike in England), and since Stephen now had a bigger child's three-wheeler, she would take him for little rides in our small community in the afternoons when there wasn't much car traffic. She was sometimes a little anxious when large dogs barked at them but soon learned which streets to avoid. Mum truly enjoyed a little exercise and liked our company but was becoming aware of a certain lack of purpose in her life. She, who had been so accustomed to ordering domestic life, missed that responsibility and felt she needed more to do. My due date, 12th July, approached – and went by. I was hardly surprised but didn't have too much longer to wait. On the evening of the 19th, as we were preparing for bed, I knew I had the early signals and thought perhaps I should check into the hospital. Michael's mum was gentle and kissed my cheek lovingly and wished me a speedy delivery, and off we went.

At the hospital, I soon realised this was not like St Josephs in Cape Town, but fortunately, the midwife, assisted by a registered maternity nurse, had no other women in labour that night. Michael was briskly dismissed and returned home, promising to look in on his way to work the next day. We still did not have a telephone. A doctor was to be called only if a problem developed. At first, I spent a few hours alone in what seemed like a cavernous delivery room with very bright lights on a very hard bed, being visited every so often by one of the two attendants. Midnight came and went, and shortly both attendants were with me all the time, but they mostly talked with each other. There came a pause in 'the action', which I hadn't experienced before and feeling very much alone; I began to cry a little. My nurses asked me why I was upset, and I replied that it had been a long night, and I didn't seem to be getting anywhere - my last baby had been born much quicker, and why had everything stopped? They told me that this sometimes happens – my body needed a little rest; everything was fine and would gather momentum again soon. As the dawn began to lighten the sky, they were proved correct; we had reached the third stage and, because I knew what to do at that point, Melanie Anne arrived at 7.00 am on 20th July 1964 weighing 7 lbs. exactly. To my surprise, she had a full head of straight, dark hair, which was very appropriate for a little girl to be named Melanie, and though quite perfect, she was a bit smaller than my previous infants. I was delighted to have another little girl.

Michael arrived as promised, on his way to work, just as I was being moved to my bed in a ward with three other new mothers. So, he had to wait a bit to be admitted. By this time, I was beginning to understand this hospital was run on protocols established in England. Michael was relieved to find all was well, although I was feeling fragile and asked him to come alone for visiting that evening. Mum was able to accompany him the following afternoon when I was feeling a little steadier. In this establishment, new mothers were allowed one week after delivery in the nurses' care. I'd had ten or eleven days after delivery in Cape Town but having help at home now and the hospital so close by, made a more extended stay unnecessary.

As usual, no matter how much I put my feet up, breastfeeding was not adequate, and when Melanie was three weeks old, we turned to a formula I had introduced to Nicola when S.M.A.

proved too enriched for this climate. *Ostermilk* was a well-known English brand of baby food, and this company produced a tropical climate formula. Michael's mother was quite impressed by how quickly and calmly I dealt with this part of baby-care and told me about her own anxious and confusing experiences as a young mother, receiving so many different opinions from her mother and everyone else. I thought being able to adjust to the situation was a regular part of my job. I'd had my 29th birthday recently and regarded my Melanie as the child of my maturity. I certainly felt like an experienced mother now. Perhaps in the 'old days', there had not been any informative baby-care books available.

Three weeks after Melanie's birth, big sister Nicola celebrated her third birthday. We had a small afternoon party with our friends' children, and this little party was an opportunity to show off our beautiful new baby and to receive our friends' congratulations. Melanie had fitted very quickly into family life.

Stephen was approaching his fifth birthday, and I was anxious to get him into regular school. A friend Anita, who came from Ireland, had secured a place for her daughter in the Catholic junior school, which was staffed mainly by an order of American nuns, and I thought if I could request a place for Stephen there too, we could share driving duties. The new school term began in September. As soon as I heard from Anita that 'The Convent' school office was open in the mornings, I braved the school Principal, Sister Damian, and asked if my son could be accepted. This school was a highly regarded private one which of course charged fees. I wanted my children to start here because I firmly believed we should always strive for the best education we could afford for our children. There was a public state school in our community, which was much cheaper, but I knew there would gradually be a higher enrolment of black children there. In Northern Rhodesia, at that time, very few black children spoke English. I had learned, from talking to a young teacher in the public school system at a Tupperware party I had attended, that in the early grades it was a very great challenge for the teacher to communicate with a good proportion of her class, which resulted in slowed progress for the whole level and school staff was concerned about deteriorating standards.

Sister Damian, an impressively large nun with brown eyes, strong eyebrows and a faint, dark moustache, wore a heavy long white *habit* with a *wimple* that concealed her hair and ears (as did the other nuns of the Order) and was not at first enthusiastic about admitting Stephen, who would be five years old at the end of September. Still, when I mentioned I had three children, my three-year-old daughter would be ready just two years into the future, she smiled and remarked that his birth date did just meet the requirement for admittance and so he was registered. Of course, I knew they might prefer to keep spaces open for Catholic children but reasoned the possibility of there being three schoolchildren in the future might be attractive. I was delighted and hurried off to Economy Stores in Kitwe to buy his school uniform clothes.

Mother had been with us for about three months when she suddenly announced that since Michael's brother Denis had arrived in Cape Town and was living in an apartment, she thought she ought to join him and maybe be of use keeping house for him. I felt a little let down because I had tried very hard to make her feel welcome, and I thought she would have liked to stay a little longer with her grandchildren. I realised that she maybe felt a bit like a displaced person in our home because she had been used to making all the everyday decisions in her own home before she was widowed. In our family, naturally, Michael and I talked together and made those decisions. So, when Melanie was about six weeks old, we drove Mum to Ndola with her luggage and saw her off on a train journey to Cape Town. It was a journey in reverse of that we had made just a few years before.

I was very sad to say 'goodbye' to her again. I wondered if I could have done more to make her feel comfortable, but eventually came to think that perhaps she needed to find her own path through making the adjustment to widowhood and ease of mind. And I had to confess life was not so easy with another person always in the house, even though we had frequently truly enjoyed each other's company. Poor Nicola missed her Nana sharply and looked very woebegone. She didn't seem to resent the new baby in any way but was a sad little girl for some weeks. She and Nana had spent quite a lot of time together.

Family life and the school routine claimed my attention.

The school day began at 8.00 am, and the younger children in the first two grades were dismissed at noon. Anita McCabe shared the driving with me as we had planned. Anita was quite a lazy person and didn't want to get up early all the time, so one week, I would do the early run, taking Nicola and the baby along, still in her nightie, and Anita would pick the children up. The alternate week she would do the early run – she was quite frequently somewhat tardy – and I would meet them at noon. Stephen didn't seem too enthusiastic about school, and I quickly discovered that he had little interest in learning to read. This revelation surprised me because he was a very bright little boy and extremely observant. When quite young, on our walks into town, he would call out the make and model name of nearly all the cars coming towards us before I could identify them – I had to wait until they were alongside us. So, I made flashcards of the homework words he needed to learn and drilled him at home. I was a bit disappointed to discover that books and reading, which were so important and enjoyable to me, held little charm for him. On the plus side, however, he was quite athletic, was good at all the sports activities, and soon learned to swim like a fish.

Melanie did well; she was a very happy baby. Lively and energetic when awake, she slept peacefully every night. Because more than a year had gone by since our holiday in England, Michael thought it time to plan a road trip to Cape Town so that we could visit our friends there. It was a very long way to drive. We had heard of many a group that had driven to Cape Town in four days in a small Volkswagen. For such a long trip, we needed to take the school year into consideration and thought we should have a better, more reliable vehicle. School children in the southern hemisphere always had their most extended holiday after Christmas, so we started to make plans for a holiday the following January.

ॐ ⚝

I don't know why I was surprised when Maureen informed me that she has once again pregnant. Was it those warm, lazy tropical afternoons? But it did seem to me that Maureen was in her element having babies and looking after young children; she never wanted to have a career outside of the home, and I wondered if she had a secret desire to have a baby or two in every country we resided. Once the pregnancy was confirmed, I was quite relaxed about it as our financial situation was improving, and the company took care of all the medical. I had been delighted with Nicola and secretly hoped for another girl, as they seemed so much easier to manage. Now that Maureen was able to drive and needed the car to ferry the children back and forth to school, it was not at all practical for her to drive me to work, so we bought a Vespa motor scooter. This was similar to the one I'd had in England, and I didn't need any additional licence to drive it. In the months following Melanie's birth, there was great excitement in the African community as talks between the British Minister for Colonial Affairs and leaders of the black community progressed towards the country becoming an independent state with an elected native government. Many of them genuinely believed this would mean the black Africans would then take over the Europeans' (a common name for anyone, not black) jobs, cars, and houses. This created some apprehension and tension among the white population, which grew as Independence Day approached.

On 24th October 1964, the Republic of Zambia was founded, and Kenneth Kaunda was elected President. One of his first acts was to declare all opposition parties banned, therefore making it a one-party state. There were no arguments or demonstrations as he controlled the police and the armed forces. Native 'tribal' culture readily accepted the idea that there should be one 'Chief'. President Kaunda was very aware that the white population was essential to maintain the economy, particularly the considerable copper mining industry, and he achieved this basically by ensuring the continued security of the mines and townships and by leaving the country's economic survival alone. We all went to see him in a parade through Kitwe, and Stephen learned at school to 'Sing a Song of Zambia, Proud and Free', the new National Anthem. For the average African, of course, it was quite a let-down as they gradually began to realise that they would have to work a long time to acquire the better conditions they had expected to transform their lives. At about the same time, Nyasaland also achieved independence, becoming Malawi, but independence was not considered by Britain for the other territory, Southern Rhodesia, at this time.

ৡ ೮೫

Because some families were already leaving the Copperbelt, we had quickly been allocated a nice Bancroft-type house at 8 Queens Street. The family leaving the house to go to the United States had installed a good quality fitted carpet in the living room. They offered it to us at a very reasonable price. We were pleased to accept, and we purchased from another couple who also were leaving, dark red vinyl tiles for the kitchen. We cleaned and installed them ourselves and were well pleased with our new home. On about one-third of an acre which sloped towards the back, the lot had well-developed lawns, and in an area at the rear of the house, adjacent to the driveway and garage, a covered patio was shaded by a large well grown purple bougainvillaea. Our houseboy James helped us move from our Geddes Street address, and I thought that as we now lived in a quieter area, I would be better able to relax and feel less stressed. But first of all, the new gynaecologist who had arrived at the Mine Hospital wanted me to have some minor repairs, which required a short stay in hospital. At that time, so many young women were having repair procedures even hysterectomies for what I thought were relatively minor problems. Michael and I believed some of them simply wanted to avoid further pregnancies, and perhaps the surgeons needed the work. Such a drastic solution was not necessary in many cases. After my minor surgery, my doctor recommended that I begin taking the newest birth control pills, which had become so popular and were regarded as very safe. I accepted his advice, and they worked well enough for us. I gained a little weight, however, but I still had mild anxiety feelings. The pharmaceutical industry had recently developed new pills for that, too! 'Uppers' they were commonly called.

Our new house was hedged by hibiscus for privacy at the sides, and there were also colourful gerbera daisies growing profusely in the front of the house. All along the back fence were young banana trees, and there were tall papaya trees, mangoes, guavas, and avocadoes. Papayas grew very quickly. In Geddes

Street, I had planted one from seed as an experiment; it produced fruit in just under a year. The space beyond the back fence had been cultivated as a vegetable garden, and there was a small patch of corn growing. Michael wasn't too interested in gardening; he was toying with the idea of learning to play golf and didn't have the time available, so we decided to let that space return to a natural state. I didn't like the growing corn as it tended to hold pockets of water in the rainy season, which attracted mosquitoes. With our gardener, I planted a lemon tree outside the kitchen door and one of the beautiful trees we called *Flamboyants*, in the front of the house, which when well-grown would create shade for the window of the living room. In the hottest part of the year, they resembled giant scarlet umbrellas when they came into flower in the town centre, where I had first seen them. I had grown dahlias for their colours in Geddes Street; this time, I thought about roses. I was pleased with this house. Michael made a colourfully painted garden swing seat for us and a tall swing for the children's play area that Melanie liked. We had brought from Geddes Street the big 'cottage' playhouse, which he had constructed from a heavy-duty packing case some machinery had arrived in at his workshop.

We bought our first TV set. Programming had been available in Kitwe for quite a few years. Like everyone else, we quickly became hooked. It was beamed from Lusaka with some locally produced programmes. At 6.00 pm every night, on would go the set, and we would start with the news which was produced locally. Then we would have canned programmes from the U.S. and other countries. We saw Sonny and Cher, and Stephen loved 'Bonanza'. He would strap on his toy gun belt and wear his cowboy hat while he watched. The night's entertainment ended at 11.00 pm. I also now had a fantastic new washing machine. It was a semi-automatic machine that stood in the bathroom where I could connect the hoses to the hot water supply. It was a semi-automatic machine because it had three foot-operated pedals, which controlled the 'start' (agitate) function, the spin cycle, and the 'empty' function. The washed clothes could be rinsed in the bathtub if I needed to wash another load in the same water as the first load; there was a 'suds return' button. It sure was an improvement on my previous method. The washed clothes were collected by James and hung on the outdoor lines to dry; he spent the afternoon ironing. We had engaged a new gardener, Jackson. He was a smallish, middle-aged man who used to clean the children's shoes, wash the car, and look after the garden. The lawns surrounding our house needed a lot of care. He didn't speak much English but was very willing. He ran about on his little legs and would become the second pair of eyes for me when Melanie was in the garden. I didn't leave her alone very much, but if something happened to her when I did briefly step inside, Jackson would run to the kitchen door and shout, 'Madam, madam come quickly' and run back to where she was. By the time I arrived on the scene, Jackson would be standing over her worriedly wringing his hands because she was crying, but never touching her. Of course, such a lively toddler would occasionally fall, but he knew I should be the one to pick her up. He regarded himself as her temporary guardian when I was not in view. We knew ourselves to be rather lucky with our help. Our black servants always loved little children.

We hadn't been in the house very long when Stephen became unwell. He had always been very healthy except for getting the measles, but he developed a severe headache with high fever, which was worse in the afternoons. He certainly was too shaky to go to school. Of course, a doctor was called. Dr O'Flynn responded. He thought Stephen was a strong boy and would get better – it was probably a virus. A couple of days later, I became steadily more concerned; I thought he was beginning to hallucinate when the fever was very high, and Melanie seemed to be sickening, too. We now had a telephone in our house, so again I called the hospital for advice. My call quickly produced another visit by Dr O'Flynn.

As he left, he said to me, 'Mrs Harbott, if we get another phone call from you, we will have to take your children into the hospital.' It sounded rather like a threat. I responded, 'Dr O'Flynn, that might be quite a good idea – we need to know why two of my children are sick.' He gave me a look and then left. There was no improvement in our children, and we were both getting very little sleep, so of course, I did telephone again – I was becoming desperately worried. I had learned from Dr Spock's helpful baby book that such a prolonged severe headache could be a symptom of encephalitis. I was advised to bring my children to the hospital where a technician was to take samples for a blood test.

The next morning Dr O'Flynn came unannounced to our door. 'Mrs. Harbott, I regret to tell you that your children have malaria.' I sat down quickly in the cane chair in our entry hall and said, 'What do we have to do now?' Dr O'Flynn said that Stephen could be nursed at home, but Melanie should be admitted to the hospital immediately because she was so young and off he went. My friend Kay Esposito, who had been a Registered Nurse before she had children, came to sit with Stephen, who seemed extremely sick to me and Nicola, who seemed perfectly well, so off I went with Melanie. I didn't know how to deal with leaving my precious little girl in the Children's Ward in the care of strangers. I wasn't allowed to stay with her, and I had to return to Stephen and Nicola anyway. When I got home, I discovered a package on the doorstep at the front of the house with a note from Dr O'Flynn advising me that the contents of the box were to be administered as directed to Stephen! I had a very poor opinion of this doctor. I thought he should at least have spoken to me directly and maybe express regret at his previous attitude. He knew where I would be. Once on the medication, Stephen improved, and we managed to begin getting some sleep. I used to visit Melanie in the afternoons, she seemed very sick for the first few days, and it was always so painful leaving her. After a while, when Melanie began to improve and was beginning to eat and drink a little, I was horrified by how poorly she was cared for. At home, she had been out of *nappies* during the daytime. Of course, it was perfectly normal that toilet training should break down when she was so sick.

One afternoon when I found her in a real mess, dirty and crying in her crib, I made a big fuss, demanded clean bedding and clothing, took Melanie to the bathroom and bathed her myself and had quite a few nurses hopping about. Then I visited the Matron's office. Matron was the Supervisor of Nursing staff, and I told her the story and my opinion of the whole episode. I felt justified in conducting this interview standing up! I was mad. Matron was not amused. At the end of my angry speech, she simply said, 'Thank you, Mrs Harbott, Good Afternoon.' Melanie was released a day or so later. I thought the whole incident very unfortunate.

Before Independence, there had been no malaria in Kitwe. The previous Town Commissioner for Health had made sure the boundaries of the townships were sprayed regularly to kill mosquitoes, which did not travel great distances. The new *black* Commissioner thought spraying was not necessary. The English doctors at our hospital had not encountered malaria before among the *white* population. I privately thought they should certainly have known about the possibility of it reappearing. We now lived closer to the Kafue River, where a small community of Africans lived. The outbreak of malaria was quickly contained and traced to that little group and proved the need for continued vigilance, and regular spraying was resumed. So, with the uncertainty inherent in our current situation and what sometimes seemed like the beginning of a gradual breakdown of our living standards, it was no surprise that we all now lived with some anxiety.

In 1966, Nicola joined Stephen at school. She took to learning like a duck to water, and all the nuns loved her. Sister Mary Crucifix told me, 'Nicola is such a little dear.' She would come home from school with her 'reading homework' words on flashcards. After our lunch and our usual short rest period she would tuck her flashcards into the waist of her swimsuit panties - the children wore very little in the hot afternoons at home - and now and then she would take them in her hands and say the words aloud and tuck them away again and continue playing. I also introduced her to dancing classes. There were two dance schools in Kitwe, and they maintained a good standard of instruction by teaching the Royal Academy syllabus. Nicola enjoyed her dance classes very much and made a new friend called Irma. Irma's father's family had all come from Italy; they were all Catholic, so Irma naturally went to the same school, and I soon met Irma's mother, Andrea. Occasionally we would meet at the mine swimming pool. Andrea, a South African, loved to swim, but her husband was in private business in Kitwe, so they didn't have a membership in the Mine Club. We could take them there as our guests. It was from Andrea that I learned how to make real Italian spaghetti sauce and lasagne, all of which she had learned from her mother-in-law.

At weekends when Michael was at home, we all had a rest in the early afternoon, and James would knock quietly on our bedroom door at about 3.30 pm and say, 'The tea is here, Madam.' James was a very attentive houseboy. On school days during the week, when I arrived back from the morning school run having dropped into the grocery store for the items we needed on the way home, I would leave the car just outside the garage to be washed by Jackson if it needed cleaning. When James heard the car, he would plug in the filled kettle, and I would lift Melanie out of the car and carry the eggs into the kitchen. James would go to the car and bring in all the other supplies and neatly put them away and then make me some tea. I still made our beds myself, but James was very efficient with managing the general housework, and he always had the house tidy when I returned from the morning school run. On Thursday afternoons, James would clean either the refrigerator or the cooking stove and oven. When I made our dinner or baked a cake, James would stand nearby and wash each utensil I put down and pass me a fresh one when I needed it. James wanted to take over the cooking, but I still preferred to do that myself. If I had a friend in for afternoon tea, he would set the small table either in the living rooms during the rainy seasons or on the shaded patio when it was dry, then make the tea and bring it to me on a tray. We valued our household helpers and allowed them to take home leftover food and discarded clothing. They particularly liked to have the discarded drippings from frying and roasting. I would harden this in the fridge and pass over a nearly full tin from time to time. They were used to living very simply and had their own traditional diet but enjoyed having some fat to cook meat when they could afford it.

The arrangement about sharing the driving with Anita hadn't lasted very long. She and Red McCabe, her husband, never got along very well, and she returned to Ireland with her children for a lengthy vacation. So, I began sharing the driving run to school with my friend Gloria Walsh. Gloria had a big American car; many of the wives of the men who worked underground had fancy cars, and her two boys went to the Convent School too. Sometimes we would have a little shopping trip together for a change of scene and visit another of the Copperbelt towns. On one of our trips, when

Nicola was in school, I had Melanie with me; Gloria brought her daughter Anne. We decided to go to Mufulira. It took a little under an hour to get there. There were two small strip malls separated by an undeveloped open space with a dusty path across it. We looked around the first area, considering our purchases. Gloria suggested it was time for a coffee, and I suddenly realised Melanie wasn't in view. We called her name and then looked in every store, and I began to feel frantic, although I was trying to be calm.

Gloria suggested that perhaps she had followed someone else that she had mistaken for me, over to the other stores. So, I asked her to remain where we were and keep looking while I ran over to the other stores and reported my missing child in all of them. I found and heard no sign of her. I ran back to where Gloria was waiting, and she said perhaps we should go to the car and begin a broader search. We backed the car from its parking space to drive slowly around the shopping area, passing the roads that led into the residential area. Coming out from one of these roads was Melanie in her pretty pink dress, holding the hand of a strange woman. Gloria slammed her foot on the brake, and I was out of that car in a flash and grabbed Melanie into my arms. Melanie smiled happily at me, and the woman hastily explained she had left her house to walk to the stores when she saw this nicely dressed little girl walking alone towards her into the residential area, and she didn't think so young a child should be walking alone. So, she asked her where she was going. Melanie had replied, 'See Mummy.' And the woman, knowing she had never seen this child before thought that perhaps 'Mummy' was at the stores. At no time was Melanie upset - she seemed an unusually self-assured little girl, but what a fright we had had. Another time a week or so later, I had a phone call from Gloria because Melanie had walked alone around the block to visit Anne. When I arrived to bring her back, Gloria very firmly told me that I must spank her. But she was such a sparkling, bright, and good little girl usually, I never smacked her. We just made sure that in the future, the hastily constructed gate to the back garden was always closed so that she couldn't escape, but she did get a good, serious talking-to, and I never ever lost her again.

Back to school for Stephen and welcoming Melanie to the family in July 1964

Rhokana Mine, Kitwe with smelter and refinery (centre) and workshops (foreground)

We spent many happy times at the Rhokana Mine swimming pool

**Zambia Independence Day parade on 24th October 1964
President Kenneth Kaunda (centre right) and
Robert Mugabe (right)**

Our new Bancroft-style house

12.
Our Great Trek

Michael

It was now 18 months since we had a holiday, and as I qualified for six weeks' leave each year, we started planning a long trip back to South Africa. Melanie was now five months old. I was beginning to feel that our days in Zambia were numbered and thought we should see as much of Southern Africa as possible whilst we had the opportunity and the money. We had purchased a better car and sold the Vauxhall Victor to an African. Our 'new' black Toyota Crown station wagon was about three years old and had been owned by a priest in The Order of White Fathers, an American missionary group operating in the northern area of Zambia, where there were mainly dirt roads. Although it had relatively high mileage, it was in superb condition and seemed to have been well looked after.

We planned to rent a caravan in South Africa and tow it down to the Cape and round the coast to Durban and Johannesburg and then drive home. This holiday was a rather ambitious trip with three children, one of them a baby. To tow a caravan, I needed a hitch for the car, but the mine workshops were quite experienced at fitting these devices. The rental company had also sent me details of additional electrical work required for the vehicle for braking and lighting. While Maureen was busy getting the children and herself and all the clothing and supplies needed ready for the trip, I serviced the car and checked it over as best I could for any potential problems. This holiday was going to be a long, six weeks trip. As we were going into areas where malaria was prevalent, we were given tablets by the mine hospital to be taken during the trip. After locking up the house securely as we had before, we left at about 5.00 am in early January (mid-summer) and took the only road south. Our plan was to travel the 500 miles across Zambia and stay the night in Livingstone, close to the Victoria Falls. The major roads in Zambia were generally very good with full tarmac; we were able to make excellent time. As we dropped down into the

Zambezi River escarpment, it became sweltering and humid, and all we could do was to open the car windows and try to deflect the breeze into the car, which had no air-conditioning. Throughout this and other low-lying areas there were usually Tsetse Fly control stations, to stop the spread of disease carried by these large insects, which can infect both humans and livestock. The fly control stations meant that you had to drive your car into some kind of enclosure and have the vehicle sprayed (with, I believe, DDT) whilst you stayed inside it. The workers wore protective clothing and masks, but none was available for us. We seem to have survived this exposure.

There were plenty of motels in Livingstone, and they were clean, well run, and always offered a friendly welcome; it was usually only *white* people that stayed in them. The following day we spent some time looking at the magnificent falls. It was a very natural tourist destination, not commercialised in any way, and visitors were able to simply walk to the edge of the gorge at designated viewing areas. It was a spectacular site with few guard rails; we had to keep the children close to us. In no time, we were all soaked from the spray. We had a memorable ride upstream above the falls in a riverboat and saw families of hippos and crocodiles on or near the banks. After two nights in Livingstone, we crossed over the single-lane bridge above the Falls, which also carried the railway track that we had travelled on from Cape Town three years earlier and reported to the Rhodesian Customs and Immigration Office.

We could see from the map that the next stretch of road to Bulawayo, a distance of over 250 miles, had no towns or gas stations except for Wankie, just 50 miles away. To make matters worse, it was a strip road nearly all the way. A strip road consisted of only two strips of tarmac, each about 20 inches wide with a bit of a gully between them. Motor vehicles and trucks contrived to stay on the strips - which often dropped away a bit at the sides. When another vehicle came towards you in the opposite direction or wanted to overtake from behind, you would have to move over to the left and have a front wheel and a back wheel inline on one strip. Keeping your vehicle on this kind of road made for careful, somewhat slower driving, and moving over for passing could be dangerous and quite bumpy. Not long after leaving Wankie, we ran into a torrential thunderstorm, and we had to halt for a while as there was zero visibility – it was quite impossible to see beyond the front of the car. We fervently hoped that all other motor traffic had also stopped. When the rain ceased, we could see the scenery was very boring as it was just fairly low bush, on relatively flat terrain, both sides of the road. There are many elephants in this area, but we didn't see any. We had a small stove with us and, at one point, decided to stop and make tea and get some boiled water for Melanie's bottle. Our tea stop proved impossible as a horde of tiny flies found us and would not leave us alone. They got into our mouths, ears, and noses, so we quickly had to move on. After a brief stop in Bulawayo, where we fed everyone, we carried on across Southern Rhodesia to the border with South Africa at Beit Bridge, which is on the Limpopo River. Here we all had to get out of the car and report to the authorities.

It was cooler in the Customs' building, and Stephen and Nicola started to let off pent-up energy and run about while Maureen and I were talking to the rather stern officer. Suddenly we heard a loud thud behind us. Turning, we saw that Stephen had run at full speed into the leading edge of an open glass door. There was an awful moment of complete silence, and then an ear-shattering scream. As we ran to him, a large bump started to swell upon his forehead. Quickly the officer stopped talking, stamped our paperwork, and thrust it back to us as we hustled Stephen outside and back to the car. After administering a cold pack to his head and soothing him, we decided we could move on to the next town, Messina, and take lodging there. But alas, when I came to start the car, it failed to come to life. I realised I had a starter-motor problem and certainly couldn't get it fixed here. We push-started the car and drove the short distance into Messina, where we found a motel for the night. Stephen had quite a bruise but was otherwise all right, and we all relaxed a little and had a peaceful night.

We were now in the Northern Transvaal, so next morning I went to the only garage in town and explained to some Afrikaans-speaking men my problem. From their broken English, I was able to comprehend that they could not fix a starter motor. It would have to be sent to Johannesburg and would be returned in about a week. This was clearly unacceptable in our situation, so I was given the name of a repair shop to take it to on the east side of Johannesburg, about 300 miles away. With another push-start, we headed in that direction. We had intended to pick up the caravan just south of Pretoria, but because of the car problem, had to pass that city and proceed through the centre of Johannesburg to Germiston, a suburb on the east side, where we were fortunate to find a nice motel. During this part of our journey, I learned that '*Joburg*' had what appeared to be the world's worst drivers. That night, although it was summertime, it became too chilly with a very brisk wind. Johannesburg is at an altitude of about 6,000 feet, and it certainly can get cold.

Very early the next morning, I was lying under the car, struggling to remove the starter motor. When I succeeded in getting it off, I took it to the shop that had been recommended to me. By the following day, the part was returned in good order. Maureen was pleased to notice the motel I had chosen had a modern laundry attached and used the time to catch up on the family washing. We stayed in the motel an extra night and then back-tracked north towards Pretoria to pick up the caravan, which had been carefully prepared for us. We were pleased with it, but Maureen was beginning to feel slightly unwell, so we quickly hooked up the car and drove south once again through *Joburg* (hell) until we reached a very scenic campsite at Vereeniging on the Vaal River. By the time we had set up our site, Maureen was quite sick with a high fever and a very severe headache; she needed to lie down, and we thought she perhaps had a bad case of the flu. We needed to buy food, but also Melanie needed her milk and semi-solid baby food, and somehow, with a little direction from my nearly unconscious wife, I managed to prepare both of these and feed her. Then I had to deal with the *nappy* change. I didn't have much experience looking after babies as Maureen always took care of our children. Melanie tolerated my clumsy efforts and seemed comfortable enough afterwards, so Stephen, Nicola, and I drove to a local store, and we bought provisions. There was not much English spoken here. We had to stay three days at this site until Maureen was well enough to travel and take care of the baby. It was challenging for me, feeding and looking after all the children's needs, but the place had excellent facilities.

Once Maureen's temperature went down, and she felt well enough to go on, we set out on the road to Cape Town almost 1,000 miles away. The roads in South Africa were excellent. We stayed at two more campsites along the way, one near Bloemfontein and the other at Beaufort West in the Great Karroo Desert. Entirely exhausted by the trip, we finally parked our caravan at Hout Bay, south of Cape Town, intending to stay for about a week. Everyone needed to relax and recover. My brother Denis was still living in Cape Town and worked for The Metal Box Company, as I had done when we lived there. He had a girlfriend, Joan, who had come out from England to be with him.

When my mother left us rather hastily in Zambia to be with Denis in Cape Town, she probably hadn't realised that he had a partner. We didn't know what their arrangements were, but by the time we arrived, my mother had left on the mail ship for England. Perhaps she had felt in the way. My brother and some of our South African friends came to see us at the campsite the next Sunday. Amid the chatter and laughter, there was suddenly a scream from Nicola. She and Stephen had been playing together; he was giving her a piggyback ride, he stumbled, she fell forward over his head, and her forehead came into hard contact with the towing hitch for the caravan. There was a nasty cut, and she was bleeding quite severely just above her left eye. Maureen thrust Melanie, who she had been holding on her lap, onto Denis and rushed to her aid. A cold compress was firmly held to the wound, and Nicola was comforted; the loud crying soon quietened. We debated whether we should find a doctor for stitches and a check-over, but the caravan site was miles from anywhere, and the bleeding soon stopped. She seemed to be all right. Patched up with a large Band-Aid, she was her usual cheerful self; quite recovered by the next day. But she still has a little scar near her eyebrow to remind her of that day.

&#x03;

From the very beginning of our relationship, I had always viewed Michael's love of adventure with interest and approval.

Now I felt that perhaps we had not thought carefully enough about the advisability of travelling so far with our three little ones. I thought I had prepared so carefully. Of course, I never expected the chapter of events that unfolded on this holiday. But I knew things didn't always run according to plan, and I greatly admired Michaels 'can-do' spirit. He never wasted time complaining about difficulties as they arose – his lively mind was always quick to devise strategies to overcome problems as we encountered them. I had become a little concerned about Melanie. She wasn't quite herself and had not slept well either in the daytime or for the past couple of nights before we arrived in the Cape Town area. Since I had recently been sick, my friend Cynthia referred me to her doctor, who thought she was well enough, but perhaps was suffering from motion fatigue. He recommended we place a pillow under her car-bed to minimise the vibration from the road when we drove those long distances to return to our home. He thought she would be fine if we could remain in one place for a couple of days. He was right. Within two days, Melanie was happily smiling at everyone and taking great interest in everything around her. I was very glad to rest for a while in Hout Bay. We planned to spend about a week at the campsite, which was a pretty place on a headland above the beach. This village-like place was close to Constantia, a wine-producing area of the Cape. Of course, we visited Joan and Alan in their beautiful new house at Somerset West. Joan had another baby girl, too. Sonya was just six weeks old. Alan had secured a great job with South African Nylon Spinners – they were happy and doing well and pleased for us that our move to Kitwe had worked out. They enjoyed seeing Stephen and Nicola again.

I felt much better after the week spent in one place but welcomed the idea of beginning the long trek back to Kitwe – which sure seemed a very long way away from where we were on the southern tip of the Cape Peninsular. I still loved Cape Town, but it was so hard to take proper care of the children under these circumstances, and I began to wonder what would happen next and whether we could make it back to our Kitwe home again in good order. Michael's plan was that we should not miss the opportunity to see 'The Garden Route' through the southern part of the Cape Province, which was widely regarded as the jewel of this tourist area. Then we could bypass Port Elizabeth and see East London on our way to Durban in Natal, where we would rest for a couple of days before returning the caravan to its depot south of Pretoria. This part of the tour would need another two to three weeks. I tried not to show any anxiety about the long journey home.

ഽ ൚

Although we never spoke to each other about it, I, too, was a little apprehensive about the journey home. Our four-cylinder car did not seem quite adequate to pull such a heavy load, and I didn't feel I could have real confidence in the braking system. There were quite a few mountainous regions to pass through. But I had the car serviced and checked over at a service station, and we said goodbye to Denis and our friends. Early on a lovely summer day, we set out across the Cape Flats, over Sir Lowry Pass and along the very scenic southern coast of Africa. Maureen had always wanted to visit Hermanus when we had lived in Camps Bay, so we planned to have a picnic lunch on the beach. We found a spot, but it was rather crowded because the tide was coming in, and all the holidaymakers were packed close to the rock wall, which formed a barrier. Without much warning, a wave washed right up onto the beach, and everyone scrambled, but a blanket Melanie was lying on, and our sandals got a little wet, so we gave up on the picnic idea and ate our lunch in the parking lot. Continuing on to Knysna, where the coast was very rugged, but there were also some lovely sandy coves and beaches to enjoy. This Indian Ocean coast is breath-taking but also could be dangerous, with sharks and whales in the area. There was no land to the south of us until the continent of Antarctica was reached. It was occasionally reported that a fisherman had been swept off the rocks by a sudden, extra powerful rogue wave in this region. We spent a couple of days here and one day on a deserted beach Maureen and I went skinny dipping, much to the surprise of Stephen. He gave us a very strange look.

The next part of our journey would take us through a region called the Transkei. Under 'Apartheid', this area was designated in 1959 by the National Government as part of eight ethnically and linguistically divided homelands for black South Africans. For much of its history, the Transkei, homeland for Xhosa speakers, was ruled by Chief Kaizer Daliwonga Matanzima, a relation of Nelson Mandela. Although I was a little nervous about passing through this area, we had no problems. It was an interesting drive. Generally, the Africans lived in round mud huts, which were decorated with a single band of brightly coloured motifs all the way around the walls, topped by a straw and mud roof. There were sparse groups of three to five huts dotted about the landscape, which was open rolling grassland with just a few small trees. The Africans seemed friendly and smiled and waved as we passed by, and we were reminded that this was the traditional way *black* people had always lived throughout this continent. Once through the Transkei, instead of continuing on the major road into Durban, our destination that day, we decided to take a secondary road east, across to the coast. We liked to be able to see the ocean; it always gave us a relaxed feeling. This choice proved to be a big mistake. After proceeding for a while along this quite broad gravel road, there was quite a steep hill up ahead, and I increased our speed to make it to the top. Halfway up, the car's rear wheels started to spin, and I realised we were not going to go up any further. After coming to a stop, the caravan began to slowly pull the car back down the hill, and after a few seconds, the vehicle and caravan jack-knifed and came to rest across the middle of the road. Maureen became very agitated. We had not seen any other cars coming along this road in either direction. It looked like we were in a challenging situation. I set the brake and got out of the vehicle. As I was pondering what to do next, I heard the sound of a heavy vehicle up ahead over the brow of a hill. Walking up to take a look, I discovered a large road grading machine operated by a couple of white men with a few black helpers. It was my lucky day! After explaining our predicament, one of the white Afrikaners brought his grader down the hill, hitched up to our car, calling out cheerfully to Maureen, 'We'll soon get you out of there, *Mevrouw*', and in no time at all had us straightened up, then towing the car and trailer over the brow of the hill, sending us on our way again. It turned out that only a short section was unpaved, and we had no further difficulties in making it to the coast, where we could once again see the ocean. There was then a good road all the way into the city of Durban.

We spent a few days in this beautiful coastal city on the warm waters of the Indian Ocean, swimming in the sea and open-air pools. All beaches and pools were racially segregated. Many sharks inhabit this part of the ocean, and all the popular swimming areas had shark nets a couple of hundred yards out to protect the swimmers, but still, occasionally, a person was attacked.

Durban borders Zululand. The native Zulu people are a well built, fine-looking race, and there were many of them in and around the city. In the tourist areas alongside the beaches, there were large rickshaws lined up, operated by very large, fearsome-looking Zulus, dressed in all their native finery, complete with large headdresses. They would whistle loudly, boldly establish eye contact and beckon the pedestrians to generate business. Maureen and the children were quite scared of them and would not chance to take a ride. The campsite we chose was quite big with good facilities. It was hot and very humid on this coast, and we had to set up the side awning on the caravan to make shade. We spent a few days here. Back on the road again, we headed toward Pretoria, where the caravan was to be dropped off. But not before we had one final scare. About an hour out of Durban on a good road, moving quite fast, we were descending a long downhill slope. I could see ahead there were two large black dogs playing on the road. I started to brake slowly but realised I would not be able to stop in time. If they did not move, I would hit them! As we approached the dogs, we were still moving quite fast, and the dogs did not move. I then did a foolish thing and swerved quite sharply to avoid them. As I did this, I felt the caravan lift the back of the car, and it lurched from side to side. In my rear-view mirror, I could see the caravan rocking violently sideways. We were fortunate that both car and caravan did not turn over. We both suffered quite a fright, and I drove more slowly from then on until we reached the outskirts of *Joburg*, where we stayed again at the same motel we had used on the outward journey. The next morning, we were up early, and I could hardly wait to return that caravan and be on our way home. What a relief that was, and I felt a significant burden had been lifted. Only another 1,000 miles separated us from our home – the very last part of our journey had now begun. We crossed into Southern Rhodesia again at Beit Bridge. We drove those strip roads for hours across rather desolate bush country, through Mashonaland, staying the night at Lake McIlwaine just outside Salisbury. On the road again the next morning, we crossed into Zambia at Chirundu. The border post is located at the bridge over the Zambezi River, just below the Kariba Dam. It is always sweltering and humid here, and we did not stay any longer than we needed to, but again had to navigate the Tsetse Fly control.

There is usually quite a bit of game in the area, but we only saw some hippo in a pool a little further up the road. One more night at a motel, and we were on the last stretch of good road toward home. Our house looked dusty and a bit neglected, but it was just the way we had left it, and our servants were pleased to see us back. We felt relieved, as we frequently heard that some people had their homes broken into while away, and sometimes they lost almost everything.

Our exceptionally reliable Toyota Crown station wagon

Victoria Falls and a return visit to the beautiful Cape Peninsular

Durban, Natal

**A colourful Zulu
Rickshaw in Durban**

13.
Changing Times

Maureen

We were both relieved to be at home again. I found the wonderful holiday we'd planned so light-heartedly had been very stressful and had built up a level of anxiety that was not easy to overcome. We soon realised that things had changed in our community since Independence Day. While we had been away, decisions affecting our future had been made. After holding meetings with government officials, Anglo-American had decreed that all ex-patriot employees were to be put on a three-year contractual basis. Certain non-technical positions were to be 'Zambianised' in stages. This Zambianisation' meant those jobs would gradually become available to native Zambians only. The people currently holding these positions were to be offered a severance package when their services were no longer required, which included a generous allowance to cover the cost of returning themselves, their family, and their personal effects to their country of origin. Of course, should anyone wish to become a citizen of Zambia, they could remain employed but would then have to accept the new, lower Zambian rate of pay. These new regulations were to become effective in stages, over quite a lengthy period. Everyone had time to consider their options.

Another mandate from the Corporation was that all the basic mine furniture initially allocated with our houses was to be immediately offered to us for the very nominal sum of £10, which would be deducted from the monthly salary forthwith. All our friends were talking about these new developments. Everyone we knew bought the furniture, and many sold it piece by piece to the Africans. But my priority, of course, was to get the family situation back to normal and resume our usual routine. Stephen returned to school towards the end of February, and Anita McCabe and I resumed our shared driving duties. We were coming up to the celebration of Easter. I asked Stephen one day what he had learned that day at school. He told me: 'Sister Mary *Goosiefix* told us about taking *'The Body up.''* The nun's name was Sister Mary Crucifix, but he certainly had learned the story of 'The Resurrection'.

Soon everything seemed more or less back to normal on the domestic scene, except I harboured a little suspicion regarding Peter. I thought money had disappeared from my handbag. I imagined he might have been influenced by the talk of the men in the townships, regarding their ambition to take over everything the 'Europeans' had; there must have been some indignation about their situation compared to that of the white people. Peter had, until this time, been a very satisfactory young houseboy. One day when I had almost succeeded in putting my suspicion aside, I returned from taking Stephen to school, placed my handbag as usual in the bedroom, which I could see had been mopped and dusted and closed the bedroom door. I took Melanie and Nicola to the play area in the breeze room and went to my sewing machine to work on my latest project. Needing something from my room, I walked through the carpeted living room, and as soon as my shoes tapped on the stone floor of the passage to the bedrooms, I saw Peter dart quickly into the children's room. My handbag was lying open on the bed, my purse beside it. 'Oh, Peter,' I said, then, 'please wait outside.' I didn't know how to deal with this, but with my recent suspicion in mind, I needed a little time to think. I gathered up my things and counted the money – nothing was missing, but the doubt I'd had before was confirmed. I went outside, and Peter was looking guilty and shamefaced. I told him to come back to the house at 5.00 pm, when *'the Bwana'* (the respectful name Africans gave to the man of the house) would be home again. Michael paid him up to the end of the month and dismissed him. Peter had been with us for about two and a half years. I was sad about this, and now I was without help. There followed several months with first one helper then another. In the native African culture, females are not highly regarded, so it was always Michael who had to do the hiring and firing. Eventually, James came by, who was older and had lots of experience, so we took him on, extending the same conditions of employment as we had to Peter. I already knew James a little; he had worked for an acquaintance that had recently left the Copperbelt.

To add to my anxiety, Melanie became sick again – there was flu about, and I saw a doctor at the hospital clinic. He was a nice young man, recently qualified, and he prescribed some medicine. Melanie became sicker and cried weakly; mouth ulcers developed, and she was in too much pain to swallow anything. The young doctor made an unexpected house call in the afternoon after seeing us the second time, 'Just to check on her', he said; his level of concern worried me. But that evening, I began to feed her with dribbles of weak milk from a spoon, thinking that might be easier for her than sucking her milk from the bottle. She accepted about half a cupful, seemed a little more comfortable, and went to sleep in my arms, and I thought perhaps she had turned a corner. On another day, she began smiling at me again, resumed taking nourishment normally, and recovered fully. I could relax once more. Later I thought the antibiotic that had been prescribed was perhaps not the right medication for my baby.

Melanie developed a light-hearted, fun-loving personality. Always smiling once she learned to walk (at about 13 months), her only ambition seemed to be to try and keep up with her sister; she copied everything that Nicola did. Nicola seemed to enjoy the role of 'Big Sister'. Stephen had always loved Melanie. When he was about five years old, he would carefully carry her through to our bedroom after lunch each day and set her down gently on the bed for me, straighten her dress 'to make her pretty' then I would prepare her for her afternoon nap.

80 03

We had arrived back home from our trek just a day or two before I was due to report for work. The mine was running at full capacity, so there was plenty of work and some opportunity for overtime. I liked the challenge of the job, and the three men I worked with helped each other, so together, we were a well-respected team. The tool room was attached to a large machine shop that handled all the heavy mine equipment needing overhaul or repair. Very well equipped with mainly English machinery, our tool room dealt with all of the smaller problems. Harold Wenman, my supervisor, had been with the company for many years and was used as an acting foreman in the big machine shop on a relief basis. At those times, I was asked to take charge of our smaller shop. Taking the lead was a good experience for me as I had always been usually quite shy and had never been in charge of other workers before.

A few months after our return, my brother drove up from Cape Town with his girlfriend, Joan, for a visit. They seemed to have survived my mother's unexpected intrusion and appeared comfortable together. They enjoyed the children; Melanie was learning to crawl, and we showed them around the town and mine, including the Mindola Dam area, which was used for water sports. They wanted to go to the Congo border, which was only about 30 miles away. Here we strolled onto the bridge over the river that bordered the two countries but retreated after taking one look at the Congolese border guards on the other side. Some years before, this route through to Elizabethville had been very popular with the white people, as the city had a very European atmosphere and enjoyed a reputation for very lively nightlife. But now, after the recent war in the Congo, it was much too dangerous to travel; some people had been attacked and killed. Within a few days, Denis and Joan left for the journey back south. I think Joan was the only female friend of my brother I had ever met.

But during 1965, there were more political events starting to evolve. With its central and southern African colonies, the British government adopted a policy known as NIBMAR (No Independence Before Majority African Rule). This policy required that those colonies with a substantial white settler population could not achieve independence except under conditions of universal suffrage and majority rule. Britain had so far refused to give independence to Southern Rhodesia, and this policy was opposed by the white minority Rhodesian Front government, led by Ian Smith, a former RAF fighter pilot during the Second World War.

On 11th November 1965, Smith's government declared the country independent from British government rule, in what became known as the Unilateral Declaration of Independence (Rhodesia) or UDI. Of course, we were all delighted and wanted to celebrate, and a few people had parties, but the black Zambian government did not look kindly on this kind of celebration. Maureen's parents in

England told us in a letter that, after hearing this news, they had lain awake all night, worrying about us. After lifting a glass, we slept well. But UDI was internationally condemned, and sanctions were imposed on Rhodesia by the United Nations shortly afterwards, which caused us plenty of grief.

For Rhodesia, 'sanctions' meant that all member nations of the UN would not allow any goods or material to be imported from or exported to Rhodesia. As South Africa and the Portuguese colonies, which were Rhodesia's immediate neighbours, did not adhere to this ruling, the effects at first were not too serious. For Zambia, however, this had disastrous consequences as most imports came through or from Rhodesia; a considerable amount came from South Africa also, including mining equipment. But worst still, most of Zambia's precious exports of copper were sent by rail through Rhodesia to the east coast ports.

The only other export route available for this commodity, now sanctions were in place, was by rail - the Benguela Railway through the Congo and Angola, where civil war had been in progress for many years. The line was forever being sabotaged. So the new Zambian government decided to buy a fleet of trucks and use the Great North Road through Tanzania to the coast at Dar-es-Salaam for exporting copper and bringing in fuel, as Rhodesia had cut off the supply. The major problem with this route was that in the rainy season, the road was often impassable. Many trucks became bogged down, and the goods were usually pilfered. Several Europeans from my company were caught and charged with stealing copper and sentenced to time in a Zambian jail. As petrol was in very short supply, we were issued ration cards, and many other items became quite scarce, including milk. We formed ourselves into small groups, taking turns to drive to a small farm just out of town and went twice a week for our fresh milk, and we kept powdered milk on hand. We adjusted to circumstances as they changed, and managed. As the work and the wages were still good, it did not seem necessary to uproot ourselves immediately.

Within the town, we felt secure; life was still pretty good here. All white expatriates (non-Zambian Nationals) were now offered a package of career options to consider, with about six months to make a decision. Many of our friends in unskilled or semi-skilled jobs were to be offered a generous 'golden handshake', paid when they were terminated, and within a few months, a trickle of them started to leave for South Africa, Britain, Europe or the States. We decided that, as the situation seemed relatively stable, I would sign on for the minimum period of three years while we tried to save as much money as we could and then return to South Africa or possibly England. In March 1966, I signed on for my first three-year contract with Rhokana Corporation.

After signing the contract, we settled into a very regular routine way of life. As there now was more overtime work available at the mine, I put in some pretty long hours. My typical work week was 7.00 am to 3.30 pm Monday to Friday, and 7.00 am to 12.00 noon on Saturdays. Overtime could be on several evenings until 10.00 pm; a one-hour break for the dinner hour at 5.00 pm was allowed, and occasionally we worked all day on Sunday. The work was interesting and often quite a challenge. Towards the end of the year, in the rainy season, conditions were sweltering and humid; the smelter frequently belched out noxious fumes, making our throats sore, but as we felt our time here might be limited we all put up with it. At about this time, a few of the men I worked with began to play golf, and I thought about joining them, but I didn't yet have golf clubs or a cart.

The Rhodesian political situation gradually worsened. Following UDI, the military wings of the two leading African political parties formed armed guerrilla groups, operating at this time from outside Rhodesian borders in Zambia and Angola. This time was the beginning of the Second Chimurenga (meaning rebellion in Shona) or the Bush War as the white people of Rhodesia called it. Zapu (the Zimbabwe African Peoples Union) was influenced and financed by China and North Korea; one of their leaders was Robert Mugabe. This group usually operated out of training camps within Zambia's southern borders. The USSR supported another group led by Joshua Nkomo. At this time, they all seemed to be just a petty annoyance to the Rhodesian security forces that patrolled the borders. The Rhodesians had a strong and well-trained army plus the support of the well-equipped South African air force.

There were several incidents in Zambia, one of which was the sabotaging of the power lines near Ndola that carried electricity to the mines from the huge hydro dam at Kariba. The culprits were never caught. The Zambian government was flirting with the idea of accepting help from the Chinese; we visited a Trade Fair they brought to Ndola. Here we saw Chinese goods and entertainment. Copies of Chairman Mao's Little Red Book were handed out at every location. Not wanting to be labelled a Communist, I declined accepting one. The always smiling Chinese were also proposing to finance and build a railway line from Kapiri Mposhi, south of Ndola, into Tanzania to facilitate the movement of Zambia's exports and imports.

In August (winter) of 1966, we decided we needed a little holiday, a break away from the Copperbelt, so we planned a three week trip through Rhodesia into Mozambique (Portuguese East Africa) to the coastal city of Beira on the Indian Ocean. Although petrol was rationed in Zambia, we were allocated extra coupons for the journey; we knew there were no fuel shortages in Rhodesia. Leaving before dawn, we again made our way over the now familiar road south to the border and crossed the Zambezi at Chirundu. We waited here for an army escort that was provided for the convoy of travellers for about 30 miles through the border area, where there had been guerrilla activity. We then found accommodation for the night at Karoi. The next day we skirted Salisbury and drove through lush vegetation heading east. This area was a very productive agricultural place with large, well-ordered farms. Soon, as we went closer to the Mozambique border, we entered a mountainous region, and our road climbed up to a beautiful resort-type hotel called the Inyanga Mountain Lodge. We had booked rooms in advance and expected to stay two nights. Shortly after our arrival, Maureen started to feel unwell and was confined to our room with a feverish cold and had to remain in bed. There was plenty for the children to do here, which was fortunate, as the weather was not too good. We were at quite a high altitude and were often surrounded by clouds, which made it quite cold. The main lounge had a massive stone fireplace, and a fire was kept burning continually. This hotel and the world-famous Leopards Rock Hotel, situated nearby, were favourite getaways for the high society types from Salisbury and Johannesburg during the hot summers. Maureen's illness turned out to be influenza, and we had to extend our stay a few more days until she was able to travel again. Unfortunately, a few years later, the civil disturbances spread to this area, and I believe these hotels were taken over by terrorists and damaged or destroyed.

Once Maureen was a little better, we drove down into the town of Umtali and presented ourselves at the border crossing into Mozambique, manned by Portuguese officials. Since arriving in Africa, we had always travelled on British passports. We had renewed them, after five years, at the British consulate in Zambia, and the children were added as they came along. At this border, we had no problems. Our passports were casually stamped, and we were on our way. Each of the Portuguese territories in Africa was considered Provinces of Portugal, but it did not take us long to realise this was a poor underdeveloped state. The road was barely paved and had huge, very deep potholes that could ruin your car's suspension. The bad roads required me to drive rather slowly and avoiding these hazards that could have put an end to our trip rather quickly. Fortunately, the weather was good and dry. I would not have liked to drive this route in a rainstorm. The journey to the coast was about 150 miles, and we only stopped once for petrol at a small place called Tete. Here the local people were impoverished but friendly. There had been some minor uprisings by African groups against the Portuguese in Mozambique, and all the bridges had soldiers casually lounging around on them, who waved cheerfully as we drove by. At last, we came to the beautiful Indian Ocean at Beira.

Accommodation had been booked in advance at an apartment complex, and since it was quite a big, modern block, we soon located it, close to a children's theme park and just across from the wide sandy beach. This small town had quite a European atmosphere, and it was interesting to try the different cuisine offered at the many cafes and restaurants. There were many unfamiliar, exotic fish dishes offered. It was not a particularly clean town, but our accommodation was adequate; our unit had a full kitchen, and the children enjoyed the warm seawater to play in at the beach. Melanie was afraid of this vast expanse of water, but on our last full day there, playing with her mother, she discovered water at the seaside was fun. We stayed for one week and then drove the same torturous road back to Rhodesia, then went on another 30 miles before stopping for the night at a motel outside Rusape. The place was a bit run down but seemed clean, with bunk-like beds for the children and a polished red floor with some cracks, which appeared to be filled with sand. Nicola was a little uneasy about this; she didn't like spiders or other *creepy-crawlies*, but we assured her that there was no need to be alarmed, and she, Stephen and Melanie soon went off to sleep. Maureen and I were in the adjoining room. Quite early next morning as we were waking, Nicola let out a very loud shriek. Maureen and I rushed into their room to find her shaking and crying on the bed. It seemed that during the night, the ants had been busy and created many small ant hills from the soft earth in several places along those cracks. Crossing the floor to the adjoining bathroom, Nicola had put her bare foot onto one of them and was frightened. We soothed and comforted her and found her socks and sandals. We thought it best if everyone got dressed so that we could get our belongings into the car and depart in search of breakfast. We were soon on our way.

After a short stop in the Rhodesian capital, Salisbury, we headed north to Lake Kariba. We left the main road at Makuti and were met here by Rhodesian security forces. They informed us the road to the lake was safe to use, and there were no known terrorists in the area. The 50-mile long road to the lake was unpaved, badly corrugated and very dusty, as we were in the dry season. There usually were many wild animals in this area, including a considerable number of elephants, but we only encountered a few troops of monkeys. After about an hour and a half of bumping along this road, we arrived at the small settlement of Kariba and found a lovely resort overlooking the lake.

The 150-mile long lake was formed in 1959 when the dam, one of the world's largest, was built across the Zambezi River to supply power to Rhodesia and the copper mines of Northern Rhodesia. More than 57,000 tribesmen and women were moved and encouraged to relocate their villages on higher ground as the level of the lake rose. 'Operation Noah' was mobilised to save wildlife. Several lakeside resorts appeared on both the Rhodesian and Zambian sides of the border. This area was sweltering and humid and barely cooled off at night. We slept in *rondavels*, which were copies of native type dwellings,(round huts with grass roofs); we required mosquito nets, which looked quite romantic when in use over our beds, but it was difficult to get a good night's sleep under them. There was no air-conditioning, of course. During the day, we spent most of the time relaxing around the well-equipped pool. The children were introduced to trampolines, one of which had a dead snake in the pit. Nicola avoided that one. It was not advisable to ever swim in the lake as the water was not safe to drink, and this was also home to crocodiles and hippos. But it was very peaceful here, and the children enjoyed the various activities that were organised for them. Every evening we always looked forward to our meal in the open-air restaurant, where we were served freshly caught bream from the lake. After just a couple of days, we were ready for the long one-day journey to our home in Kitwe. We passed through the Rhodesian border point at one end of the Kariba Dam, drove across it, and presented ourselves to the Zambian immigration official on the other side.

With little formality, we were soon on our way on a short gravel road and then the main road through Broken Hill and Lusaka, which was paved all the way through to the Copperbelt. From all of the long trips we had by car, I cannot recall any of the children ever being car sick. Maureen provided plenty of toys and books for them, and generally, they were very well behaved. But there was the odd time when we were all tired that we lost our composure. I remember one time on a long stretch of road in Rhodesia when Stephen and Nicola were arguing and fighting over something, I stopped the car, opened the back door and gave them both a good slap, which made Maureen laugh because she said it looked like I was swatting flies. In a better mood, we continued on our way. It then remained quieter in the back. On another occasion, I was exasperated with Stephen. In the middle of nowhere, I made him get out and told him to walk home. Once he was back on board, we had peace.

We were always glad to be home again and relieved when once again, our house and belongings were intact. It was time for me to get back to work, and Stephen and Nicola to resume school. Nicola had one more fright with African creatures in our own home. One day she shrieked and came running out of the toilet with tears running down her face, saying there was a giant frog in the bowl. I immediately went there and saw nothing. I calmed her down, assuring her this could not be possible and persuaded her to use it (we had only one). Later that day, I went into the bathroom, and sure enough, there was a large frog in the toilet. It disappeared on my arrival, and I put some disinfectant down there and never saw it again. I kept my sighting a secret from Nicola as I thought if I told her about it, she might refuse to ever use that toilet again.

Shortly after our return home in September 1966, the Prime Minister of South Africa, HF Verwoerd, one of the architects of Apartheid, was assassinated at his desk in the House of Assembly in Cape Town. He was succeeded by BJ Vorster, and South Africa continued to hold just as firmly to their policy of Apartheid.

Back at my work, we were still very busy. The mine was at full production, and spare parts for machinery were in very short supply, so we had to fabricate replacement parts in the workshops. The government was insisting that all companies must become *Zambianised*, which required all businesses to employ and train more Africans. The apprentice training school was enlarged, and my colleague Brian Lowe was appointed to run it. The African apprentices were chosen from some of the best students in high school and after some training were assigned to various departments on the mine where the trades were performed. We had two in our department, and although they had a good command of English, were pleasant and clean, it was difficult to get them to understand many of the technical skills required. After a year, they could take two weeks' vacation; usually, they returned to their family village where they again lived according to the tribal traditions that had existed for centuries. Upon their return, it seemed that they had forgotten most of what they had been taught, and it was back to the beginning again. When the school first expanded, I thought of getting a job there, but later decided against this move.

A growing problem with some of the Africans was that they smoked *dagga* regularly, a type of cannabis, so those people appeared stoned much of the time. It was never considered an illegal substance in Zambia. Occasionally our work took us into the native township of Wusakili, where white folk generally never ventured. Usually, two of us would go together, and as we were driving a company vehicle, we felt relatively safe. Our work here involved fixing some part of the mine shaft venting fans, which were installed at various locations all around town. These fans were used for circulating air into the mine shafts and tunnels, thousands of feet below the surface. We had also developed a procedure for resurfacing the commutators on large DC electric motors that were utilised on the mine headgear, to raise and lower the cages that carried men and ore from the bowels of the earth. This work was always done on a Sunday when activity at the mine was reduced, and this meant double-time pay for us. As we were the only team on the Copperbelt able to make this repair, we occasionally went to other mines at Chingola and Mufulira to perform this duty. On one occasion, I went to a fan shaft at Mineola, close to Kitwe, to work on a surface fan. The electrician assigned to the job, a German named Gunter Czerwinski, told me that he was thinking about going to Canada with his family when his contract expired the following year. He had been a young soldier during World War II, was captured in Normandy, and taken as a prisoner-of-war to Canada. He had been so well treated there during this period; he thought Canada a wonderful place, and perhaps one day, he would like to return and live there permanently.

I met many strange and interesting people at work. One fellow was Algerian and had been in the French Foreign Legion for many years. Although his English was poor, he had many intriguing stories to tell. Another man, a Belgian, had been a mercenary in the Congo. He, unfortunately, had lost his arm below the elbow when a car he was repairing fell on him. But this did not stop him from working. Attached to his stump, he had a heavy piece of tapered round metal. He used his stump as a hammer. In the end and around the sides of his 'hammer' were various holes that accommodated screwdrivers, files, and other tools. He worked as well as any other man. Jokingly, he would nudge you with his steel arm to make you understand what a weapon it could be.

Although it was illegal to buy uncut diamonds in Southern Africa, there were always plenty of people, both white and black, trying to sell you rough diamonds. Unless you were an expert, it was very difficult to know the value; I stayed away from any of those deals.

Since Independence, some of the African workers had become more hostile towards the white workers, even though they realised they were not capable of doing the kind of work that we did. However, I thought life there was still reasonably tolerable even though we knew that the situation could worsen.

Another year passed, and we felt the need for another short break from the Copperbelt. Petrol rationing was no longer necessary as ample supplies were coming in now from Tanzania. We had no other shortages. We had enjoyed our last visit to Lake Kariba, and as it was only a one-day drive away, we decided to go there and stay for one week. This holiday was to be our only break that year; the rest of my vacation time, I was able to bank. When we eventually departed from Zambia at the end of the contract, I would be paid cash for unused vacation time, and this would add considerably to the money we had managed to save. We were assured that although there was considerable terrorist activity in the border area between Zambia and Rhodesia, the roads and the resort area were perfectly safe. So, we set off early again one morning in our faithful Toyota station wagon hoping to make the border crossing on the Zambian side of the Kariba Dam, which we knew closed at 6.00 pm. There were some delays along the way, and we arrived at the turn-off too late to use that entry into Rhodesia. The alternate route was to continue along the main highway and cross the Zambezi river at Chirundu. The border crossing here was open 24 hours every day. After the border crossing and the climb out of the escarpment, we took the dirt road we had followed the previous year. We were a little apprehensive of using this route as there had been reports of terrorists on the Rhodesian side. But we had no other choice as it was now getting dark quickly. As we made the turn onto the dirt road, a large Impala (I believe), with an impressive set of antlers, startled me; he seemed to freeze in my headlights, but I managed to avoid him. Maureen and I were now both quite tense, and the children absolutely quiet in the back seats. The narrow road was lined by fairly high bush, and the headlights seemed to shine down a tunnel. Suddenly a little way ahead, my headlights picked up a small elephant, about five or six feet high, walking down the road in the same direction we were going. As I slowed down and caught up with him, he started to run, but could not leave the road as the bush on each side was too dense. He lumbered along ahead of us for several minutes, and then, seeing an opening between some small trees, he disappeared off the road to the right. This was the closest we had ever been to an elephant in the wild.

Together with the excitement, there was tension. Several more miles down the road, just after rounding a bend, we were shocked to see armed camouflaged Africans standing in the road with rifles pointing toward us. As we drew to a stop, we were relieved to see white officers appearing from the surrounding bush. Both black and white soldiers were part of the Rhodesian Security Forces, and they advised there was no cause for alarm. There had been some activity in the area, but the road through to Kariba was now safe. After a short chat, we completed our journey to the resort and fell into bed that night, relieved that we had survived all the nervous tension and excitement of the day. We spent a relaxing, peaceful time at the lake and had an uneventful journey home a week later.

Once again, South Africa was in the world news, but this time it was a matter for congratulation. On 3rd December 1967, Dr Christian Barnard and his surgical team performed the world's first human heart transplant procedure at Groote Schuur hospital in Cape Town. Everyone in South Africa and around the world celebrated this magnificent achievement.

Our Christmas was spent with friends Jill and Otto, and the main topic of our conversation, as with most expatriates at that time, was what to do and where to go at the end of our contracts. For us, this was just over a year away. The company had made it quite clear that they wanted many of the skilled people to stay on for a further contract and were offering attractive incentives to stay. These included paying the cost of private education overseas or in South Africa for our children, as well as overseas holidays with all travel expenses paid by the company. We still had plenty of time to make up our minds, but returning to South Africa or England, seemed to be our most likely possibilities at that time. For the past six months, I had been trying my hand at golf. I had joined a small group who all worked on the mine, and we became a foursome. None of us had played much before, although some had received coaching; for me, it was all new, and I soon found out what a challenging game it was. I had purchased some second-hand clubs and used to carry them around until Bill, who was in charge of the welding shop, had a cart made for each of us using mine materials. The course was very lush and ran close to the Kafue river, from which it was well watered. At times crocodiles were seen on the banks, and there were a few baboons in the trees, which occasionally would come down and playfully steal a ball. We did not take our games too seriously but had a good time together. In the rainy season (October to April), we often got caught in a downpour but usually played on. I sometimes played after work during the week and often at the weekends. We always finished our game with a visit to the club bar. Two of my colleagues seemed to be becoming alcoholics, but I usually had just a couple of beers before leaving them. At weekends Maureen would often bring the children out to join us for a drink at the end of the game. She said sometimes it was the highlight of her week. After having three children, Maureen at 32 was still a very nice-looking woman. She would dress herself and the children beautifully and drive out to meet us. I could tell by the comments my colleagues made that they appreciated her joining us. Bill's wife occasionally joined us too, but the other wives stayed away.

At the beginning of 1968, the Zambian Government introduced its new currency called the *Kwacha* (meaning 'dawn' in Bemba). One Kwacha was divided into 100 *ngwees*. Two Kwachas had the value of one Rhodesian pound. It seemed very strange at first, but we all soon became used to it.

My mother raised the question with me of the possibility of making another visit to see us in Africa, and we agreed she should come. We realised that time was passing, and it could be the last chance we would have for one more holiday in the south. We hadn't yet been able to see much wildlife. My mother arrived in early February for an extended visit. We set up her room and oiled up the bike she had used on her first visit. She liked to just cycle around the town, which was reasonably flat terrain, and this time Nicola was able to accompany her sometimes. It was late summer, so it was not too hot during the day, and it never rained, but there were still just a few clouds in the blue African sky. I had only had one week's holiday in over 20 months, so we decided to take my mother to Durban and perhaps visit a game park too. Although we still had not come to a decision about what we were going to do at the end of my contract, I believe in the back of our minds the idea was growing that we would leave Africa; this could be perhaps our last long African trip. So, on yet another early winter's day, we set out for the now-familiar journey south. There was only one road; there was no alternate route. The guerrilla war in Rhodesia had escalated a bit. Although there had been some isolated attacks on outlying farms, the security forces seemed to have the situation under control, always with special attention to the security of main roads. We were again escorted in convoy for a short distance south from the Rhodesian border, but we spent a peaceful night at Karoi.

It was customary on these trips to get up and get going quite early, so we were in Salisbury for an early lunch. Salisbury seemed to be in a holiday mood. The streets were thronged with happy, smiling Africans, and we were told that it was payday at the farms and missions; everyone had come into town to celebrate and joyfully spend their money. We didn't want to spend too long here, so after a quick meal, we were once again on our way. We had an uneventful drive through Rhodesia to Beit Bridge, the crossing over the Limpopo River into South Africa. Stopping for the night, just over the border at a motel in Messina, we were made most welcome by a couple of happy and respectful South African black men who waved our vehicle into a parking spot then when we had registered, guided us up to the door of our rooms. Of course, they were anxious to wash our car, carry in our suitcases, and clean all of our shoes in the expectation of a small payment. It was encouraging to see happy Africans. My mother was heard to murmur, 'So these are the downtrodden blacks we have heard so much about in Britain!' The situation between blacks and whites in Zambia was beginning to feel generally more tense. Driving south the next morning, just outside the town of Louis Trichardt, we encountered a group of Africans milling around an accident scene. A black man was lying by the side of the road, presumably struck by a car. Many more Africans were converging on the scene, running in from all directions. Maureen, perhaps sensing a moment's hesitation on my part because someone was hurt and maybe needed help, said firmly, 'Drive on, Michael.' I did. In Zambia, there had been some rather nasty confrontations between Africans and whites at accident scenes. It was best to take no chances.

To avoid Johannesburg, we left the main road at Petersburg and found some secondary roads through to Middleburg. Along one very straight stretch, we saw several native women dressed in very colourful tribal costumes and later a large iguana, about two feet long, just sitting in the middle of the road. By nightfall, we had reached the outskirts of Pietermaritzburg in Natal, and we looked for overnight accommodation. We stayed in a family-size *rondavel*; our bathroom was next door. There was a large double bed for four other single beds and us. We all slept with our feet, almost meeting at the centre. This amused my mother very much; we all prepared for sleep giggling. By early afternoon the next day, we had completed the journey to our booked accommodation at Umhlanga Rocks, just a little north of Durban. It was a three-bedroom holiday apartment in quite a tall block overlooking the ocean. Once again, we could bathe in the warm blue waters of the Indian Ocean.

ಉ ಅ

We had been living in a time of growing tension. All my friends who were mothers like me, pushed anxieties into the back of our minds. We calmly continued creating family life in our usual way without even mentioning it as we were all determined not to cause our children any concern. I thought of my mother's attitude in wartime and followed her example. My daily life was full. We had two children in school now and little Melanie at home. Nicola needed picking up at noon, Stephen, who was usually free at 1.00 pm, often remained for an extra hour as he was quite athletic and joined in school sports. So, I was frequently in and out of the car on weekdays. I took care of the grocery shopping, etc., ran the house, and we did a little entertaining.

We didn't talk very much about the uncertainty ahead of us. My life was full and satisfyingly busy. I thought Michael as the family wage-earner must be the one to make the decision about our plans for the future. I wasn't too thrilled about the golf-playing idea, however. Golf is a game that takes up a lot of time. Michael worked long hours and was tired when he came home. I don't think he knew how I arranged our domestic life and how much work went into it because his time at home was for relaxation. His 'home-life' experience was quite a different thing from mine. He didn't spend much time with the children and hardly ever went to their school. I thought of his golf game only as boring hours that I had to endure at the weekend, while most of my friends were enjoying their husband's company. But with as good grace as I could muster (Michael did deserve some pleasurable activity with his friends after all), on Sunday afternoons, I would bathe and dress the children and myself and join him at the golf club where I would enjoy one gin and tonic. The children would enjoy a plate of chips. It indeed WAS the high point of my weekend! He would always encourage me to bring the children to meet him there, and I think it might have been his way of finding it easier to leave this rather hard-drinking group.

Naturally, I much enjoyed our holidays, and I thought it a good idea when Michael's mother asked if she could pay us another visit, and we decided we should make a holiday trip altogether. In the meantime, I joined other women from time to time. We learned to make hats, we went to Tupperware parties, and we also took an excellent course of cake decorating. That year the children all had fabulous birthday cakes.

It was a pleasure to welcome Michael's mother again. She joined in our routine as much as she could and sometimes helped with getting our evening meal on the table. She truly enjoyed her granddaughters as she'd had experience only of raising boys. She thought our life vastly different from what she was used to, as of course, it was. When we had a few friends in for drinks etc. she would usually find someone with an English background to talk with. After any little gathering, she would have a little 'post mortem' chat with me the next day over coffee. She would talk about the people she had met and how different these young people had so quickly become after just a few months of living in Africa. I thought she didn't quite approve of the tone of our conversations, which were all about travel, our clothes and servant problems, new cars, the political situation, etc. and what was on our local television programme. It sure wasn't a bit like 'Coronation Street' type living! I thought she would understand our life could be no other way; it was hard for her to accept the difference. Things in England never seemed to change much.

I think she was keen to experience a little more of Africa when we set out on our 'safari'. She always said she longed to travel, but it must have been difficult for her to be in the car with the family for such long periods, although we thought things generally went reasonably well. We always made sure she had comfortable accommodation when we halted for the night. Even this was somewhat outside her usual experience; she had never stayed in a hotel or motel before, but she always said she had slept well when we met at breakfast time. When we got to Durban, after seeing so much of the vast and varying terrain of Rhodesia and South Africa, she seemed quite pleased with our holiday apartment. The weather was perfect, and the children always had a good time at the beach, which was well guarded by shark nets that had been recently installed offshore in the distance. This area was the home of the great white shark, and there had been some awful attacks a few years before our visit. We met an acquaintance there who had arrived from Kitwe and who was happy to chat with our mother occasionally. Nicola gave us all quite a turn one day when we returned from a morning at the beach. She had collected many beautiful shells of various sizes and went immediately to the bathroom to wash them. We heard a loud scream, and Michael rushed to her. Nicola was in shock, staring at the shells in the hand basin. A hermit crab had taken up residence in one of the shells, and exposure to the freshwater had made it think exiting was a good idea. A large claw was visible and poor Nicola, who feared *creepy-crawlies*, was frightened and shaking. She quite lost interest in shell collecting. Aside from these incidents, it had been a most pleasant little holiday, but the very best part was yet to come.

శ్రు త్రు

After about a week at the coast, I checked over the car as best I could before the journey home. We intended to head north into Zululand as we wanted to visit a large game park. We had visited a small private one just outside Durban on a scorching day, but the animals there all seemed old and tired, and it was more like a rehab zoo. The road along the coast passed through sugar cane plantations for miles. There was a village by a river, and many children came running with carved wooden snakes in their hands.

Further along this narrow road, still in sight of the river, another group of clamouring children appeared as we rounded a corner. We realised they wanted to sell their carvings. We stopped the car and soon were surrounded by this happy jabbering group, all thrusting small carved wooden crocodiles at us through the open windows. After some negotiation, we bought two for 25 cents each and proceeded on our way. It was a one-time opportunity as we didn't see any more crocodiles or snakes for sale, and those primitive carvings must have been those villages' speciality. In Zululand, we stopped when a friendly-looking black lady with bold eyes offered us beads for sale. She was dressed in traditional costume, naked from the waist up except for many strands of beads. We bought her Zulu beads, took a few pictures, and were on our way.

Soon we were at the border with Swaziland, a British Protectorate, which is bordered by South Africa and Mozambique. It was one of the world's last remaining absolute monarchies, ruled by King Sobhuza II, who was believed to have had more than 60 wives. The royal family was often criticised for living so lavishly, spending millions on luxury cars and mansions for the numerous wives, while the majority of the population lived in abject poverty. Border formalities dealt with, we moved on, and as it was now approaching nightfall, we wondered what kind of accommodation might be available in this remote area. Soon we saw what looked like irregular but carefully cultivated areas and then saw lights ahead. We pulled up to a small hotel, seemingly in the middle of nowhere. We were so surprised when we noticed the interior was just like an English hotel, and the receptionist spoke with a cultivated Oxford accent. In the corner of the well-appointed lobby, an unusually disreputable-looking black man squatted, looking like a bundle of dirty old rags. No one took any notice of him. This was the only available accommodation in the area, so we stayed one night and had nicely appointed rooms and very good service. The next morning, we drove across Swaziland, a small but scenic country and exited at Kamatiepoort, back into South Africa. We were now quite close to the southern entrance to the Kruger National Park, one of the world's great game reserves. Our plan was to enter the park here and travel north almost the entire length of it. The park is 350 kilometres long by about 60 kilometres wide. The ranger at the gate advised us that there was accommodation available at Skukuza and at Olifants campsites, which we should book with him. We would not have been able to gain entry if accommodation for the night was unavailable; it was just too dangerous. We booked two nights at Skukuza and another at Olifants. A strict list of rules was handed to us. All animals within the park roam freely, and at no time were we to get out of the car while on the roads. The ranger said the lodge would be informed we were on our way. It would take quite a while to get there as the speed limit within the park was only 20 mph.

Skukuza Lodge impressed us when we arrived and drove through the large gates in the 20-foot high circular, heavy wooden fence enclosing the camp. There was a large lodge building with a covered outdoor kitchen and a small circular lecture area with low benches. Close by our accommodation there was a sort of picnic area and we were asked if we required a cook-boy. We hadn't brought along supplies as we planned to eat at the lodge, so we didn't need one, but the question caught my mother's attention! Shortly after we arrived, it was dusk, and the gates were closed for the night. We could feel safe here. The rooms, round huts with straw roofs, were clean but serviceable. We had a meal in the rather spartan outdoor dining room and then listened to a ranger tell us about the park's history, and he added some advice about game viewing.

As we walked under the stars back to our cabin, we could hear the night noises of many wild animals from the other side of the fence. But we all slept well that night. After a good breakfast, we drove a circular route from the camp and saw many different animals. Except at certain specified places, we always remained in the car, but we saw plenty of giraffes, zebra, wildebeest, antelope, and even some lions. After the second night, we left for the next camp. As we drove north, the terrain changed from quite lush tropical vegetation too much drier bush country. Here we saw a small herd of elephants at a distance. The park is vast, about the same size as Wales or Israel, and it is possible to see the 'Big Five' of Africa - elephant, lion, rhino, buffalo, and leopard, but we didn't see a rhino or any leopards here. Arriving at Olifants camp, situated high above a river gorge about mid-afternoon, we again settled into our rooms. We generally took two rooms, keeping Melanie with us, and Stephen and Nicola went in with my mother. The Park staff was as always very accommodating and offered a warm welcome to families. Looking down from the veranda of the lodge, one could see crocodiles on the banks of the river below and a large number of elephants across the river valley on slightly higher ground. Here Melanie, who generally skipped or ran headlong everywhere, tripped and fell on the sloping gravel pathway, landed on her face, scraping a sizable piece of skin from the end of her nose. Once the crying was over, we cleaned her up, but she had a Bandaid dressing on the wound for quite a few days.

Early the next morning, we were on the road again, and soon we saw two juvenile lions crossing the road behind us. They looked purposeful as if they were out hunting. After about 20 miles, we came up to a massive bull elephant standing alone right next to the road. We slowly passed him, and then I stopped the car; I thought this was too good a photo opportunity to miss. As I had both cameras, I took several still shots and then reached for my movie camera. Suddenly my mother started to hiss, 'Michael, Michael, he's coming after us.' With both cameras in my hands, I managed to put the car into gear and move forward, stopping again after a short distance. Then I had a good look at the huge beast, which was walking toward us with his ears flapping in a very threatening way. I took just a quick movie clip and decided it was time to leave. There was a massive sigh of relief from everyone in the car as we drove away. Elephants of that size had been known to overturn and damage vehicles. A few weeks before our visit, one rogue elephant had stomped on a small Volkswagen Beetle and turned it over; the people inside had been injured. Shortly after that little episode, we exited the park at Letaba and met up with the main road to the north. We had a lump in our throats, and Maureen murmured a soft 'Tot Siens, Suid Afrika' (Afrikaans) as we crossed the Limpopo River at Beit Bridge; we were leaving South Africa, we thought, probably for the last time.

After crossing the rather desolate southern portion of Rhodesia, we made a detour, as we wanted the opportunity to visit the mysterious ruins at Great Zimbabwe, near Fort Victoria, where we planned to spend the night. Great Zimbabwe, the most extensive ancient stone construction south of the Sahara, was built between the twelfth and fifteenth centuries by the ancestors of the Shona, one of Rhodesia's many Bantu speaking groups. It was believed to have housed up to 40,000 people at the zenith of its influence and had been an important cattle-raising area and slave-trading centre. When the Portuguese traders first encountered the vast stone ruins in the sixteenth century, they believed they had found the fabled capital of the 'Queen of Sheba'. Until recently, various theories were offered as to the identity of the people who built it. The Phoenicians, Arabs, Romans, even the Hebrews had been considered the possible builders. It was thought, taking into consideration the generally perceived abilities of the present indigenous people, the Bantu would not have had the technical know-how to build such an empire. Great Zimbabwe has now been recognised as a UNESCO World Heritage Site. It is the most mysterious and unique place; we enjoyed the day exploring the ruins where there were surprisingly few other people, just a few baboons to keep us company. The thick, high stone walls definitely had an Arabian look about them; no mortar was used in the construction. My mother was fascinated by the place. The next day, while the children stayed with Mum around the hotel pool, Maureen and I spent some time playing a round of golf on the Great Zimbabwe Golf Course, which was moderately challenging, and we had almost to ourselves. Many of the holes had trees down each side of the fairway, which seemed to be the home of lively monkeys. Off one tee, I hit a particularly good shot uphill, right to the green. But when we got there, no ball was to be seen. After searching for a while, we realised it must have been stolen by one of the many baboons that were chattering in the branches. The next morning, after a short stop at Lake McIlwaine, one of our favourite places just outside Salisbury, we again started on a very familiar journey home.

As we wanted to show my mother as much as possible, we again took the dirt road turn-off to Kariba. We were advised it was relatively safe to do so; there were no terrorists in the area. Again, we stayed at the same resort and sweltered through a rather hot night under the nets. The next morning after crossing the dam wall to the Zambian side, we had an unexpected delay. There was only one black Customs and Immigration official there, and he spent ages going through our declaration item by item, inspecting all of our personal effects, and asking stupid questions. I started to get impatient with him but realised this would not help. After almost two hours, he allowed us to go. I realised afterwards that this was the new regime, and he was waiting for a bribe. We completed the long drive home; our faithful Toyota had performed very well, and once again, we found our home in perfect order.

Olifants Rest Camp, Kruger National Park, South Africa

Some of the many animals we were able to see in the park

Beit Bridge over the Limpopo River; the main border crossing between South Africa and Rhodesia

A visit with Michael's mother to the Great Zimbabwe Ruins in Rhodesia

Kariba Dam on the Zambezi River - This was a border crossing between Rhodesia and Zambia (background)

The new Zambian currency

A rural Zambian scene

14.
'Tot Siens, Afrika'

Michael

After we had been at home for a week or so, my mother became restless again and somewhat depressed at times, as had happened toward the end of her last extended visit to us. Maureen and I, of course, had to get back to our everyday life, working and caring for the family, so she was sometimes left to her own devices for short periods. She also seemed to miss my brother back in England very much. I thought they had an odd sort of relationship and relied on each other for far too many things. At the end of May, we took her to the airport in Ndola, and she left for her home in England.

All our friends who were under contract to Anglo American Corporation were now either leaving Zambia as the term of their contract expired or were making plans to do so in the future. Some neighbours in Queens Street left for Tasmania; many were returning to South Africa, and some were considering moving to the United States. Among this group were our friends Peter and Gloria Walsh. I had a question mark in my mind about the U.S. From early in 1968, the war in Vietnam had escalated, and there was considerable opposition to it in America. Racial tension there seemed to be at an all-time high when Martin Luther King was assassinated in April, followed by Robert Kennedy in June. Maureen was concerned about the growing *hippie* counterculture and escalating drug use among young people living in the 'Western' world. She and I were now in our mid-thirties and felt that it was time to settle for the sake of my career and also to provide a more stable future for our family. The cheapest and easiest move would be back in South Africa, and there was plenty of work available there. We all felt a little uneasy. 'Was there going to be a future for the white man in Southern Africa?' We had lived with racial tension, always knowing white people were greatly outnumbered by black. There had been some serious incidents lately.

One Saturday, coming home from work on my scooter at noon, I saw a huge column of black smoke rising in the clear blue sky at the north end of town. I said to Maureen I wanted to go and see what was happening. She wisely said she didn't think it was a good idea, so I never went. We found out later that a fuel storage tank had caught fire, and the Africans, blaming the white people, had attacked cars on the Kitwe to Chingola road by throwing large rocks; one white woman had been killed and some other people injured. Maybe it *was* time to leave.

Maureen really felt we should return to England, buy a house or cottage in the West Country, which she loved and live happily ever after. But I knew there was very little work for me in that area and I still remembered my working days in the London area and had no desire to return there. We had become accustomed to a different way of life here, appreciated the freedom the vast spaces allowed and the easy way of life, all of which I am sure we would miss if we returned to England.

Some people at work seemed interested in Canada, and we learned from a small Zambian Times newspaper advertisement that a Canadian Consulate representative would be in Lusaka in June to interview prospective tradespeople for possible immigration to Canada. I phoned and made an appointment for 5th June 1968, which happened to be Maureen's birthday. Taking Melanie along (Stephen and Nicola were in school), we drove down that morning for an interview with an official from the Canadian Embassy in Beirut at the Lusaka Hotel, which was the best one in town. I filled in some forms, we had a brief discussion, and he informed me that we would be accepted for immigration to Canada, subject to a medical, which we should have in London. All documents would be forwarded to London, and we could pick them up there. I was delighted, but Maureen, in her usual cautious way, seemed quiet and thoughtful about the enterprise. We had a delicious lunch at the hotel, and to celebrate, I bought her a bracelet made of local semi-precious stones set in silver, which cheered her up considerably as she had not had many presents. We happily drove home.

୫୦ ଓଃ

I was happy when we arrived home from our South African holiday with Michael's mother. It had gone quite well, but naturally, there had been some small difficulties. We were a little more crowded in the car, and mother had caught a bad cold as we left Durban, which made her feel miserable and quite unwell for a couple of days. She was intrigued by Swaziland and couldn't understand how the staff at the hotel there could allow 'that beggar' to remain in the lobby, and she was not too sure about the Game Park as it was a kind of camping. Fascinated by Great Zimbabwe, she was interested and amused by the Lake Kariba experience. Along the way, she had learned something about the pleasures and stresses involved in living where we did. So altogether, once we arrived home safely, I thought we had given her quite a good time and an exciting experience of life in southern Africa.

Before we went away, she had shown me a beautiful length of blue silk her sister Hilda had given her, which she would like made into a two-piece dress, and once I got the house in order, I was able to start work on the project. My house-servant James had not returned to work for us; perhaps he had found another place. As people were beginning to leave, it wasn't hard to engage another servant. George appeared, and we took him on. I had come to rely significantly on help in the house, especially as my life became busier with the children's activities. Mum's outfit was completed quickly, and I gave her the instructions as to its care. She had never had a fine silk dress before, and I knew it would require careful laundering. Once that project was completed, she thought she should return home. She wanted to tell her sisters about her adventures, and Denis was living alone in her flat, and that was where she now wanted to be. Michael wanted our life to return to normal and was beginning to think about plans for our future when his contract period was up. So, he despatched his mother at the end of May, and we could once again concentrate on our everyday life.

Michael has mentioned his reasons for deciding we should leave Africa. They were good reasons, but I couldn't quite believe that we would leave a comfortable life that had evolved. I had become very attached to our home and my now familiar lifestyle in

Kitwe. But Michael seemed to think Canada would be a good choice. It certainly was a large and spacious country, and as it was his technical ability, which provided the income that supported our family, I thought I should listen to his ideas. I knew when the time came we would have saved up quite a nice sum, and having a little financial security while we sorted out the next stage of our life, meant we could take our time over the final decision. So as always, I concentrated on looking after my home and family and here and there taking time to look after myself. I had quite nice clothes now. I always made some of them myself but would purchase a few good quality outfits and shoes a couple of times a year. I was in the habit of having my hair done every six weeks. I usually took Melanie with me for short hair appointments but made the ones that took more time when Michael was at home so that he could spend a little time with his children. Just a week or two after Mother left, I needed a completely new 'hairdo', which would take a bit more than three hours. Michael was at home, lunch was prepared, and Stephen was playing with a friend nearby. When I returned, there was poor Michael, looking a little shaken, limping out with blood running down his left shin. 'Your family needs you', he said, 'I've had an accident. I'm wounded!' The girls came running, beginning to cry when they saw me. They were fine, but they had also been involved in the accident. Michael had arranged to pick them up from a birthday party, so they had been wearing their nicest dresses and new shoes. He put them both on his Vespa scooter, Nicola, on the back seat, holding onto his belt and Melanie standing between his knees. Near a friend's house, a dog appeared, barking threateningly. In an impulsive moment, Michael, thinking he would give the dog a warning, swerved a little towards the animal, which was running beside him snapping and barking. The dog was right alongside the front wheel, which bumped him, and off he ran yelping. Michael lost control of the scooter at the collision, and all three of them were suddenly on the road! I was horrified to think of my lovely little girls being spilled into the road, but fortunately, Michael hadn't been going very fast, and he managed to protect Melanie a little. Nicola too was all right; being quick on her feet, she had probably been ready to jump when the scooter went over. She was always nervous about barking dogs. Our friend Pam

Clelland heard the noise, ran out to help, and comforted the girls, but poor Michael had a very severely scraped ankle. I would have bathed his leg for him, but it looked pretty bad to me, so I said right away, 'Hospital!'

Michael wouldn't hear of it. He said he had bathed it thoroughly and thought it was not as bad as it looked. Later, in the early evening, Michael decided he would go to the hospital, where they cleaned him up and gave him a tetanus shot. But the following day, things didn't get any better for him. A couple of days later, when a scab had formed, he simply had to return to the out-patients' clinic because we could see there was an infection present, and he was in great pain. He worked every day through this but needed a couple of days off after that second clinic visit. He could barely walk. After the rather painful treatment on that day, his injury gradually began to improve, and he was soon back at work again. Michael was always thin while we were in Africa; perhaps he didn't have much resistance to infections, but he had become a regular blood donor, so I had always regarded him as a vigorous and healthy man. I usually never needed to worry about him.

With the departure of our friends, Peter and Gloria Walsh, and having watched them dispose of their belongings, we realised we had to think seriously about planning for our eventual departure. Michael's contract would be completed in March 1969. We began to consider the possibility of my having a Christmas in England with the children. This opportunity would give the children time to enjoy a traditional English Christmas and make life somewhat easier for Michael to dispose of the items we couldn't take with us. The two older children were involved in their school activities, so we gradually came to the decision that the end of the school year, in December, would be an appropriate departure date for us, leaving Michael to finish his contract period. Stephen was immensely enjoying the athletics' programme at school. We decided to stay until after Sports Day, which came during the final week of school so that our son had the pleasure of taking part. I put the idea of disposing of my home out of my mind – I hated the idea of leaving Queens Street and Michael behind, even though I was keen to see my family again. Sharing a beautiful family Christmas with them was an excellent idea. I thought it best to keep my negative personal feelings about our immediate future from the children. Always a regular correspondent, my sister Pam had promptly offered to accommodate us all in her home as soon as she learned of our plans. Pam and Ron were now buying their own house. It was a three-level townhouse with four bedrooms, with a view of a large park in a fairly new development in Basildon, Essex. To help Pam prepare, we sent a sum of money to buy bunk beds and bedding for the girls to use and asked her to buy three warm jackets (*anorak-style*, preferably) because we would be arriving during their winter. My children had never needed winter clothing until now. Naturally, we would also share the grocery bill. *Dear* Pam was sure she could fit everyone in.

So that part of the plan was in place, but there were still a few months in which to enjoy our African lifestyle together. We used the time in the same way that we had lived. I took the same care of my home, garden and children, Michael worked hard, and we entertained, perhaps a little more because we would soon be parted from the good friends we had made. We made a few more visits to Cheeseman's Farm, sometimes in the company of some of the newer contract people that had arrived from England, to show them the recreational amenities which would add something to their adjustment to life in Zambia. The young women seemed a slightly different breed to me. They understood from the beginning that the people they would meet in Kitwe were 'ships that pass in the night'. And I noticed these women mostly were a little more 'liberated' and more vocally forthright about women's rights. Living in Southern Africa had kept me insulated from what was happening in the rest of the western world during the sixties – we'd had other tensions in our daily lives. We stopped going to Cheeseman's Farm after a young Greek teen drowned in the lake. Michael and Stephen were among the people who were asked by anxious family members to help look for him. They witnessed him being discovered under the water and rushed away to Ndola hospital. We read in the newspaper the next day that he had been pronounced dead on arrival. The water was not very deep at Cheeseman's Farm; we never heard what the cause of death was.

The children celebrated their birthdays. Melanie was four years old that July, Nicola was seven in August and Stephen, nine at the end of September. Their birthdays were celebrated with outdoor children's parties and a *braai* in the evening. Melanie had joined Nicola at dancing school at the first level, and Nicola passed her first Royal Academy syllabus dance examination. She had worked very hard and was just a few points below the Honours mark. Stephen had been doing well at school. This year he had a lay teacher named Mrs Greig who took a great interest in him and helped him. And after the school swim meet, where Stephen did very well, we finally came to Sports Day at school. Stephen was everywhere; he seemed to be in almost every event, and at the end of the day to my complete surprise and delight, he was announced the Top Athlete for the year with the title '*Victor Ludorum*'. I was genuinely thrilled for him, and Stephen was very proud too! Mrs Greig, who was a quiet, somewhat shy person, sought me out afterwards and told me that Stephen truly deserved the honour because he always tried very hard. She wished us well for the future. I visited Sister Damien's office and thanked her for the service the school had provided for my children and said, 'goodbye'. I also said 'goodbye' to Sister Joan of Arc, who I had helped teach swimming of an afternoon and Sister Mary Crucifix too. Our departure from Kitwe suddenly seemed very real.

For many months now, the conversation at every gathering had been all about departure plans. I had met another woman who, with her husband, was considering Canada. She loaned me a couple of newspapers, one published in Toronto, the other in Vancouver. We studied these papers carefully and found the cost of housing seemed a little high, but food and many other goods and services cost much less than we were used to paying. Except for accommodation, we thought living expenses in Canada would be lower than in England. I wasn't exactly fully committed to the idea of starting a new life in Canada but figured it would certainly be interesting to see North America. Together we decided we would aim at moving to the West Coast because we had quickly learned winters there were much milder than east of the Rocky Mountains and the rest of this enormous country. The average temperatures in the Vancouver area seemed rather like weather conditions in the south of England, so feeling encouraged, I had been able to support Michael's ambitious idea. Before we left, we were invited to several farewell parties. My friends had always been very important to me. We had dinner with Jill and Otto on our last weekend together, and at the end of the evening, I kissed them both 'goodbye'.

And so, we came to the last few days in Zambia. Michael had a large wooden packing case placed in our entry hallway inside the front door, and it was my job to begin packing it. I lined up the things I needed in the living room. We couldn't take furniture or electrical items, so it was small household goods, our blankets and linen and some of each of the children's toys and a few things that had been wedding presents. I carefully packed up my beautiful *NECCHI* sewing machine. Since it had been built in Italy, I knew it could be modified to run sweetly wherever we ended up. I left my ironing board and iron because George was going to remain Michael's house servant and would look after his laundry. I was to leave the packing case open for Michael to add his tools and things. It was a very sad business. On my last day in my home, I put in the canteen of cutlery Michael's mum and dad had given us for a wedding gift. I was very depressed and wept sadly at night – I didn't want to leave my home without Michael. But the plan was made, and our departure loomed. When the day arrived, somehow, I managed to smile and tell George to take good care of my house; I shook his hand and thanked him and walked out of that house, got into the car with Michael and the children, and we drove away. I couldn't look back.

At Ndola Airport, our British Caledonian VC-10 aircraft was at the gate. I had to relinquish my Zambian identity card on exiting the country. We waited a short time before boarding – there was nothing much we could say to each other – Michael talked a little to the children, and they nodded solemnly, and soon it was time to board. There was no covered jet-way at Ndola, so we kissed goodbye and walked out to the aircraft on the tarmac and mounted the stairs; I had Melanie by the hand and was carrying my old camel coloured winter coat that I had kept for ten years in Africa. It had never been worn there, but I would need it in England. I managed to turn at the top of the stairs before entering the plane and wave in the direction of the people at the departure gate; I couldn't see Michael. We were shown to our seats and made comfortable. In the language of our Afrikaner South African friends, it was time for us to say, '*Tot Siens, Afrika*'.

৷৹ ৫

This parting was difficult for both of us. Since marrying ten years earlier, we had not been apart for a single day. Suddenly three months seemed an awfully long time. I had never done much cooking, washing, or ever made a bed. The mine did have a big restaurant called Ernie's, and they had pretty good meals, so I went there most evenings. I did manage to make a quick breakfast for myself and then throw together a sandwich to take to work for lunch, something Maureen had always done for me. She had only been gone a few days, and I was beginning to miss her already. But our friends were very understanding, and I did get plenty of invitations out, particularly at weekends. As we had been accepted for immigration to Canada, I had to make all of the arrangements. The travel agent I went to in Kitwe was excellent and had lots of experience with travel plans all over the world. I booked my flight for a couple of weeks after the end of March, when my contract expired and arranged for all of our possessions to be shipped by sea to England. The company covered the cost for all of this, so I never had to put down any *Kwacha*. Although Maureen and I had discussed going to Canada, I knew she was not sure that this was what she wanted to do, but knowing it was a beautiful country I believed that if we got there, she would probably like it. So, I went ahead and booked the journey from the U.K. to Canada as well. The travel agent informed me that we could travel by a Canadian Pacific ship from Liverpool to Montreal and then by rail with the same company to Vancouver, which was the only destination in Canada we would consider. I paid the full cost of this journey, but as new immigrants, our personal effects accompanying us would be transported free of charge on the ship to Canada.

Conditions at work seemed to be deteriorating quite rapidly now, and the Africans were not able to learn quickly enough how to manage the complexities of running a section, the mine, or the country for that matter. At Independence, the United States Government had given Zambia four new (and powerful) GM railway locomotives. By this time, most of them were out of service due to damage or mechanical failure, and many of the train crews had been arrested and jailed for driving them while drunk. The time went by slowly, so I tried to work as much overtime as possible. For the past two years, Harold had been acting foreman in the main machine shop, and I would then be upgraded to charge hand in the tool room. From time to time, if he were away, I would also be in charge of the big shop. This promotion was a big responsibility as there were about 20 white artisans and a smaller number of African helpers. But I learned to handle it. I also played a lot of golf, although I never really became very good at it. I should have taken the time to have lessons. I was invited out for Christmas dinner at a friend's house, but I did miss the family and wondered what kind of party they were having.

Once into the New Year of 1969, I started to sell a few of our belongings, knowing we could not take them with us. By now, many Africans had better jobs, so they were anxious to buy almost anything people who were leaving had to offer. I sold my scooter first as I now had the car to use every day. Then it was the children's beds and the furniture in their rooms. Slowly the house emptied, and it seemed far lonelier. My Scottish friends invited me to a Burns' night supper in February, where we drank rather too much, and I sampled the Scottish *haggis*. A fun night and it helped to pass the time.

I was now getting close to the end of my contract. Having quite a lot of tools to take with me, I had a wooden box made for them in the carpenter's shop and gradually sold off the rest of our possessions. It was the tradition for anyone leaving to host and pay for a party at the mine club. The party turned out to be quite an expensive event. It was planned for the day after I finished work, and a good number of my friends and colleagues came, some with their wives. It was an open bar with food supplied. Praise and gifts were lavished on me, and many happy people celebrated the time we had spent together. During the next few days, I had to sort out my finances, my wages from the mine plus the holiday pay owing, and make arrangements to have it all transferred in *Kwacha* to Barclays Bank in Basildon, the town where Maureen was staying with her sister Pam. I then had to finish packing the crate and have it picked up. This crate was to be shipped to the U.K. to await our further instructions. A problem developed with the packing when I realised that there was just not enough room; I still had to get my small but heavy toolbox in. Unfortunately, I had to remove some of Maureen's precious items as there was just no room for them. I sold them to one of the many Africans who were always at the door looking for bargains.

I was now down to the last day. I had a customer for the car, who came early that morning with a pocketful of paper money in small bills. That same morning, I sold our bed and the rest of the items in the house. George was paid off, and he seemed so sad to see me go. I gave him quite a number of smaller items. My golfing friend Bill Clelland offered to take me to the airport, and on the way, I stopped at the bank in Kitwe to deposit the additional funds I had acquired, adding to the sum to be transferred to England. There was a limit to the amount that could be transferred out, but we were well within it. Shortly after we left, this limit was drastically reduced, forcing many people to leave much of their money behind. When we arrived at Ndola Airport, Bill quickly left, and within a short time, I was aboard the British Caledonian VC-10 departing for London. After take-off, the aircraft banked sharply as we turned to the north, and I took one final look at the lush vegetation of Zambia below me before the ground disappeared under the clouds. It was a sad moment. We had spent just over ten happy, eventful years in Africa, producing three wonderful healthy children, and those years had been very good to us.

I wondered what the future would hold for this beautiful but troubled continent. The 'Wind of Change' had certainly created many changes. The potential was there for all of Southern Africa to be successful, so rich in manpower and resources, with a wonderful climate, but as we left, the situation in Rhodesia had escalated into an all-out guerrilla war spreading across the country. Zambia's economy was starting to falter, and although apartheid was still in effect in South Africa, one wondered how long that regime would endure. I also thought about the many friends we had made who intended to stay; many of them, not emigrants like us, but those whose families had helped to build up these countries over many generations and what would become of the black Africans who had touched our lives and whose future now looked uncertain.

After a while, my thoughts turned again to our future. We now had no house, no job, or even a country of residence. But we did have enough money to begin buying a home of our own, wherever that might be. Our life in Africa had given me so much more confidence. I had learned a lot, not only about my work but about how to relate to and even manage other people, and I felt, given the opportunity, we could be successful anywhere.

The plane took off, and it truly was 'Goodbye Africa' for my family.

Our final days in Africa, before boarding a British Caledonian VC 10 to London

15.
Another New Beginning

Maureen

The journey went well; the children were very good and went to sleep as it got dark, but I seemed to retire inside myself for the first part of it. Reviving when we reached Rome and thinking they needed to stretch their legs, I suggested that we all take a walk to the main concourse. The walk turned out to be not quite such a good idea because it was quite a long distance to walk. Rome is a massive airport. My feet were a little swollen, and my tight new shoes made blisters on my heels. But the children were glad to escape the confines of the plane's cabin and ran and skipped along quite happily. When we arrived at Gatwick, London's second airport, my brother-in-law, Ron, was there with a very warm welcome and three warm jackets. We lost no time in stowing our suitcases in his car and leaving the airport for the two-hour ride to Basildon.

My Mum and Dad were waiting there with Pam with a joyous, loving welcome. It had been more than five years again since we had been together. Four-year-old Melanie had never seen these grandparents or any of these other people; she was welcomed and made a great fuss of. In the years since our last visit, my mother had experienced many episodes of poor health. We had a lovely reunion, and the conversation was all about arrangements for Christmas Day, which was just a week away. Mum and Dad would be coming to share our Christmas dinner, traditionally served in our family at about 2.00 pm and some of my brothers and their families were to join us for an evening party. The weather was reasonably pleasant, although I sometimes felt rather cold. My heels were still so painful because the blisters had become infected; I couldn't wear outdoor shoes for several days, but on Christmas Eve, I walked up to the town centre to buy my Christmas gifts, wearing my heel-less red slippers. My children had very few toys of their own with them, so I bought the girls Barbie dolls and various outfits, etc. and construction sets for Stephen and something for every other family member, too. I hadn't had so much pleasure buying Christmas gifts for a long time. One purchase was three 'nighties' from Marks & Spencer for my female relatives, which my mother thought wildly extravagant behaviour. For once in my life, I felt I didn't need to worry too much about the cost of family gifts.

I missed Michael, especially in the evenings, although I knew he wouldn't much enjoy being surrounded by his wife's relatives. I wanted to make the most of this time and enjoy being with my family since he seemed quite determined that we would not spend the rest of our lives in England. We exchanged letters, and he urged me to visit Canada House as soon as I could after Christmas – since my feet still hurt so much, I put that suggestion aside. We had a wonderful Christmas Day, and the following afternoon Ron took us all to a pantomime. It has long been a tradition in England that after Christmas beginning on Boxing Day, families take their young children to see a theatre production of a *pantomime* as a special treat. It is usually a colourful musical story based on traditional fairy tales such as Cinderella, Puss in Boots, or Dick Whittington. The female lead is a young and beautiful girl; there is always somebody representing a Prince Charming sort of person and an evil female character who is very obviously a man in drag. Audience participation is encouraged so the little ones can *boo and hiss* when this character appears. Our children had never seen anything like this before, so we all had a good time, especially the girls. Pam and Ron both made us feel so welcome, and this warm feeling carried on even though occasionally the children had small disagreements. It was rather hard for Pam's children to have to share their space with us. After the celebration of Christmas, it was time to take the children to see Michael's mother in Hainault. Denis very kindly came to collect us, and we had a pleasant visit. Mother seemed fairly happy with her new home. Naturally, she wanted to see her grandchildren frequently while we were in England and told me where the nearest '*tube*' station was so that I could work out a route. I explained I would be registering Stephen and Nicola for school locally, but I was sure Melanie and I could make the rather complicated journey to see her when the weather allowed. I was glad to hear all the news from Michael's side of the family. I really enjoyed my time with my sister and with Mum, who lived nearby. I was able to walk round to her house for a little visit with Melanie when the children were in school. I kept our rooms tidy and took care of our laundry when Pam was at work and helped with the simple cooking Pam did when necessary – it all worked very well. Along the way, I saw some rather lovely new houses near where Mum's sister, Olive, lived. I thought we could easily afford one of them, but Michael reminded me, when we exchanged letters, I should be going to see someone at Canada House. To be able to tell him that I had tried to move things forward, I made the journey up to London with Melanie and presented myself at Canada House.

I took a number in the Immigration Hall and waited for my turn for an interview. When my number was called, I approached the desk and related the history of our interview in Lusaka seven months before, to the female officer, and requested appointments for the medical examinations we had been advised we needed, adding that my husband would be available early in April. Without ceremony, I was informed they knew nothing at all about our case, and when my husband, Michael, arrived in England, we should both begin the application process again for permission to become immigrants. I was taken aback at this, but there clearly was no room for argument, so we left and went home to Pam's house. My parents were there when we arrived. They were wearing their outdoor coats, about to leave, but asked me how I had got on. I told my story and finished up with, 'I am not going there again; Michael will have to do something about it if he really wants to go to Canada!' I was quite tired and dejected from the long journey to London and back; it had been a difficult day. I think they guessed I didn't really want to go to Canada. My Mum and Dad exchanged a look with each other and departed Pam's house.

Stephen and Nicola accepted the routine of going to school in Basildon quite well. I had bought them some warmer English-style school clothes, although the weather never got very cold. They stayed for school lunch, and I would sometimes meet them coming home at 4.00 pm. Their accents were changing a little; they were trying to fit in with the slightly *cockney* speech of Basildon, which as a 'New Town' constantly received an influx of new residents, who were displaced tenants from the overcrowded, run-down, old communities of London that my mother called 'the Slums' and which were being cleared before being rebuilt with modern apartment towers. Basildon probably would not have been my choice of a place to live permanently, but there were other options in the surrounding areas, and I would have loved to be able to live in the West Country. So, I settled down to routine chores, seeing my mother and occasionally going out with her for a shopping trip. I had learned how to get to Michael's mother's flat, too. Pam and Ron sometimes invited me to go out with them on Friday evenings, when they would go to a pub and meet their friends. I was never a fan of the pub scene when I was a young woman before I married, so I usually declined and said I would stay with the children and watch the television with my knitting, but I went with them occasionally. Because houses are small in England, there was never very much entertaining attempted in the home. This is one reason why the British pub is such an important part of so many people's lives. It is where one meets friends to exchange news and keep in social touch with one another.

Not having a home of my own, I sometimes felt like a poor relation within the greater family circle, and my thoughts often dwelt on what Michael was doing and thinking and when we could be together again. We exchanged letters but had not been able to talk. My sister had a telephone – I guess Michael didn't think a telephone conversation would be very satisfying. The winter weeks dragged on, but my mood brightened as the little green leaf buds on the trees in Basildon signalled spring was coming, and the day Michael was to arrive at Gatwick approached. On the weekend before he was to arrive, I took the children to see their Nana and let her know we had agreed that I would meet him by myself because we wanted to spend the first night of our reunion in a hotel near the airport, but we would come to Hainault in the morning of the following day. We had been apart for three months; the separation had been hard for both of us because we had never been apart for a single day since our marriage. I have no memory of getting myself to Gatwick Airport – it was quite a complicated journey. I do remember waiting very nervously on the 'Arrivals' level for my husband to appear – I was fearful something terrible might have happened to prevent his arrival. That reunion is one of the fondest memories of our life together. Michael was as happy to see me as I was to be reunited with him. When he appeared, it was as if there was no one else in that meeting space. We both still smile when we speak of that day.

True to our word, the next day, we went first to Michael's mother's home where we had lunch with her, and then it was on to Basildon and the reunion with the children, who were very excited to see their father. He was taken aback because Stephen's and Nicola's accents had changed. They now had a bit of the London sound; it hadn't bothered me very much.

⁎ ⌘

I was very excited to be reunited with Maureen and the family again after over three months of separation. The journey on a British Caledonian VC-10 aircraft was uneventful. After a brief stop in Entebbe, Uganda, we soon headed across the Sahara Desert. I was able to go onto the flight deck for a short time and spent a little while talking to the crew. I took some photos with my new Canon camera and briefly thought this must be a fantastic industry to be in.

I was surprised and thrilled when I saw that Maureen was alone to meet me at London's Gatwick Airport. She had obviously made an effort to look her very best, including new clothes she had bought, wearing her favourite '*Shalimar*' perfume and of course we were both delighted to be once again in each other's arms. We took a taxi to a small country hotel she had booked and spent a wonderful, passionate night together. After a leisurely breakfast, we caught the train to my mother's flat and then went on to Basildon for a reunion with the children. They were all excited to see me, and I noticed a little of the local accent was creeping into their speech. After a few days in England, I was anxious to finalise our immigration plans to Canada. Maureen told me of her unsuccessful visit to Canada House, and I could tell by the tone in her voice that she was not sure whether she wanted to leave England again. But I had the ship and train already booked for our journey, so off we went to London for an interview with the Canadian officials. I explained to them that we had already been accepted and just needed a medical. Without even looking, they said they knew nothing about us and handed me a lengthy application form. After completing it and showing them my apprenticeship papers, they said we should go ahead and have our medicals, but there was no guarantee we would be accepted for Canada. I explained about our ship and train bookings, but they were quite unimpressed. Feeling very discouraged, we made our way back to Basildon. Although she didn't say anything, I think Maureen was not at all concerned it had not gone well; her dream of staying in England might come to pass after all.

But I was determined to get those medical tests done as soon as possible. Having come from tropical Africa, we were required to have somewhat more extensive tests than the usual English applicants. I took all five of us to Billericay Hospital, where we were to provide blood, urine, and stool samples; we also had chest x-rays. The hospital staff was quite cooperative, but certain members of the family could not provide stool samples. I went back several days running with the children's samples, but Maureen's system seemed to have shut down. I started to get impatient with her, thinking she was somehow holding back as she did not want to go to Canada anyway. But I knew that sooner or later, she would have to produce, and as soon as she did, I rushed off to Billericay Hospital with the final specimen in hand. The completed test results would be forwarded to Canada House. After a few days, I called them but was advised they would not have any more information for me for several weeks. The delay would bring us very close to our proposed departure date. I was getting very anxious.

My brother Denis had returned to England about one year earlier, having now finished with the British Merchant Navy. He had moved back in with my mother and had been helping her purchase the new flat in Hainault after selling 187 Browning Road. He was now working in the tool room at Plessey's, and I thought this rather strange, as he had also worked in the same company as I had in Cape Town. I met him at the Plessey plant and enjoyed meeting many of my old colleagues again. Everything seemed the same after ten years of absence. Shortly after our arrival, I had rented a small car in Basildon and, at Maureen's suggestion, we decided to take a trip around the southwest part of England and show the children some of the areas we had travelled to as teenagers on our bikes. We were both very fond of this part of the country, and I think Maureen thought if I would perhaps want to stay in England, we could settle in this beautiful area. Our journey took us first to Stonehenge, where the children were able to climb and wander about the ancient stone pillar circle and then drove across Exmoor to the north Cornish coast. The weather was quite damp and chilly. Maureen's Aunt Louise and new husband, Harry, had a small hotel on the rugged coast. Here we stayed for a few days, and the children had quite a nice time, as it was a resort type hotel with a discothèque where Stephen danced with the young local girls. We then drove down to the extreme western tip of England at Land's End. Maureen had not been here before, and we were both disappointed when we saw how commercialised it had become, including a casino with flashing neon lights. For us, this, together with the driving rain, just spoiled the rugged beauty of the place. After staying one night we drove to Plymouth where it was still raining. We spent some time on Plymouth Hoe, from where Francis Drake sailed for his round-the-world voyages. We also visited the Naval War Memorial, where we found my Uncle Reg's name inscribed. This day seemed to make quite an impression on Nicola.

The return journey to London, via the south coast, was uneventful, and we were soon at Maureen's sister's home again. The trip had not changed my mind about going to Canada, as I realised that although the West Country was one of the nicest parts to live, there was very little work in the area for me. Upon our return, I called Canada House; it was now only one week to our intended departure date. They gave me an appointment for two days before the ship sailed and said I would then be advised whether we were accepted for entry into Canada or not. Although I was very anxious during those days of waiting, Maureen was calm, often going shopping with her mother. On the day of the appointment, off we went to Canada House. After a short interview, I was informed that we had been accepted for immigration to Canada. We were advised that, with my qualifications, we should proceed to Windsor, Ontario, as there was plenty of work in the motor industry there. They advised us against going to Vancouver as there were few jobs in my trade. I reluctantly agreed we would do this. The entry papers were not yet available, but after reminding them the ship sailed in two days, they said I could pick them up the next day. Such a relief, for me anyway, but I was still unsure about how Maureen felt. I could now go ahead and make the rest of my arrangements. We had transferred our money (Zambian *Kwacha's*) to a branch of Barclays Bank DCO in Basildon, and after withdrawing the amount I thought we needed immediately, I now requested them to transfer the balance to Vancouver. I had no intention of going to Ontario. There were strict restrictions about transferring funds out of Britain at this time, but as we were not domiciled in Britain and considered to be in transit, the limits did not apply to us. Also, our crate of personal effects I had sent straight to Vancouver from Zambia. And now we were almost set to go. We all had to go to Canada House the next day as they wanted to see the children, and we were given our immigration papers for entry into Canada. I booked the train from Euston to Liverpool. My brother came to Liverpool with us. No other members of either family offered to see us off yet again.

On 17th April 1969, we boarded the Empress of England in Liverpool and sailed for North America.

16.
A Welcome to Canada

Maureen

Michael knew perfectly well I was not exactly thrilled about his proposal to try Canada next. I had a strange heavy feeling in my chest, a kind of anxious disappointment. I had always wanted our children to have an English education – I wondered if our lives were to be disturbed periodically by his restless nature. It annoyed me more than a little that my husband could so casually brush aside and ignore my feelings. At the same time, I thought I ought to be a supportive wife – there were no heated arguments. He knew I always enjoyed a little adventure with a change of scene, and he was the one whose hard work supported us all. Therefore, I tried to accept his plan as the head of the family and didn't keep repeating my concerns. I loved him and had to admit our life together so far had not been humdrum. So, even though I loved my family and wanted to stay in England, I accepted that as Michael was our bread-winner and was prepared to finance this next adventure, at the very least, we would all enjoy a kind of holiday trip and see something of Canada and the United States. Perhaps everything would fall into place as Michael hoped, maybe not. We knew one person just a little in Canada. My mother's youngest sister, June Hambleton, lived in the Vancouver area. More than 25 years earlier, she had met a Canadian soldier towards the end of the war and became a *War Bride*. My mother and I had kept in touch with her by mail just once or twice a year. My aunt June had been a closer friend to my sister Pam, who was five years older than I was and that much closer to June in age. We hadn't seen her since she left England; Vancouver was far away.

We had kept in touch by mail with our good friends Peter and Gloria Walsh after they left Kitwe. They were now living in Rhode Island in the U.S. (on the east coast near New York), where Peter was working hard on a three-year course in the developing highly technical electronics field. To help support the family, Gloria was working in the beauty industry, selling cosmetics for a drug store chain. Together we planned that we would visit them when we got to Montreal, so, after a miserable British Rail train journey to Liverpool, when we were served a perfectly awful lunch, we boarded the ship headed for Canada.

It was a rather rough crossing. Spring had not yet arrived in the North Atlantic, and a moderate gale blew as soon as we left the shelter of the tired and shabby old port of Liverpool. The wind blew so hard that it was quite impossible to remain on deck, and the ship seemed to lean over at a 30-degree angle the whole way across the Atlantic. But I set myself to enjoy the voyage and the attention of the crew. There were some families on board, mostly new immigrants like us, as well as many returning Canadians. By the second day, there were very few passengers in the dining salon for breakfast, so many were afflicted with seasickness. Michael was one of them, but the children and I seemed perfectly all right.

Nine-year-old Stephen would escort his sisters to the Children's Lounge to enjoy the various activities arranged for young passengers there. Michael soon discovered he could have an injection to deal with the seasickness problem, which would cost £1 and joined the long line-up at the sickbay. After that, he was able to eat a little at the mealtimes, which I was thoroughly enjoying. I had purchased new warmer clothes for the family in England, and we felt we were properly equipped for the weather, but I feared the weather in Eastern Canada, which I knew could be brutal. As we intended to rent a car upon arrival and drive south, I hoped Montreal wouldn't be too cold, and spring would soon arrive. We made friends with another couple from England and met for a drink on some evenings – they were planning to settle with their young son in the Hamilton, Ontario area. We learned that most of the new immigrants were planning to stay in Eastern Canada, where there were more employment opportunities. There was a little entertainment arranged onboard some evenings, but we didn't often keep late hours. The rough seas helped us decide our stateroom was the best place to be at night.

The time on the ship soon passed. The Captain was not the party animal that our Captain on the Pretoria Castle, the Union-Castle ship on which we had travelled to South Africa, had been, but he appeared at the children's fancy-dress party. We had spent some time creating the children's costumes, and they had quite a lot of fun. Stephen dressed up in western gear with his toy gun belt and western hat, Nicola went as a Hawaiian dancer, Melanie wore a green crepe paper robe with a paper crown to represent an Irish Empress. All the ships in the Canadian Pacific fleet were named 'Empress' of somewhere or other. Every child received a little treat, and Nicola was interviewed briefly by Captain Williams. She was quite thrilled to be speaking into a microphone for the first time.

Eventually, we were advised we would make landfall the next morning, so we got up early to take a look at the country, which was going to be our new home. We could only take a very quick look because it was a freezing cold morning, with a clear light blue sky but a very bracing, cold wind. Looking north the shore of Newfoundland was visible and a cold, bare, inhospitable sight it seemed. About five miles away, the land rose from the Atlantic Ocean. The snow-covered slopes had a soft look, but there were absolutely no trees, just a few bare, black, rocky surfaces dotted the snowy slopes - a cold, cheerless prospect that did not look inviting. After breakfast, we entered the calmer St Lawrence River estuary and anticipated arriving at Quebec City at around 6.00 pm. It was 23rd April 1969, and just as it was getting dark, we prepared to officially enter Canada as new immigrants.

I felt a little nervous about this and dressed the children and myself with care. I thought we needed to make a good impression, but I should not have worried. After an early dinner, in family groups, we were escorted off the ship, and the passport formalities were quickly and efficiently completed by male Immigration Officers at the nearby Customs and Immigration building, which was at the quay adjacent to the Old City, below the very imposing Chateau Frontenac, a landmark Canadian Pacific Hotel. Afterwards, we were invited into another large area where French-speaking women smiled at us and offered refreshments, hot coffee, and tea, cool drinks for the children, and a great variety of sweet cakes and other goodies. They were the Welcoming Committee, all volunteers and everyone admired the children and treated us very kindly. As we were not very hungry - we had already had an early dinner - we were soon back on board ship for the overnight trip up the Saint Lawrence Seaway to Montreal, our destination. Montreal is a very large cosmopolitan city, and it was a somewhat intimidating experience to realise we were going to be on our own now in a foreign land and had to make our way, beginning to put into effect the plans we had made so long ago. We had set aside two weeks in which to rent a car, visit Gloria and Peter in Rhode Island, and return to Montreal via Niagara Falls, where we were to board the Canadian Pacific cross-Canada train to Vancouver. Michael had booked that part of our journey before leaving Zambia.

ℬ ℭ

I was beginning to feel at this time that we should not have planned this two-week side trip to see our friends in Rhode Island, as we now seemed to have a nomadic existence, and it was time to provide some stability for my family. I thought of changing our train reservation and leaving earlier for Vancouver, but Maureen was keen on seeing our friends and a little of the eastern US. It was instead an ambitious program for newly arrived immigrants, but we decided to stay with our plan. After we had eaten a good breakfast and upon leaving the ship, we had to locate our large packing case, which had been shipped from Zambia. To our utter amazement, the packing case was where it was supposed to be, and I arranged for it to be transported to Vancouver and held there until we arrived. Next, we had to locate a car-rental place close to the Canadian Pacific Railway station, which would make it simpler for our eventual return to Montreal and the cross-country train trip. Trundling along with our suitcases and cabin baggage, we managed that with the help of a friendly cab-driver and soon discovered how odd it felt to be driven along on the WRONG side of the road in noisy, busy traffic in an unfamiliar city. All the motor vehicles and trucks seemed to be so big and fast-moving in Canada. We were deposited outside a large Tilden Car Rental establishment where we rented what was called a mid-size, two-door grey Chevrolet, which seemed a pretty big vehicle to us. We were all glad to have our own wheels again, but now I had to instantly learn to drive an automatic vehicle, whilst we had always been used to manual gearshift cars.

Montreal is not the easiest place to begin the North American experience. It is a beautiful city on the St Lawrence River, with many bridges to islands in the river and some of the other suburban districts. The first thing one notices here is that all road signs and street names are in French, the second official language of Canada. To safeguard the cultural heritage, Quebec is the only officially French-speaking province, although many residents also speak English in the cities. We had a good map, and I wanted to get the family out of the downtown area of the city in the direction we wanted to go, which was south into the United States. We were all rather anxious! The three children seated in the back seemed frozen – they were so quiet. With our luggage stowed in the trunk, Maureen was fumbling in my holdall for a sweet treat for each of them when we all lurched forward as I hit the brakes rather hard; I had not used power brakes before.

We eased into the traffic and, seeing from our map that Montreal was all one-way streets, I suggested we drive around the block a few times, turning right at each corner so that I could get the feel of this strange vehicle. Maureen's head nearly hit the dashboard one more time, but after that all was well and once we had made a complete circuit of the block we all calmed down and were able to navigate ourselves onto a street which led to an appropriate exit from the city so that we could proceed in a southerly direction. Somehow, we managed to leave the downtown core of the city, travelling south on a major road over Jacques Cartier Bridge, until we came to the suburbs. Here it was apparent that absolutely everything was definitely French-speaking only. We were looking out for a drive-in motel with a nearby restaurant. The road traffic decreased, and we found ourselves in a community called St Lambert, where there was a clean, new-looking motel with a nearby coffee shop type of restaurant. We needed two rooms at the motel, of course, but we needed a good meal more, so we registered and moved our luggage into the rooms and walked across the road to the restaurant. We quickly discovered that amenities for travellers in North America are very well organised and of a high standard. Here nearly everything to eat at coffee shop type travellers' restaurants is served with *french fries*, which we called '*chips*'. This meal suited Stephen very well. He immediately fell in love with hamburgers and fries; Nicola was a little fussy about food but took to hot dogs (*wieners*) with a side of fries, and little Melanie didn't have a very big appetite. We were to discover that Melanie could live very happily on a few fries and apple pie and ice cream. I too, was delighted with the array of freshly baked fruit pies that were displayed everywhere we went. Returning to our motel rooms, the children watched television until bedtime, and we all relaxed. We felt very strange in this place but slept reasonably well. Occasionally we heard heavy trucks rumbling past, but daylight eventually came.

Our plan for this day was to leave the car safely parked outside our rooms and return to Montreal for a look around. We hadn't been relaxed enough to explore Montreal at all the previous day, and we needed to take things easy to recover from the stress of that day. I wanted to get used to the currency, and we needed to buy some extra underwear for the children. There were so many strange things to get used to. Many things worked quite differently here. We had not known how to lock our rooms when we left them to find food the day before and felt so stupid asking the porter in Reception for help; even the bathroom taps and drain plugs functioned differently. We had noticed buses on the streets the day before and decided to use public transportation to return to the city. We even encountered a little problem with this idea because we had to have the exact change in coins to put into the farebox beside the bus driver upon entering the bus, and there were five of us to pay for. No bus conductors to take the fare here, just drivers and it seemed no one spoke English. We really had trouble with currency. When asked for a nickel, I had simply held out my hand with various coins in it. There were pennies, dimes, nickels, and quarters, all terms unfamiliar to us. Then after a few stops, we all had to exit the bus to enter a subway station; the journey into the city would be completed by an underground train. A friendly plump lady indicated we should follow her – she beckoned to us and showed the way; the fare already paid included this part of the trip. We realised the local people recognised what we so obviously were – newcomers to Canada. We had such a lot to learn – we needed to keep our wits about us; it was stressful, but we made light of it, people were kind to us, and it became quite good fun.

There was plenty to see in the city, and we strolled around wide-eyed because everything seemed different from what we had been used to on the other side of the Atlantic, and we were a very long way from Kitwe. For the first time in my life, I felt a bit like the country bumpkin come to town. I scrutinised the petrol filling stations (that we should now call 'gas stations') so that he would know what to do when we needed to fill up the car. We carefully watched how everyone managed things, and we made our first purchases, the extra things we needed for the children, and paid in Canadian funds. We visited a bank to exchange some of our traveller's cheques for U.S. funds. The day quickly passed, and we managed to retrace our steps back to our motel rooms in St Lambert in good time for an early night so that we could make an early start the next morning. It was exciting to think of entering the United States, the country we had only seen in movies and newsreels at the cinema.

Our visit to Peter and Gloria in Rhode Island went very well, but always at the back of my mind was, 'I need to get my family settled.' The return journey to Montreal, via the 'splendid' Niagara Falls, Toronto, and then driving alongside the St Lawrence River through Quebec did not disappoint us, but we were anxious to head west to our final destination. After a further night in Montreal, we once again had to navigate carefully through city traffic, but after a quick lunch, we found ourselves at the large Tilden Car Rental office. The grand Canadian Pacific Railway Windsor station was within sight, and we quickly unloaded our large suitcases and baggage from the Chevrolet. We reported to the office and waited briefly while I paid the bill, and we were soon getting organised for the short walk to the train station. I was carrying two large suitcases, and Maureen had a couple of lighter bags plus Melanie by the hand and Stephen and Nicola each had a smaller bag.

We walked for just a few minutes and then soon came to the imposing station entrance. I checked our booking at the office, and we proceeded to our platform. Immediately, we saw our train; it looked huge! In England, we were used to entering station platforms that were elevated a few feet so that passengers could easily step up right into their compartment, which was almost level with the platform. Trains here were entered by climbing up steep steps from ground level. We trudged past the huge wheels, which we never noticed on English trains. Melanie began to shake and cry – this train looked a most fearsome thing to her. A man wearing a top hat and a scarlet coat was coming towards us. This man was the station master, and he, seeing our little family trundling along with a frightened little girl, wanted to help. What a kind gesture! He picked Melanie up and asked me for our compartment number and then escorted us to the right entrance and handed us over to another uniformed attendant, lifted his top hat in farewell and wished us a pleasant journey. A wonderful welcome; we felt like royalty! We were shown to our accommodation, which I had booked months before while I was still in Africa. It was quite impressive – first-class accommodation. We had two adjoining staterooms; each had a small bathroom. Facing picture windows were two comfortable upholstered chairs, one of which would fold out at dusk to become Melanie's sleeping cot, and there were two fold-down bunk beds in each stateroom. We kept the dividing wall folded away to make the most of our space. We were advised we would have access to the nearby observation car, which had a glass 'bubble' roof. Our steward asked which seating for dinner we preferred and offered tea immediately. It was about 3.30 pm. This clearly was the best way to travel. We could relax on this four-day trip and enjoy a little luxury. We heard the other passengers settling into their accommodations; Stephen was anxious to leave the compartment and see what was going on, but we made him be patient until the train started. We enjoyed our afternoon tea and biscuits, and then the whistle blew, and once again, we were off!

At precisely 4.00 pm, the Canadian Pacific Transcontinental train pulled out of Windsor station, Montreal, taking us to our new life in Western Canada. Maureen was properly impressed by the accommodation and wonderful service on the train, and I felt we could now relax a little and enjoy the journey. Although we did not have anyone to meet us in Vancouver, or any kind of a job lined up, I was relieved to be on the final leg of our long journey from Africa. I wondered what the future held for my family. Having always enjoyed train travel, we settled down to savour this part of our journey. We had several hours of daylight, and after our first meal, beautifully served in the dining car, which we all seemed to enjoy, it was time to open up the beds, which chore was taken care of by a porter. I don't think I realised when I booked the train that we would actually be in first class, or maybe I just wanted to impress my wife. We were advised that the train would be stopping for a while at Sudbury, to connect with the carriages coming from Toronto. At about 1.00 am, this took place, and both Maureen and I were awoken by noisy clanging and banging before we were again on our way. We had left Montreal in relatively mild weather, and the next day as we proceeded northwest around the northern shore of Lake Superior, we were reminded that winter was not over yet as there was still plenty of snow; the lakeshore was frozen. We slept well through another night, and after stopping at Thunder Bay, the train set off for the long straight, rather boring ride across the Canadian prairies. The children were very good. Stephen was very inquisitive and highly sociable. We were not too concerned about him while the train was moving, but as soon as it seemed like it was going to stop, Maureen would send me to look for him. We didn't want him to get off. He must have investigated all the different carriages, and when he took us to meet some new 'friends', we found that in some instances, people actually sat up for the whole journey. Not everyone had a comfortable space like we did. The train had two glass-domed observation cars, and I would sometimes find him seated next to strangers telling them our family history. They seemed fascinated by him and his South African accent. Nicola and Melanie preferred to remain with us, usually playing with their dolls. They only left our accommodation when we did.

After the middle of the night stop in Winnipeg, the train moved steadily on across the barren prairie landscape for hour after hour, finally arriving in Calgary during the late afternoon. A two-hour stop was scheduled here while the train was cleaned and prepared for the journey through the Canadian Rockies. Our train was powered by a powerful diesel-electric locomotive, and an extra one was added here for the steep ascents and descents in the mountains. We were able to stretch our legs, and we took pictures of the train. Although it was quite cold, the sun was shining. Calgary seemed a nice kind of place and the people were very friendly. We realised we were now truly in Western Canada -

Cowboy Country! Leaving Calgary at about 4.00 pm, the train had barely left the station and was moving very slowly. Looking out the window, we saw that we were to pass through a giant train wash-station. At this point, we proceeded to the Club Car at the rear of the train to have a drink and watch the procedure. Looking back toward Calgary station, we noticed a mature woman running at the side of the track after the train, carrying a suitcase and waving.

The train conductor was nearby, and we drew his attention to the woman's plight. He calmly took out his watch and made us all laugh when he checked the time and announced like the seasoned railwayman he was, 'She's making pretty good time, too!' He then disappeared and caused the train to stop for her. The lady caught us up and was assisted into the car, very much out of breath. For the next few hours, we sat in the glass-domed observation carriage and watched the most fabulous scenery we had ever seen unfold as we passed from the foothills of the mountains into the Rockies. By the time we reached Lake Louise, it was beginning to get dark, and before we settled down for our last night on the train, we saw Kicking Horse Pass, which was identified for us by the conductor. As we had travelled from east to west across this vast continent, we noticed that winter still gripped the landscape, and in Alberta, although there was little snow, everywhere had been very brown and dull; there were no leaves on the bare trees. Imagine our surprise when we awoke the next morning in British Columbia's Fraser Valley, and spring had arrived. Overnight the season had changed. The air was softer, and fresh young leaves were on the trees. Everywhere was so clean, so green and it was very sunny. We had our final breakfast in the dining car, and the mood was one of celebration – our spirits were high. The train moved quite peacefully along the banks of the mighty Fraser River, through the spread-out suburbs of Vancouver, eventually arriving at the original CPR Pacific Terminus on Burrard Inlet. We had reached our destination at last. It was 12th of May 1969.

After tipping our steward, who helped us remove our bags into the station building, we stood for a moment or two trying to get our bearings and considered what our next move should be. Maureen had the phone number of her Aunt June, and she called her, but she seemed to be too busy to see us, so we were left to fend for ourselves. Studying a Vancouver accommodation guide I had picked up along the way, we picked out a hotel that seemed to be central, and I called them and requested accommodation (two rooms) for a few days. The Niagara Hotel on Pender Street said they had room for us. We trundled our bags through the impressive station hall and walked out into the sunshine on Cordova Street, where there were taxi cabs waiting. After loading our bags, I told the driver we wanted to go to the Niagara Hotel. He gave me a somewhat strange look and proceeded to drive just around to the other side of the block to the entrance for the hotel we had selected. We quickly realised that it would have been just a short walk from the station.

Our first impression of the hotel was somewhat mixed. It seemed to be close to a seedy part of the city, where a drunk or two littered the pavement. But the rooms appeared to be clean; the staff seemed respectable, so we decided to stay anyway; we didn't know if there would be better accommodation available and didn't want to trundle our bags and baggage around anymore. We first needed to get our bearings. We were all a bit cranky and tired after the long train journey, and although it was a noisy part of town, we all managed to sleep well enough when evening came. We did hear some police car sirens in the night, which made us think of Hollywood movies.

The next day we went to the Canadian Imperial Bank of Commerce, which was nearby on Hastings Street, to see if our money had been transferred there. To our great relief, it had arrived, and we were immediately able to open an account and receive a chequebook. Then we decided we should take a look at the city. Using the bus system, we did a little exploring and realised that the reports we had of Vancouver's beauty had not been exaggerated. This city was the most impressive. The sun shone, and the sky was very blue; the weather was perfect. We thought Stanley Park and the panoramic views across to the north shore mountains were spectacular, so we took a bus across the Lions Gate Bridge to West Vancouver and thought this was the kind of place in which we would like to live. Maureen liked this community. The scenery reminded us of the first place we shared together in Cape

Town. We spent one afternoon at the beach where the children could play, but we soon became somewhat restless probably because we felt we had more important things to pay attention to. That day we bought newspapers and studied the classified columns for places to rent, quickly realising that West Vancouver might be a little beyond our means. It was generally regarded as the most affluent and, therefore, the most expensive community.

Within a short time, it became urgent that we should have our own wheels to view the rental accommodation advertised. It had quickly become tiresome, always having to find enough small change for fares when shepherding my family on and off buses. I felt we should get our children out of the downtown area as soon as possible. We noticed from the newspaper advertisements that there were a few auto dealerships situated on Burrard Street, so the next day we walked there and went into the first large place we saw selling cars, which was called Bowell-McLean. The dealership office was fronted by an impressive line-up of clean, reasonably new-looking vehicles. From our rental experience in Montreal, we knew we liked the larger, more powerful American-type cars, and gas was only about 49 cents a gallon. We knew we wanted a four-door vehicle. The salesman talked about the features of a few vehicles, and I indicated we would take a test drive in a cream coloured Chevrolet Acadian four-door car with a V8 engine – quite a sporty looking car, which was about a year old. After just one short drive around the block, I decided to buy it. The salesman and manager were all smiles when I wrote the cheque for the asking price of $2,300. I had not given any thought to haggling over the price, and they must have been delighted with such a quick sale, believing we were country bumpkins just come to town, which was close to the truth because we had such a lot to learn about this new country. But it turned out to be a good vehicle which gave us great service for many years. Now that we were able to get around more easily, we started to explore further afield. With the aid of a good map, we saw it was easy to get on to the Trans-Canada Highway going east to the Surrey area beyond the Port Mann Bridge, where we looked at apartments for rent. As I had no idea where I might be working, we felt that at least it would be easy to get into the city from there. We decided to take a three-bedroom apartment on the third floor of a nice-looking, somewhat new building on 108th Avenue in North Surrey.

I checked with Canadian Pacific and learned that the crate I had shipped from Africa had arrived safely in Vancouver. It would be stored for me until we were ready to pick it up. To do this, I reserved a U-Haul truck for the end of the month. Since arriving in Vancouver, the weather had been wonderfully warm and sunny every day. The winter had been quite severe, and there were still piles of snow in some of the large parking lots at the shopping centres, which were melting fast. It was now nearly two months since leaving Kitwe, and I still felt like I was on holiday. The thought of going out and looking for work wasn't exactly appealing to me.

℘ ℘

What an adventure our journey to British Columbia had been. It had been easy for me to regard it as a holiday period, and now we were in Vancouver, we began to feel somewhat overwhelmed by the many details we had to deal with to set ourselves up for regular family life once again. I was quite disappointed when I called my aunt from a telephone booth as soon as we arrived in Vancouver. I hadn't expected her to meet us, but I did think she would have been able to say or suggest something to make us feel welcome. When I later spoke to June, she explained she had spent the morning saying 'goodbye' to her husband Les, who had just left White Rock, near Vancouver, on a long-planned voyage alone on his sailing boat. Les was planning to become a 'Round the World' yachtsman. She had sounded high spirited, quite excited, maybe even a little 'high'. At the time I called, I could hear there were several people nearby who had come back to her house for a drink after the 'farewell'. This event was quite a big thing in White Rock and a significant event in her life. Naturally, I clearly understood I should wait a few days before contacting her again. We were entirely on our own. But we were reasonably resourceful people so soon got ourselves reasonable accommodation. I thought the city of Vancouver had made a very nice first impression on us. We were fortunate that the weather was so good. Since we initially had no car, we explored on foot and learned how to use public transportation, but after three days of that, Michael just had to buy a car. Having our own vehicle made things much more manageable; Michael wanted to get out of the city; he especially didn't like our family staying in the downtown area.

It didn't take long for us to find our way about. The Vancouver area was enjoying an expanding economy. There were road building and housing construction going on to accommodate the expected population surge, and there were plenty of choices when we came to examine the rental situation. We soon found a spacious light-filled apartment with a great view in North Surrey. The children were thrilled it was a family-oriented development; there would be other young folks to play with, and Stephen mostly was pleased that there were a covered swimming pool and a large play area. It seemed a well-appointed and well looked-after place. There was a coin-operated laundry facility on site. The Manager kindly allowed us to move in as soon as the newly painted walls and the steam-cleaned carpets were dry. We were finding Canadians were generally very kind and ready to be helpful. Having purchased beds for the children at a Hamilton Harvey department store, we chose for ourselves a good quality queen-sized bed, which was on sale in the Sears catalogue. All these things were delivered free of charge on the day we moved in. The bedrooms had built-in closets; we could keep our underwear etc. in our suitcases for the time being. The well-appointed kitchen was fitted in the American style with numerous built-in cupboards, plus a chocolate brown, almost new stove, and a large matching refrigerator; I couldn't believe my good fortune. I had to buy a new iron and ironing board plus some inexpensive lamps and dishes. There were good budget-price stores in nearby Whalley, but otherwise, everything else we needed was in our big packing case, which we had to collect.

The lovely weather continued, and Melanie and Nicola played together with their dolls. Stephen, however, liked to be outside where he could be with other boys and either joining in their games or swimming at the pool. It was here Stephen met a young woman – Angela, with two little children, and soon got into a conversation with her. She had noticed his accent and asked where he had come from. He soon brought Angela up to our apartment to meet me. She was English and delighted to meet another English woman. Naturally, I was pleased to make a friend too. Angela's husband, Murray, was Canadian, and we found it helpful to have social contact with this couple because they could quickly answer our questions about all things Canadian. I explained to Angela that we had to collect the large packing case Michael had despatched from Zambia, and she offered to keep an eye on the children while we were taking care of this errand. So off we went!

Why Michael chose to rent a small truck for this trip, I never asked. He could be impulsive sometimes; perhaps he thought truck rental would be cheaper than having our packing case delivered. We did seem to be spending quite a lot of money. But since I usually accepted his way of doing things, I simply took charge of the street map of Vancouver on our way to the truck rental depot, where we left the car. We were still learning how to navigate around the city, and while Michael concentrated on driving an unfamiliar vehicle, I could follow the route chosen and indicate when we should make a turn. We needed to go right downtown to the Canadian Pacific Railway depot. All went well, our packing case was loaded into the truck, and we very cautiously drove out to the apartment in Surrey, realising we should open and unpack it outside – we'd never get that large wooden crate up to our apartment. So, we drove around to the back of the building. The truck was equipped with a lifting platform, so unloading was not too much of a problem. Once opened, I could see that things had moved around. Michael said he had to change things around a bit to make room for his heavy toolbox, which he had brought home when he left the Rhokana Mine and suggested I go upstairs and make some tea while he and a helpful neighbour emptied the crate. I had an idea the friendly neighbour had plans for that packing case.

When everything had been brought into the apartment, and we'd had tea, I wanted to sort out and put away our belongings. I was dismayed to discover some of the bed linens, table linen and towels were gone. When I came across three loose serving spoons from the canteen of cutlery Michael's parents had given us for a wedding present, I realised the wooden case containing our best table cutlery was missing too, along with several other wedding gifts and parting gifts from friends. My precious, relatively new sewing machine was there safe and sound. I was sure I had packed all our belongings carefully. I wondered to Michael if the 'friendly neighbour' had taken anything, and he explained he'd had to make room for his toolbox and some other things when he quit the mine and gave away the discarded items. I was distraught, but there was nothing to be done. For a few days, I mourned the loss of those missing articles. Naturally, I understood Michael's toolbox was essential, but so were some of those things that had so lightly been put aside. I knew Michael, like a lot of men, wasn't attached to 'things' in the same way I was. I just hoped that one day I could replace some of the lost belongings that had been so casually given away to the native boys when he was leaving our home in Kitwe.

The Canadian Pacific 'Empress of England'

The 'Canadian' travelling through the Rockies to Vancouver

17.
A Land of Opportunity

Maureen

Putting aside my disappointment over the lost possessions, I thought I should rather keep in mind that what was remarkable was that so much had gone right. Our permission to enter Canada as immigrants had arrived in the nick of time; the journey here had been an enjoyable travel experience for us all, and now we were settled in comfortable, affordable, and very suitable accommodation. The children were well and happy, our neighbours seemed friendly, and we already owned a nice car. The sun shone each day; this seemed like a beautiful place to live, and Stephen especially seemed enthusiastic about making friends and getting to know more about the new environment. Nicola and Melanie played together happily, and they didn't talk about their changed life.

It was early summer, and I didn't immediately try to replace those missing items. The children were always happy to play on the carpeted floor, but we did need to buy some budget-priced basket chairs to sit in and a few dishes, etc. We had some cheap but sturdy, made in Korea, stainless steel knives, forks, and spoons that we had used in the kitchen in Kitwe. Not knowing what the future held, I thought it best to adopt a sort of careful 'camping at home' style of living; it was summertime, and it wasn't difficult.

During the first week or so in our new apartment, we took the opportunity to take the children to the beaches and explored our environment a little more. Still, on a Monday morning after breakfast with the children, I made Michael a package of sandwiches and indicated that perhaps it was time to begin looking for work. I thought the past two months must have made quite a dent in the savings Michael had accumulated in Zambia. Although he was never entirely comfortable discussing financial matters with me, I understood that the success or failure of this enterprise depended on him re-establishing income. I felt the most helpful thing I could do was to hold back on spending and live very

320

frugally, at least until he was employed again. We had grown up in the 1950s, and men's and women's roles in society were still fairly clearly defined; the man was the breadwinner, his wife, the homemaker. He, still feeling in the 'holiday' mood, didn't much like my suggestion about looking for work, but demonstrating little enthusiasm, he decided to take the car and go and begin the search. Perhaps he thought avoiding another argument was the best course.

80 cs

As Maureen has suggested, I did not have a great desire to go looking for employment, but with a wife and three children to support, I also knew very well that we should not chip away at our hard-earned savings. I realised every penny would be necessary when the time came to buy a house. I had never enjoyed looking for a job; probably very few people do. In my trade, where many of the better jobs were unionised, it was always a case of starting again from the bottom of the ladder and working one's way up. I soon realised from the newspaper advertisements that Vancouver was not a highly industrialised city, and the only work for my kind of trade was in the repairing of logging and pulp mill equipment. I wanted to get back into the lighter, high precision work for which I had initially been trained. I had always reserved the thought that if I couldn't get a suitable job in the Lower Mainland area around Vancouver, there were many mines in the interior of B.C., and I had plenty of experience of that kind of work. But that idea would only have been utilised as a last resort.

My first day out looking for work was not very encouraging. I drove to the Fraser River waterfront at New Westminster and visited two very dark and dirty machine shops involved in marine work. The equipment was ancient with one overhead pulley system run from a single motor, for driving all the machinery. I thought this method had gone out of style in the 1940s. It was quite a warm day, but I could imagine in winter these places would be unbearably cold. Although they were offering work, I felt there must be better places than these. Scanning both daily papers the next day, I saw they were looking for toolmakers at a company called Windsor Chain Saws in Lake City, Burnaby.

I phoned for an appointment and visited the Works manager within a few days. He offered me a job on six months' probation, and I started on the following Monday. There was something about this place I did not like. The workforce was mainly from Europe, many with very little English. I had been used to having some authority in Zambia, and I think I resented the 'come-down' to the position as the man on the bottom of the seniority list, which seemed to have great significance in this part of the world. I soon understood that this was because when work was short, most companies would lay off the junior man, no matter how good he was at his job. I thought this to be very unjust, but the trade unions were powerful. The work at this place reminded me of my early days serving an apprenticeship in England. On a Friday morning, being thoroughly unsatisfied with the type of work, I told the foreman I would be leaving. He was surprised and said he had some better work for me starting the following week. But I quit anyway. I knew this was just not the right environment for me.

On our travels into New Westminster, I had noticed a small business called Surrey Engineering, and on the following Monday, I ventured in and asked about work. Although cramped and untidy, I was impressed by the modern equipment in the shop and the friendly manner of Hank, the owner. He explained this was a jobbing shop, meaning they would attempt to fix any item that was brought in, and I assured him I was used to that kind of work. I seemed to hit it off with him right away, and he introduced me to the other three employees. The pay rate was to be $2.50 an hour, which seemed relatively low, but I felt I could live with it for the time being until I had time to look around.

Up to this point, I had been driving legally on my South African driver's license. I also had one issued in Northern Rhodesia, but both were only valid for six months here. I had found driving very easy with so much room on the roads and having an automatic car helped, but I decided I should get the local B.C. license. I obtained a copy of the Highway Code, spent a few weeks studying it, and then went for the test in Cloverdale, a small quiet town close by, passing with no problem.

୫୦ ୯୪

As Michael adopted a normal working man's routine, the atmosphere of our home changed from the casual 'holiday' mode we had enjoyed for some time. We had to adapt to real-life again. It wasn't too big an adjustment for the children and me. The schools were to close soon for the summer, but as they were in session for a few more weeks, we registered the children nearby at Hjorth Road Elementary so they could get to know some of the local children. The school year ended early in June. All children would then have a long holiday and freedom. Our children soon began to make friends with others their age in our apartment complex. There were new games to learn.

I contacted my Aunt June once again. She was quite pleased to hear from me this time and asked me how we were getting along. We arranged to meet and made a date for when Michael was available on the next Saturday afternoon. She now lived in a small beach cottage overlooking Semiahmoo Bay in White Rock, close to the border with the United States. It was an easy drive south. She gave clear directions; we also had a good map of the area. June had not met any of her family since leaving England as a War Bride, shortly after the war, almost twenty-five years earlier. I was surprised when we reached her home because she had sent me pictures from time to time during the few years we had corresponded. The little snapshots had shown her with her husband, Les, on holiday in Hawaii. The pictures of her children showed them at her attractive family home on a lovely pastoral property that had been made by her husband and a golfing buddy into a Par Three golf course on Coast Meridian Road in South Surrey. Their current home was clearly a rather dilapidated holiday cottage in a row of other similar beach cottages, but it had a fantastic view over the bay, and I always admired a water view. When I saw June get up from her chair to greet us, I suddenly saw my maternal grandmother again; I was quite moved. She shared exactly the same physique, mannerisms, and facial features. I forgot about the surroundings and greeted her with affection. Michael said afterwards that June seemed nervous about meeting us. I was so busy taking in this experience, and everything was so new to us, I didn't ever imagine she, a Canadian, could be uneasy about us.

My grandmother had been a forthright, confident woman. We just stayed a couple of hours and had tea in the garden and got to know each other a little. I heard the story of Les' recent 'Lone Yachtsman' departure and how anxious June was about him. And what a difference this idea of his had made in her life. She deeply regretted having to leave the family home on the golf course. It had been sold to provide him with funds for this adventure, which would take many months. There had been several men who had attempted to sail alone around the world in the 1960s. Some of them hailed as heroes upon their safe return became famous and were lionised by the media and newspapers. June very seriously told us that if he were successful, Les would become a 'Big Man' in this part of the world. I realised she still loved her husband; he had persuaded her to agree to his plan and wanted to be a 'Somebody', but now she felt betrayed by his absence and the niggling worry that all might not be well. I called June again a week or so later, and she was overjoyed to be able to report Les was safe, but the prevailing winds and spring storms in the Pacific approaching the west coast of North America from the islands of Hawaii, had punished him severely. He had been hospitalised and was resting on the island of Maui, where he had friends, having had hardly any sleep at all. The boat needed a great deal of repair work. She told me their son Steven, who was about 22 years old, would be going out to meet his father when the repairs on the boat were underway to help him sail the boat back home again. Les was in very poor condition. He had been sick and wet for the whole voyage; she would let me know when he was expected back in White Rock, and she seemed to look forward to our meeting the rest of her family.

Michael was beginning to believe this country had real possibilities. On a weekend outing, we drove into the city. A special event was to take place in Stanley Park. We found parking and discovered the event was called an Indian Day and was crowded with groups of North American Indians wearing their native dress. There were all kinds of displays and dancing, but I particularly admired some of the women who were wearing beautifully coloured long gowns, which didn't look to me like a native dress. But they did look elegant. The event was hosted by the Capilano Indian Band, who had their home just across the bridge on the North Shore. We soon noticed that there weren't a large number of white people present – this event was indeed for the aboriginal tribes, so we soon collected our car and made our way home again.

We began to discuss the possibility of finding a house. While Michael was working, I made inquiries at some real estate offices in our current locality to learn how much average family homes cost. He wanted us to have a home but wasn't very keen on the 'shopping around' process of finding one. I would have preferred to continue to rent for a time, but since the price of a house was increasing all the time, I also understood that putting our savings into a new home was probably a better idea. The Municipality of Surrey was expected to experience an economic boom and a considerable rise in the total population because the economy of British Columbia was gathering steam. House prices were rising in all locations. Surrey, a large, once rural municipality, had plenty of room to accommodate the increase in population.

At about that time, Michael remembered we had the address of another expatriate from Zambia. Cathy and Jimmy Cash had been friends of Gloria and Peter and had left for Canada almost two years ahead of us. I called Cathy, and she was pleased to hear from us and immediately suggested we should come to see them the following weekend when her husband would be at home. They lived in an interesting waterside community of Beach Grove, Delta, which had many summer cottages. They were pleased to see us, although I had only met Cathy a few times in Kitwe. We had so much to talk about. They hadn't found settling in Canada very easy but were determined to make a success of their migration. Their big news was that they were about to buy a house that was being constructed in nearby Ladner, originally a fishing and farming village community on the south bank of the south arm of the Fraser River. Their home would be ready in time for the beginning of the next school year in September. On the way home, we decided to try a new route following the Fraser River upstream towards Surrey. It was a lovely scenic drive beside the river in the early evening with the sun setting behind us. As we were motoring uphill, a car appeared up ahead, coming around a bend towards us, and the driver seemed to be having difficulty keeping on their side of the road. We almost made it past her, but she clipped the backside door of our car where the children were sitting, causing our car to fishtail a bit, and the children bumped their heads against each other and the side windows. With a steep grassy slope very close to our side of the road, we stopped to assess the damage. There were houses above us, and people who had heard the collision very kindly came down to help. It wasn't a serious accident but was a bit of a shock for the children; the girls were crying but were otherwise unhurt. We were glad to take refuge in a nearby home while Michael dealt with the situation. Delta Police responded quickly, and we were soon on our way again; the driver of the other car admitted her vehicle caused the collision, but our beautiful new car now had damage. We soon learned how well things were arranged in Canada. While repairs to our car were taking place, we were given a courtesy car, so we were never without a vehicle. We thought this wonderfully efficient service and with so much to think about, when we got our car back in perfect condition, soon forgot there had ever been a problem.

18.
Settled at last

Maureen

Our mishap, while returning from visiting our friends, gave us insight regarding the open friendliness of Canadians. We were impressed by how quickly complete strangers had responded so kindly to our moment of difficulty.

We decided to actively look into the idea of buying a house. On my next visit to White Rock, producing our map of the area around Vancouver (generally referred to as the Lower Mainland), I asked June if she had any thoughts about which community would be a good area for us to consider. To my surprise, she simply said our map was more help than she could be as Les had always decided where they should live. Michael believed White Rock was too far from where he might be working to be seriously considered and in any case he wasn't happy with the idea of our children being drawn into the free and easy drug life-style of the local teenagers and biker gangs which we had observed in this seaside community. Now that it was high summer, we found the air quality in the river valley we overlooked from our Surrey apartment, could become somewhat smog-laden, when the weather remained sunny with little wind for several consecutive days. Out in Ladner, on the other hand, on the Fraser River, the air quality was a little like White Rock since it was also close to the ocean. We could see the mountains on Vancouver Island in the distance, and every time we visited, the air seemed fresh with occasional gentle breezes. We thought it would be a healthy spot to raise our children.

Ladner was an interesting little 'village' community. This part of western Canada had been developed initially as part of the fur trade. The coast had been peopled by aboriginal 'Indian' inhabitants for many hundreds of years. Eventually, white men settled in the area, and they developed as a farming and fishing community. We visited Cathy and Jimmy again soon after they moved into their new house. It was a three-bedroom rancher-type dwelling very similar in layout to Gloria and Peter's home in Rhode

Island. Our new friends advised that house prices were rising at more than $500 *every month*. We should not delay our decision for too long. Since we had always been used to having the ability to move about easily, Michael was pleased to see the major road system included a second motorway south of the city. This freeway started at the Oak Street Bridge at the southern boundary of the city and came through Delta, connecting Vancouver to the United States and Seattle. In fact, it continued all the way south, down the west coast to Mexico as Interstate 5, which impressed us. To the north, through the city of Vancouver, it was known as Highway 99 to Squamish, Whistler, and the interior of B.C. We liked the idea of being able to move quickly into and out of the city.

While we were debating the pros and cons of house purchase, June telephoned in a state of some excitement. Les had called her from Neah Bay on the Pacific coast of Washington State at the entrance to the Straits of Juan de Fuca. He and their son Steven had managed to sail his boat back across the Pacific and was expected to sail his sailboat into White Rock later that afternoon. When Michael came home from work, we had a quick meal and thought we should be on hand to welcome the sailors, so off we drove to White Rock. There was no-one at home at the cottage, so we went down to the pier on Marine Drive and parked the car. We soon saw June's daughter Jennifer, and she pointed to a tiny sail far, far off in the distance to the west. 'That's my Dad', she said very definitely, 'he's coming home.' She seemed so sure - we walked together along the White Rock pier. Her eyes were shining; she appeared to be almost trembling with joyful anticipation. The light evening breeze brought the sailboat towards us, and finally, they tied up at the little floating harbour at the end of the pier. Stephen stayed on board, and we saw a gaunt, sunburned figure leave the boat and purposefully stride up the gangway looking neither to the right nor left. June's husband, Les, was on his way to report to the Customs Officer. June was nowhere to be seen. He looked to me rather like a character from 'The Old Man and the Sea'. His demeanour seemed to illustrate the trauma of the expedition he had undertaken. When he returned, June - flushed and excited - was with him. I sensed the electric emotion of this reunion, and that probably this was not the time for us to be re-introduced. We watched as Les and June boarded the 'Lemming', and he set sail to bring the craft around the breakwater into the calmer water on the south side. There was quite a tide running now plus a pretty strong breeze blowing onto the shore; I worried that they would be 'shipwrecked' on the big rocks of the breakwater, but all was well, and they berthed. I was happy for June that her husband had returned safely, and we gathered our children and drove home. We would see Les and June on another day.

We resumed our discussion regarding buying a house and agreed we should muster our courage and take the plunge into homeownership. We knew nothing – we had always rented accommodation. Fortunately, we had funds for that vital down-payment. We visited the on-site mobile office of a new development on 45th Avenue in Ladner and picked up an impressive-looking brochure detailing house plans etc. There were six different house plans to choose from, each with varying floor plans and amenities. While we were looking around the various models already built, we were advised we had to 'qualify' for a mortgage – we knew nothing about that either, but the friendly salesman said he could help us when we were ready to make a decision; we needed to learn a whole new financial language. The architectural style of homes in western Canada followed North American design and were all constructed with a timber frame. We studied that brochure for about two weeks. These detached homes were vastly different from the English terraced housing we were accustomed to and different again from the shaded, well-spaced brick-built homes we knew in Africa.

But Canada was the New World – many things were different here. It was interesting to absorb all this information. I naturally leaned towards one of the bigger homes offered, because the plans included useful extras and larger rooms. We were a family of five people. The master bedroom suite included a neat, small en-suite bathroom; having more than one toilet was essential to a family of five. A large walk-in closet was also included. All the rooms were a little larger than in the other designs. The largest home was priced at $24,300. We visited a bank manager in nearby Richmond recommended to us by our real estate salesman. This friendly man educated us regarding mortgage terms and how much a loan payment would cost monthly, considering the principal sum plus interest and taxes. It wasn't easy to understand. But when we mentioned we had about $10,000 for our down-payment, he immediately said he would have no hesitation in recommending us for the loan we required. This was encouraging news, but we had to think carefully about this; the most important investment a young couple ever make. We went back several times to look at the houses being built, and a week or two later decided we should go ahead and buy.

Immediately it all became exhilarating. We were plunged into appointments with various people. We were able to choose the plot of land, called a 'lot', that our house would stand on. I wanted a south-facing lot – we had been used to lots of sunshine in Africa, and there was a nice corner lot available on 45th Avenue and 47th Street (in Delta, avenues always ran east-west and streets north-south). My mother had always believed a corner house to be a bit more worthwhile than one in a row. We would have a space on each side of the house to cultivate, plus a large front lawn. We visited the principal office of the builders, and there were a great many choices to be made regarding finishes for the fireplace and feature wall in the roomy living/dining room; a basic carpet style in several colours was offered, plus linoleum and tile colours for bathrooms and kitchen fixtures to be selected. We needed to purchase a good quality refrigerator and cooking stove, and these could be ordered through our builder at a slightly lower price than department stores offered and added to the cost of the house. We were unfamiliar with all these things but applied ourselves to our 'homework' and made the decisions. We included some of the basic selections and decided avocado green would be our feature colour. It was regarded as very fashionable at that time. We added extra insulation under the aluminium siding in the walls, which would help save energy (and money) when winter came, and we included a slightly more expensive shag-style carpet for the living room. With these additions, our final cost, with the smart new General Electric kitchen appliances, was a little over $26,500. It seemed a tremendous financial responsibility. I worried just a little that perhaps we were going into purchasing a house too soon; Michael wasn't yet satisfied with his work situation and income.

But it would take about three months for our home to be built; we still thought the right, good job for him was still out there somewhere.

On our second interview with the bank manager, we signed on the dotted line. Our bank account had been administered from the downtown branch of the Canadian Imperial Bank of Commerce, and we asked to transfer the account to the Ladner branch. We had arrived in Canada with about $15,000. This sum had all been earned and saved by Michael, working in Zambia. I fervently hoped we were not risking losing our money. With the impressive number of new houses being built everywhere, we could see that the economy of the Province of British Columbia was thriving.

ᛒ ᛃ

Now that we had committed ourselves to buy a new house, it suddenly became crucial that I seriously look for work which would pay a better wage. I liked the work and the people that I worked with at Surrey Engineering, but the hourly pay was just too low. Since arriving in Canada, I'd had to learn that the employment situation here was different from everything I had ever experienced. Throughout this province, the economy was based mainly on fishing, mining, and lumber, all basic industries. Many of these jobs were seasonal, and the workforce was always strongly unionised in the larger companies. Unions regarded all their members as equals, traditionally maintaining a strict seniority system. Historically, whenever there was a downturn or slowdown in the economy, the junior men were let go or 'laid-off' as it was called here. This policy never seemed quite fair to me; I had always felt that ability was the most important criteria for employing a person. After a brief look around and interview, I accepted a job at CAE Industries on Broadway in Vancouver. It was quite a large company with several branches across Canada. In Quebec, they were well known for designing and manufacturing airline flight simulators, but on the West Coast, were only involved in equipment for the lumber and pulp industry. The pay was a little better here, and one of the first things I had to do on my first day at work was to join the union, The United Steelworkers of America. I have always had an aversion towards unions, but one had no choice if one wanted to work. I was, of course, now the junior man. My journey to work from North Surrey was an easy drive with very little traffic. I soon found I could manage the work well, and they seemed happy enough with me, assigning me to a brand-new piece of equipment after only a few weeks. The work was quite heavy, but I had been used to that in Zambia, and many of the pulp mill parts in for repair let off an obnoxious smell when machined. But again, I was used to bad smells from Africa too. This same smell was evident around Vancouver, from pulp mills located along the Fraser River, in Howe Sound, and on Vancouver Island. As well as lumber products, B.C. is a massive producer of paper, which is made from woodchips and chemicals. To produce power, many mills burnt wood chips in a beehive burner, which created a great deal of pollution around the city when there was little wind to blow it away.

Visiting Jimmy and Cathy again, we met friends of theirs, Brian and Donna Carney. Brian had once also worked on the mines in Zambia. I had quite an interesting conversation with him and learned that he was an instrument technician who currently worked for Canada's second-largest airline, Canadian Pacific Airlines. He suggested that I apply there, as a large newly built maintenance facility had just been opened at Vancouver International Airport. I visited the company offices in Richmond and filled out an application form but was advised that there was nothing available at present. I thought I should keep in touch with them and carry on at CAE for the time being. But with the mortgage we were about to assume responsibility for, I definitely needed to find that better-paying, more secure job.

೫೦ ೮ಃ

We drove over to Ladner frequently to check on the progress of our house. On our corner lot, we saw trenches had been dug, to bring in the services and to provide for the cement foundations. The streets were marked out but were simply dirt roads on what had previously been farmland. Then the next time we came, the timber framing for our house was partly in place –

houses seemed to be built at a fantastic speed here, and we were fascinated by the process. The framing method looked rather insubstantial – so different from the sturdy brick-built dwellings we had been used to. But we learned that the West Coast was sometimes subject to earth tremors and timber framing made for flexible homes. On the next visit, the cement gutters either side of the streets had been installed, which were soon followed by tarmacadam 'blacktop' finishing the street layout. We saw that 45th Avenue came to an abrupt end on the west side of our property, extending into farmland.

We all enjoyed that summertime, especially the children. We visited White Rock frequently and saw June sometimes. The children loved the beach and the 'seaside holiday' resort atmosphere. On one occasion, when the tide was entirely in, it was late afternoon at the end of our visit, Stephen dived into the deep water from the pier. That was not exactly something I encouraged, but he was a pretty good, confident swimmer, and he seemed quite fearless. They were almost as happy at the apartment complex, where there were other children to play with who taught them new games like 'kick the can' and 'tether-ball'. It was an amazingly warm, sunny summer. Stephen would happily talk to just about anyone, and before long, we acquired a television set; it came about because one of his new friend's parents had purchased one of the newer colour TV sets, and they passed their old black and white one to us. Canadians were so friendly and generous. We hadn't been paying much attention to the local news, but our kind neighbours provided that television set just in time for us to witness a fantastic event.

Except for the advertising material, which I always examined to see where the bargains were, I hadn't paid much attention to the newspaper we regularly had. I was interested in everything I saw around me. On our drives to White Rock along King George Highway, I was always amused by large signs advertising 'English China' and 'English Toffees', but I didn't notice that things 'English' were actually of great interest to the average West Coast citizen. England seemed so far away. Everyone, men and women alike, were so intent on living their own lives – moving about their daily lives energetically and at such a fast pace, I thought it was going to be hard to keep up with them. What a significant change from my leisurely past life in Africa! This new country was going to take some getting used to! The 'amazing development' burst into my consciousness when we were watching that television set we had been given.

ઠ લ

In the second half of the 1960s decade, the United States and the U.S.S.R. had been competing fiercely to put spacecraft and humans into orbit around the earth, but the ultimate goal had still eluded them both. During July 1969, the Americans announced that their next mission into space would be an attempt to land a man on the moon. We sat in front of our small donated black and white TV as the spacecraft was launched and put into orbit around the earth. July 21st occurred on the weekend, and we all watched excitedly as the small lunar landing craft left the mother ship and went into orbit around the moon. The pictures we were viewing of the landing of the spacecraft on the moon's surface seemed unbelievable, and when Neil Armstrong descended the stairs and said 'That's one small step for man, but one giant leap for mankind,' we were moved and had tears in our eyes.

But even with this success story, the mighty 'neighbour' to our south seemed to be somewhat out of control. The previous year 1968 had seen the assassination of Bobby Kennedy and Martin Luther King and an escalation of the war in Vietnam. This year saw the birth of the hippies and 'flower power' at Woodstock and the horrific Manson family murders in California, much of it drug-related. U.S. draft dodgers were heading north, and Canada had felt a very safe place to be.

ઠ લ

The moon landing event was so memorable after witnessing it; it seemed unreal. We went out for a little walk afterwards, and there weren't many people about. Perhaps they, like us, were somewhat shocked and needed to make sense of what we had seen. Along with many others, we wondered if it had actually happened, or was it some kind of a hoax? However, after a very few days, it was 'business as usual', and our everyday life resumed. The newspapers returned to devoting space, which had pictured that incredible event to, 'back to school' sales, and we had to register Stephen and Nicola for school. Hjorth Road Elementary School was just a few blocks south on 104th Avenue. So, there I had gone with my children in tow to see how to go about introducing them to the British Columbia school system. There were no difficulties. The teachers and administrators at schools in Canada were quite used to the movement of new immigrants and were not at all surprised when I informed the office personnel of our current address and that we would be moving to Delta very shortly when our home was ready. The school would resume on the first Tuesday after Labour Day in the first week of September. The children accepted the situation calmly enough, but I felt a little concerned for them. They had experienced tremendous change in their young lives, and change was still ahead. Melanie was such a contented little soul. She was always perfectly happy if I was in view, but it must have been harder for Stephen and Nicola, although I never heard a word of complaint. Perhaps because we had always kept them with us as we travelled about to see new things in the various countries we had visited, they felt secure enough not to have any worries. We had all enjoyed regularly going to see our new house. Finally, the day came, after we had completed the financial arrangements when we made the final inspection prior to moving in.

No. 4689 - 45th Avenue, Delta was ours! Everything looked beautiful, all brand new. The lot had been cleared of debris, ploughed and levelled. The carpets were laid, and the kitchen appliances were in place. It was a fine October day. With our brand-new keys in our hands, we opened the front door of our home and spread out to examine everything. The lower level was a bright empty space, except for the entry hall containing the front door and the carpeted staircase, which led to the living space on the second level. We all took off our shoes and tiptoed about. I admired the colour scheme; the children were introduced to their bedrooms. The house was ready and seemed to be waiting. I had very strange mixed feelings – this was serious – this might just be permanent. This place was where we were to live now to make our new life in Canada. England and my family were very far away, and I realised I might never show them this house. It was a solemn moment. When it was time to leave - we were going to move in at the weekend - we couldn't find Melanie. We called out to her, and there was no reply. Everyone was waiting to get in the car, which was parked on the pristine blacktop of our new driveway. I went back inside the house and looked in every room and found little Melanie hiding in the closet in the bedroom, which she was to share with Nicola. She was in tears. 'Why are you crying, Melanie?' I asked, helping her to her feet and picking her up in my arms. 'I want to stay here – I don't want to leave these lovely carpets', she replied with a sob. Melanie and the other children too, clearly were ready to adopt what was going to be their home and settle down. Our job now was to keep them safe and happy while they grew up!

Our new house under construction in Ladner

Ready to move in and learn how to manage Canadian winters

19.
A New Chapter in Our lives

Maureen

The weather remained fair, and we were all anxious to make arrangements to move from the apartment after our new home had the final inspection. It was now mid-October. We needed to move on a weekend as we planned a 'do-it-ourselves' move. Michael couldn't take any time off from work. Now, having some experience of seeing how things were done here, he made arrangements to rent a small U-Haul truck. We had minimal furniture to move, and Murray, our friendly neighbour at the apartment, was happy to help. Michael parked the U-Haul truck at the back of the apartment complex, and the loading commenced. In very little time, we handed over the keys to the Manager, who made a quick inspection, and in a convoy of three vehicles, we drove west to our new home. Upon arrival, I parked our car on the street in front of the house, so that Michael could reverse the U-Haul truck onto the driveway. We could move our beds, mattresses, and small pieces of furniture into the house through the side door located in the open carport under the sundeck. Everything was pristine and new in the house, so I thought it best that we take off our shoes to move things upstairs into the living and bedrooms. We didn't yet have a vacuum cleaner. Everything was soon unloaded, and we had a light lunch with a cup of tea before Murray took his leave to return to his own family. I promised I would be in touch – we would very shortly have the telephone connection.

As always, through so many changes of address, I followed the routine of making up the beds as my first job. What a joy to unpack everything and complete that chore in the very first home we could call our own. We were determined to be happy, even with so little furniture, in this lovely new sunny house. We needed furnishings and window coverings, but our new kitchen appliances were impressive, and I couldn't wait to get to grips with them and learn to operate them successfully. Outside all was very bare; the lot on which the house stood was like a ploughed and levelled field, but we realised it needed a lot of work – we could see that it was going to take some effort to devise landscaping; it was quite a big lot. But gardening could wait until spring. That weekend we made many lists. We had the vital fridge and stove in the kitchen but no laundry equipment or vacuum cleaner. I knew I could always revert to washing the bed linen and children's clothes in the bathtub but didn't want to have to do that for too long. So, the first purchases at the local hardware store were some pegs and a collapsible clothes dryer, which opened up like an umbrella and which we planted just beyond the carport. I would be able to hang up the clothes while standing on the solid cement surface. Any shower of rain turned the ploughed field into a quagmire; this, after all, had been farmland.

That first night we all went to bed very happy and slept very well – it was so quiet. We thought that living in Ladner was going to be so peaceful. When Monday morning arrived, the peace was quickly shattered. Since there were many other new houses being built all around us, trucks and men arrived on site soon after Michael left for work, and there was a cacophony from much loud hammering and heavy mechanised equipment in use. But the children and I had an appointment at the local Elementary School. Once again, I enrolled them at the school office and, after I handed over the small lunch bags I had prepared for both Stephen and Nicola, they were escorted to new classrooms. I was given the list of school supplies they would need. It had not been too long a walk for them – maybe 15 minutes from our home. On the way there, I promised Nicola I would be waiting outside for them after school and walk home with them. For the first week or two, I suggested that Stephen and Nicola should walk home together; I knew they would soon make friends and learn the route quickly as they had in England. It was a very safe area; every house we passed as we got closer to the school seemed to contain a family with young children. With optimistic excitement, we looked forward to the settling-in process. For now, Melanie and I were on our own in the daytime.

ℬ ℭ

After we moved to the new house in Ladner in October, my journey to work was somewhat longer. Shortly after starting this route, I received my first speeding ticket ever, when I was late for work one morning. This job required clocking in and out, a procedure I had never had to do before and something I loathed. On another occasion, I cut my hand rather severely and could see it would require some stitches. Enquiring where the First Aid Office was, I was told there was no one and that I would have to take myself to a clinic several streets away. I drove myself there and returned with six stitches and the impression that this company did not have much consideration for the workers. I was beginning to dislike this job and the people that worked there. It seemed to be an 'every man for his self' kind of place.

ℬ ℭ

Within a very few weeks, we had achieved much. Stephen and Nicola settled into the school routine and began to make friends. Their strange 'foreign' accent made them a little conspicuous, but they had experienced that when they went to school in England and once again set themselves to fit in. We all went to the local drugstore after school that first day to buy the necessary school supplies. Although daytime was extremely noisy, I had many things to do and soon forgot about the chaotic din outside. Meeting some of my neighbours, I soon discovered Canadian women were very hospitable and friendly. Morning coffee gatherings were popular and frequent, and even though these women were busy housewives, their homes were always immaculate.

I soon learned that it was vital to become a Simpsons-Sears' customer. From this old and well-established business, one could order, before 10.00 am, nearly anything home and family could require and usually have it delivered after 4.00 pm the same day. Large appliances might take a little longer. The Simpsons-Sears company seemed like a fantastic service to me. I was soon examining their fat catalogue and when the telephone had been connected, was able to become a customer. Sears even extended credit – as newcomers to Canada, it was set at a reasonably modest amount for us. Our first purchase was a good quality Sears vacuum cleaner.

We also were investigating laundry equipment. We still had a little money available, but as Michael was not yet satisfied with his work situation, we planned to be cautious. Fresh milk and dairy products were delivered twice weekly by Dairyland in a big truck. I had never experienced such a cheerful and friendly service from so many hard-working people. The lovely summer weather continued through October as we adjusted to our new routine in our Ladner home. The days passed, and the children were made aware of the North American tradition of celebrating Halloween. We'd certainly never experienced this before. It was quite a festival and children everywhere were anxious to enjoy the celebration. As the night-time weather cooled, we suddenly noticed the farmers' fields were littered with bright orange pumpkins. I knew pumpkins were a North American vegetable but was amazed to learn that everyone would carve a weird face on their pumpkin and set it with a candle inside in a window, as an invitation for the neighbourhood children to visit calling 'trick or treat' on the last evening in October. I was pleased that many children, ours included, also carried collection boxes for UNICEF. Having lived so long in Africa, we knew very well how badly needed funds were to help less fortunate children in the world.

November was a very dull month; it rained dismally day after day, and it became apparent we simply had to buy laundry equipment. This was soon installed in the section of the basement area already designated for the laundry, at the side entrance to the house. The services, water, and electricity had been 'roughed in' when the house was built. I thought our new equipment was marvellous; well-built and incredibly efficient. As the weather changed with the season, we experienced wind and rainstorms. One night there was a tremendous storm; high winds, heavy rain, thunder, and lightning. As there were several partly finished houses on 45th Avenue when I looked out the next morning, I expected to see an area of devastation; the shell-like look of the construction process here looked rather flimsy to eyes used to brick-built homes. But to my surprise, all was more or less as it had been the night before. This 'foreign' way of constructing houses really had merit! We had purchased a table tennis table for our basement. Michael and Stephen, who was learning to play, would have a little game while I cooked our dinner each evening. Part of the basement area in these houses usually was finished by the owner as a recreation room – very helpful for a family when the winter weather set in. Our first Christmas in Canada was celebrated with friends Cathy and Jimmy and all the children. There was a lovely turkey dinner at their house, and gifts were exchanged. On New Year's Day, 1970, we entertained a few friends. We hardly had enough chairs, but we had purchased an unpainted wooden kitchen set, a round table with four chairs, and Michael had set to work and very quickly painted the set avocado green to match our kitchen appliances, so we just had enough. After our meal, the 'ping-pong' table and our new dartboard provided us with entertainment. It was a wonderful evening.

80 CB

Once settled in our Ladner home, I wrote to Canadian Pacific Airlines (CP Air), reminding them I was still interested in working for them, giving them my new address and phone number. To my delight, several weeks later, I received a letter inviting me to come in for an interview. I made some excuses with my present employer for time off and once again made my way over to the airline's sizeable new maintenance facility close to Vancouver International Airport. After a short interview with the Personnel Department, I was escorted to the Power Plant manager's office. Here, together with the manager and Machine Shop foreman, I was quizzed about my background. It seemed that they favoured men who had served apprenticeships in the U.K., and I felt the interview went very well, except for one small part. When asked where I had taken my training, I told them, The Plessey Company. The manager then advised me that the Britannia aircraft that the company had until recently flown were equipped with Plessey hydraulic and pneumatic pumps, and they were the '*shittiest*' he had ever encountered. Somewhat taken back, I explained that I didn't design those devices; together with others, we simply made the tooling to manufacture them. After the interview, I was shown around the Machine Shop, Engine Overhaul, and hangers. The building was brand new; I was very impressed by everything I saw there. The people I met seemed very friendly, and I felt this would be a good place for me. I drove home, a short 25-minute drive, and told Maureen all about it.

A week later, I received a letter saying I did not get the job. I was deeply disappointed. But, at the interview, it had been mentioned that additional machinists were going to be needed, and in early April 1970, I was called in again. This time after a short interview, I was offered a job. Maureen and I were really pleased. Having a good, secure job with a very reputable company was extremely important to us both. The fact that it was in the Vancouver area and just a 25-minute drive from our new home made it ideal. The job came with attractive medical, pension, and travel benefits – these last two would take some time to qualify for. My starting date was set on 6th May 1970, several weeks away. The new job offer couldn't have come at a better time as the company I was currently working for was experiencing a slow-down of orders, and people were being laid off. The following week the foreman asked me if I had another job lined up. Replying that I had, he told me he had to let someone go on Friday, and would I mind if it was me since I had another job to go to. Of course, I said it would be okay, and I left at the end of the week.

We now had two weeks to fill before I started my new job at the airline, and as it was Spring Break (for all school-children), we decided to drive down and explore the coast to Oregon. I knew I would not get much vacation time for at least another year. Driving had always been a pleasure to us, and the roads both in Canada and the United States were not too busy and very spacious. Gas was about 46 cents a gallon, and there were good diners and attractive rest-stops along the way. Entry into the United States was very easy for Canadians; just a valid Canadian driving license was required for identification. We could only afford a short break, so after spending a few nights on the Oregon coast where it was rather chilly and wet, we soon decided to begin the long drive back to our home.

I started at Canadian Pacific Airlines on 6th May 1970. The airline was the second largest in Canada, with about 70 aircraft. The national (government-supported) airline, Air Canada, had about 120 aircraft. Vancouver was the headquarters for CP Air and housed its only heavy maintenance base. The newly constructed Operations Centre building included huge hangers for overhauling aircraft of all sizes, an Engine Overhaul Department, various shops for the overhaul of all components and accessories, training facilities for pilots (amazing highly technical flight simulators), flight attendants and mechanics. The second floor was mainly storing parts, and the third was all administration offices. The airline flight kitchen was also located in a part of the building. My department, the Machine Shop, had only six employees at this time and was supervised by Norm Vaux, the foreman. We were attached to the main engine overhaul shop, which also had welding, plating, and Non-Destructive Testing facilities. Our department's job was to manufacture and repair all types of engine and aircraft components. We worked shift-work hours with four men on day shift and two on afternoons, rotating every two weeks. The hours were Monday to Friday from 7.00 am to 3.00 pm and 3.00 pm to 11.00 pm. Weekend work and extra hours were paid overtime rates. The fleet consisted of McDonald Douglas DC-8s and Boeing 727s and 737s; the company had only recently converted to an all-jet configuration. The airline had extensive routes to Europe, Asia, Australia, and South America, as well as covering all of Canada and some of the United States. It was a fascinating industry to be a part of. The aircraft were mostly all-new, with the latest technological improvements, and the engine shop was just getting set up for complete engine overhauls in-house. The Machine Shop's equipment was quite good, and some new additions were on order. I had to learn all about the new exotic metals used in this industry, but I did feel with my experience, I could handle the expected work assignments relatively easily. As were most large companies in Canada, CP Air was strongly unionised, and I had to join whether I liked it or not. The union was the 'International Association of Machinists and Aerospace Workers (IAM).

80 03

To earn a little extra money for me, I decided to become an Avon representative to cover all the new homes being built in our area. I could cover the whole of it on foot, and I accepted this might be an excellent way to meet my neighbours and maybe make friends, so I looked forward to receiving my first 'Campaign Kit'. Since Melanie was not yet old enough for school, she would come with me on my 'working' trips when I was looking for customers. She was a good little girl, happy to walk along with me and when I was lucky enough to find somebody at home to my 'Ding Dong! Avon calling!', she was sometimes given a cookie, while my customer browsed through my colourful brochure. I was sometimes a little successful, but it was slow work finding people at home and introducing them to the products and persuading them to buy. It took me a few months before I made any money at all, but I still hoped one day to buy a small car. My friend Cathy tried selling Avon but then decided that she should be trained for a career with the Canadian Imperial Bank of Commerce. I was quite shocked at this development, as we had always agreed that although so many women were clamouring for 'liberation', looking after our home and family was the very best job that we could do. But that idea became old-fashioned. Women everywhere were joining the workforce. The 'Women's Liberation Movement' was gathering steam. I personally didn't perceive 'going out to work' as becoming 'liberated'! I had felt so much more comfortable with my *unliberated* South African friends. Some friends had also invited us to join them to learn to play badminton in a small hall.

After the first 'season', we moved to the High School, which had a much larger gymnasium, and soon a club was established. We met on Friday evenings, and some quite good players joined. Stephen had been a Cub Scout in Zambia, and there was a group established in Ladner. This group was headed by a Mrs Willis, who encouraged him to proudly continue wearing his Zambian uniform because he was nearly old enough to be promoted into the Scouts the following year. We made enquiries regarding something for Nicola, and there were several Brownie packs and Guide troops. Of course, all these activities relied on some parent participation, and we were quite happy to help. Gradually our children were becoming involved in everyday Canadian life.

When spring came, we noticed that a new open-air swimming pool was being built in Ladner, just across from the library. The rapid residential development taking place in Ladner required more facilities for the mainly young families that were buying the new homes. This new pool was attractive to Stephen, mostly. He and Nicola had learned to swim well in Africa. When the swimming pool opened in the summer, we were approached by other parents, who invited us to help them set up a swim club for interested young swimmers. There would be meetings with other interested parents, and the objective was to set up a committee to manage the affairs of the swim club, which would then be recognised as eligible to take part with other clubs in our area. We were learning that organisations supporting children and young people's activities were extremely dedicated and hardworking in this part of the world. Long ago, I had been to just a few Girl Guide meetings when I was about 12 years old but hadn't stayed long. I was so much more involved with my school life. However, I liked the idea of our daughters having access to Guiding to help them find friends, so I became a 'helper' at meetings and was introduced to other mothers who formed the support groups.

The following year, I was given the task of running the Girl Guide 'cookies' drive. I think this is a North American tradition – I don't remember it happening in England. It serves in Canada as a significant fundraiser because the proceeds from the sale of cookies trickle down and are shared by the individual Guide and Brownie packs. It is usually quite a small sum but is always very welcome to the Guiders in charge of the groups. Within the Girl Guide community, over a few years, I was to progress until I later became the District Commissioner for Guiding in Ladner. Perhaps it was a job that no one else wanted to do! I understood I needed to accept and make the adjustment to Canadian life and tried to overcome my feelings of being disconnected from my previous existence. We all began to be happily involved in normal family life in Western Canada.

When I had been living in Zambia, my gynaecologist had suggested I manage birth control in the future utilizing 'The Pill', which was making so many women's lives easier. This innovation was helpful, but there were side effects. For me and many others, it caused a mild depression and some feelings of anxiety – perhaps made a little worse because we lived in politically troubling times. I had brought with me an adequate supply of my medication to remedy depressed feelings. Early in 1971, when my supply ran out, I decided I was living in a perfectly safe environment in a beautiful country and should not need them. But of course, I was still on 'The Pill'. So, my mood wasn't always sunny, especially as Michael, busy with finding his way with a new and exciting airline company, like most young men, wasn't 'tuned in' to my difficulties. He likely thought I would 'get over it' and eventually settle down in the new environment as I had in the past. And I certainly tried.

In early 1971, Michael's mother had suggested she would like to visit us – she was feeling rather sad because she was now living alone. Of course, we invited her to come to Vancouver in the summertime when Michael would by then have a little vacation time. He was not yet eligible for airline 'Parent Passes'; that would come when he had been employed for several years. So, Mum booked her trip with Wardair Canada, which at that time was a charter airline, very popular and very good. I felt a little diffident about this visit – life in Canada was a vastly different thing from our life in Africa – she had already visited us twice there, and I would have liked my own mother to be able to visit us. I wasn't quite reconciled to Canadian life, and Michael's mother could sometimes be a little difficult, especially as the time away from her own home lengthened, but as she was now alone, I thought it better if we encouraged her to come.

Michael had been working very hard during the winter months 'finishing' the basement area of our house. During the previous summer months, we had tried to establish our lawns and garden. We were amazed at what *'do-it-yourselfers'* could achieve in these open basement spaces – it seemed that nearly everyone was a good 'handyman' with tools and wonderful family recreational rooms were created in the above-ground basements, which added much to the total living space (and the value) of the homes. Ours was still unfinished, but the area had been divided by Michael and walls were 'framed' to define the spaces. Then it was quick and easy to add pre-finished wall panels to the area. We purchased a sofa which included a fold-out double bed. It was called a 'Hide-

A-Bed'. Now we had somewhere for mother to sleep. We explained to her when she came we would be making that area more comfortable as finances allowed – we thought she might enjoy a place where she had her 'own space' and a little privacy, but it was very bare down there; the floor was plain cement with just a small bedside rug.

Andrew Hannay, a friend of Michael's at CP Air, had also offered to lend us his camper, a tent-trailer if we needed a holiday when mother came. Michael, knowing our powerful car could comfortably tow a camper, thought this a good idea, although I was a little doubtful about camping with three children plus mother-in-law. We had never camped in a tent together before. When we asked Michael's mother about this, she expressed interest. She always enjoyed a road trip and had always liked to understand and experience our new environment; we had been relatively successful when we took her on those other trips when she visited us in southern Africa. Our car had a powerful V-8 engine and seated six, so we thought we could attempt a trip to a campsite Michael had heard about from another friend at work. The trip would be through the scenic Fraser River Canyon to 100 Mile House in the Cariboo and into the wilderness at Canim Lake. At that time, many young families used a camping experience as their summer holiday; few families could afford airline travel overseas. All campsites in British Columbia were well maintained, equipped with open fireplaces for cooking, and there were always excellent clean toilet and bathing facilities. If we had fine weather, it could be delightful.

Michael's mother arrived in July, and after the first week, while she adjusted to the time change we prepared to begin the camping trip. We packed the camper with sleeping bags and blankets, food, and a portable outdoor cooking stove, and off we went. The scenery leaving the coast on Highway 1 (of the Trans-Canada Highway) was spectacular, and the weather was fair. We stopped just a few times at breath-taking locations to stretch our legs and enjoy the view of mountains and lakes; Michael took pictures. Each time we got back into the car, we changed seats to give everyone time in the front seats of the vehicle, although, of course, Michael was always the driver. Six people in the car felt a little crowded. The children were reasonably good. We spent one night in the Okanagan at a campsite, and Mum was enthusiastic about how clean and well organised the facilities were. The next day it was back into the car for the drive to Canim Lake. We were almost into Cariboo country, and we saw nothing but the road in front of us, trees and scenery – there were few communities. Eventually, we reached our destination and got organised for our first night at Canim Lake.

There was an extensive covered area like an open-sided rough timber auditorium with tables and benches, plus a good fire pit for cooking. The community area was surrounded by a big circle of nicely laid out camping spots with fireplaces, camp tables, and benches. There was a nice large washroom block and a good supply of firewood. We had our provisions, and soon, everyone was fed and bedded down. The next day we woke up to rain, and it was rather chilly. Stephen and Nicola sat in the car playing card games; Michael, Mum and I, with Melanie, put on our jackets and went for a walk to keep warm. We also spent a lot of time close to the fire burning in the fire pit in the open-air 'people space'. There was another family camping, and I struck up a conversation with the mother of that group while we each cooked dinner. We asked the Park Ranger when he came by if the weather was going to improve for us and he smiled and said that it might. So, we decided to see if we could stay another day. We had been warm enough in the tent trailer the first night – it was pretty close quarters for six persons, but the second night was darn cold. The next morning Mum wasn't looking very cheerful, and I was beginning to think that camping was jolly hard work. It was difficult keeping everything organised and off the wet ground, and I also had to cook and keep the hot drinks coming for everyone to help keep warm. Michael still wanted to persevere. But eventually, we managed to convince him we should perhaps return south to the Okanagan where it would be warmer and drier.

So, everything was packed up again. Seeing Mum looking so glum, even though she didn't complain, I had a private chat with Michael before we set off and suggested we must find accommodation when we got to a warmer spot, and maybe we could still enjoy a bit of a holiday. Michael didn't want to do this because of the cost involved but reluctantly agreed, and we stayed for a couple of days in a rather run-down motel in Peachland in the warmer Okanagan Valley, where there was a playground for the children. The weather was better, but things were not going well. I suggested we spend the next day at the beach so that the children could have a swim in the lake and play on the sand with other kids, but somehow everyone was out of sorts, and even the beach failed to lift our spirits. Michael's mother became upset, the children were cranky, and we realised that the best thing to do was to simply drive home so that everyone could be comfortable again. The general feeling in the car returning home was certainly less convivial than on the outward journey and going home was the right thing to do. Michael and I were hardly speaking to each other, and we were all glad we gave up on the camping idea and came home to our civilised sturdy, warm house. We never tried a tent-trailer camping holiday again. After a little more than a week, Mum returned to her home again. I felt our relationship had been somewhat damaged, but in hindsight realised we were not well enough established in our new environment to properly manage a successful visit.

While we were recovering from Mum's somewhat less than a successful visit, we heard from my Aunt June again. Les had made good the repairs his boat 'The Lemming' required meaning to complete his 'Lone Yachtsman' mission of sailing around the world. June was miserable. She told me Les had behaved through the summer as if he couldn't stand his turbulent teenage family and was determined to make a name for himself. June indicated that she had to get a job and earn her living. Les had almost bankrupted them with the cost of his preparations. June said goodbye to her husband, Les Hambleton, at White Rock Pier in August 1971. He never came back – she never saw him again.

℘ ℭ

It seemed to me that no matter which country we moved to, a political or racial crisis erupted, and Canada proved to be no exception. For many years, the mainly French-speaking province of Quebec had been seeking independence from the rest of Canada. To further the cause, in October 1970, a terrorist group called the

FLQ (Front de Libération du Québec) kidnapped several government officials. The Prime Minister at the time, Pierre Trudeau, who hailed from Québec but was adamantly not a separatist, invoked the War Measures Act and declared a State of Emergency. Troops were assigned to all government buildings. The Deputy Premier of Quebec, Pierre Laporte was eventually found executed and stuffed into the trunk of a car. British Trade Commissioner James Cross was released after 60 days in captivity. Ultimately many members of the FLQ were arrested and some convicted of murder. The state of alert was in place for just a few months.

Back at work in August 1971, I was given a new challenge. A large new sophisticated milling machine had arrived from Germany, to be used mainly on jet engine overhaul work. Because of union seniority requirements, the opportunity to work on this machine had to be offered to those with the most length of service. All the men ahead of me refused this opportunity, and when it was offered to me, I jumped at the chance. To me, it seemed to be an interesting challenge. Some of the required assignments which I found most interesting involved working directly on aircraft at the airport ramp, or in the hangers where aircraft were undergoing regular maintenance servicing or complete overhauls. The normal work in these areas was carried out by aircraft and engine mechanics or other technicians. When they ran into problems beyond their capabilities, a machinist was called. As these areas were operational 24 hours a day, we could be called upon at any time, day or night.

My first venture working directly on an 'in-service' aircraft involved repairing a damaged screw thread that held a small inspection panel in place. This repair was carried out using a helicoil thread insert, and there were choices to be made whether to use a locking or non-locking type. As they were in a hurry to get the aircraft back in service, I had to make a quick decision. I completed the job, and the aircraft went on a trip right away, but I worried all night that the part might fall off and hurt someone or cause damage. We all were required to sign off paperwork for every task completed, and I soon understood that minor repairs like this one, did not jeopardise the safety of the aircraft in any way, so I learned to relax about it. I had been with the company for about six months when a fellow machinist did not show up for work one day, and we were informed he had died of a massive heart attack. Norm, at 48 years of age, was the most knowledgeable and respected person in our department, and he was hard to replace. Together with all my colleagues from work, we attended his funeral service, my first one where the casket was open, and the deceased visible. Norm's death was the second from heart disease affecting personnel in the machine shop in 18 months, and the company became concerned that work-related stress was a factor. During the first six months of employment with the company, all new employees were on probation. I had just received my final appraisal, which was very good, and I was now considered a permanent employee.

We were now into our second winter in Canada; the first had been mild with only a trace of snow in the Lower Mainland. But this winter proved to be quite different. Late in January 1971, the snow had started to fall one day, and it continued throughout the night into the next day. I was on the afternoon shift and managed to get to work quite well as the main roads to the airport were kept clear. Leaving work at around midnight, with the snow still falling, I made my way slowly home. There was very little traffic, and I was relieved when I finally made it off the freeway and into Ladner. But just a few streets from home, I became lodged in a heavy snowdrift and had to abandon the car. I had phoned Maureen before leaving work, so she knew I would be late. It was now after 1.00 am, and the streets were deserted; I was quite prepared to leave the car where it was until morning. When I got to the house, all the lights were on, and Maureen was looking out the window. She insisted we retrieve our car, so armed with a shovel and broom, we proceeded to tramp through quite deep snow back to the car to dig it out. It was snowing hard. After about 45 minutes of snow moving, I managed to drive it out of the drift and onto our driveway. This was our first experience of real Canadian winter. On Saturday, we tried skiing on our streets with equipment lent to us by our new friends, Inge and Assad Bishay and by Monday, all the snow had disappeared.

Michael spent
many years
working for
Canadian Pacific
Airlines at their
Operations Centre
in Richmond, B.C.

We enjoyed the beauty and culture of Vancouver and
British Columbia

20.
A Brand New Canadian

Maureen

The winter of 1971-72 was indeed a Canadian winter, but I appreciated being safe and warm at home. I was a little lonely and missed chatting with Cathy, who had shared with me the familiar bond of our 'old life' in Zambia. I spent time with a new Danish friend, Inge Bishay, occasionally. We both agreed that our Canadian neighbours were friendly enough, but they viewed us both as 'different', and of course, we were different. We didn't get excited about Vancouver's professional American-style football or ice-hockey teams, as almost everyone else did. They seemed very rough games to us – we weren't used to seeing professional sports teams actually roughing up their opponents. It never happened at soccer or cricket matches. We both felt our past experience in other countries was what set us apart. I hoped we would eventually 'fit in', and we certainly wanted to. I realised it would take time. I was putting away the minimal sums I made from my Avon work, and my bank account grew very slowly; it was quite demoralising. I really wanted to enjoy more freedom of movement by having my own car. So, I persevered! Michael was pleased he had found the kind of employment that was challenging and exciting, and I was pleased for him, especially as, in time, we all would be able to enjoy airline pass privileges, which was an event to look forward to. It would make having a holiday so much more exciting. In the meantime, he concentrated his attention on his work, and in his spare time at home, he continued finishing the basement as funds permitted, also helping to keep the children busy with their homework and after-school activities. Our unsuccessful camping trip in the summer and Michael's mother's visit was seldom mentioned, but I was still rather depressed about what had happened.

From the time we had first left England, my sister Pam and I had maintained very regular correspondence. From her, I learned that my mother, always in rather delicate health, had not been at all well. Pam mentioned Mum had recently had stomach surgery, and my worried sister explained the situation. I was sad and deeply concerned. Without telling me what he intended to do and knowing he had not been at CP Air long enough to qualify for pass benefits, Michael explained the situation to his boss, Mr Norman Vaux.

He must have liked Michael because, within a couple of days, he handed him a 'Compassionate Pass' for me to fly to Amsterdam and on to London so that I could visit my dear sick mother. This kindness pleased me. I yearned to be 'at home' with my parents and sister for a while. Of course, I had to make sure my children and Michael would be looked after while I was away.

I decided to cook and freeze many dinners for the family, and made arrangements for Melanie, who was now seven years old and in Grade Two, to go to her friend Kelly Dean's house after school. Pat Dean, Kelly's mother, who was friendly, promised to help keep an eye on her. She always walked her own daughter to and from school every day, so I had no safety concerns. Nicola and Stephen were instructed to help Melanie get ready for school each day and to support their dad keep things going by assisting with the household chores, and so, early in February, off I went. Once on my way, Michael telephoned Pam to advise her about my approximate time of arrival in England, if all went well. In Amsterdam, I would have to find my way to the British Airways' departure gates. It was a short 'hop' from Schiphol to London Heathrow, and I'd never travelled entirely alone, so it was an adventure; I had no problems.

My brother-in-law, Ron, who was such a good friend to me, was waiting to meet me when I got to London Heathrow airport. Ron had always been my friend and 'brother' since before he and Pam married. He happily took charge of my suitcase and drove me to Basildon, where we picked up Pam and then carried on to my parents' home, which now was a new ground-floor apartment not far from the house in Delimands where she and Dad lived when we were last in England. My mother had always been too restless once she and Dad had left the family home in Dagenham, and together they had had many different addresses since we had all lived there. Along the way, her restlessness and the many removals had caused her to suffer quite a few accidents, the worst being one that affected her back for many months. But this time, her problem was internal; it was a form of cancer – she was so frail she needed a wheelchair for use outside her home, but she was able to carefully walk about inside her present one-level home. Mum was thrilled to see me and insisted I sleep in her room, which was furnished with twin single beds. Dad, who was now retired from Standard Telephones & Cables, seemed not to mind – he had a bed in his workroom, where he continued to work on his model boats.

After the difficulties of the past year, I was so glad to be able to relax quietly with my beloved parents and sister and to tell them a little about the problems I'd encountered during the past couple of years in yet another 'foreign' environment. I also told them how well the children were adjusting and what a good and exciting job Michael had now, but when Michael called at the end of the first week and asked me how long I would remain in England, I wasn't ready to answer. As the days passed, I realised my mother was recovering very slowly from her surgery and was not in any immediate danger. She was as frail as a little bird. Nutrition was challenging for her, and Dad and I would take great pains in devising simple, nutritious meals that she could eat. She liked to go out every day, and we were happy to take her in her wheelchair whenever she wanted an outing, even though the weather was quite cool - it was early spring. I introduced her to flavoured yoghurt and made her some egg-based dishes and custards. Of course, Dad had never learned to cook at home or how to undertake any other type of housework. Pam was a working woman, and she was therefore not able to help very much daily, and her free time at weekends was devoted mostly to looking after her own family. But she always managed to spend a little time very regularly with Mum to help with chores that Dad could not manage.

At the end of the second week, Michael called again and asked me if I was ready to come home. I still didn't feel ready. He then asked if I would like him to fly over and travel home with me. It sounded to me as if he wanted me to return - perhaps he was missing me more than I thought he would, so I replied that he might make arrangements for me to fly home after one more week and to please let me know when there was space available. Persons travelling on Employee Travel Passes always were on a 'stand by' basis, which means there is no point in attempting to fly if the plane is already fully booked. Towards the end of my visit, Ron made the telephone call to 'list' me on the flights I needed to get home, but I prepared sadly to depart. It was very hard to say another 'goodbye' – I never could leave my mother without a tear leaking, and it was hard for her too. She looked so frail and tried to smile. My dear Dad, always the gentleman, with tears in his eyes insisted on carrying my suitcase out to the taxi. He said gruffly, 'Goodbye, Duck' and kissed me. It was a short ride to the train station. I started the journey back to my home. I wasn't sure how I felt; was my mother going to be all right? Had I stayed by her side long enough? Would I ever see her again? I wasn't genuinely sure I wanted to go to our home in Canada yet. In Canada, it was altogether harder to work caring for the home and family than I'd experienced in my African home where help was readily available. But I understood I really couldn't expect Michael to manage everything. The children were young and needed a lot of attention, and I was sure the frozen dinners I had prepared would not have lasted long. I thought about my children; I knew I shouldn't be absent from them any longer – I had always loved and cared for them – I had truly missed them.

Michael brought them all with him to meet me. It was a very happy reunion, and in no time at all, I knew I had done the right thing in returning to my family. Michael too, was pleased to see me and the next day he asked me if I was ready to look for a car! My Avon fund had grown a little, but I knew I only had about $300; he thought a little help from him would make it enough, so we agreed to start looking around on the following weekend. Having my own car would add interest and flexibility to my life. I also understood that having two cars to look after would add to Michael's 'at home' chores, but in this instance, I recognised he truly wanted to help me to be happy. There were several used car lots in New Westminster at that time. We had frequently driven past them when we were in the process of buying our house in Ladner. We made a couple of trips there and made the acquaintance of a nice young man who understood exactly what we were looking for. Some of the older salesmen seemed a bit 'pushy' to me – I didn't want anyone like that telling me what I needed. Our younger guy, Ken, gave us a call when something came in that he thought might serve my needs, and off we went to see him. His choice was right on! It was a little red Sunbeam Arrow, a British import in really nice condition. It cost just $350. I was pleased to have wheels and to feel independent again. Now I could drive myself to Oakridge shopping centre in Vancouver, on 41st Avenue and Cambie, or even to the shopping centres in Surrey – I'd driven to those places often enough with Michael, I was quite sure of the route. I was going to enjoy the next summer and perhaps be able to settle down better in my Canadian environment.

Michael and I resumed our twice-weekly badminton evenings. I remained a part of the local association that supported our Girl Guiding activities, and Melanie was now a Brownie, Nicola had 'flown up' to Guides, and the fledgeling swim club committee meetings also took up a little of my time. It was a challenge to find a suitable, competent swimming coach. We were looking forward to our first swim meet; Stephen was doing quite well, always going to practice regularly. I thought this a wonderful sport – it took up quite a lot of his leisure time, and he always came home tired and clean! Stephen had also become friendly with the young man who lived in the newly built home opposite our house. Gary and Edith Wright had recently moved from Alberta and had an adopted baby girl. Stephen was always interested in everyone and was soon chatting away to Gary, who kept horses on the farmland to the south of us. He began teaching Stephen to ride his horse on Saturday mornings. Naturally, I was a little worried about this at first, but as we got to know Gary and his wife and Stephen was able to show us what he was learning, I realised he would come to no harm under Gary's instruction. Gary had a very calm demeanour, he was a good, steady man, and Stephen learned to love riding horses.

The first swim meet went off quite well. Of course, many parents turned out to watch the action and cheer on their swimmers. A swim meet requires quite a lot of parental involvement. In no time at all, Michael was hauled in to hold a stopwatch and be a 'timer', and I was recruited as a stroke judge. I had always liked to swim myself, although I never was good enough to be competitive. But with instruction, we both soon learned what we had to look out for. Our first 'fun' competitive meet was with the Boundary Bay Bluebacks; they had been in existence for a few years and, at first, had practised in the cold water of Boundary Bay. Of course, their swimmers were superior to ours, but it was merely a 'fun' event, and our swimmers quickly understood they needed to work very hard to catch up. There were to be many years of summer swimming, which required Michael to be up early on weekends to drive Stephen to the swim meets, which were held all over the Lower Mainland. Fortunately, sometimes Stephen could get a ride with another team member's parent. We actively promoted the swimming because it certainly kept him from getting into mischief. All our children were enrolled in the Red Cross 'Learn to Swim' programme. I discovered this was a very worthwhile programme leading eventually to obtaining National Lifeguard Certification. Since we now lived in an environment that was well provided with recreational bodies of water, it was entirely appropriate that our young people should learn to swim well. Boating also was very popular here.

That spring, we all soon became involved in various activities, so we were beginning to get more involved in Canadian community life, but a slight complication became evident to me. I was pregnant again. Michael could hardly believe it – perhaps he thought I was too old at thirty-nine to have another baby and wasn't too sure if he was pleased about it. I, however, was delighted – I'd always loved having a new baby – it had always been the best and happiest thing I could do. And I was determined to enjoy this pregnancy as much as I could, although we kept the news private at first. I thought at my age it was best to be a little discreet. I also thought it would probably be some months before my condition became apparent. I didn't immediately go to my doctor – Ladner was a village; word could quickly get around. I knew how to manage pregnancy. As usual, I felt a little sick, but that meant I ate lightly and so didn't immediately put on much weight. I did write to my mother and tell her. I was like my mother in the matter of having babies, she was happy for me, and I made up my mind I would go and see her again the following year so she could see my infant – it was something she would be happy to look forward to. She was still very frail.

ЄꙨ Ꮸ�3

Maureen seemed to be happy enough to be at home in Canada after her lengthy stay in England, and I was greatly relieved to see her. It was not easy trying to look after three children and attend to my work, which was demanding because our department had increased in size, so there now was a greater volume of work and a larger number of aircraft that were brought into the hanger and to the expanding airport. Because of this, management decided to put everyone on additional afternoon shifts, from 3.00 pm to 11.00 pm. The new rotation required four weeks of day shift followed by two weeks of afternoons. The afternoon shift period was extra tiring. Naturally, during the week, the children rose quite early for school, so I seldom 'slept in'. On Saturday mornings, I would take Stephen to ice hockey in an old disused hanger at Boundary Bay airport. This place was cold and damp, but Stephen enjoyed learning the game. We were amazed at how quickly he became quite proficient at it. The following year a new ice rink was built in South Delta, and this place was eventually heated for the spectators but, as ice time was in great demand, Stephens game or practice would often start at 5.00 am. Later, when summer came, he became involved with the swim club, and this also meant many early mornings, which often included driving great distances at weekends for the competitive swim meets.

When Maureen had told me she was expecting again, I was initially quite shocked, as I thought she was still on 'The Pill'. Now I felt that I could never keep up with the demands placed on me, but after a while, seeing how happy she was to be having another baby, I had to acknowledge we would find a way to manage. However, money always seemed to be in short supply. With a new baby coming, I needed to complete finishing the basement and moving Stephen into a bedroom downstairs, as well as installing a toilet and shower stall for him there. With the idea of making a little extra money, I built a bench in the final free space on the ground level of the house, which currently housed a large closet containing the hot-water heater and the furnace; here, I could set up my watch repairing equipment. We bought a couple of unpainted chests and created a work area in the laundry for Maureen's sewing machine. She had always made some of her own and the girls' dresses and was also good at keeping our clothing and other household things in good repair, which saved a little money.

After two years with CP Air, I was entitled to family passes anywhere in North America, including Hawaii. I was pleased to be able to reserve two weeks' vacation for July. We had heard many wonderful things about Hawaii, so we decided to attempt a trip there. This vacation was an exciting idea as we had not had a relaxing holiday since coming to Canada. In May, we made reservations at the Marine Surf Hotel in Waikiki and could not do anything about the flights as we would be on standby. As we needed five seats, I was somewhat anxious about this, but other employees assured me that because of 'no shows', they very frequently took all the standby passengers. We had not been able to save much money for this trip, but we now had a new Visa credit card, so I knew we could pay later for some items. There were three flights a week to Hawaii, all continuing on to Australia, which utilised a stretched DC-8 aircraft.

Close to the departure date, I made a listing with reservations, and they informed me our chances were good. CP Air had a strict dress code for employee travel, and on the appointed day, Maureen had all the children properly attired, and I told them they must behave well at the airport, or we may not be accepted for the flight. They sat like angels at the gate, and after a few tense moments, we were assigned seats, and at 11.00 am on 4th July 1972, we departed Vancouver for the first of many trips that we made to Hawaii. Seated toward the back of the aircraft, we were all delighted to be offered a steak dinner with wine for Maureen and me. The five-hour flight seemed to pass by quickly, and we could soon see the islands from our window seats. I thought of those early explorers finding these tiny places in the middle of the vast Pacific Ocean, with minimal navigational aids. We approached Honolulu from the north down the centre of the island of Oahu, the same route the Japanese took when they surprised the Americans at Pearl Harbor, and then there it was below us. We came in over the water and landed at Honolulu airport, noting how warm and sweet-smelling the air was as the aircraft door was opened. It reminded us of Africa. After clearing U.S. Customs and Immigration, we decided to take a taxi to Waikiki, a distance of about eight miles; as we were five, this seemed to be the best way. The first taxi in line was a Cadillac, which we happily took, and during the ride, the radio was playing traditional Hawaiian music. With the sun shining, the beautiful scenery, and the music, we thought we must be in paradise.

We arrived at our hotel, the Marine Surf on Seaside Avenue, and were pleased with the room, which was on the tenth floor. We had a small kitchen and balcony overlooking the famous International Market Place. In the distance, we could just see the sea. We were now quite tired, and as it was beginning to get dark, we decided to call it a day and prepare for bed. Just then, we heard several huge explosions that echoed through the high-rise buildings of Waikiki. It was the 4th of July, Independence Day – a memorable holiday for all Americans, and we were treated to a fabulous fireworks' display that lit up the sky outside our floor-to-ceiling windows. What a view we had, and what a welcome!

We spent our first few days on the beach, exploring the famous sights around Waikiki and just enjoying the variety of mixed races that make up the beautiful Hawaiian people, who we found to be warmly friendly and polite. Most mornings, we would go to the beach, and Nicola, who loved the water, would sit and play at the edge of the waves, only coming out when it was time for us to leave. She would then be quite wrinkled. Melanie usually played in the sand with a bucket and spade, never far from her mother's side. We let Stephen rent a surfboard, and he was soon out of sight, off into the big waves which were some distance from the shore. After about an hour, Maureen would start to get anxious about his whereabouts and wanted me to search for him. I would find him, among many other people in the big waves, where he was making progress in the art of surfing. We had gone on this holiday with very little money and usually had breakfast in the hotel room and then something light at lunchtime. We discovered an ice cream parlour in the International Market Place that also made wonderful Belgian waffles, and this became one of our regular places for a snack. Perry's Smorgasbord became another favourite place to eat for dinner, and Stephen could satisfy his growing appetite here, as this was an 'all you can eat' establishment. It did seem that most of the money I had brought with me was required to feed my growing family, just buying ice cream for five cut into the budget. As always in world-famous places, there was plenty of information available regarding places of interest and special free events to go to.

The large hotels were very spacious and featured groups of performers playing traditional music and dance, which entertained anyone who walked by or paused to have a drink. They seemed such beautiful happy people. One large free event we all attended was the weekly colourful Kodak Hula Show held in Kapiolani Park, a 10-minute walk from our hotel. The Kodak Hula Show was a popular show which had been running for over 30 years, with traditional Hawaiian and other Polynesian singing and dancing. The girls all loved it. On another occasion, we took the local bus to Pearl Harbor. Here we visited the museum run by the U.S. Navy and saw a movie about the 7th December 1941 attack on the Pacific Fleet in Hawaii by the Japanese Air Force, which brought the United States into the Second World War. A naval launch took us across the harbour to the USS Arizona memorial, which is built across the sunken ship, still visible in the clear water. It was very sad to think that this was where 1,300 sailors lost their lives. We were quite surprised by the large number of Japanese people who also were visiting these sites. Wanting to see more of the island of Oahu, we rented a car in Waikiki one day, driving around Diamond Head, visiting the 'Blowhole' and Hanama Bay. The drive along the coast northward was stunning and reminded us again of the Cape in South Africa. The Polynesian Cultural Centre was our next stop. The cultural centre is operated by the Mormon Church and recruits young people from all over the Pacific who demonstrate their culture, arts, and crafts. Unfortunately, we did not have the time or money to enter the showground on this trip but promised ourselves we would on another visit.

After driving to the northern tip of the island, we stopped at the newly built Kuilima Hotel (now the Turtle Bay Hilton) situated on the rocks overlooking the ocean and dreamed that one day we might come back and stay there. (We eventually were able to.) The famous North Shore surfing beaches were just a little way further on, and we were very impressed by the size of the waves and the bravery of the surfers. Returning to Waikiki down the centre of the island, we passed through miles of pineapple fields and stopped at a roadside stand to sample. The fruit was delicious, and we all over-indulged, an act we regretted later when everyone complained of stomach pains, and there was a big demand for the bathroom. That was a restless night for everyone.

Our last day was to be a very long one, as our flight did not leave until 1.30 am. The hotel extended our check-out time until 2.00 pm, and we rented a car in Waikiki for a half-day with a drop off at Honolulu airport. The rental car enabled us to keep our baggage with us and for Maureen to rest, as she could not always be on her feet. I had checked with CP Air, and they said the flight did have some seats, but it was always a concern as there was no other flight for three days, and we never knew how many 'standbys' senior to me there were. But we passed the day partly at the beach and extended the time by eating and admiring the goods on display at Ala Moana Shopping Centre. We arrived at the airport around 8.00 pm. We all had to change into suitable clothes in the washrooms. After check-in, we still could not be assured that we would get on the flight and had to wait until after midnight before there was any activity at the gate. Honolulu airport at midnight is a fantastic meeting place for aircraft from North America, Asia, and the South Pacific. It is a hub of activity at this time. The airport is open to the elements, and warm scented breezes blow through, mixed with the smell of jet fuel. Just a few minutes before our flight was due to depart, we were relieved to be given five seats and in no time were on our way home, with a feeling of contented relief. We landed in Vancouver at 6.00 am and retrieved our car, which was parked at the CP Air Operations Centre.

ဆ 03

By the end of the children's summer holidays and our wonderful trip to Hawaii, we were all well-tanned. It certainly wasn't possible to hide my pregnancy any longer; my health was good, and I was happy when the children went back to school so that I could begin to make my preparations for the new arrival. The children all knew about the impending event, and Stephen had very solicitously asked me one day when we were at the beach, 'How are you really, Mum?' as we were walking together with the incoming tide back to our towels at the water's edge. He was then nearly 14 years old. I replied that I was absolutely fine, but since I was a somewhat 'older' mother-to-be, I sometimes felt more tired than usual. I was pleased with his quite mature attitude and remembered how much he had loved and cared about little Melanie when she was a baby. Michael had spent time during the summer finishing off the basement rooms with indoor/outdoor carpeting and adding a shower cubicle and toilet, next to a space that would become Stephen's new bedroom. The small bedroom upstairs between our room and the one the girls still shared, which he had previously occupied, would be perfect for our coming baby. I had a passing thought that this baby might be a boy, which would make the family even, and I secretly chose two names, Alex and Abigail. Michael wasn't too interested in choosing names, but he carefully painted the second-hand crib we purchased and tried to be interested in all the other items and supplies I gradually collected. My due date was deemed to be mid-November – I thought if it were to coincide with my mother's birthday on 17th November, she would be pleased.

As usual, my due date came and went, and when we got to the end of November, I was wondering if this pregnancy would ever end. I had been very well, and Dr Jones, our local physician, had taken good care of me. On my regular (now weekly) visit to his office, he thought that if there was no action from me over the weekend, I should be admitted to Richmond Hospital on Monday morning the 4th December, for a consultation with a gynaecologist who would determine what should happen next. That weekend it snowed hard, and Michael thought it would be a good idea to take the car and the children up to Seymour Mountain on Sunday afternoon to enjoy the beautiful new snow which had fallen. He had read that taking a pregnant woman to a higher altitude could induce labour. I wasn't too comfortable about this little outing but thought if anything should happen I would already be in the car and could be driven to the hospital. So off we went – it was a gloriously, bright, clear winter's day. Once at the top parking lot, I wasn't able to get out of the car because the parking lot was a sheet of ice, and I didn't think I should walk on it, so I stayed nice and warm in the car while the children romped in the deep snow. It was freezing up there and within little more than 45 minutes or so they all came back, ready to go home. I was relieved to be off that mountain.

The next morning there was still no sign of anything happening with me, so we called Dr Jones and were soon on our way to Richmond hospital. He joined us there and introduced the gynaecological specialist he had called. This man, Dr Jynn, asked the pertinent questions and then conducted a very searching, thorough examination, and both doctors retired to confer out of my hearing. It was decided that labour was to be induced, and Michael was allowed to go home. I was transferred from what would become my room to another bed close to the nurse's station, and an intravenous drip was slowly started. I was left alone. I was a little apprehensive being alone, but in the early afternoon, labour pains commenced, and I was soon transferred to the Delivery Suite. Once there, Dr Jones appeared, and together with a midwife-nurse, I was well taken care of. I wasn't conscious for this birth. I think Dr Jynn had determined this was quite a large baby because when birth was imminent, a mask came down over my nose and mouth, and I was o-u-t. When I came to, I heard newborn baby noises to my left, and I turned my head, and there was my baby in a bassinet some distance away. 'It's a girl', Dr Jones was joyfully telling me, 'and now we have to put in some stitches'. I started to say, 'Give me my baby.' But I was out again for a few minutes.

I came to again being wheeled into the first room I'd been in, which had a view of the snow-covered North Shore Mountains. It was such a lovely sunny day. Of course, I wanted to know where my baby was, and a nurse was sent to bring her to me. Because of the medication I had required, my baby was somewhat sleepy and needed monitoring I was told, but I held her for a little while – I was feeling a bit bruised myself and soon let her go back to the special nursery. Michael arrived with the children when school was finished for the day, and they all inspected the newcomer through the nursery glass window. She was a beautiful, rather big baby, weighing nine pounds. She had dark hair; we named her Abigail. Nicola told me later that as soon as she saw her, she knew this was *her* little sister. They didn't stay long, and Michael came back alone that evening. He seemed pleased with our baby too. The next day I had some 'tidy-up' surgery in the morning, so I didn't see him that day, but the baby was brought to initiate breastfeeding. I had taken with me to the hospital some little fine cotton, back fastening 'angel' shirts I had made, and some blue and pink floss to embroider the finishing details. Since I'd had surgery, I was in the hospital six days and peacefully spent my time adding her name and decorating them. When we came home, 'Abby' wore those little shirts with pink embroidery for the first few weeks. It was a precious peaceful time.

Since the older children were in school, I determined to try to make a real effort at breastfeeding. I did quite well for about two and a half weeks, but then Christmas was upon us, and once again, I was busy as any woman with four children would be. Melanie liked helping out and would often bottle-feed our baby for me. I look back on that time with great pleasure. I have always thought of Abby as my reward. That year we spent time with friends, Inge and Assad – they and their little girls were very interested in our baby. Inge took great pleasure in creating Christmas in the Danish tradition. It was a wonderfully warm and loving celebration. I felt like a fortunate woman to have such caring friends and such a loving, close family.

Abigail's birth that winter gave me a whole new perspective on many aspects of our life together in Canada. Caring for a new baby naturally always keeps the caregiver very busy. When the needs of four other family members are included, there are seldom any spare moments. Fortunately, as a healthy, active woman, I had little trouble adjusting and was always able to relax a little when feeding my beautiful baby when the older children were in school. It is a natural thing to be a bit less active during the colder weather, and one is grateful for a warm, comfortable home with efficient domestic appliances to help with the chores. It was a peaceful time for me, and Michael never complained about the shift work. He, too, always came home with a smile and relaxed when he could. 1973 became a hectic year. When spring arrived, I was able to take

Abby out in her stylish baby carriage, and on the traditional May Day parade in Ladner, we all attended when Stephen rode a horse with his friend, Gary. Shortly after May Day, Mother's Day comes along. Michael had got to know there was a small local tennis club which met in Ladner, where municipal courts were reserved for adult tennis players. He had decided that as I had asked him not to continue playing golf in our new country, as golf is such a time-consuming activity, he would take up tennis. He had agreed to help run a little tournament for the group on Mother's Day without telling me, leaving this mother at home taking care of family business. I was not at all pleased. He arrived home to a somewhat silent wife in time for dinner.

The very next day, Monday, I put Abby in the baby buggy, and off I went to our local tennis courts and registered with Barry Sanderson, a long-time local tennis teacher, and had a brief lesson. I had been turning over this course of action in my mind after reading a 'tennis lessons' advertisement in our local newspaper; I'd had just a little tennis experience when I was a schoolgirl. It was clear to me that I had to make an effort to join in. The exercise would be good for me, and I might make new friends. I had six lessons with a new group of ladies and began to accompany Michael to tennis practices. I was determined but had to be patient about my progress while Abby was still so young. Initially, I didn't make good progress because the small Ladner Club had very few competent players. At least Michael and I were able to begin to play a friendly game of mixed doubles together.

Later, when Abby was in school, I had quite expensive lessons at the indoor facility at the Town and Country Inn on Highway 99. This facility had recently been built nearby, with a good teacher, Don McCormack; one of Canada's best Davis Cup players. I had studied the game and wanted to improve.

Abigail Ellen arrives on the scene

Michael

Before we departed from Africa, my brother Denis had returned to England from Cape Town and was living with my mother in her small apartment in Hainault, Essex. To my surprise, he went to work at the same company, Plessey, where I had served my apprenticeship, and he now worked with many of my co-workers in the Tool Room. Denis was still unmarried and had lived with an earlier girlfriend, Joan, in Cape Town, but I believe when my mother arrived there, this relationship came to an end.

During the spring of 1973, Maureen's mother again became very sick, so we decided to visit England as it was suggested to us that she may not live much longer. Maureen, Abby, and I left in mid-July, and as I had only planned on being away only one week, the older children were looked after by friends. We spent some time with Maureen's family, and I then returned to Vancouver, leaving Maureen and Abby to spend more time with her mother. Upon my arrival in Vancouver, I was shocked to learn that the Machinists' Union had gone on strike, and the airline that I worked for was virtually shut down. This strike was the first in the history of CP Air. As an apprentice, I never had to join a union, but in Africa, I was obliged to, and they did look after the interests of the expatriate employees in Zambia. Here at CP Air, it was mandatory to belong if you were not in management. Talking to some of my colleagues the next day, I learned that to receive any strike pay, I would have to report for picket duty at the union office. Upon arrival, I was signed up and told to go to the company's main gate at noon for duty with three others. Here, I explained to them that I was not happy being caught in this situation, as I had a wife and four children to support on my salary alone, and the strike pay would not go very far. Their response bothered me as they indicated this could be a long strike, and they intended to 'bring this company to its knees', all for an increase in wages. Their wives were working, the weather was good, and they seemed to have no concern for others. The very next day, I went looking for another job and found one, working for three German guys who had just started a small machining and fabricating shop in Richmond. The airline had cancelled all travel passes, so Maureen and Abby were stuck in England another two weeks. Thanks to my cousin Pat, who had worked for Pan American Airways in London, tickets were arranged for them to return home via Seattle. When the labour dispute was finally resolved after ten weeks, the small company I was working for asked me to stay, but I declined and went back to the airline for the security and benefits. CP Air had managed to keep its international services flying with management personnel, but most domestic flights were cancelled. The machinists' union returned to work with about the same offer made to them before the strike.

I vowed I never wanted to be put in this situation again. Promotion was always by seniority within the union ranks, and as I had only been there a few years, to advance to a supervisory position would take forever. For any management job, I would need further qualifications. In September, I decided to go back to school, signing up at B.C. Institute of Technology for one evening a week after work. The first year I took Mechanical Drafting, followed by a Metallurgy (study of metals) course. The company policy allowed for reimbursement of half the cost of the course upon completion. So, at nearly forty, I was returning to the classroom.

Following our somewhat rocky start in Canada, in both our domestic life and my workplace experiences, I was beginning to feel that we could indeed settle down in this beautiful country. The children seemed happy here, and Maureen was more contented now that she was back to being a full-time mother with a baby to look after. The visits to see her own mother, made possible by my company, also helped her to feel that this was the best place for our family. As the older children grew into teenagers, they became involved in many sports and pastimes. For Stephen, it was soccer, swimming, hockey, and some horseback riding with a friend, Garry Wright who lived across the street. Both Nicola and Melanie took part in figure skating, tennis, and also some swimming. Both girls were in Brownies and Guides, and Maureen became involved when they needed a District Commissioner in Ladner. These activities kept us very busy, transporting them around during the evenings and at weekends. Stephen had befriended a recently married young man across the street, and he spent quite a bit of time chatting to

Bill and his wife Carole and throwing a football around. He was often invited to stay for supper. Although he seemed to be struggling somewhat with his schoolwork (the parent/teacher interviews being quite painful), overall, he was a well-behaved teenager and did not give us too much call for concern. When he was fifteen, he wanted to return to England and meet up with our family again, so we decided if he continued to act responsibly, he could go alone in the summer, which he did. Stephen was very keen to drive at 16, and after he obtained his learner's license, I took him out and let him drive our car. I soon realised that he seemed to be very good for a beginner and learned that his friend Bill had given him a few opportunities behind the wheel. He soon had his full license and then, of course, wanted his own car.

During our time in Africa, we had retained our British passports and renewed them with the various embassies as required, adding the children as they came along. I thought that as our children (except Abby) were born in various African countries, it would be best if we all became Canadian citizens, and in August 1975, we did, except for Maureen, who felt she was not quite ready. Almost twenty years later, when Britain joined the EEC, and the British passport was no longer used, she decided to become a Canadian. We all watched proudly at the ceremony as she swore allegiance to the Queen of England and Canada.

As we moved into the mid-seventies, we realised that Maureen's mother's health was very fragile and that we should try and see her as often as we could, even though it was not easy leaving the children alone. Several times we were given the impression from England that she may not live long, so in January 1975, we again made the long trip to London via Amsterdam. We had to go this way as CP Air did not have landing rights in London at this time. Abby came with us, and she turned out to be a very good traveller, sleeping most of the time we were in the air. We repeated this journey again in May 1975. Maureen's mother had several operations for stomach cancer and other problems, but she pulled through each time. She had a strong will to survive and told us on the last visit that she wanted to visit us in Canada. We, of course, thought this was just a pipe dream. In 1983 we sold our home in Ladner and bought a rather English-looking Tudor style house in Tsawwassen, a few miles further south of Vancouver, very close to the United States border crossing at Point Roberts. The name Tsawwassen is from the aboriginal people (now known as First Nations) and means 'Land Facing the Sea'. Although Stephen had brought home girlfriends, from time to time, none had seemed very special to him until he met a girl in his cooking class at Delta Secondary School. He talked about her quite a lot and then invited her to come back to our house and share their lunchtime with Maureen. Her name was Teresa Wright.

Stephen went on to marry Teresa, and they now have three children. He has a successful electrical contracting business in Delta, British Columbia. Nicola met and married a young American attorney, Barry Franklin, and they live in Florida with their three children. Melanie lives close by in South Surrey, B.C., with her two children and new partner Bruce. She has a successful career in the financial investment community. Abby also lives in South Surrey after a short time in Ontario and is now a part-time working Mum with husband, Spencer, and two delightful young children. Both Maureen's mother and father did come to visit us in Ladner, but her mother passed away in October 1986 at the age of 78 and her father William the following year at 84. My mother, Florence, died four years later. Following some years of poor health, Maureen's sister Pam died of heart failure at the young age of 64.

After many years of travelling the world, my only brother Denis met Christine, a lovely English lady. They married and settled down living at Hatfield in England; he, working for British Aerospace and her for a large drug company. He was 50 years old and had lived with my mother on and off for many years. After the death of our mother, he was devastated and was deeply disappointed when, several years later, his job was terminated. He had a supportive wife, a lovely home, and no money worries. They never had children. He was 64 when Christine found him dead at home upon her return from work; he had used his scouting experience with ropes and taken his own life. We had no idea he may do this, and I have never been able to understand why he needed to perform this desperate act. Later, Christine told me several things I never knew about my brother. First, they both desperately wanted to have children but were unable too. Also, during our evacuation years in Shropshire, he had willingly worked hard on the farm, and the family wanted him to stay and work for them. How different their lives would have been if either had taken place.

In our story, we have tried to accurately and honestly portray our thoughts and adventures, for what we believe has been an incredible and rewarding journey. As we reflect on the different and difficult choices we made, I truly believe that we made many good ones that resulted in a better life for ourselves and our family. It is satisfying at this time in our lives to have no serious regrets about the path we chose and to believe that a person's life is created by the decisions one makes, with a little good luck thrown in as well. As I grew up in the dreary east side of London, I always believed there was a more exciting, rewarding world out there, and I wanted part of it. I was fortunate to have met and fallen in love with Maureen when I did, and if she had not wanted to leave England, or if she had had a child early in our relationship, we may never have left. I believe that having a good trade also opened up many opportunities for us both in Africa and Canada.

Our decision to go to Africa, so soon after we were married, fortunately, proved to be a good one, especially as many of our family and friends thought it was foolish to go to a place that was, in their opinion, very dangerous. Africa helped me overcome much of my insecurity, and I believe many of the people we met there, of many races, nationalities, and beliefs, helped us both to conduct our lives differently from what we had been exposed to while growing up in England. The people of Southern Africa I worked with contributed a great deal to increasing my engineering skills, and together we shared many interesting and difficult challenges. Africa has a way of getting into your blood, and the many friends we made there will always be remembered for their warmth and generosity.

Since we left in 1969, there have been many changes. Apartheid ended in South Africa in 1994, and with the release of Nelson Mandela from prison, it seemed to prosper. Following his death, the country appears to be once again in disarray. Rhodesia became Zimbabwe, and under corrupt leadership, the population, both black and white, have suffered immensely. It is said that when you have lived in Africa, you leave something behind, and a part of it rests in your soul. We have always had a desire to return and help the people there in some way. Many there of all races certainly deserve a better life.

As we have mentioned, Maureen was somewhat reluctant to come to Canada and wanted to live in a rural setting in England, but life has been very good to us here. My working life with an international airline gave us many opportunities to travel and helped us keep close ties with our parents in England until the end of their lives.

We also feel that we have provided better opportunities for our children in this country, and all of them have made a successful adult life for themselves here and love this beautiful land. They have also blessed us with ten wonderful grandchildren.

And so, dear children and grandchildren, this has been our life, your heritage, and the reason for being where you are today.

The rest of the story, we leave up to you!

Our Fine Romance - The End.

Our English Tudor-style house in Tsawwassen

Enjoying our retirement with family and friends

Michael

At the Care Home, I reached the last page of '*Our Fine Romance*' and slowly closed the book.

Over several weeks, I had quietly read to Maureen, trying to see if she could remember some of the moments of our wonderful life together. Sometimes a smile made me feel that she recalled events as I read about them, but these were few and far between. More often, the sound of my familiar voice just seemed to calm her.

I wondered again, 'Are these memories really all gone for her and only captured in our book, or are they still hiding somewhere in her brain, possibly waiting to be retrieved one day.'

'Perhaps they come to her as dreams?'

21.
Our Greatest Challenge

Michael

This was the point where we initially concluded our story; we had no intention of writing about the trials and tribulations of our children's teenage years or our retirement in Canada.

But our incredible journey together started to take a different course in 1996, at about the time I retired. My career at CP Air (later Canadian Airlines and then Air Canada) had gone well. After taking further technical courses, I was promoted into management, firstly in aircraft/engine maintenance planning and later in overhaul support shop activities. After many years of managing about fifty unionised tradespeople, I decided to take early retirement at age sixty and set up a small business at home, repairing antique clocks and watches, an activity I had always enjoyed. However, life can have unexpected twists and turns, and I was not prepared for the changes that would start to occur around that time. Little did we know we were about to face the greatest challenge of our married lives. The children were all now conducting their own lives, and we had no concerns about them. We were both in excellent health and had planned to enjoy our family, travel, and leisure time together, and as we were both still playing tennis, we hoped to spend many occasions on the courts together. Our finances were adequate after we were able to pay off our mortgage. Maureen had always been a wonderful seamstress, making many of the girls' and her own clothes and was in great demand at the tennis club for her custom-made tennis panties. She took up quilting, and nothing but perfection would do. She had also mastered the computer and regularly e-mailed friends and family around the world, as well as joining a writers' group and creating several short stories. Maureen was accepting our elder years well and was still a fine-looking woman.

My first indication that something did not seem right occurred some years after I took retirement and started the clock repair business at home. I have always hated accounting and bookkeeping, and I asked Maureen if she would be part of my business and look after the books for me. She somewhat reluctantly agreed, and we started doing it together.

As Maureen was not familiar with this, I asked a friend to show her how to keep our records, which were straightforward addition and subtraction. But she had difficulty comprehending, and I passed it off as lack of interest and took over the task myself.

A few years later, we decided to go on a cycling trip in Europe with a group from our tennis club that entailed a journey down the Danube from Passau in Germany to Vienna. The trip, although quite arduous, was a wonderful experience, but I had a feeling that Maureen's self-confidence was not as it had been, and she was more nervous than I had ever seen her on a bike before. I guessed it was just part of ageing. The following year started with distressing news from Florida that our daughter, Nicola, had been diagnosed with Non-Hodgkin's lymphoma, a blood cancer. This news, of course, was a significant concern to us all, but with her courage and determination, months of chemotherapy, and with the help of family and friends, she managed to get through it. Maureen and I made many trips to Florida to help her and their family, and I took several alone. During these trips, when I went without her for a few days, she seemed very anxious and desperately wanted me to be with her. I felt her dependence on me to be not quite normal and that again, it must be signs of old age approaching. Nicola thankfully went on to make a full recovery.

Maureen now seemed to be having some trouble with her eyesight, and after a visit to our local ophthalmologist, she was sent to a specialist at Vancouver Eye Clinic. Here we were told the bad news that we had expected. Maureen had Macular Degeneration and was advised not to drive anymore. She was very distraught and cried bitterly on the way home. I tried to comfort her and convince her that it was not so bad, and many people function very well with failing eyesight. For the next few weeks, I noticed that she seemed to not have much interest in her usual activities. Although I was prepared to drive her anywhere she wanted to go, she did not seem to have much incentive, and there was a noticeable sadness in her demeanour. She tried to continue with tennis, but failing eyesight did not allow her to see the ball well enough. I made an appointment for her with our regular doctor, and he prescribed some anti-depressants, but I had a feeling that maybe there was something else causing this state of mind, and more help was needed. After about a month, we returned to our doctor, and I reported that I felt that Maureen was experiencing more than usual memory problems; he advised she should be tested for this. So, we then saw a memory specialist, who after testing, referred her to a specialist at Delta Mental Health. I knew then that the situation was not good. Our next interview was with a Geriatric Psychiatrist, who seemed to take a very encouraging interest in Maureen, and she related well to him. He initially diagnosed that she could be clinically depressed, gave her some medication for this, and wanted to see her in two months. At this appointment, he gave her a cognitive assessment test and came up with a number, which he relayed to his assistant. He called up a CT scan of her brain, advising us that he needed to see us in two weeks. I had an uneasy feeling all was not well, even though the scan results showed there was no tumour, evidence of a stroke, or other abnormalities in the brain. We were not told directly what Maureen's condition was, but as we left the doctor's office, he said he wanted to see Maureen again in a month, and I was handed an envelope. The contents contained all the information I had dreaded to hear; it was apparent that Maureen had Alzheimer's disease.

It is now many years since the diagnosis, and as we have always been a very devoted couple, I was determined to look after Maureen and stay in our present house, enjoying our garden, which we both loved so much. But this disease is progressive; it gradually changes the personality, and the ability to reason and make sound judgements is severely diminished. Short-term memory gradually becomes more of a problem, and one finds oneself repeating the same questions and answers over and over again. Time did not seem to mean much to Maureen anymore, and although we tried many simple activities, her attention span was very short. I was getting more concerned about her safety in the house as she did not appear to be paying much attention to her own or others' well-being, and she always wanted to leave our home and search for a previous dwelling.

On 20th September 2012, before breakfast, she missed her footing on our stairs, fell, and broke her leg. I knew by the angle of the leg that it was terrible and called 911, but Maureen seemed more concerned that she had no panties on than the nature of her injury. The two cups she was carrying at the time were unbroken. It took three weeks in hospital and surgery to install several plates before she was allowed home. This time was an incredibly difficult time for us both as she did not understand the seriousness of her injury and just hated me leaving her at the hospital. Upon her return home, I knew I could not manage this alone, and through our local health services, I was able to secure some funding for hiring a Live-in Caregiver.

Arlyn Aquino came from the Philippines, where she was a trained nurse, and she had spent many years in a nursing home in Taiwan and then as a caregiver for a family in Richmond B.C. She had considerable experience of people with dementia. After much paperwork with Labour and Immigration Canada, I secured a contract which enabled her to stay in Canada and would eventually lead to Canadian citizenship for her. She was with us for over 15 months, and without her help, I could not have got through that difficult time. We were now getting into another phase of this terrible disease, as Maureen's ability to function and take care of herself became more difficult. Alzheimer's was tormenting her brain, whereas the rest of her body remained youthful and healthy. She became confused about her house, her family, and often not sure where she was, or even who I was. In January 2014, with my son Stephen present, I was told by her psychiatrist doctor, that I could no longer look after Maureen at home as she was at Stage 6 out of 7 of this disease and that she should be put on an urgent waiting list for residential care. This decision was a tough decision to make. Maureen was admitted in March 2014 to a Care Home in Vancouver and then transferred, two months later, to Delta Life Enrichment Centre, which is about 20 minutes from my home. Ironically, it is owned and operated by a wonderful family who came here from East Africa; she is provided with the very best possible care we could wish for.

Epilogue

Maureen's confinement has been as hard on my four children as me, but they all visit her as regularly as they can. We all miss her, especially on special occasions, when we would have all been together. Abby particularly regrets that her mother will not be able to follow her children's progress in life. Maureen now has very little recognition of her children or me, but she does seem comforted by my presence, my touch, and the sound of my voice.

After such a beautiful life together, what more can I do than love her and be by her side for as long as it takes?

Maureen's ability to recall her memories has now disappeared, but we are blessed to have captured them in this book for our future generations to enjoy.

The End

Our grown-up children: Abigail, Melanie, Nicola and Stephen

Delta View Life Enrichment Centre, B.C., Canada, Maureen's 'New Home'